The Ari Laurel Garam— with me (High School) + later married Vernal Floen (also in our class) who was Obert Floen's son — Ernie's 1st Cousin.

T 182 N R 40 W 5th Mer Mer

North	Between section 27 & 28	
		Var 12° 39' E
20.00	Leave timber & enter prairie bears N & S	
35.00	Enter a poplar grove	
40.00	Set a post for ¼ section corner from which	
	Br Oak 10 in diam bears N 29 E 281 links dist	
	No other tree convient	
80.00	A White Ash 10 in diam corner to	
	sections 21, 22, 27 & 28	
	Land 1st rate mostly prairie	
East	On a random line between sec 22 & 27	
		Var 12° 39' E
10.00	Enter prairie bears N, W & S. E	
40.00	Set temporary post for ¼ section corner	
80.74	A point 5 lks S of the corner to 40 22	
	23, 26 & 27 from which corner I run	
S 89° 39' W	On true line between sections 22 & 27	
		Var 12° 39' E
40.37	Set post in mound for ¼ section corner	
80.74	To corner to sections 21, 22, 27 & 28	
	Land 1st rate level prairie	
	Nov 7th 1866	
North	Between section 21 & 22	
		Var 12° 39' E
22.00	Leave timber & enter a Large prairie	
	bears N 29 S. W.	
40.00	Set post for ¼ section corner from which	
	Br Oak 6 in diam bears N 83½ W 153 lks	
	No other tree near	
80.00	Set post in mound for corner to	
	sections 15, 16, 21 & 22	
	Land mostly 3rd rate 2nd on S end	
	timber Br Oak & Wh Oak rest of the	
	line prairie	

T 132 N R 40 W 5th Mer Minn

East	Random line between section 15 & 22
	Var 12.31' E
40.00	Set temporary post for ¼ section corner
80.00	A point 30 lks N of corner to sec 14,15,22,23
	from which corner I run

N 89°47' W	On true line between sections 15 & 22
	Var 12.39' E
40.00	Set post in mound for ¼ section corner
80.60	Corner to sections 15, 16, 21, 22
	Land 2nd rate rolling prairie

North	Between section 15 & 16
	Var 12.39' E
25.00	Leave prairie & enter a grass marsh
40.00	Set post in the marsh for ¼ section corner
	Blk Ash 7 in diam bears N 53° E 252 lks dist
	Quaking Asp 6 in diam bear N 72° E 310
45.00	Leave marsh & enter timber
50.00	A marsh with shallow pond on the south
	bears E & W & cross the Lake on ice
80.00	Set post in pond for corner to sec 9, 10, 15 & 16
	from which
	Bl Oak 8 in diam bears S 25° E 90 lks dist
	Wh Birch 6 " " " N 35° W 317
	Land 1st rate 1st 25 chs rolling prairie
	rest mostly marsh the marsh where
	the section corner stands extends north
	to the W
	Nov 8th 66

	The line between
	Lake & the rail
	& therefore run
East	On the true line
	Var 12.31' E
25.00	Leave marsh

The end papers were photo-copied from the surveyor's original field notes.

Courtesy Bureau of Land Management.

Ever The Land
A Homestead Chronicle

by

Ruben L. Parson, Ph.D
Professor Emeritus in Geography
Saint Cloud State University

Published by

Adventure Publishing
Staples, Minnesota 56479

Printed in May 2004 by

McCleery & Sons Publishing
Gwinner, North Dakota 58040

Through the Otter Tail County Historical Society
with permission of the Parson family.

Original book cover from 1978.

Copyright © 1978 by
Ruben L. Parson
Battle Lake, Minnesota 56515

Paperback Reprint Edition
August 1980

Printed in May 2004 by

McCleery & Sons Publishing
Gwinner, North Dakota 58040

Through the Otter Tail County Historical Society
with permission of the Parson family.

Library of Congress Catalog Card No. 78-71174

International Standard Book Number: 1-931916-33-0

Dedication

To the revered memory of Lillian
and E. E., whose patronage made this
book possible.

Frontispiece

Discovery Hill as seen looking eastward from the kitchen door of the "Big" house early of an autumn morning. Setting of grain stacks and two-bottom gang plow with a five-horse hitch recall fall plowing about 1925.

(Reproduced from an oil painting by the author.)

Preface

This book had a period of gestation several decades in length. Indeed, some time before World War II I had determined to attempt it. When I sat in Burma after the Japanese surrender simply accumulating sufficient overseas points to be shipped back to "Uncle Sugar Able," I sent my father a long list of questions, to which he promptly returned more-or-less complete answers that now, ultimately, appear in this book.

After the war and return to college teaching, my spare time became fully devoted to a textbook and its two revisions before I retired from teaching in 1973. Then I revived the long-latent project, and with the slow pace of an old man, completed the manuscript in three years. I hope my efforts will yield some pleasure and information to my readers, be they many or few. In either case, I will deem myself well rewarded.

The most salient facts, events, and circumstances set forth in the volume herewith are recounted truthfully, to the limits of the author's perception and ability. Elaborations to enhance readability do not compromise any main truth. To better comprehend and appreciate Pehr's Swedish origin, the author traveled to Middle Skåne in August 1974 and for three days, from headquarters in the Stora Hotellet in Hörby, by taxi and with Swedish cousins, examined as carefully as possible the entire vicinity of Pehr's home before he departed for America. The author walked some of the ground walked by Pehr more than a century previously.

Many of the major characters in this book, relatives or intimates of Pehr, are identified by their true names. All other characters are entirely fictional and were given fictitious names. Every major character mentioned in the text is long since deceased.

The story commences near Huaröd in eastern middle Skåne with the marriage of a happy young couple, who would within a year become the proud parents of our principal character, a son named for his father, Pehr.

The book traces the life of young Pehr through his youth, marriage, parenthood, and tenant farming in Sweden; then his emigration to America, his homesteading in Minnesota, his development of a quarter-section farm with standard accouterments, and ultimately (for due consideration) his transfer of the freehold to his only son, Nels, before he, Pehr, a venerable patriarch, died in 1914 at a ripe old age.

Multifarious simple joys and woes, and one deep constant sorrow accompanied Pehr to his grave, his coffin borne from the very church that he had helped build and had served as its first Senior Deacon.

This work is thus an historical chronicle, and not a novel. It is in the main factual, and not fictional. It is couched in simple wording and style, becoming the level of sophistication and erudition with which its characters were endowed.

Acknowledgements

In addition to all public and private sources listed in the Appendix, to each of which I am grateful, I wish to thank more especially certain persons and officials for lending me assistance that greatly improved this work and facilitated its completion.

Dr. Henry A. Coppock prepared, most meticulously, thirteen original maps and diagrams toward illustration of the book, though heavily preoccupied with teaching duties and preparations for assuming the departmental chairmanship of Geography in Saint Cloud State University. His cartographic skills are obviously exemplary.

Mrs. Julie Wolters, geography and art graduate of Saint Cloud State University, contributed four creative charcoal sketches that add much to the character of the book.

Mrs. Janet Neubert, Secretary of the Geography Department at Saint Cloud State University, typed and mailed for me some two hundred letters of inquiry and acknowledgement; with the kind permission of her Chairman, Dr. Philip L. Tideman.

The Administration of Saint Cloud State University extended to me, as to all Emeriti of the University, the privilege of using for professional correspondence official letter-head stationery, and the mailing of such correspondence at the expense of the institution. This has been a most gratifying kindness and honor.

I would further express my gratitude to Mrs. Rita Buntje, who took my longhand manuscript with its multifarious interruptions, transpositions, deletions, and other mutilations, and with patience (and gnashing of teeth) transformed it into a coherent typed copy. Equal credit is due Mrs. Greer Stene for copy-reading and correcting faults in the manuscript before its delivery to the printer.

Thanks also to my daughter, Mrs. Mary Luanne Dignin, for lending me her Smith-Corona typewriter, adaptable to accommodate the Swedish alphabet with its three letters more than in the English. The machine certainly got a "shake-down" trial.

For photographic reproduction of almost every illustration in the book—halftones, documents, maps, and sketches, I am indebted to Mr. William F. Ash, Proprietor of Photos, Inc. of Minneapolis. To several old and faded prints, Bill applied his skills to make them appear clear and new, thus adding much to the visual quality of the book.

Finally, for reading proof with me at various stages of production, I am much indebted and equally grateful to my wife, Mary Louise. Ideas and encouragements came from so many friends and relatives that I cannot thank each one by name. I am, however, greatly indebted to every one of them.

All the above mentioned contributed much of its worth to the book; its failings are entirely my own fault!

Ruben L. Parson
Battle Lake, Minnesota

March 1978

Table of Contents

Frontispiece

Dedication

Preface

Acknowledgements

	Page
Chapter 1: Skåne to Minnesota	9
Chapter 2: Sojourn in Litchfield	48
Chapter 3: Choice of Four Forties	63
Chapter 4: Preparations for Frontier Subsistence	85
Chapter 5: To the Claim by Covered Wagon	97
Chapter 6: Home on the Prairie Border	111
Chapter 7: First Winter in the Wilderness	135
Chapter 8: Spring in the New Land	163
Chapter 9: First Summer and First Harvest	179
Chapter 10: Tragic Second Year	193
Chapter 11: Mixed Blessings of the 1870's	217
Chapter 12: Era of Progressive Affluence	243
Chapter 13: Sons of Pioneers Assume Proprietorship	277

Appendix:
    Part I: Printed Sources Consulted 311
    Part II: Personal Contributors 315

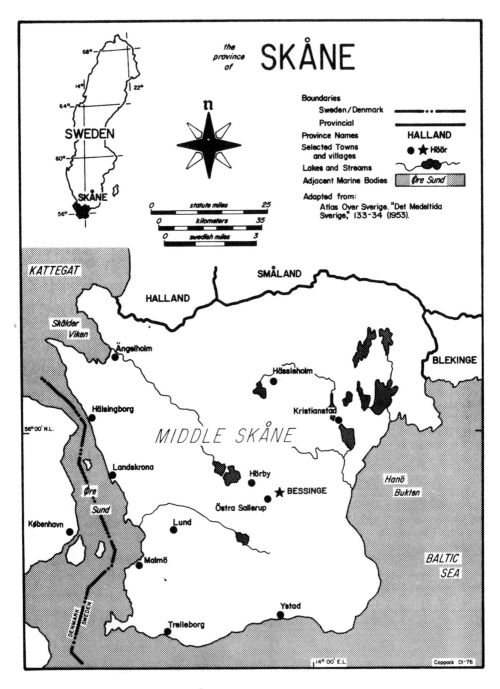

Figure 1.1. Orientation map of Skåne, southernmost province of Sweden. Note situation of Bessinge, our major area of interest.

Chapter 1

MIDDLE SKÅNE TO AMERICA

Our story begins on a festive note, with a wedding in the large steepled church in Huaröd, Skåne, Sweden.

United in marriage were the stately twenty-nine-year-old daughter of Torkel Olsson, Sissa, and twenty-five-year-old Pehr Pehrson from Oderup. Oderup lies some twenty kilometers by road southwestward from Huaröd; so Pehr was pleased to make a considerable winter trip to Huaröd the day before the affair *(Figures 1.1 and 1.2)*.

Pehr stood two inches shorter than Sissa and was known as something of a tippler, but Sissa had attained an age at which she feared indefinite spinsterhood—and this she could not countenance. She was grabbing at straws! Pehr was well-built and quite handsome in good clothes. He might have caught a woman younger and prettier than Sissa; but he knew from much experience that all women were fundamentally alike, and few could yield him a dowry such as would come with Sissa. Indeed he lacked the means to support a wife and family, as did most Swedish men of his time and age.

The ceremony took place at noon on 2 January 1831. The church was crowded, elaborately festooned with spruce branches and cones; and the housewives of the parish had arranged blooming houseplants about the altar. In mid-winter cut flowers were too dear to buy in quantity, but Pehr dutifully procured a dozen yellow roses as Sissa's bridal bouquet. The scent of spruce pitch permeated the church.

Father of the bride, Torkel Olsson, a huge, raw-boned, red-bearded man, made his large daughter seem almost small as they strode down the aisle arm in arm.

Waiting at the altar, Pehr stood on shaky knees, weaving gently,—partly from excitement, but more from carousing and drinking with friends too late the night before (New Years Day, to boot).

After the ceremony those in attendance by formal invitation went to the bride's home for the customary wedding dinner. As the party drove from Huaröd to Trokel's farm, beautifully toned sleigh bells attached to hames and harness rang out miles about on the crisp winter air. People living along the way stepped outside their doors to hear the joyous symphony. The dinner was replete with 'akvavit,' pork rib roast, scalloped potatoes, baked beans, hot buttered hard rolls in cloth covered

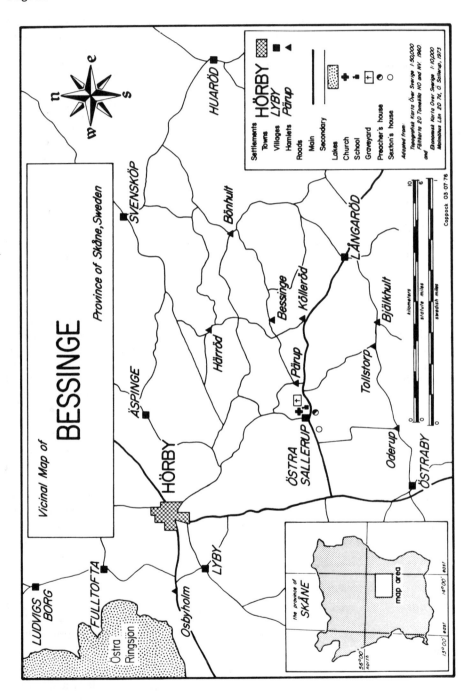

Figure 1.2. Vincinal map of Bessinge and surroundings.

baskets, rice pudding with lingonberries, and 'spettkaka' (a many-tiered wedding cake) three feet tall, which Sissa and Pehr sliced and served together. Sissa's mother's extended table seated twenty, and there were three sittings. Soon as one group arose from the table they were served cognac from serving trays carried about by the bridesmaids.

Before the dinner was quite over, and the bridal couple had changed to travel clothes, darkness was descending; but Sissa's younger brother cheerfully hitched a pair of prancers to the cutter and delivered the honeymooners to the Hörby hotel. Three days later he returned with the rig and fetched husband and wife to their new home on a farm at Bessinge, a mere two Swedish miles from Hörby *(Figure 1.2)*.

The honeymoon had been thoroughly gratifying to both partners, and they went to their new home much in love with each other. Their first night of love-making was somewhat less than satisfactory, but mainly because Pehr was exhausted by two days of travel and carousing. After he had finally consummated their marriage and moved aside, Sissa said "I may be too old to bear you any children. Would you love me less for it?" But Pehr was by then sound asleep and heard not a word of her apology. The apology proved entirely unnecessary; over the ensuing years Sissa bore several children, as we shall see.

When the young farm couple became promised, one to the other, half a year before their marriage, they immediately set about to select and purchase a farm to their liking. They found such a one at Bessinge and pooled their finances (mainly Sissa's from her father) to pay cash for it—the staggering sum of 900 riksdaler-riksmynt; assessed valuation was only 875 riksdaler. The fired brick house and the log stables were, indeed, both spacious and in superb condition. Few clumps of beech-birch and oak timber remained; most non-crop land was predominantly of large crowded boulders of granite, schist, and other crystalline or metamorphic acidic rocks. In the soil accumulated between the stones grew coarse grasses, sedges, bracken, heather, junipers, and birch coppice. So massive and thick was the glacial boulder-till that it imposed an absolute limit to the area of land that could be cleared for cultivation. Where boulders lay two, three, or more deep, one simply could not pile them high enough to reach arable earth. The relative area of arable land, cleared by carrying and rolling stones into huge piles and thick walls, bore witness to centuries of backbreaking work with crude tools, wielded by sturdy determined men *(Figures 1.3 and 1.4)*. The cultivated fields so laboriously cleared were remarkably free of stones and comprised excellent fields to till with animal-drawn implements. The soil, derived from acidic crystalline rock, tended to be acid; but there were marl pits within reasonable hauling distance, and the frequent spreading of marl to sweeten the soil was a common and routine practice.

Pehr's little fields lay scattered outside the hamlet. His cattle grazed communal pastures in the vicinity. His was the only well in the village. The disgusting stench of many animals in restricted space and the numerous dung heaps compounded a noxious air pollution. Eighteen families lived in the village.

Sissa and Pehr were obliged to borrow money to equip and stock the farm—by mortgaging the land for two hundred riksdaler. This, fortunately, they managed to

Figure 1.3. Thick glacial boulder till of crystalline varieties, and large rock piles ('sten rös'), in stony permanent pasture at Bessinge. Rock piles in fence rows and corners and atop knolls in the middle of the small fields are prominent landscape features.
Photo by E.A. Vievering, 18 August 1974.

pay off in a few years. Their annual taxes in the beginning were only 1 riksdaler, 36 shillings (less than 50 cents American).

A neighbor's wife gave Sissa six hens and a rooster of polyglot ancestry for a wedding present. Pehr bought a team of good sturdy work horses, a brindled cow recently freshened, a heifer large with calf, two young ewes that would lamb in spring, and two fall pigs that would be ready for slaughter before March. Sissa soon arranged for sharing beef and veal butchered by neighbors from time to time, until such time as Pehr would have his own steer to slaughter in late fall or early winter. Sissa would veal the heifer's calf; Pehr would butcher it; and they would distribute cuts and parts to those who had given them fresh meat earlier. Only salted or salted and smoked meat could be kept in summer.

From neighbors about, Pehr acquired on loan sufficient hay, grain, and beets to carry his animals until his first crop came in. Then he would return all feed loans in full and of his best quality.

Equipment requirements were simple: harness for the horses; a two-wheeled cart mounting a large box, with tongue, neck-yoke, and whipple-tree for a two-horse hitch; a wooden plow with iron share, a wooden harrow with oak pins, a wooden wheelbarrow, a scythe for mowing hay and grains, and the numerous hand tools with which to operate and maintain a farm establishment.

During the cold, dark, and snowy months of winter remaining before planting time, the young couple did much love-making and little work. Indeed there was little work to be done and long nights for sleeping and philandering. Darkness of winter must be exploited, because the extended daylight of spring and summer (at 55½° N. latitude) soon to come would demand long days of labor and short nights for sleep. Work would come before play, and fatigue would dampen romance.

Sissa tended her chickens and milked the cow twice a day. Pehr fed all the animals morning and evening and cleaned all the pens and stalls once daily, removing the dung and replacing it with fresh (straw) bedding. The manure accumulating in the square closed on three sides by the stable grew into a mound so high that Pehr laid planks up one side of it so that he could push a loaded wheelbarrow to the top and dump it. This was his most strenuous winter work, discounting Sissa's more pleasant demands. It was important that the manure be piled high in the middle of the stable lot so that one might later drive the horsecart around it, load the manure onto the cart, haul it to the fields, and spread it before spring harrowing or fall plowing.

Pehr had wisely demanded of the previous owner that all the fields be properly fall-plowed, so that he need only cross-harrow the furrows and have a seed bed fit for sowing. The kind of plow then in use did not scour, and turned no furrow either on edge or clear over; it merely pushed a ridge of earth to the side, so that a plowed field with straight plow-ridges had the semblance of a giant rubbing board. But one or two harrowings perpendicular to the ridges left a remarkably smooth seed-bed.

While he waited for spring, Pehr canvassed his neighborhood for seeds that he could borrow against his coming harvest in August. He would then repay in kind, with a specified weight added as interest on the loan. He carefully recorded each loan and kept the record in a secure place on the mantel.

He elected to plant each of his six fields to a separate crop and commence a regular rotation, omitting rotation pasture, but including hay or other forage. He borrowed from neighbors; wheat, oats, barley, and potatoes. The clover and grass seeds he needed were not available so he bought these in Hörby. The largest of his

Figure 1.4. Stony, boggy brush pasture with junipers, heather, birch copse, sedges, and coarse grasses. In background is a young plantation of Norway Spruce, probably publicly owned, and land purchased and planted by the Commune. This scene is just south of Bessinge.

Photo by author, 18 August 1974.

fields, at the south end of the farm, was inclined to be a bit soggy in spring. This he would sow to oats after all other crops were in.

His fields varied in size from less than an acre to one or two acres each, so his rotation was not without complexities, nor could he actually rotate more than six crops, unless he split a field or two. This he would not do, deeming each small enough as it was, for ease of cultivation.

Sissa prepared to make maximum use of the garden patch south of the orchard (apples and pears). She did not beg or borrow her seeds, but purchased them from a seedsman in Huaröd during one of their visits to her home. She would plant a row of early potatoes for summer use; cabbage for kraut and for winter storage in the cellar, wrapped in paper; Brussels' sprouts, carrots, rutabagas, table beets (for greens and roots), beans (notably brown beans to dry and store for winter use), cucumbers for pickling in a stone crock with brine, vinegar, and generous stalks of dill fully headed, etc. etc. No one would have a garden better than Sissa's!

Eventually the long winter ended. Came a day so warm that men went about their chores in shirtsleeves. And summer was almost instant. In one week the landscape changed from white to black, and a few days later the fields were dry enough for working.

Pehr hired the brawny son of a neighbor to assist with manure hauling. The boy was Johan Erickson, who lived a mere kilometer east of Pehr's place. Thither went Pehr one Sunday evening to hire the boy, with his father's permission.

"I will pay Johan one riksdaler per day and furnish him bed and board while I need him."

"That's a generous offer, and he will take it. When do you want him?", spoke Johan's father.

"We can begin hauling tomorrow morning. Perhaps, Johan, you'll come with me now and be ready for work tomorrow morning after breakfast?"

"I'll come right now. Just give me time to bundle up a change of clothes. I'll not sit to table with manure on my shoes or pants."

"You may be sure of that," laughed Pehr. "Sissa would show you the door."

They hauled and spread the manure in five days—five long days of diligent labor. They manured the field southwest of the farmstead, south of the high-road. Pehr would manure one field each year in a strict rotation, to maintain fertility in all; this in addition to a rotation of marling.

A goodly spring rain postponed field work for two days; but on the third day Pehr was busy early to late with his horses and a two-section harrow—with a swath of about ten feet. He harrowed all his plowed ground in two days, including Sissa's garden plot and the big south field, which was, indeed, scarcely dry enough to work. Another spring shower delayed his sowing two days again; but then he sowed in one day, broadcast by hand, all the small grains. Next day he "after-harrowed" all of them to bury the seed. Then came potato planting, for which he prepared the field with a marker that laid off rows with uniform width between them. This done, he called on his good wife to help him plant the potatoes. These they had cut into suitable pieces two days before and left spread on a stable floor to dry. Pehr dug with a spade, Sissa dropped in a cutting, and Pehr covered it and stepped it in with his heel. They worked rapidly and smoothly as a team, but before the field was half planted Sissa suggested that they sit and rest a spell.

As he sat down beside her, Pehr said, "You are usually the tireless worker, Sissa, and now you wish to sit. You are keeping a secret from me no longer. I have suspected that you are pregnant. Am I not right?"

"You are, indeed, and I'm ever so proud. Are you happy about it too?"

"I am delighted." He held her to him and kissed her gently. "You will bear me a son, and he shall become a man we can be truly proud of. When will he arrive?"

"Whether son or daughter, the baby should come about the end of October. I've been pregnant since early February, and it is now past mid-May. I thought you knew weeks ago and felt unhappy at the prospect. I'm ever so glad that you are pleased. If I bear a son, his name shall be Pehr!"

"Come, my pregnant woman. To the house with you! I'll do both digging and dropping for an hour or two, and we can quickly complete the planting tomorrow."

He walked with her to the house, hugged her and kissed her, and then returned to the field, whistling a song remembered from his youth.

Sissa helped Pehr in the fields throughout the summer. She hoed, and later heaped the potatoes, side by side with him; each doing one row at a time. Without his sturdy wife, Pehr should have had to pay out considerable wages to a hired hand. Sissa tended her garden independently, not once asking help. And she kept it literally weedless. Even her row of flowers next the south edge grew luxuriantly, and she had fresh flowers in the house until frost. When she harvested all her garden truck, Pehr did all the lifting and heaving—and carrying into the cellar.

In August, when the grain stood ripe and ready, Pehr again hired Johan as before, having spoken for his harvest help when they were hauling manure in the spring. Johan was young, but he was wiry and willing; and the Pehrsons became genuinely fond of him. He and Pehr took turns swinging the scythe and tying the sheaves. Each evening before departing the field, they built all the sheaves into shocks—the bundles stood up against each other in groups of eight or ten, so the heads were all in the air and would dry quickly after any normal autumn rain. (Lying flat on the ground, they would have sprouted.)

Working diligently, with only brief stops for food and water, the two men together could reap, tie, and shock three acres 'tunnland' in a LONG work day. (Earlier, when Pehr harvested his sown hay crop, he mowed two acres a day. When it was dry Sissa helped him rake it into cocks and haul it into the stable. They filled the main loft.)

Johan and Pehr, their work interrupted twice by rain showers, harvested all the grain in two weeks—before the end of August. In the first week of September they hauled the grain into the stable and flailed it out on the threshing floor. This tedious work took them another two weeks. The hot strenuous work of harvest was done!

Yields and quality of the crops were excellent, and Pehr proudly returned all his seed loans, with extra weight for interest.

Immediately after the first frost, potato digging commenced, and Johan was recalled to help. They dug the potatoes with forks, picked them into wicker baskets and emptied the baskets into the horse cart. Then they drove the loaded cart to the community distillery a kilometer to the northeast and sold the load. They dug and hauled an entire week and finally carried the last cart-load into the cellar for family use. After supper Pehr paid Johan his wages, thanked him for his superb help, and begged him to come back for manure hauling next spring. Johan committed himself: "I've enjoyed working for you and Sissa because you have never driven me and you have treated me as an equal. Few farm owners ('bönder') do that. You can count on my coming back."

After Johan's departure, Pehr sat down at the table with a bottle and a glass in front of him. Sissa knew what would eventuate: He drank himself stupidly drunk; and she helped him to bed.

Next day was rainy, a good one for recovering from a hangover. Sissa feared that Pehr would resume drinking, as he had several times before; but this time he had plowing on his mind, and he would begin in the morning. The time was mid-September, and hard ground frost could come in less than a month.

Pehr drove his horses hard as he dared and put in long days. He fed the animals generous measures of oats morning and night and kept sweet new hay in their mangers. Before mid-October, all his fields lay black—ready for spring harrowing.

After completing the plowing, Pehr celebrated with a drinking spree that lasted three days. Sissa wisely held her tongue, and on the fourth day Pehr sobered up and became himself again. He would not get drunk again before his son came!

Sissa, with Pehr's help, gathered all her garden produce and stored it properly, most of it in the cellar. Pehr did the back bending and lifting; Sissa could not reach the ground without squatting.

She grew tremendous in girth as the healthy fetus grew, but she did all her household chores much as before. She knew that exercise and control of weight were factors of importance to her prospective birth-giving. Pehr had to do the milking, because Sissa could not hold the pail.

Impending events soon enforced a respite from his labors while he drove to Huaröd to engage a midwife; Sissa was too far along to ride with him.

"Ask Ma to get Lundström's wife, Else, to come. She's the best midwife I know of," admonished Sissa.

"That I will," said Pehr. He kissed her goodby despite her protrusion, mounted the cart, and clucked the horses to go. He called back to Sissa: "You take care of yourself while I'm away. Do little work and no lifting. Johan will do all the chores and any odd job you ask of him. I will pay him accordingly. With him asleep in the spare bedroom, you need have no fear of prowlers at night." He was now out of ear shot, so Sissa missed part of his lecture.

He reached Huaröd at dusk, and before night his in-laws had driven to Lundström's and made arrangements with the wife, Else, to come to Bessinge on the 25th of October as Sissa wished.

On 24 October, Pehr drove again to Huaröd, but this time with a sleigh, on three inches of new snow. Two snowfalls previously had each melted in a day, but this he hoped would lie longer—which it did. He supped, slept, and ate breakfast with his in-laws—Torkel Olsson and Elna Mårtensdotter.

"I will ride with you and show you where Lundström lives. It is nearby and on your way home. I'll walk back after you are safely off with his wife, Else," said Torkel at breakfast.

"Tell Sissa that I will come and help her after the midwife goes home, since she has only one spare bedroom," said Elna.

Pehr and Else arrived at his Bessinge farm before dark, and Sissa was delighted to greet them and serve them a delicious supper: roasted pork chops with boiled cabbage and potatoes, hard bread with fresh-churned butter. After supper, Sissa showed Else to the spare bedroom—a small chamber, but adequately and nicely furnished. Johan had returned to his home.

"Have you had any pains or new feelings yet?" inquired Else professionally, as she unpacked a wicker basket of clothes and personal items. "No," said Sissa, "I feel well as ever. I have been getting plenty of exercise so the little one should arrive on time."

"Yes, yes! time! how many know the right time to count. I've never met one. But we'll simply wait it out."

Wait they did, until finally, on the morning of 4 November, came into the world a strapping squawling son who would be named Pehr—the hero of our story. Else stayed for three days after the birth to ensure Sissa's full recovery. Then Pehr drove her home, in the horse cart this time, because the ground was bare again. After handing her down at her home, he gave her twenty riksdaler, or two a day—twice the wages of a laborer. She bowed and thanked, and walked into her house with the wicker basket swinging at her side.

Pehr drove on to his in-laws. Torkel helped stable and feed the horses. Pehr, Torkel and Elna ate a hearty supper of beef roast, brown beans, potatoes with brown gravy, and home-made bread and butter. Elna asked dozens of questions about Sissa and her first-born. Pehr assured her that all was well with mother and heir and that delivery had been easy. Pehr scarcely had time to chew and swallow between answers. After early breakfast next morning Pehr, accompanied by Elna, drove home, arriving in premature dusk, with snow falling. This snow lay on the ground several weeks, as days became shorter and temperatures lower. He had made his last trip with the horse cart until a mild spell in November rendered sleighing so poor that wheels served better.

Elna returned with Pehr to spend a week with her daughter and new grandson. Torkel would come to fetch her at the end of the week, thus sparing Pehr a third two-day's journey. This delighted Pehr, but he was less pleased with a mother-in-law in the house. He hid his bottles in vacant barn stalls, burying them under old hay and straw in idle mangers.

Next day when Pehr came in from his stable chores to eat dinner he told his busy women, "On Sunday I shall go and confer with Pastor Olander. I must arrange for Pelle's baptism six weeks from now. Sissa, you must get word to your brother Emil and his wife if you wish them to stand up and become godparents. We must also see that Torkel and your sister, Minna, come."

"I'll ask Emil and also send word to Torkel soon as you have assurance of the date from the pastor," answered Sissa.

Next Sunday when Pehr returned from church he reported loudly, "The christening is set for the second Sunday in December, and if we get a bit of new snow riding in the cutter will be fun."

Before the second Sunday in December, the day of little Pelle's baptism, there was snow in abundance both on the ground and in the air. Emil and Lisa came to

---

Under Swedish church law abiding in 1831, a woman was deemed unclean for seven days after bearing a son and was denied church attendance for forty days following the birth. When she bore a daughter she was unclean for fourteen days and denied church attendance for sixty-six days following the birth. These rules came directly from the Old Testament, third book of Moses, chapter 12.

Customarily, farmers paid their church dues with flax fiber prepared for spinning in a special community building that served all. Pehr would give the Pastor an extra skein of flax for the christening.

Both parenthetical statements above courtesy of Göran Börjesson of Guddastad.

stand as godparents; Torkel and Minna came to join in the celebration. The baptism would be in Östra Sallerup Church. Emil and Pehr drove rigs to church. Emil, Lisa, and Minna rode together in a cutter; Pehr, Sissa, Elna, and Torkel rode in Pehr's farm sleigh. All enjoyed the mile long ride (6½ American), viewing the clean, white landscape all about. Minna commented; "There's no horizon; earth and sky simply meet and merge."

At the church Emil and Pehr unhitched and carefully blanketed their horses and put before them armfuls of hay that they had carried along. The sky had cleared, but the weather remained mild.

Inside the church, the entire party was ushered into the front pew on the left hand side, near the baptismal font before the altar. The font was sculptured of basalt centuries ago, but its brass lining was not so old. (Except for certain ceremonies, males and females sat apart in church, women left of the center aisle and men, right.)

Little Pehr remained asleep until the pastor, the child on his left arm, arrived at: "In the name of the Father," and dribbled water on the child's head. Then the infant awakened and made his presence vociferously known. Sissa felt as if the floor were giving way under her. But "Amen" came quickly, and when the preacher returned his name-sake to Pehr's arms, the little one quieted as by magic and caused no further disturbance during the entire church service.

Eventually our party drove home and enjoyed a delicious dinner of celebration. The guests from Huaröd did not tarry after eating, because they would be enroute until late night as it was. They did not travel in total darkness; the snow rendered night more like dusk than dark. When Sissa bade her mother goodby, she whispered in her ear: "Pehr's folks are coming to spend Christmas with us. They chose the holiday for a visit instead of the baptism. If you'll have us, we'll come to Huaröd for New Year's."

"Come, by all means. You will always be welcome in your parental home," whispered Elna in return. Before departing, the guests and hosts shook hands all round, as was the custom of saying farewell.

Sissa and Pehr agreed that their infant son was too young to appreciate the celebration of Christmas. They would defer the erection of a tree in the "big" room until he was a year old. But they celebrated with Pehr's parents, Per Jonasson and Cherstina Månsdotter, who came by sleigh from Fränninge, and spent three days with their son and his family. They fondled little Pehr whenever he was awake and took great pride in so perfect a grandson. Jonasson vowed he would become a strong and rich farmer.

The group celebrated Christmas Eve with a traditional supper of lutefisk, aqua vit, and rice pudding with lingonberries. On Christmas Day they drove to Östra Sallerup Church to attend 'Julotta,' the pre-dawn worship by candle-light, a tradition honored to this day in Swedish communities in Sweden, America, and elsewhere.

They returned home by daylight, and while Pehr milked the cow, the women prepared a breakfast of fried side meat, fried potatoes, bread, butter, and coffee. Each filled to capacity, they retired to their respective rooms and slept until noon. Pehr did no barn cleaning that day; he merely spread fresh straw in each stall on top of the dung. He would sweat tomorrow, but today was a day of rest and contemplation. He contemplated the bottle of aqua vit several times.

Little Pehr thrived on his mother's milk, which, from her ample breasts, came in abundance. But at five months he commenced biting the nipple when he fed, and Sissa was thereby so provoked that she often slapped him sharply during a feeding. The time had come to wean him she determined, and toward that end she commenced. At first she chewed for him only a small part of his ingestion, but she gradually reduced his access to her milk and increased his consumption of solid food at meal time. He sat in a high chair built by Pehr, who was clever with hand tools. Sissa fed him by chewing thoroughly a small portion of food and then conveying it from her mouth to the child's with her fingers. He soon learned to open his mouth for each delivery, much as a young bird in the nest.

Nor was Sissa his lone contributor; Pehr often gave him a pinch of what he deemed particularly tasty. Indeed, visiting mothers might help Sissa with her chewing, winning friendship with the child and sparing Sissa's teeth at the same time. Saliva tasted the same to little Pehr whomever it came from.

By the end of his sixth month, Sissa had her son completely weaned from the breast, but her chewing for him had increased as his breast feeding had declined, so that Sissa's jaws were over-worked for several months. Not long before his first birthday the little boy ate independently, chewing his own food, or swallowing it whole, as he chose. Sissa was careful to slice his meat very thin or chop it into small pieces.

Pehr was a doting father, proud of his little blond-red haired, blue eyed, rosy-cheeked son. Whenever it was feasible to do so, he took the little boy with him—even into the village saloon; but when the boy drank lemonade, Pehr, with a wink to the bartender, had his drink diluted to fill a similar glass. He drank sparingly when little Pehr was with him, obviously sensing the responsibility.

On Sunday, it was Pehr by whose hand the little boy entered church, and he sat beside his father with such decorum as was scarcely believable by his own mother. "My son is no sissy," pronounced Pehr, "and he shall not sit on the women's side!" The closeness between father and son endured even after the arrival of a daughter, Else, born 30 November 1833, and named for the midwife who, with difficulty, delivered her. It endured beyond the birth of a second daughter, 9 July 1837, named Kerstina after her paternal grandmother, and a third daughter, born 29 February 1840, and named for her paternal great-grandmother, Ingar. Finally, on 22 February 1843, Sissa bore a second son, Nils, so named because Sissa fancied the name, and for a favorite neighbor ('bonde'). *See map & notes on page 20.*

At Nils' birth, young Pehr was eleven, so the brothers had little in common before both were quite grown. Indeed, Pehr was often charged with caring for Nils, and keeping him from danger at play or roaming the fields and woods. On one occasion, Pehr may have saved Nils' life. Nils, only three, had blundered onto a striking adder ('huggorm') before the snake could escape into a stone pile nearby. Nils screamed in terror, and brother Pehr came on the run to his aid. Nils stood as frozen while the viper coiled to strike. Pehr quickly picked up a sizeable stone and threw it forcibly at the venomous snake, striking it so accurately that it uncoiled sluggishly and crawled uncertainly into the great stone pile. Pehr shook Nils to his senses and gave him numerous additional shakes for his foolhardiness. "I've told you to be careful in brush and near stone piles, because such places are the homes of the only venomous snake in Sweden. A bite from this one might have killed you. From now on, I shall always walk or run ahead when we are in field or wood."

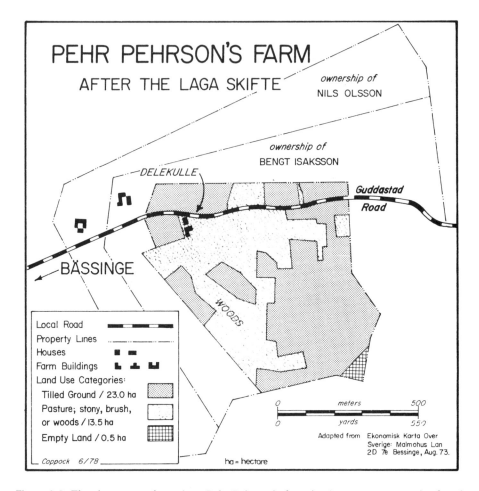

Figure 1.5. The above map shows how Pehr Pehrson's farm lay in one compact unit after the (Laga Skifte) legal shift, concluded on 16 September 1839. By King's edict proclaimed in 1827, most farmers in the village of Bässenge (later Bessinge) were obliged to surrender their scattered parcels of land and select, several hundred meters away from the village, individual, whole farms of such area and quality of land as were their former aggregates.

Pehr chose and was granted the above depicted farm. The building of a new brick house with brick-walled cellar and a brick oven and chimney, removal and reassembly of out-buildings (one used in good part for storage of peat cut and dried to fuel fireplace and oven), and the sinking of a new well cost him 85 riksdalar, 32 shillings. One-third of costs, he was reimbursed from a public fund, one-third from five farmers permitted to remain in the village, and the remainder came from his own pocket. Thirteen families were removed.

In 1841 the family moved from Delekullen to a farm west of Tormastorp, but in 1847 they repurchased the Bässinge farm and remained there for the remainder of Pehr's and Sissa's lives. (Sissa sold a portion of the farm about 1865, with her heir's approval.)

Map and notes courtesy of Göran Börjesson of Guddastad.

Nils hung his head and cried quietly, partly for having endangered himself, and partly for having violated Pehr's care. Pehr, in sympathy, held his little brother's head to his chest and stroked it gently, saying: "I wouldn't want to lose my brother, so please stay closer to me from now on. We can have just as much fun." The incident was kept secret several years.

After attaining the age of fifteen, Pehr had little time to spend with his little brother; he had man's work to do. He helped his father with all the field work in summer and all the stable chores in winter. He milked three cows morning and evening (there were now six.). When his father went on a drunk, he did all the chores alone, but Sissa did half the milking. Though strong and diligent, he remained a boy, earning his keep and helping his parents. Pehr and Sissa gave him a few öre (penny equivalent) now and then, but he was not regularly paid anything. This arrangement prevailed until little Pehr passed his twenty-first birthday. Then it ended abruptly.

Sissa had prepared for his birthday his favorite—fried pork chops with boiled potatoes and thick sweet cream. He ate less heartily than he ordinarily should; and his mother sensed a tension unusual in her elder son. She waited until the others had quite finished, and then asked: "My son, your appetite is not normal. Something is troubling you. If you will tell us, perhaps we can be of help. What is it?"

"Yes, my son," seconded Pehr the elder, "do not be troubled under the roof that will someday be yours, as my heir."

"All right," said Pehr, pushing back his plate, "I will tell you what is troubling me, and the troubles are several. In the first place, I have never felt myself to be the sole heir and life support of my parents in their old age. The girls have reminded me that the law is changing in other Provinces of Sweden, and it may change in Skåne before I become affected. Please understand that I love you all dearly; and would like nothing better than to stay on at home, as I have, indefinitely. But this I cannot afford. As you well know, Monson at the distillery has hired me several winters past. He has now offered me hire every winter, November through March or April, at one rikesdaler per day six days a week. Hauling potatoes in a large wheelbarrow and dumping them into the washer is hard work, but the off-season pay is good. Where else could I find paying work in winter?"

"No place on the land, surely," prompted his father. "Perhaps in the woods."

"I now feel that I must earn a similar wage year round in order to save some every month of the year against such time as I may wish to marry and rent a place of my own. Nils is now big enough and strong enough to help here at home as I did when I was his age. Pa, you really need a hired man only at harvest time; Nils can sow as well as you or I can."

"I have completed my military obligation to the King; I'm a voting member of the Östra Sallerup parish; I must be my own man. Mårtenson over near Pärup, who owns much land, has offered me full-time summer employment at the same rate as I'm paid at the ('bränneri') distillery. I ask your advice."

Instantly his mother asked, "Would your lodging be a clean kept room in the manor house, or in a stable stall? Find that out before you agree to anything! Before you live as a swine for hire elsewhere, we will hire you here at the same wage. Will we not, Pa?"

"Indeed we will; but get the particulars from Mårtenson, and get the conditions in writing over his signature."

Next day young Pehr walked to Pärup and hired out to Mårtenson for the coming summer. Mårtenson was glad to meet Sissa's requirements for her son, and he signed a paper such as Pehr's father had defined. Pehr came home in a happy mood, rushed to the kitchen, hugged his large mother, and lifted her right off the floor.

"By God, my firstborn is a man," thought Sissa. "We will be proud of him always."

The elder Pehr was less than excited by the prospect of operating the farm with Nils his sole helper. One consoling thought came to him: Sissa is a strong woman and apparently going to bear no more children; she will help me much as she did when we were young. And this she did.

The evening after announcement of his independence, young Pehr had further to say about his status: "Now that I shall be earning wages regularly I should not be at home without paying for food and lodging. You, Pa and Ma, what do you wish me to pay you?"

"You speak foolishly, my son," spoke up the father. "None of mine shall pay for food and lodging in my house so long as I have the roof over my head and the fare to go on the table! Should I come into hard times, only then would I accept payment. You may consider your keep earned whenever you can stay with us. It will always give us joy to have you home."

"I would ask something of you for your staying," added Sissa. "I urge you to continue your observation and practice of your father's wood craftsmanship. A degree of mastery of his art might one day stand you in good stead. Kindly do this because I ask it."

"That I will," replied her strapping son. "I take great pride in that which I have learned, and I shall work diligently to learn more whenever time affords." Young Pehr did, as will become apparent later, master the art of making by hand with simple tools almost every wooden article or implement used in a home or on a farm. It gave him an independence, which at the time seemed of little importance, but which later rendered possible his successful homesteading in Minnesota. Though as a youth he had no thought of his skills as vital accomplishments; he acknowledged them as such when, years hence, he determined to go with his young family, to America.

Now employed almost year-round, young Pehr saved one-half of his earnings. During his first two years with Mårtenson, he worked as a field hand—long hours and strenuous labor. But when some implement or other piece of equipment broke down, it was Pehr who repaired it and made it serviceable again. Noting this, and observing Pehr's late hours devoted to the readiness of a failed implement for use the following day, Mårtenson relegated him to the shop full time to repair worn equipment and to build new as needed. He also raised his wage from one riksdaler per day six days a week, to thirty five riksdaler per month, and employed him every month of the year. Fully employed throughout the year, Pehr's savings accummulated at a goodly pace. He thought himself most fortunate; as indeed he was, for in his time and place a young man had difficulty making a living, not to mention setting anything aside. (In 1854, all community distilleries were shut down permanently by a national law.) *(Figure 1.11)*.

Almost every Sunday, he met his parents and siblings at church, and almost invariably went home with them for Sunday dinner. Knowing full-well that her elder son was not fed any delicacies during the week, Sissa contrived to offer him a virtual feast every Sunday. Others in the family appreciated his coming almost as much for the cooking he inspired as for his pleasant companionship during the few hours they could have together. In fair weather he walked back to Mårtenson's in the evening; in foul weather, Nils delivered him in a horse-drawn vehicle with some covering against the weather. Once a snowstorm compelled Nils to stable the horses for the night, with Mårtenson's ready permission, and sleep the night with Pehr, returning home next day when the storm abated.

Indeed, Mårtenson commanded them to "water, stable, and feed the horses," then turning to Nils he greeted him thus: "Young man, I will not permit you to attempt the return trip at night. We shall see that both of you have a good meal before going to bed."

To Pehr he said, "Use those old blankets hanging in the stable to dry off the horses. Then come in and dry yourselves off before sitting to table. You must be hungry after driving in this heavy weather."

The young brothers thanked profusely and went about attending to the horses.

Since the time was long past supper, the brothers were seated to table alone and ate what seemed a feast.

Herren Mårtenson sat in an easy chair facing them and conversed with them while they ate.

Of young Nils he inquired, "You're not neglecting your school work, now that Pehr is away and more responsibility falls on you? That you must never do!"

"No indeed," replied Nils, proudly, "I'm doing well in school and intend to complete the entire seven year course. Pehr got in three years before he became fourteen and had to quit." (Sweden instituted free and compulsory education for children between seven and fourteen years of age in the year 1842.)

The over-night stay together gave the brothers ample opportunity for exchange of confidences. Nils began: "Pa is drinking more and more, Pehr. And now he gets sick from drink and runs out to vomit. I fear for his health. Ma and I do almost all the work about the place, except as the girls are able to help. Else and Kerstina often do all, or at least Ma's half, of the milking, and Ingar churns the butter and slops the swine. Ma spends more and more time in the kitchen attending to our food—and keeping a watchful eye on Pa when he sits about drunk. She is under such strain that she might break at any moment."

"I have become increasingly suspicious of just such conditions," replied Pehr. "And I regret exceedingly that affairs are becoming worse. Perhaps next Sunday when we return from church and Pa is sober I should have a quiet talk with him. Could you arrange for me to be alone with him immediately after dinner? Perhaps I can talk some sense into him."

"Remind him about the drunken murder in our house in 1846, when Nils Anderson was killed in the brawl and the farmer, Mårten Persson, was convicted of the crime. But for Pastor Olander's deposition on Pa's behalf, he might well have been condemned. The tragedy sobered him for awhile, after which he drank harder," Nils said bitterly, almost crying.

"I can assure you of this, my young brother, I shall never partake of any alcoholic beverage—NONE!" vouched Pehr.

"I have tasted enough to know that I shall never be a slave to it. I see no wrong in a man's sociable nip now and again, but a drunk man is to me utterly revolting. And so is my own father now, most of the time. It cannot last indefinitely," said Nils.

The sorry exchange between the brothers took place during a blustery night in April of 1854, and their observations would soon prove prophetic. On 5 November 1856 their father died at the age of only fifty years, victim of a liver ailment probably caused by excessive drinking over a long period.

On 7 November the Pehrson patriach was buried in the beautiful Östra Sallerup churchyard with due solemnity and many mourners. Pastor Olander delivered a burial sermon crediting the deceased with deep faith and scrupulous honesty during his normal years, and begged forgiveness of his later failings. A churchful of parishioners came to pay their final respects.

Also came the in-laws from Huaröd to share their daughter's sorrow. They stayed for dinner but did not linger. On parting, Sissa's mother held her to her and said quietly: "You must now have your elder son at home to set things in order and revive the farm's full productivity. I beg you not to delay!"

So it was that Pehr, the elder son and heir, returned the following April (1857) as manager of the farm and head of the household. Sissa, despite his objection, gave him all implements, tools and other appurtenances, paid half the seed costs and wages of Nils and other seasonal laborers, and insisted that Pehr have one-half of all profits at year's end. Pehr accepted, knowing his mother's determination to realize her late husband's wishes; but Pehr secretly shared generously with his sisters and brother. Indeed, he kept for himself less than one-half the proceeds that became his. Even so, he was well rewarded for every summer's work. Nor was Sissa idle. She retained both health and will, and bore her full share of household duties: carding, spinning, weaving, sewing, cooking, baking, and overseeing the regular cleaning and scrubbing of the house. She ran the home; Pehr ran the farm.

It was not his innate generosity that prompted Pehr to share liberally with the other siblings. He knew that he was envied his inheritance and could not peaceably claim it. On this Else was most out-spoken: "In other provinces survivors share and share alike, and the law will soon be changed in Skåne. I shall hasten that day. Pehr, you needn't count on being sole heir when Ma dies. I intend to have as much as you." The other sisters may have felt the same, but they said little about it, perhaps because they held their elder brother in extraordinarily high esteem. They felt that he was giving them more than they deserved! Nils deemed his share and earnings entirely satisfactory. He was secretly saving for emigration to America, though he was only 16. He would go before his call to military service!

Pehr was gifted with a strong and naturally well modulated voice, and could often be heard from some distance as he worked in his fields, singing Swedish folksongs ('visor'). Some were epic, such as one relating the strength and bravery of Sweden's warrior king, Karl the XII (whose victorious warring over Europe for several years was finally stopped by the Russians at Poltava, 8 July 1709, where he was beaten by Peter the Great). Some were suggestive and sexy; some downright vulgar; but sing them he could, and that with full-throated melody.

He was repeatedly encouraged to join the church choir, but yielded only when a certain cute little brown-haired soprano in the choir caught his eye one Sunday during services. He came to the very next choir rehearsal and missed few thereafter. He joined the choir in spring, and by mid-summer he was quite regularly walking the brown-haired girl, Anna Olsdotter, home after choir dismissal. This was no puppy love!; he had to walk one and a half kilometers to Omsed and as far back to the church, and then more than as far again to his home in Bessinge. (One walks such distance only if it bears on a serious matter!) The year was 1860.

As a Casanova, Pehr was an utter clod. Only after walking Anna home a third time did he venture to kiss her goodnight, and then he was somewhat startled by the eagerness with which she turned her face up to him and threw her arms around his waist. He disengaged quickly, lest his rising manhood embarrass her, and said 'good-night' as he walked away.

Pehr walked home with extra springy strides that night, delighted with Anna's ready response to his advances, wondering whether she would yield all the way to him if he wished, and whether she had ever gratified any other swain—a most revolting thought. As he strode along he mused: her passions appear potent and readily aroused. She should make a wonderful wife!

Thereafter, whenever they were alone they kissed vigorously; and he felt, and stroked, and patted, until Anna would have yielded all the way. Then he caught himself up, desisted, and explained that he wished to marry a virgin.

"You haven't asked to marry me!" exploded Anna.

"Well then, I'm doing so now! I love you as a man should love his wife, and I believe we can he happy together."

"I accept," said Anna emphatically. "I'll tell Papa your intentions so he can prepare himself for your asking."

"Do that! I will talk to him at the first opportunity. We shall consider ourselves 'promised' meanwhile."

Ola Olsson was not overly enthusiastic when his daughter told him that she intended to marry 'Pehr, Pehr's son.' "Do you know that his father was a drunkard, however honorable the son may be?"

"I know that, Papa, but Pehr does not drink. Indeed, he abhors liquor and refused to taste it, even when he worked in the distillery until six years ago. He is a kind, gentle, understanding young man; and I ask that you welcome him as a son-in-law. I'm in love with him as I could never again be in love with anyone else."

"All right, daughter, let him come and ask. I will defer to your judgment and yield to your wishes."

Next Sunday, Pehr was at Olsson's for dinner and after the meal, sitting with Anna and Pehr together in private, Ola first volunteered much good advice, and then gave them and their contemplated union his blessing.

Instantly the announcement reached every room and every ear in the house. Everyone, except Pehr, drank a toast of red wine. He drank water.

Next came Anna's invitation to dine at Pehr's home—an event somewhat less exhilarating. Pehr's sisters embarrassed him putting on airs. (They felt themselves in the presence of one with more wealth and sophistication than they could truthfully boast.) Sissa was herself, and she endeared herself to Anna from the start.

Pehr introduced Anna as, "My promised, my future wife. I trust that we shall always be good friends as well as relatives. Please welcome Anna into the family as a regular member!"

The company responded affirmatively, and as one. Aqua vit went round for a toast, but Pehr toasted with water.

At mid-afternoon, sensing the strain among the young women, Pehr announced his desire to set out for Omsed, that he might return well before dark (daylight would prevail until nine o'clock, or later since it was still summer, so the cause of his hurry was obvious).

Once on their way, alone with the horses, Pehr turned to Anna and said in well chosen words: "Do not think that I would have you live in my home. My sisters would make life miserable for you."

She interrupted heatedly: "And don't think for one minute that I would. Your mother I could bide, I liked her. But Else and I would soon be at war. I would not marry you if I had to live under the same roof as your sisters."

"Calm your fear, my dearest," replied Pehr. "I've already arranged to rent a small farm about one kilometer east of home, the cash rent estimated to approximate one-half of what I get for sold produce only. We shall owe the landlord a few eggs when the hens lay, and some meat when we butcher. It has a small, but durable, set of buildings. The house has kitchen, bedroom, and living room. The stable has more space than we shall need to keep a cow, a sheep or two, swine for our own meat, and chickens for eggs and meat. The buildings are of logs, well layed and chinked. The house I will give a coat of whitewash on the inside. We shall have to buy, beg, or borrow furnishings; there is a fireplace, all of stone, with a broad granite hearth to catch sparks. I will take you to see the place one day soon. Oh, I forgot, there's also a good-sized garden patch and a small apple orchard. It will be our honeymoon retreat—before I acquire more than a cow to tend. Will such a place please you?"

"Of course, with you it will please me. Now I am happy instead of gloomy. I'm glad that you knew we must live alone." She pulled his free left arm tightly to her side.

"Then I shall rent it beginning next fall, say October first. You have said that you wish to be married on October 23rd, assuming that your father and all his tenants will by then have their harvest in and most, if not all, of their plowing done—so they can witness the ceremony without falling asleep. The date suits me well too; I can take possession after the present tenant has completed the plowing of the ten acres of plow ground—certainly by October first. I shall insist upon this promise in my contract to rent. We shall have three weeks in which to make the place ready for moving into."

Pastor Olander, after conference with the amorous young couple and approval of their selected date, read the Banns on three consecutive Sundays in August in compliance with Church law.

Anna and Pehr spent a romantic summer and autumn. They met and were together whenever possible. They went to the Hörby Mid-summer festival (24 June), viewed all the exhibits, rode most of the rides, ate of the delicious foods and sweets, and returned home bone-weary. They went and returned in Tufvason's spring wagon behind his shiny black trotters.

Every Sunday they ate dinner together, either of Sissa's or Anna's mother's Bolla's, culinary masterpieces. One Sunday afternoon when they were walking, Pehr chided Anna about growing fat before marriage, to say aught about middle-age. "If you weigh more than I do when you are forty, I shall have to get ahold of another, less bulky woman."

"That you may," replied Anna tartly. "No-one in my whole family has been obese at any age. Watch your own girth, Mister! I may have to leave *you*!" They continued their walk, laughing.

On their Sunday walks, Anna often gathered a bouquet of flowers for a vase on the table. Her favorites bloomed in autumn—heather and goldenrod—of which she would select an armful.

"Today I must bring home my best bouquet of the summer. I fear this may be my last opportunity. We shall be too busy to stroll the countryside and make love to each other," she spoke her thoughts aloud.

Retorted Pehr: "We shall be busy, sure enough, but we will certainly take time to walk the land over on Sundays. If marriage should terminate our joy of life, then I say we stay single!"

"We shall always stroll the land together, Pehr. The Sabbath will come as regularly after our marriage as before. But we must guard against becoming too work-weary to walk out and see the beauty of nature!"

"Huh," snorted Pehr, "I appreciate nature every day I work on the land, whether I'm plowing, sowing, or reaping. But with you beside me the appreciation is always greater, and I trust it will always be that way."

On October first, their date for taking possession of the tenant farm, Anna rode her father's most gentle saddle mare to Pehr's home, whence they walked to the little place they had rented. They were well pleased with its condition of repair and general cleanliness. (Under the law then pertaining to land tenancy, a tenant must leave the place in as good or better condition than it had been when he first occupied it.) Yet, they devoted many days of hard work to have it as they wished—a honeymoon cottage should be shipshape! Anna scrubbed floors and hung curtains. Pehr white-washed all interior walls of the house, and chinked every crack on the exterior of both house and stable.

Then they moved in the essentials for keeping house, many items contributed by their mothers and Anna's father—bed, stove, churn, chairs, cooking utensils, etc. etc. Items lacking after the deluge of gifts, they bought together in Hörby, barely making the round trip from first crack of dawn until darkness. Pehr bought and borrowed an ample supply of seasoned stove wood so they might cook and keep warm. By evening of the 20th the place stood ready for occupance; and the young couple were proud to admire their renovations. The last three days before they would wed would go for proper fitting of fine clothing for the ceremony. Anna would wear a plain white gown of silk, and Pehr a brown suit, with vest of finest worsted. (He hoped that the day would be cool.)

Anna chose to be married in her own home, which was amply spacious. She invited only near relatives and special friends—her own and Pehr's, and all were invited for supper after the ceremony. More than a hundred came, requiring three sittings to table and a long row of hitching rails built under Ola's supervision. A stable boy fed all the horses oats and hay, so they too could celebrate.

In the double ring ceremony, Anna and Pehr exchanged plain yellow gold bands—the choice of both.

Pastor Olaf Lars Olander ate with the first sitting, after which he drank one sip of aqua vit to the bride and groom and excused himself. He would not stay and possibly dampen the spirited revelry that would rock the house before midnight. The hour was quite late when Anna's mother drew her aside and persuaded her to spend her bridal night in the spare bedroom upstairs. "Don't go home to a cold house," she urged. "You can go at your leisure tomorrow and have the house warmed before evening."

"I'll ask my new husband," replied Anna. "You are very kind to invite us."

Pehr had no objection to staying. Indeed, he had wondered whether the most ardent love-making could heat a house with a fire just kindled.

But Ola, Pehr's new father-in-law would not tolerate his wife's foolish idea. Before she could order the stable boy to put up Pehr's horses for the night, Ola, who had overheard the plan to sleep over instead of going home, fairly exploded: "Bolla, have you forgotten your wedding night? We were to ourselves, away from home; and although the weather was cool, we certainly didn't freeze. I seem to remember that we got too warm. It was May, of course, and not in October, but if Anna and Pehr can't keep warm in that feather bed we gave them, their marriage should be annulled tomorrow. They won't even need a fire, I'll warrant."

To Anna and Pehr he said, more calmly: "Tonight you will make memories that will last your entire lives. Those memories should be made in your own, quiet, private place, not here in crowded surroundings and a noise that may last until morning. Of course you're welcome to remain here, but I cannot countenance your cheating yourselves."

Anna and Pehr stole out and drove home before any of the merrymakers missed them. Pehr stabled the horses and unharnessed them before entering the house. Anna had kindled the fire and laid out her new nightgown chosen for the special event. Now they undressed quickly, in the dark but for flashes from the fireplace; and they were soon in the feather-bed, energetically consummating their marriage. Before morning they had numerous times proved themselves husband and wife. Both were content and happy.

They slept in until quite late. Then Anna bestirred herself to prepare breakfast, while Pehr went to water and feed the horses. They returned the team to Sissa's place that afternoon and led the borrowed cow back to their place. Sissa was pleased to lend the cow and sent them off in a happy mood. Next morning they returned to reality. Pehr fed the cow and cleaned her stall, then spread it with new bedding. Anna milked the cow and set the milk for the cream to rise. In a few days she would churn a goodly batch of butter; the cow gave milk quite abundantly (for those times).

That night their frolicking in the feather bed was rudely interrupted by a large band of neighbors come to charivari. The abrupt violation of the night's quiet was almost deafening. The bridal pair arose and dressed quickly; then opened the door, which provoked a stop of the beating on noisy objects such as tin pans, and a boisterious call for 'brännvin' liquor. Pehr had anticipated the event and had an ample stock of akvavit in readiness. He handed out four bottles, which went quickly from hand to hand and mouth to mouth as the noise subsided. When the bottles were empty, some of the less genteel of the crowd called loudly for more, so Pehr handed out two additional bottles—his last. Before these were entirely consumed, the band staggered and swaggered away, wishing the newlyweds a long and happy life in voices audible two kilometers away. Anna and Pehr, glad the customary nuisance was over, returned to their bed and resumed their love-making. When they rested from their delightful exercise, Pehr commented, "There must have been a hundred or more revelers. I believe we are welcome in the neighborhood."

"It would seem so," agreed Anna. "I saw faces all the way from Pärup, Östra Sallerup, Omsed, and Bjälkhult. They have a long walk back home, and I'm proud that they would come so far to wish our marriage a success." They turned apart and went to sleep.

The long Swedish winter seemed short to the newlyweds. Finally, before the end of April, the landscape changed in color from white to black and gray. The storks and lesser migratory birds returned, busily singing and building nests. Pehr planned his crops for all the fields, at home and on his tenant farm. Anna planned the use of the garden patch. Both were collecting seeds for planting. Pehr borrowed seeds from his home place to sow his rental. Anna got her garden seeds (vegetables and flowers) from her mother and mother-in-law. When the soil dried and warmed enough in May, they worked from first full light until dark every week day. Pehr used the farm equipment on his home place also for tilling his tenant farm. Soon after mid-May he had cross-harrowed, sown, and after-harrowed every field. His spring's work was done. The year was 1862.

Brother Nils was serving out his military term, because Pehr had denied him money for going to America while the Americans were fighting a bitter sectional war. "You'd better do your compulsory service here rather than go to America and become involved in a real shooting war. When that war ends I'll see that you have enough money to go over."

In 1863, Pehr planted his tenant field to sugar beets, a new crop that arrived in Sweden in 1850 and became concentrated in Skåne. He grew the crop only one year, however, because it demanded too much hand harvest labor and distance hauling of a tremendous tonnage per hectare. The nearest refinery was miles away.

Anna was too large with child to assist with the harvest. She bore a daughter on 11 September, and Pastor Olander christened the infant, Elna, when she was six weeks old. She was named for her paternal great-grandmother, Elna Mårtensdotter (Sissa's mother). Little Elna was a beautiful child whose blond child's hair turned brown such as her mother's, hazel eyes widely spaced, a pretty mouth, and round, rosy cheeks.

Said Pehr, "This one is pretty and without fault, but the next must be a son. You have your instructions, wife!" he added laughingly.

In 1865, after the civil strife in America had ended, Nils set out for the United States with 200 riksdaler riksmynt given him by Sissa and Pehr. He had his miserly savings in addition. His savings were small; he had just completed a two year apprenticeship under a well-known blacksmith in Hörby and departed for America a journeyman blacksmith. Someone in Paxton, Ill. took advantage of the naive Swede and employed him as an apprentice again. (According to death records of Östra Sallerup, "The blacksmith's apprentice, Nils Persson "Rosenquist" died in Paxton, Illinois on 22 September 1868.) His fortune-seeking in America failed, as it did for an untold number of other Swedes who staked their all for a better life in a new uncrowded land. Also in 1865 the sister Kerstina went to live in Linderöd Parish, at 28, a housemaid in desperate search for a husband.

The year 1866 became notable for two major events in Pehr's life: the birth of a daughter on 9 January and the marriage of his eldest sister, Else, to Anders Olsson of Östra Kärrstorp on 29 June. The dark-complexioned daughter was named Hanna, not for any ancestor but because Anna liked the name. A typical Swede, Hanna was born blond and remained so until she attained the age of about five years, at which time her hair commenced darkening and was finally almost black. She was, by comparison with her sister Elna, a frail little child, who would grow to womanhood much dependent on her elder sister and would die of consumption (tuberculosis of the lungs) at middle age.

For several years past, Pehr had given much thought to the prospect of migrating to America. It became the subject of many arguments with his wife, but her observations always prevailed. The American Civil War put aside his intentions for its duration, but the war ended, and his brother Nils reportedly prospering in America, he thought of little else. Nils' description of the fertile virgin land, virtually given away for little more than the asking, so intensified Pehr's land hunger that he could scarcely contain himself.

"Think, Anna!" he lectured his reluctant little wife, "We could have in America 160 'tunnland' (acres) of land; ours without owing anyone; ours to make fruitful for our own profit. How can any intelligent Swedish peasant, restricted to a few arable hectares, deny himself and his family such a fabulous opportunity?"

"My dearest Pehr," came Anna's ready rebuttal, "so many Swedes are going to America that we shall soon have abundant land available to those remaining at home. Well you know that a dozen or more neighboring tenants have already departed, and that little farms are in the process of being merged, two, three, even four or more, to comprise sizeable operational units. Many farmsteads stand vacant even now because the landlord has no need for them. Be patient, and you may have 160 tunnland to operate right where we are."

"Such patience I lack," replied Pehr. "I have struggled on small patches of plowable ground, restricted by rocks that defy removal; I've already strained against stones enough to do myself permanent injury. (He got an inguinal hernia the spring following their marriage.) The damned rocks have done me hurt, but I swear they shall do me no further injury! I will not further jeopardize my health in a futile attempt to provide properly for you and our children! If I become crippled even America will be unattainable."

"Would you truly leave our safety among friends and relatives to go where the American savages continue to rape and murder and burn entire villages, one after another? Would you have us cross the ocean in the bottom of a filthy, half-rotted, rat-infested ship; risking disease, starvation, even death during the ocean crossing? Have you not heard how the shippers pack emigrating peasants into the steerage hold, concerned only about those who die, because the dead must, by law, be cast overboard? Have you, my Pehr, thought about all those sordid conditions, and would you still expose your family to the hazards? Would you have us hauled to America as a shipment of swine?"

These arguments erupted repeatedly, but without conclusion.

Pehr discussed his emigration plans with his mother, thoroughly and considerately; and she encouraged him to emigrate.

"Lonely as I shall be without you, my son, I cannot discourage you from going to America. You may go with my blessing, and I will help you get together the sum of money you will need. As for me, I will live out my days where your father and I set up housekeeping and I bore all my children. The farm will yield me more than I shall need, so you must not be troubled by the 'life's support' for which you are traditionally liable as your father's heir. You may take what you wish of the tools and implements I gave you when your father died. The animals also belong to you, so you may sell any you wish to raise money for your travel. Ingar is promised to Hans Pehrsson of Vitaby, as you know, so she will soon go away too, leaving me all alone. But the farm is good, and I can quickly get a suitable tenant to operate it. If I become too lonesome, I will join you in America. The ocean may not always separate us." So spoke Sissa to her beloved firstborn.

"You are kind and understanding as ever, Ma," said Pehr, almost in tears. "I shall be grieved to leave you, but I cannot deny my family the great American opportunity. If you will come with us or join us later, you will be heartily welcome. Please consider this seriously! The farm should bring you a good price, should you ever wish to sell. I will not permit you to mortgage it heavily on my account!"

Pehr completed the plowing of all his fields in mid-October 1868. He smeared his plow with tallow and stowed it in its accustomed corner of the stable. He unharnessed his team and stabled them, then walked to his tenant house where Anna was busy preparing supper.

"The plowing is done once again," he announced casually, and then dropped the bomb that Anna had been anticipating. "I have plowed this ground for the last time! Try as I might, I could never much improve our status. Next spring, after planting, I shall go to America. You and the girls may accompany me or join me later."

"If you must go, you shall certainly not go without me and the girls. But know this, Pehr Perhson, there will be no love-making between you and me before I feel safe in the Wilderness. I will not carry or bear a child while I live daily in fear for my own life. Last night was your last of me until I tell you otherwise!"

"For America, I will even be celibate. You shall not be bothered by me again before you invite me to do so. It will be difficult to keep my hands off you, but do it I shall! Now let us think and do toward the end of emigrating next spring."

"Since the issue appears settled, I should like to go and tell my family in Omsed tomorrow. They have a right to know our plans; and they will help us assemble such items as we should take with us."

"We can walk over and tell Ma and Ingar after supper. Ma has already made generous provision for our expenses, in lieu of the farm as my birthright. We shall have enough money to reach Minnesota and set up housekeeping in a new log cabin."

"What is Minnesota?" inquired Anna innocently. "I thought we were going to America."

"You know very well what Minnesota is and where it is! That's where the best surveyed land is now available for homesteading under the American law of 1862. There should be much empty land to choose from. That's where we shall go," replied Pehr, irritated!

They notified Pehr's mother and sister that evening, and drove to Omsed the next day to inform Anna's parents. Both fell to crying quietly and wiping away their tears as Anna related their plans.

"You are a determined young man, said Ola to Pehr, "and I will not attempt to deter you. I will give Anna some money to help with expenses of getting settled in a new land." (Pehr never asked how much she got, and she spared it for emergencies, as he learned later.)

"You have always been kind and understanding," replied Pehr, "and we shall be ever so grateful for your help."

"What happens now to your birth-right, the farm on which Sissa lives?" asked

Bolla, half in anger. "Are you giving a good farm away to go and starve in a wilderness?"

"Dear Mother-in-law, one or two of my sisters so resented my inheriting the farm that I have paid sums of money to each of them and to my brother, Nils, already in America. On my account, my mother will mortgage the farm to help me get settled in America. She gave me all the equipment and animals when Pa died. These I shall sell in order to raise some of the money for passage and settling in. Ma has a good man ready to rent the farm when I depart, and she will keep her room and garden and enjoy the freedom of the entire place. In case she wishes to come later, I have invited her to America."

At supper Anna sought to cheer her mother: "It's not as if we were going tomorrow, or as if we were going to America to die. You will hear from us, although letters take a long time between Sweden and America."

"That's the idea," said Ola, pretending bravado, "we might even join you in America. I shall count on you, Pehr, to tell me whether we too should emigrate."

After they were seated for supper the conversation became more cheerful as the meal progressed, and promptly after eating the young couple departed amid customary exchanges of "God speed" and "goodby." Anna was now quite resigned to accompanying Pehr to America.

In his father's shop at the back of Sissa's house Pehr set about building a huge chest in which to convey family belongings to America. He built it strong, with inch-thick seasoned oak, tongued and grooved, screwed onto a 2 x 2 inch frame, bound with several metal straps, and protected with metal on all corners. The lid had at the back three long stout strap hinges on the inside, and at the front a stout metal strap and staple to receive a sturdy pad-lock. Into this container would go his precious hand tools and other prized possessions, including clothing, kitchen utensils, and a selection of seeds.

Anna busied herself assembling and choosing items of clothing and utensils that she would need in the new land. She had difficulty distinguishing between utility and sentiment, but in the end did remarkably well.

After an errand to Hörby late in February, Pehr came home with news that would cancel Anna's worst fears—the conditions they would suffer in the hold of a ship. Pehr stopped the sleigh before the door and called to Anna: "Come out and hear my news at once." She appeared at the door in moments, and he called to her from the rig: "Your worst dreads you may now lay to rest. The king has issued a proclamation setting forth conditions under which shippers may carry Swedish emigrants to America. They shall henceforth be adequately fed and given sufficient clean space in which to live aboard ship. Furthermore, in event of any delay, the emigrants must be furnished adequate food and quarters without additional cost to them. The tickets we buy in Malmö will take us all the way to New York without any additional charge. You needn't even worry about carrying any food with you. I'll tell you more after I stable the horses." *(Figure 1.6)*

Anna fairly jumped with delight when her husband came in from the stable. She threw herself at him and kissed him hard on the mouth. "Kisses you shall have, if nothing else. Perhaps my fears will vanish sooner than I think, and we can again live normally as husband and wife. I yearn for love-making as much as you do. My self-denial is no less than yours!"

Said Pehr quietly, "If I am not man enough to deny myself the pleasures of sex

Figure 1.6. Facsimile of formal contract between Swedish emigrant and carrier as prescribed by King and Parliament 5 February 1869. Specimen is from Göteborg, but the law applied also to Malmö and every other port of exit.

temporarily, I am no match for the American wilderness! Continue your yearning, but please do not test my resolve unduly!"

In Hörby Pehr had also been informed about tentative sailing schedules from København and Liverpool, and listed his family for departure from Malmö on 11 May. In this he made a grave error: He would have no spring planting to do; new tenants would do that: They might have sailed a month or two earlier. However, he justified his error by telling himself that the seas would be less stormy in May and that they could be better prepared for departure. He had funds to assemble to a considerable sum and several legal papers to execute before they could depart with all affairs in order.

Sissa, defying her daughters' objections, mortgaged the farm and paid Pehr 2,000 riksdaler for his birthright. Sissa's holdings now had an assessed valuation of 5,000 riksdaler, and could have been sold for somewhat more. Her taxes remained modest, in compliance with royal decree by King Karl XV, continuing the reforms of his two predecessors in distributing equitably the taxation of iron mining, lumbering, manufacturing, and commerce, as well as that of land. Before fairly recent times Sweden had little taxable wealth other than land.

Pehr signed a release to his mother, legally executed before witnesses. From his farm equipment and animals he realized a sum of 800 riksdaler, selling most of the items to the tenants that would rent the two farms. He withdrew from the Hörby bank several hundreds of riksdaler saved over the years by denying his family and himself more than bare subsistence. Anna got several hundred riksdaler from her father. Of his father's hand tools Pehr took those he deemed most essential in the new land and of sizes the great chest could accommodate. Between him and Anna was much choosing and discarding before the chest was full of articles deemed by both most essential. Furniture and household articles given them at their marriage they returned to the donors, including Bolla's feather bed. Articles they themselves had acquired, they sold to the new tenants for a pittance. The chest stood ready and locked 1 May, boldly lettered on top:

**PEHR PEHRSON
MINNESOTA, U.S.A.**

The chest was a light blue, the printing jet black.

On that very day came notification to be at the "Out Migration" Center in Malmö on the morning of 10 May and prepare for departure from Sweden on the midnight ferry to København.

Next day Pehr, Anna, and their little daughters drove to Omsed to discuss the travel schedule with Anna's parents. Ola determined that they must go to Höör, north of Hörby, on the 9th and take the night train to Malmö, via Eslöv, Lund, etc. so they would have a full day for clearing all formalities required of emigrants departing Sweden. Höör was their nearest rail station *(Figure 1.7)*.

Ola came to Sissa's place by spring wagon the evening of 8 May so they could have ample time next day to reach Höör, almost three Swedish miles from Bessinge. The train was scheduled to depart Höör soon after midnight and arrive in Malmö before daylight *(Figure 1.7)*.

Next morning Anna roused her daughters at a sinful hour, Sissa roused Ingar, and all ate breakfast by candle light. Pehr and Ola then hoisted the great chest into the

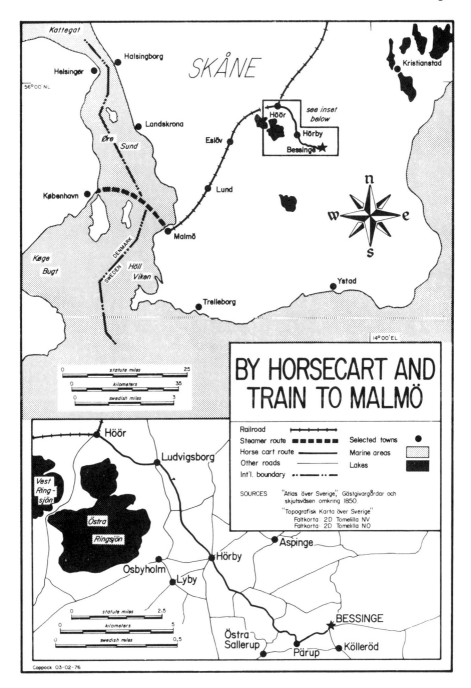

Figure 1.7. Map showing route by which Pehr and his young family departed Sweden, 11 May 1869.

rear of the wagon. Anna, Elna, and Hanna hugged and kissed Sissa and Ingar by turn; Pehr helped them up to the back seat and set their wicker baskets on the floor in front of them. His own cardboard suitcase, secured with two leather straps and containing one complete change of clothes, his razor, shaving mug, and small mirror he set in beside the chest. Then he kissed his mother final goodby, amid a copious flow of tears—his and hers. He turned and fairly sprang to the front seat beside Ola, and they were off. Anna and the girls waved to Sissa until she was out of sight. Sissa's blessing: "God be with you," was heard only by herself and God.

The party stopped at the Hörby hotel for lunch at noon and reached Höör at ten o'clock—before dark *(Figure 1.7)*. In town, Ola hauled his rig up alongside a uniformed policeman and got directions for finding the railway station. The stop and loud talk wakened the little girls who had slept most of the way from Hörby, one leaning against each side of their mother. Now they came wide awake to gawk at wonders never seen before.

At the railway station Pehr bought tickets to Malmö and supervised careful tagging of the great chest for the same destination. Their train would depart Höör soon after midnight.

This business attended to, Ola found the, reputedly, best inn in Höör and stopped squarely in front of it. A stable boy appeared as by magic to care for the horses. "I shall spend the night," Ola told him, "these animals have come a long way today, and will travel as far back tomorrow; give them an extra measure of oats and bill me for it."

"Yes, 'Herre,'" answered the stable boy, "it's a pleasure to care for horses the calibre of these."

The company went in to supper in an elaborate dining room. "My last chance to treat you," said Ola gravely, "so let us smile while we eat." He and Anna drank wine together, and Anna gave Elna and Hanna each a sip. Pehr kept them company with water, while gloating over an entry on the menu, "stuffed pork chops." All ate heartily, Ola paid the waiter, and all others expressed their sincere thanks.

Ola stepped to the desk and registered for the night. "I shall be in after the night train departs for Malmö," he told the clerk.

When they had walked back to the station the clock showed 11:30, so their wait was brief. The train came in, whistling and blowing, immediately after midnight, frightening the girls almost out of their wits. Hanna dropped her basket, but Anna grabbed it before it rolled off the platform and under the cars. Pehr and Ola shook hands and looked deeply and sadly into each other's eyes. Ola lifted each of the girls in turn and hugged them to him. Then he bent and embraced and kissed his departing daughter amid a flood of tears. Through his weeping he managed to say as the young couple mounted the train: "God be with you and bless you always!" When the train steamed away, he turned and walked back to the inn, feeling twenty years older than when he had departed Bessinge a few hours before.

They arrived in Malmö at dawning (3 o'clock) and got directions from a tired policeman to the out-emigration station, which was nearby. Next to the station was an all-night restaurant (for obvious reasons of location), in which they ate an early breakfast of fried potatoes, fried side meat, bread and butter. Anna and Pehr drank each two cups of coffee and the girls each a glass of sweet milk.

"We'd better eat well," advised Pehr, "because we may have a busy day once the offices open for business. How I can be hungry so soon after that heavy supper I ate last night, I don't quite know."

"The train shook it down," suggested Anna, trying to seem less sleepy than she was.

When they could eat no more, Anna escorted her daughters to the toilet for relief and a quick wash of hands and faces. When they returned to the table Pehr took his turn. He had carefully lectured his women folk: "No baggage must be left without someone to keep an eye on it. We cannot afford to lose any of the sparse belongings we have with us." His money he carried in a large leather bill-fold, tucked into his inside jacket pocket, secured with two tight buttons and a metal clasp. He would have been a poor target for a pick-pocket! Before 7 o'clock the cobbled walk in front of the out-emigrant station was crowded with people, and the doors opened on the first stroke of the steeple clock. (By special arrangement with the transport company, the place opened an hour earlier than otherwise.)

Once inside, the crowd of a hundred or more was herded into four groups and each group lined up before four desks. Behind each desk sat a clerk with a specific duty. One collected fares, one noted town of origin and probable destination, one noted the sum of money and other valuables declared by each head of family, and one executed the "carrier-emigrant" contract decreed by the king, handing one copy to each head of the family with this admonition: "Keep this securely on your person and surrender it to no one. It is your real ticket to New York and you may not be charged anything extra" *(Figure 1.6)*. When all the people had been cleared at the four desks, a uniformed agent of apparent authority called out: "Now hear this! You should now have in your possession the following papers: (1) a ticket to New York, showing names and ages of your family members, (2) a "carrier-emigrant" contract such as this (he held one up to show), (3) passes for boarding the *Ocean Queen* in København, the boat train in Hull, England, and the ocean steamship, *France*, in Liverpool. Does everyone have in hand every one of these items?" There was no correction.

Pehr had paid 405 'riksdaler riksmynt' for passage money; he paid half fare for each of the girls. He put all the papers into a compartment of his large billfold and secured it in his inner pocket. He had a claim slip for his chest.

The uniformed authority continued in a clear, loud voice: "You are all bound for America by the fastest means at our command. You should arrive in New York in about two weeks. You will assemble here at 11:30 hours and we shall see you safely aboard the ferry for København departing immediately after midnight. Get such sleep as you can sitting up; the trip takes three hours. Your official date of departure from Sweden will be recorded as 11 May 1869. Farewell and good luck!" The emigrants applauded! *(Figure 1.7)*.

When they were seated (uncomfortably) and under way on the ferry, Pehr ventured to say, "One couldn't sleep on this thing even if he could lie down on this hard bench! At least we can sleep on the ship, after only a few hours." He was trying to divert Anna's thoughts from the sea, the jiggle of the ferry, either pitch or roll, was enough to turn Anna green. Only by sheer determination did she keep from vomiting. Until now she had sailed in no vessel larger than a row boat on the large lake northwest of Hörby. Pehr felt no discomfort, and the girls were too young to become sea-sick.

When the ferry entered the slip at København the rays of the morning sun were just creeping down the towers and steeples of the great Port city. Daylight came to the dock as the sleepy group of some hundred and fifty were guided from the ferry slip to the quay beside which the *Ocean Queen* lay tied.

Hanna could not hide her fright. "Are we going on the water in that monster? It's bigger than many houses put together."

"Don't be afraid, dear," soothed Anna. "We will soon be comfortably inside her. And then we can sleep."

The crowd of passengers were hustled up the gang-plank and quickly escorted to their assigned quarters. The shipping company was obviously wasting no time.

Pehr, Anna, and their daughters were ushered into a compartment, cramped but adequate, and near toilet facilities down the passageway. Indeed, stowage of hand baggage presented a problem, but they solved it by pushing Pehr's crude case under a bunk and placing the baskets at the foot of the bunk occupied by the girls.

The iron-screw driven *Ocean Queen* cast off and got under way before three thirty. By four o'clock Pehr and his dependents were asleep, on their first ocean voyage.

The trim little ship steamed cautiously through the narrows between Denmark and Sweden, but once she entered the Kattegat the captain ordered, "full ahead all engines"; the sea lay smooth, and this was the place to do maximum knots. Between København and Hull were six hundred eighteen nautical miles that he must traverse in consideraly less than two days, so he could spare neither coal nor engines. The bunkers were full and the engines all drove without undue strain. He could cruise at fourteen knots and do almost two more at full power.

Before the *Ocean Queen* made a forty-five-degree turn at Skagen and entered the Skagerrak, her passengers had all eaten breakfast, half of them to a sitting, in the main deck dining room. The food was good and plentiful. They ate dinner on the North Sea, on which a swell was running high enough to slow the ship to cruising speed and cause several passengers to quit the table without eating—Anna among them.

By supper time the sea lay smoother, in the lee of England, and those empty since noon took nourishment at the table—including Anna. Both Pehr and Anna praised their daughters for being excellent voyagers. The Captain steered to portside of the Dogger Banks to avoid the numerous fishing boats.

They entered the Humber estuary about seven o'clock and docked in Hull at eight. The boat train stood ready on the quay, and they were herded onto it quickly. It was crowded and smelled strongly of coal smoke. All got seats, but Pehr and Anna were obliged to hold their duaghters on their laps. The locomotive spun its wheels to get started.

At eleven o'clock the train came to a screeching halt alongside the docks in Liverpool. Once again a guide directed and led the passengers to their waiting ship,

---

The Ocean Queen *was an iron-screw steamer: tonnage 218, length 137.5 feet, breadth 18.2 feet, depth 9.8 feet, 50 horsepower. Master, T. Huttan, crew—about 15, passenger capacity between 100 and 150. Burden: 156 tons. Usual voyage between Hull and Rotterdam. Built at Hull in 1854. Owned in 1869 by Tyne Steam Shipping Company. (Source: Lloyd's Register of Shipping: 1868-1869, Courtesy of J. Smith, Liverpool Record Office, England; and Henning Henningsen, Director, Danish Maritime Museum, Helsingør, Denmark.)*

the steamship *France*. As they climbed the gangplank onto the great ship, it was Elna who expressed the thoughts of all. On viewing it silhouetted against the weak moonlight, she exploded: "Can such a monster float on water, and with all of us inside?" *(Figure 1.8)*. The great ship loomed so high above them that it appeared taller than the tallest building.

Figure 1.8. The Steamship France, pictured above, was carrier of Pehr and his family across the North Atlantic. The S.S. France was an iron-screw steamer of 3,572 registered tons, built by Thomas Royden and Sons on the Mersey at Liverpool in 1867. Her length was 385.6 feet, her breadth 42.4 feet, and her depth 28.7 feet. Her engines were of 400 horse-power, built by J. Jones and Son. She carried a crew of one hundred and could accommodate some twelve hundred passengers. She was replete with stout tall masts, and great yards for hoisting a very considerable area of canvas—whether to complement the engines in a favorable wind or as a precaution against engine failure. (The combination power—sail and steam—was not uncommon during the era of transition from wind to mechanical propulsion.) She was owned by the National Steamship Company, Ltd. of Liverpool. She was broken up in 1896. Commander during the Pehrson's voyage was Captain R. W. Grace. Photo reprinted by permission of Craig J. M. Carter, Editor, from Sea Breezes *P. 422, Dec. 1956, Vol. 22. Considerably retouched by Photos, Inc.*

With incredible speed and efficiency the passengers were installed in their compartments, the great hawsers cast off fore and aft, and a few minutes before midnight the ship, almost imperceptibly at first, moved away from the quay pushed by a tug. A pilot steered the ship through the busy port channel, at the end of which he debarked into an attending launch, and the giant entered the Irish Sea under her own power, in command of Captain R.W. Grace *(Figure 1.9)*.

Before she cleared the Skerries and changed course to southward and St. George's Channel, Pehr and his little troop were sound asleep. Breakfast was served as they cruised St. George's Channel, and they had a light lunch of bread, cheese, and tea as they passed Cape Clear at the southern tip of Ireland. After the cape dropped from view, they would see no land for thirteen days. The ship would be their home; sea below and sky above would be their world.

The first three days out from Ireland were sunny and pleasant. Passengers from all levels in the ship, including steerage, were given one hour on the sun and promenade decks so they might stretch their legs and breathe the fresh sea air. The Pehrsons made full use of these outings and walked about the ship the entire hour. How much better they slept after exercising!

On the evening of the third day a cyclone approached from the west, and the sea commenced getting choppy. By midnight the ship was riding across deep troughs and tall crests, and eventually the bow rode high into the air and crashed down again with a report like that of a giant rifle. This, as Captain Grace well knew, no ship could endure very long without breaking up, so he changed course to angle across the troughs and crests.

This gave the ship a motion combining pitch and roll-corkscrew, a sure test of resistance to sea-sickness. Anna lay vomiting into a container provided for the purpose. Pehr grew nauseous but did not throw up. He soothed Anna with cool towels to her forehead. The girls slept. Pehr never dared mention that their quarters were well below the water line—bottom steerage.

The storm raged for two days, and a considerable sea ran an additional day. Then hours on deck resumed and most of those who had been sick recuperated, including Anna. Some remained flat in their bunks until they landed in New York. These ate well the day after they departed the ship.

Another cyclone met the *France* when she was only three days off New York, but this blow was less violent, and the Captain held to his course. But walking and sunning were suspended until the sea leveled out again—near the end of the voyage *(Figure 1.9)*.

In a morning fog early on 26 May, a Pilot came aboard and brought the large ship to her assigned berth. Our Swedes had arrived in America, safe and sound, little the worse for their long tiring journey.

Our small company of poor Swedish peasants entered New York at night, without fanfare. The ship had slowed to a few knots at the roadstead entrance. A few bells and whistle blasts wakened Pehr, but he remained still so that his family might remain asleep. They were warped to a pier and tied up, and lay still in the water when passengers were awakened by the customary blasts from the bosun's pipe.

The little family arose, noted the stillness of the ship, and went with unusual ease to their morning ablutions. Breakfast call came an hour early, and the meal consisted of a fresh bun with butter, fresh coffee, cream and sugar—all brought aboard while the passengers slept. It was good advertising to discharge contented passengers! During breakfast a crewman stuck his head into the dining room and announced loudly that the "guests" would remain in their places until summoned

---

A cyclone is a low pressure center about which, in the northern hemisphere, winds blow counter-clockwise and toward the center. It is an ordinary phenomenon of mid-latitude weather and usually passes without violence. It must not be confused with the tornado! Mid-latitude cyclones travel from west to east, on curved rather than direct courses. The North Atlantic is infamous for its frequency of strong cyclones in winter; relatively few cross in summer.

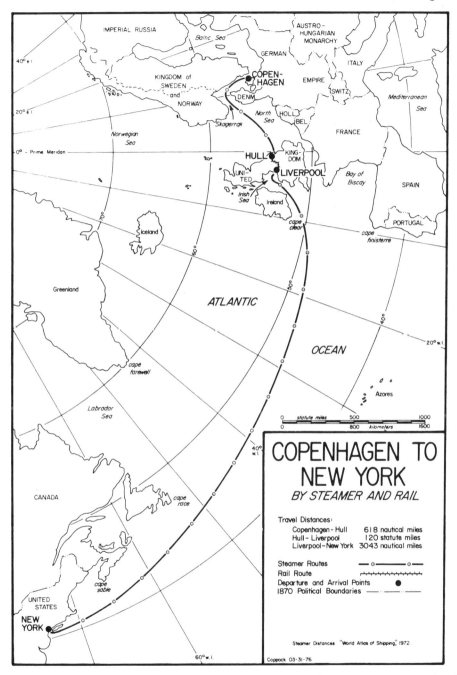

Figure 1.9. Map of sea voyage that brought Pehr and his family from København to Hull and across the North Atlantic from Liverpool, England to New York in less than fifteen days, arriving in America early morning of 26 May 1869.

for disembarking. They would be conducted top-side in small groups so no one need be lost on board.

After returning to their own quarters of almost two weeks, Pehr and his brood knelt and thanked God for safe arrival in the Promised Land.

They waited an hour without complaint, and then the little girls began to whimper. Eventually came their turn. All hefted their bulky burdens and followed their guide in silence. They climbed three flights to the main deck, on which rested the gangplank. To the plank came two streams of people from oppostie directions, and the streams joined to descend. For his band, Pehr led the way, the girls behind him and Anna bringing up the rear. Despite the inevitable bumping and crowding of heavy bulky burdens, no one showed either discomfort or anger. (Crewmen pondered whether European peasantry might not be less crude and vulgar than commonly portrayed.)

They were directed into a large room and instructed to set their baggage down. Almost at once came a loud voice from a corner of the room (in Swedish) "All Swedes headed for Minnesota this way!" It seemed that almost a quarter of the crowd responded. In the corner was a tall blond individual who quickly instructed his group of newcomers. (This was one Colonel Hans Mattson, immigrant agent for Minnesota, and connected in like capacity with the St. Paul and Pacific Railroad.) "Your trunks and chests will soon come off the ship and be set down on this floor. When you see your own, go to it and sit on it until I get along to help you on your way. This will take some time; if you need to relieve yourselves, there are facilities over there (he pointed). They are for your use!"

Pehr kept his eye on the door through which came the heavy baggage; after about an hour came his treasured chest, carried between two muscular sweaty dock workers. He went promptly and sat upon it, glad to be off his feet. He lifted the girls up beside him. Anna felt silly sitting without touching the floor with her feet, so she half sat and half stood, braced against the chest. Soon tiredness of feet overcame feelings of pride, and she climbed up beside the girls—with a helpful boost from her husband.

After what seemed a long time, the uniformed Swede came up and addressed them: "And where do you intend to go in Minnesota?"

"To Litchfield, in Meeker County," answered Pehr, instantly.

"That will be at the end of the railroad then?" queried the agent.

"That may be. I know only the town name. A friend told me where I should go."

"Ah, so. I'll tag you for the Central Railway of New Jersey. One of their men will come and get both you and your baggage and see you safely on the train. When you get to the ticket window, ask to be sent all the way on one ticket. It will save you time and confusion *(Figure 1.10)*. There were now two dozen persons in Pehr's group, all destined for Litchfield, Minnesota.

Now, as an afterthought, Mattson asked: "Does anyone here have Swedish money with him?"

"Yes," said Pehr, and several others.

"You will need to have it exchanged for American. See the window there (pointing) where it says 'Pengar Växel' (money exchange). I will go with you and see that the cashier gives you fair exchange. Perhaps you know the rate, if not I will help you."

Pehr knew the rate well enough. He had studied it many weeks, reading from a

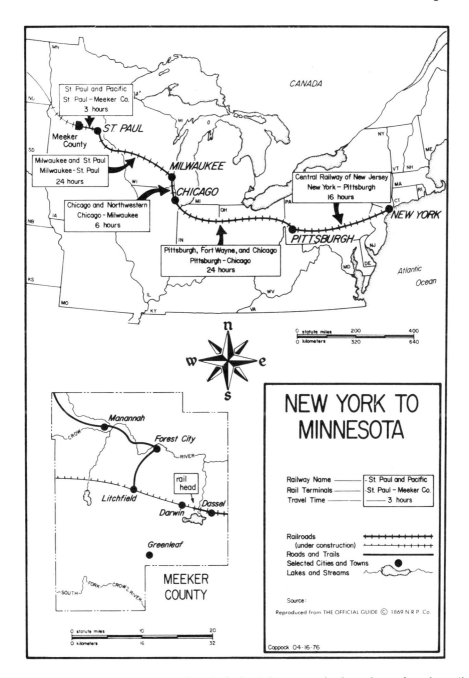

Figure 1.10. Map of railway route by which the Pehrsons made the arduous four-day rail journey from New York to the end of construction some distance west of Dassel in Meeker County, Minnesota.

notice he had got at Hörby. When came his turn at the window he counted out his Swedish notes and pushed them forward. There were 3,195 riksdaler; he should have in exchange 852 American dollars. Mattson kept an eagle eye on the cashiers, lest someone be short-changed. The rate of exchange was 3 riksdaler and 75 öre for one American dollar-gold standard. The cashier counted back to him exactly the sum he had figured. He tucked the bills into his large leather wallet, put it carefully into his inside pocket and secured it there with the flap with two buttons and the stout metal clasp. Anna's secret came out when she planked down 500 riksdaler and had counted out to her $133.33. Pehr grinned at her.

When all had exchanged their money, the Swedish speaking Mattson had a final word for the group: "Each one of you now wears a tag which says that you are a Swede going to Litchfield, Minnesota. Keep that tag on you until you arrive. The man from the Central of New Jersey will soon be here to see that you and your belongings get on the right train. Ah! here he is now. Follow this man's instructions, and you will go where you should. Good luck to all of you!" *(Figure 1.10).*

The train man was tall and clean shaven, in a uniform shiny with wear. He said (though no one understood him), "I shall mark your trunks and chests so that they will reach your destination." Pointing to Pehr's he asked, "Whose is this chest?"

"That is mine," said Pehr. "I have it marked, as you can see." Apparently the official understood Swedish because he made ready reply: "That is good, I'll just sharpen the lettering a bit." He took from a pocket a small brush and a can of paint. He went over Pehr's lettering with a bright green: "PEHR PEHRSON, LITCHFIELD, MINNESOTA." (That paint lasted the life of the chest.) One by one the thin man got owners and trunks coordinated, and soon all the heavy baggage stood clearly marked.

"Do not expect to see this baggage again before you arrive at (he read off a tag) Litchfield. I shall now give each of you a slip with which to claim his property at the other end." While he wrote these out and handed them round, the green paint appeared to dry. In any case, a heavy green wagon drawn by two large horses backed up to a wide door, and two burly draymen loaded all the heavy articles into the wagon and drove off. Pehr took out his large wallet and carefully inserted his claim slip in the most secret compartment. Then he buttoned it into his pocket as before.

"Now we are ready to go to the depot," said the thin man. He motioned them to the street. "When I signal you, climb aboard the horse car that I stop. Do not fumble for money, because I'll pay your fare (Courtesy the Central of New Jersey). The station is not far away."

The little girls were utterly awed by the large city and its constant turmoil. Indeed, they were frightened. Hanna cried a little, quietly. Elna pulled at Pehr's trouser leg until he bent to hear her, and she asked, "Papa, are we going to live in a place like this?" Her ingrained vision of America was of beautiful flowered meadows and tall forests.

Pehr reassured her, "No, my dear girl. I would not live here at any price. We are going where we'll have peace and quiet and fresh air." (Without the pervading odor of horse manure.) Elna felt better.

At the ticket window Pehr caught the agent's eye, pointed to his tag and said, "All the way, please." The agent grasped his broken English!

The agent commenced flipping thin pages in large books, noting times and prices and jotting down lengthy entries. Finally, after about fifteen minutes he stopped writing, re-examined the entire accumulation of passes, signed each one, slipped them into an envelope marked "Central Railway of New Jersey," and pushed it to Pehr across the counter.

"That will be $84.00 for you and the missus; the children less than six go free. The fare averages only three cents per mile because you will travel mainly in emigrant coaches."

Pehr thought: "Our fare across an entire ocean was not much more; this must, in truth, be a mammoth country. And we go only halfway across it." He hauled out his wallet again, withdrew a hundred-dollar bill, and returned to his wallet the sixteen dollars he got in change.

Eventually everyone had his tickets and commenced thinking about hunger. One of the party, slightly schooled in English, asked the ticket man how soon their train would arrive, and was told it should be there within an hour.

"Can we buy food on the train?" he then inquired.

"Yes, the train will have a complete diner, but food in it is expensive. You may wish to buy from a vendor who comes through the coaches selling sandwiches and drinks at moderate prices."

"Thank you, we shall do that. We cannot afford luxury."

As an afterthought, the ticket agent said, "Get on the coach marked Pittsburgh. That will be your first stop, and your first change of trains. There will be a person to help you get on another train where you should." Indeed, Hans Mattson would shepherd his little flock the entire distance.

In due time a steaming clanging locomotive rolled past the station and stopped. There was the coach marked Pittsburgh, and the group crowded into it. It became full, and several men, including Pehr, were obliged to stand in the aisle. With the sudden jerk as the locomotive started forward the standing men grabbed for the hand-holds in the corner of the back-rests. A few sprawled almost to the floor. When the train had gotten up what seemed fantastic speed, the uniformed conductor entered from the front end, calling, "tickets please." From each envelope handed him by a head of household he extracted a slip, punched certain holes in it with a tool for the purpose, and crammed the mutilated slip into his large pocket.

In due course came the sandwich and coffee vendor; and he did a landslide business, though his sandwiches (without butter) cost ten cents a-piece, and his black coffee a nickel a cup. Anna borrowed Pehr's cup to fetch water for the girls from the corner cooler. There was no milk for them! By the time they reached Pittsburgh sixteen hours later the vendor had quite exhausted his supplies.

In four days, after riding five different railroads and waiting many hours in depots between trains, they would almost reach their destination.

Their itinerary looked as shown on the map *(Figure 1.10)*. Central Railway of New Jersey, New York to Pittsburgh - 16 hours; Pittsburgh, Fort Wayne and Chicago Railway to Chicago - 24 hours; Chicago and Northwestern Railway (Milwaukee Division) to Milwaukee - 6 hours; Milwaukee and St. Paul Railway to St. Paul - 24 hours; St. Paul and Pacific (under construction) to end of line about 3 miles west of Dassel - 3 hours; eight miles short of Litchfield.

Anna vowed later, in retrospection, that the journey inland from New York was a greater ordeal than the crossing of the North Atlantic. Pehr agreed readily. Worst trial of all were the "emigrant coaches" on which they came most of the way. These monstrosities were entirely of wood (excepting the underpinnings and wheels, of course), built over a frame of heavy timbers bolted together. Huge straps of iron ran from the mid-point of the bottom on each side to the upper end corners—as main supports. They were furnished with benches almost entirely devoid of padding. When utterly fatigued, parents sat asleep leaning against each other, their children across their laps. Sanitary facilities were comprised of two 2-hole privies, one at each end of the coach.

The coaches were heated with coal stoves, which appeared to emit more gas than heat. They were, in truth, more suitable for hauling swine than for transporting humans. But rates on them were only 2 to 3 cents per mile, often the limit of a poor immigrant's meagre resources. In 1869 the Central of Pennsylvania operated 52 such abominations. The predecessor of the Great Northern (St. Paul, Minneapolis, and Manitoba) once built emigrant coaches almost one hundred feet long, with five decks. (It would be difficult to design a more colossal fire trap.) Railroad men commonly referred to them as "Zulu" cars — reminiscent of slave trafficking.

Three miles west of the small town of Dassel the train stopped, and well it was that it did; there was no more track for it to go on. Litchfield lay eight miles farther west, and would be a railroad town before the end of the summer. But now it remained attainable only, and barely so, by ox-or-horse drawn vehicle; and of such had come to the rail end a number estimated to accommodate the passengers destined for Litchfield.

This was a rare spectacle to behold: there in front lay the obvious end of the rails with loose fill beyond; and in the wide open country, there did indeed reign the quiet the little girls had wished for in New York, but for the greetings called from men atop an assortment of wheeled vehicles of various descriptions. Pulled up alongside the train was a whole row of assorted stagecoaches, buggies, wagons, and buckboards, waiting the pleasure of the travelers bound for Litchfield. One coach was artistically identified in bold letters on the side spelling out "Litchfield Hotel."

The women and youngsters were milling about, stretching their weary legs, and scratching themselves wherever their dirty woolen underwear commanded their attention. The men searched the baggage coaches for their trunks and chests. Pehr soon found his, and with the help of another kindly Swede, lowered it to the ground. One of the wagon drivers came quickly and helped them load it into his wagon. Pehr told him, "Litchfield Hotel," and turned to lend a hand to the man who had helped him lift it from the train. He found him and reciprocated in kind. He elected to hire space for his family and himself in the "Hotel" rig, and this he accomplished. It was crowded, but the air outdoors was getting the evening briskness of spring, and a contraption more or less closed against the elements was a good choice. Going was slow because the road, if such it could be called, was deep with mud and mire. The jouncing swaying trip took more than two hours; and Pehr paid the coachman his announced fee of three dollars ($1.50 per person, children less than six free) the instant the rig stopped and he got down. A quarter hour later the wagon with his chest drew up; and when the chest was safely stowed indoors, Pehr paid the drayman his required fee of one dollar.

The hotel was newly built and rough, but spacious. The entire crowd from the train were accommodated, and duly assigned to rooms. Pehr, Anna, and the girls got a room on the second floor, with toilets at the end of a long corridor. Thence Anna, with her daughters, repaired immediately, stopping at their room only long enough to deposit their baggage and ask Pehr to fetch a pitcher of warm water. This he did willingly, anticipating his own turn to wash himself.

When the mother and girls returned to the room, Pehr knew without asking that Anna was greatly irritated. She volunteered the answer to his unasked question: "I found lice in Hanna's underwear. I thought she kept scratching herself more than usual. She caught them, no doubt, in one of those filthy coaches we rode in. Everyone of us has them, more than likely. If you will absent yourself, I'll wash the girls with the water you brought and get them into clean underwear."

"You needn't drive me out," replied Pehr. "I'll stretch out on our bed, my face to the wall. Go ahead with your washing, and wake me for my turn, please." He was soon asleep.

Anna's facilities were the customary ones: a large pitcher for water, a large bowl in which to pour it for use, both atop a wash stand, with threadbare towels on a spool at the back, and a large covered pail for wastewater on a shelf beneath, hidden behind a flimsy flowered curtain drawn across the opening.

She turned to! She stripped the girls naked and laid all their clothes in two separate piles (they might not both be infested). Then she washed each of them with soap and water from head to toes, using one of the flimsy towels as wash rag and the bar of soap furnished in a flowered dish—matching in design the pitcher, bowl, and slop jar. The girls dried themselves after their mother's scrubbing and donned clean clothing that she extracted from their bundles.

This done, she waked Pehr and suggested they go down for food while some might still be available; and so down they went to the dining room, and barely in time before closing.

After their simple repast they returned to the room, and Anna tucked the girls into bed. They were asleep almost instantly. Pehr now descended the stairs with both pitcher and bucket and returned with warm water for Anna. She washed herself as she had the girls, and Pehr politely turned his face away. When she stood dried and dressed for bed, Pehr was sound asleep again. Reluctantly, she waked him a second time, and he made another trip to empty the bucket and fill the pitcher. When he had washed and dried himself and donned a clean suit of underwear, he blew out the lamp and crawled in beside Anna without waking her.

Figure 1.11, The distillery in which Pehr had off-season employment as a young man stands in good repair today, as here shown, though about a hundred and fifty years old. Under it are large cellars for potato storage.

Chapter 2

SOJOURN IN LITCHFIELD

Early on 1 June 1869, Pehr Pehrson and his little family awakened in Litchfield, Meeker County, Minnesota. Railway construction northwestward that would reach the Dakota line about two years later, was for a time, focussed on Litchfield. The town was wilder than the wildnerness, what with a gang of a thousand men, most of them young bachelors who could labor all day (12 hours) and carouse half the night. The boardwalk town, with dirt streets had its brief taste of glory; with glaring raucous saloons and shabby secreted whore houses, and various retail stores all doing a landslide business.

Snow melt and rains of the spring just past had valiantly cooperated to flush away the winter's accumulations of animal dung and other nauseous filth, but the conspiracy had quite sadly failed. Housewives who frequented the stores by day waded across streets in mire; the barmaids and their more professional cohorts came and went with ease, driven in closed carriages after dark and before full morning light.

The town stood on land too flat and low for adequate drainage. The otherwise balmy breezes of spring were spoiled by the noxious odors with which they were burdened.

On Saturday night the town fairly rocked and roared; by daylight Sunday morning it lay hushed as if asleep, which, indeed, it was. Those carousers of last night who could not sleep were so hung-over that distant church bells seemed to ring within their heads, and they needed cold packs more than any sermon. They might toil until Monday noon without taking anything more substantial than black coffee and water — much water, but by evening most could eat and be jolly again.

The little immigrant family arrived quite sober, and they sobered even more when they beheld the dreary aspect.

Pehr looked out the window aghast! To himself he said: (and he swore rarely even to himself), "What a hell of a place to bring a family. In all of Sweden, poor as we were, I doubt one could find a single town or village so dirty and ramshackle. Perhaps we should have stayed home as Anna wished." He said nothing aloud; but he sensed also Anna's disgust, which she also bore silently.

They had awakened to the noises of the street. Anna shook the girls to consciousness, and quickly steered them to the toilet. She stood blocking the door while each little one relieved herself in turn. Herself also relieved, she ushered the girls back to the room; and then Pehr went to take his turn. He then washed and shaved before the dull mirror over the wash-stand. Between razor strokes he said: "We must pack up all our belongings, ready to move out of here. Surely we can get a place for less than two dollars a day. After a bit of breakfast, we shall all walk out together and see what we can find. I believe that a decent family can have a decent place in which to stay, at a price they can afford."

Breakfast was truly a mere "bit"—flour mush with skimmed milk and sugar. Pehr and Anna had coffee with it. The whole bill was fifty cents.

In their search for quarters they commenced a systematic inquiry on side streets near their outer termini, and were soon rewarded. They rented from a Swedish housewife, quarters prepared for exactly such as they, on the edge of town almost in the open country. The good, inexperienced landlady showed them how meticulously clean were her premises, what she would furnish, and what they must procure for themselves. They would have a fair-sized bedroom with two double beds; a dining-sitting room to themselves; and kitchen privileges, including cooking and baking, with free use of all kitchen utensils. They would pump and fetch their own water from the well on the back porch and carry their own wood from the stack on the back of the lot—next the two-hole privy. (The privy had the luxury of a duck-board walk all the way from the house, so one needn't step in mud or dew.) Anna might use such tubs and kettles as she needed for washing clothes. Bedding now on the beds would be furnished.

Anna and Pehr exchanged knowing glances, and Pehr asked: "How much rent must you have? Your accommodations may be more costly than we can afford."

Mrs. Jönson replied: "My family and I were in your circumstances only two years ago, so we know your needs. Furthermore, we would not take advantage of our own countrymen. You may have these accommodations, under the conditions I have told you, for just fifteen dollars a month, payable weekly in advance. You will find nothing else like this for less."

Now Anna spoke up: "Your price is certainly reasonable, but we must be no less fair with you. We will not be long-term tenants, Mrs. Jönson. Pehr hopes to settle us on a Homestead before the end of June. Will you rent to us, knowing that we may stay only a few weeks?"

"I certainly will," replied Mrs. Jönson, "most people in Litchfield are transients, and when railroad construction passes westward there will be little demand for rental housing. Indeed, I fear that many buildings will stand empty. You may well be my first and last tenants. I'd rather not have renters here in summer, in any case."

"Then we shall move in," said Pehr. "Here's your first week's rent as earnest money." He took out a five-dollar bill and handed it to their new landlady.

The good woman puzzled, then said: "Let us simplify this rent business. You will pay me four dollars a week or part of a week. You will owe me on the first, seventh, fourteenth, and twenty-first of each month. Do you mind if we figure that way?"

"That will raise the rent a dollar or so a month," replied Pehr, "but I'm entirely agreeable."

Mrs. Jönson hurried to the kitchen, and returned in a moment with the dollar

Page 50

change and handed it to Pehr. He thanked her, and they shook hands to seal their contract.

As they moved toward the door, Anna said: "We will go and fetch our belongings from the hotel and be back soon. We do so thank you for your considerate disposition toward us."

"We shall be pleased to have you," said Mrs. Jönson. "Won't you leave your daughters here with me while you do your errands? The street mire is especially bad for little ones." She bent down and asked the girls: "Will you stay with me awhile? I have fresh-baked brown cookies for you."

"I'll stay with you," said Elna, but Hanna stood silent, looking at her shoes. Elna took her sister's hand, and thus reassured, Hanna looked up and smiled. She would stay too.

Anna patted each girl on the head and instructed them: "Be good girls! Papa and I will be back soon." Enroute the hotel, Pehr said, with obvious relief: "We are lucky to have found a comfortable place to live at so reasonable a price. Perhaps this town is better than it looks. Maybe it has a good heart despite its ugly face."

"I am tremendously relieved," said Anna. "I feel more confident now than I have at any time since we departed Sweden."

"Now, that does make me happy!" asserted Pehr, almost too loudly for a public street.

They got their things from the room; Pehr paid the bill and they went out. At the boardwalk in front stood a one-seated buck-board ready for hire. Pehr placed the baggage in the shallow box, helped Anna up beside the driver, and motioned him toward the hotel entrance.

Pehr and the drayman, midst much straining and grunting, man-handled the great chest into the vehicle; and by Pehr's signaling each turn, the rig was quickly in front of the newly-rented quarters. With a few more grunts and groans the chest came into the living room. Pehr said in English, "How much?"

The man said, "Fifty cents," and Pehr understood. Unable to haggle in English, he handed him the half-dollar. The immigrants had attained another milestone on their long road to independence!

Anna named off a considerable list of groceries they must have to resume their own food preparation; Pehr went to the stores on Main Street and bought her requirements. He returned heavily laden and was extraordinarily hungry at noon.

After noon, Pehr unlocked the heavy padlock on the great chest, and they examined their possessions brought across the sea. They needed a careful recounting to determine more certainly what their additional needs might be. The chest was stuffed so compactly that it must have weighed at least three hundred pounds, a weight equal to Pehr's estimate in Swedish units. It contained clothing and bedding (arranged to cushion fragile items), a few dishes (one piece was broken) and copper kitchen ware, two bow saw blades, two wooden planes, one hammer, one axe, a one-inch wood auger in wooden cross-tree, one draw-knife, one steel square, one wooden plumb and level, a variety of small knives, chisels, and gouging tools, a few flower and vegetable seeds, two small dolls, and a well-oiled double-barrel musket with a quantity of shot, balls, and a box of priming caps (baggage must not contain gun powder!). The hand-tools were of high-carbon Swedish steel from Eskilstuna, the kind any journeyman would wield with pride. (Pehr's collection would still be serviceable in the hands of his great-grandchildren.) In his skilled hands they would build and furnish a cabin and make and mend numerous farm implements and other equipment. That which could be wrought from wood with simple tools, he would never buy.

There were lacking several necessities for homesteading which must be procured locally, but there remained several weeks before he should need them. He would go and choose his land when the prairie lay clad with new verdure. Then he could see where sloughs stood in summer, where the boulders cropped out, and where any sand pockets lay. He would choose his land carefully.

Meanwhile, to augment rather than deplete their meager funds, he needed remunerative employment. Waiting would cost a dollar a day for food and shelter, and this he must off-set immediately. Essential additions of equipment and supplies would cost several hundred dollars; considerably more than he now counted out and stowed deep in the chest. He would seek work tomorrow, hopefully at a good wage. Who might use a steady willing laborer?

Railway construction answered the question, as it did for many another "green-horn" newly arrived from Europe. In summer the grade bosses took on anyone strong enough to push a dirt-laden wheelbarrow and smart enough to tip it where the boss pointed. It was work for brutes, and the human kind was more readily available than work-cattle or horses. There were, in fact, horses and oxen by the score, but each kind had its peculiar handicaps. Horses required considerable stabling, care, and attention; and became mired in deep muck. Oxen were slow and plodding, though sure-footed. A yoke of oxen needed no pampering and could haul heavy loads or snake huge timbers about. They required no money for women and whiskey on Saturday night. They slept on the ground without being drunk, and their gait was steady on Monday morning. Little wonder that they were more highly esteemed than the Swedes, Germans, and Irishmen who, ostensibly, stretched the "civilizing rails" across Minnesota—completing the traverse in three places during 1871 and 1872. Wonder it was that the gigantic projects were so soon completed, what with hot-headed "Irisher" and hard-headed Swede working and sweating side-by-side. A taste for hard liquor and soft women was about all they had in common. They quarreled soon as the Swede could understand an insult in Irish brogue. They fought when he learned to counter the jibe. And, when he became quite proficient with profane invective, one or the other might end up at the bottom of a high earth fill, his head cracked with a spike hammer or smashed with the back of a shovel. (When one travels this landscape by train, he might give passing thought to the bones that, in places, help support the track.)

Pehr and his fellow Minnesota land-seekers in the era of the late sixties and early seventies came at a most propitious time. Railroad construction was progressing apace on three major lines, and the northern pineries were in full swing, as well. One could earn good wages both summer and winter, and many homesteaders did so. But for these employment opportunities, many would have become delinquent in "proving up" their claims. At the very least they must have a yoke of oxen and an iron plow, and these were costly items. Few arrived with sufficient money to buy them, and must first earn and accumulate the requisite sum. Many husbands left their wives and children alone on the claim while they spent the winter in a logging camp. Then they returned home in the spring to work and sow their land. Some worked on the railroad between sowing and harvest.

The logging camps got an unsavory reputation for profanity and vulgarity, whiskey drinking and brawling; but all lumberjacks were not so rough and wicked as they were wont to be painted. Among them were many honest decent men who abhored cursing, gambling, and drunkeness, and most particularly the bedbugs with which most bunk-houses became infested. In spring when logging stopped, the married men sought to shave and bathe—and leave the bugs behind—before heading for home. The single Karls hastened to the barbershop in a town nearby—for haircut, shave, and bath—and then dressed in new clean clothes in which to paint the town. This they did in riotous fashion. For a brief season, quiet sedate towns and hamlets became dens of iniquity. Raw whiskey and loose women became cause and object of skull-cracking brawls; buildings and other physical property became high risk. Wives and young women of good repute remained indoors after dark, seething with both overt disdain and secret envy of their less circumspect sisters out on the town and having all the fun.

Snow and frost of winter interrupted earth moving for four months or more. When the daily minimum temperature fell far below zero (Fahrenheit) the ground froze too deep and hard to penetrate and break up with a pick. At "forty below" the new green, or half-green, cross ties became too brittle to take a spike without splitting. Winter was off-season for excavating, filling, and track laying; but there was much else to railroad building. There was right-of-way to clear; there were trees to fell, buck, and snake out, to be peeled and hewn into timbers for trestles and pilings; there were crossties to be cut 8 feet long and hewed to 8 by 8 inches, some 2700 of them for every mile of track. (Later, 3000 ties per mile became standard.)

Logging was the winter work of railroad building and the Swede from Skåne had virtually cut his teeth on an axe handle. In the woods Pehr was as much at home as an Irishman in a saloon. He could notch a tree so it would fall exactly where he wanted it. He could saw and wedge heavy timber with the ease born of experience.

Not so the Irelander! He'd get one tree hung up in another so only an expert woodsman could undo the tangle. He would fell a tree crosswise onto the logs and splinter it, and get everything so generally balled up that he often became less help than hindrance. He could pile tops and limbs out of the way, and he could roll logs together after he learned how to manipulate a peevy; but with an axe or as a partner on a two-man cross-cut saw he wasn't worth his salt. In the woods, the Swede was boss. His indignant Irish helpers cast their insults and oaths toward the lee of the Swede, lest they suffer more ridicule.

By inquiry of Mrs. Jönson, Pehr learned the approximate location of logging operations west of town and took himself thither early next morning, his axe on his right shoulder and a lunch sack in his left hand. He walked a considerable distance from town, following the construction scars on the land. He found the logging foreman's shack without difficulty. Most of the men appeared to be Swedes, and he got directions he could understand. The foreman himself was a Swede, about Pehr's age by appearance, and Pehr was delighted.

"Are you looking for work?" asked the foreman, motioning Pehr into the shack.

"Yes!" said Pehr. "I was hoping to find work in the woods. Is it too late in spring?"

"We have a requirement to meet, leaves or no leaves. Have you done any logging before?"

"Yes, I have logged both conifers and hardwoods such as you have here. I assure you I can earn my wage!"

"I believe you can," asserted the foreman. "Do you have a yoke of oxen or a team of horses that you would also like to hire out?"

"That I have not," answered Pehr. "I have only my axe, and that I brought with me, as you can see."

"Which part of the work would you prefer to do, then," inquired the foreman, "felling, trimming, and bucking; peeling and hewing; or helping the teamsters and ox-drivers snake out and stack the timbers?"

"I would prefer not to work at yarding; and you would have to furnish me with broad-axe and adz if I were to split and hew. I believe I should prefer to fell, clear, and buck the logs. I assume you have cross-cut saws and steel wedges."

"We furnish all the necessary equipment, including regular axes, but you are free to use your own axe if you wish. Right now I need a good man to take down big trees, so that's where I'll put you. I see you brought a lunch; are you ready to go to work?"

"I'm ready right now," replied Pehr, confidently. "I came to work."

"Come along then, and I'll show you where we are now cutting. You can leave your lunch here in my shack, and join me at noon." He led off, in the direction of the central activity.

Arrived at the momentary felling site, the foreman stopped and turned to Pehr. He said: "You see we are felling mainly white oak and elm. The oak is the best, for both sleepers and trestle timbers; but since we have to cut elm to get at the oak, we cut and use both species. Back in there a short distance you'll come on blazed trees. They mark our boundary. That man over there notching the big oak (he pointed), he will be your partner. You will, of course, use a two-man cross-cut." He cupped his hands and called: "Nils, 'kom hit,' " and Nils quickly joined them. The foreman introduced Pehr to Nils Johnson and the two slipped off their right-hand gloves and shook hands.

"Can you two Swedes work together?" asked the foreman laughingly.

"If we can't," said Nils jovially, "we'll turn the whole damn woods over to the Irishmen."

"You will, like hell," said the foreman, and turned to walk away. Then he turned back, facing Pehr, and said: "You didn't ask about our wage. Wouldn't you like to know?"

"Of course I'm interested," replied Pehr, "but I've been told that you pay well; and I assumed that I would be paid according to my worth."

"Our base pay is one silver dollar for a ten hour day, but men such as Nils here, get 25 cents a day more. We begin work at seven o'clock and knock off at six; hour for lunch! If you are as good a woodsman as he is, you can expect the same wage as he gets. I'll tell you tomorrow."

By twelve o'clock Nils and Pehr had taken down half a dozen large oaks, whacked off branches and tops, and bucked the main trunks into sleeper lengths. One of the trees had sufficient girth and clear length of bole to make a dozen sleepers 8 x 8 inches and 8 feet long. But it had a tremendous crown, with main branches thick as a man's waist—large enough for squaring into crossties. Nils had observed, with real pleasure, the power and accuracy with which Pehr swung his axe and the large chips he made fly. He had first tried the new man on an 18-inch oak, and Pehr had notched it almost half way through in little more than ten minutes. Nils brought the large cross-cut saw, and smiled broadly at Pehr as they pulled the saw back and forth, smoothly and easily. Ten minutes of sawing, with one interruption to drive a wedge behind the saw, and the tree toppled.

When he stopped puffing, Nils said to Pehr, most earnestly: "You have done more logging than I have, and you shall certainly get the same wage as I do. I only wish you'd come last fall. I've had a tough time with bragging amateurs. I hope you stay on this job as long as I do."

Pehr turned the compliment aside by saying: "You and I, Nils, we make a team hard to beat. It's a pleasure to work with a man who knows exactly what he is doing, one who wastes no motion. I hope to stay on about two or three weeks, if the season lasts that long. I hope we can remain felling partners."

"Now it's lunch-time," announced Nils. "Did you bring food?"

"Yes I did," answered Pehr, "it's in the foreman's shack. He told me to come and eat with him! Won't you join us?"

"Thanks! Ordinarily, I would not, but in your case I shall. You see, the foreman eats with a fellow the first day if he thinks the man may be a good hand. Otherwise, the choppers eat on the log pile. Come on. I'll go with you."

They entered the shack together, and the foreman handed Pehr his lunch sack. They commenced eating. After a few mouthfuls, Nils stopped chewing and spoke to the foreman: "Karl, we have a good man here, and I hope you will pay him the same wage I get. Pehr and I as a team can really lay down the timber. He's the best woodsman I've worked with all winter."

"I saw you work together," said Karl, "and I had in mind to ask your opinion on the matter of wages. Pehr shall have his $1.25 a day, beginning today. "All right, Pehr?"

Pehr arose, and without a word shook hands with his fellow woodsmen. Then they all sat down again and finished their lunch.

The afternoon went as well as the morning; and before seven o'clock, Karl was storming at the ox and horse drivers for falling behind. He would have to get more work animals on the job.

(By no means did railway right-of-way and "grant" land in the vicinity yield a sufficient quantity of timbers for railroad building. Most such materials were purchased from local land owners at fixed unit prices payable on delivery to designated yarding areas. Round wood pilings, squared timbers and crossties were largely procured in this manner. Delivered to a yard, cross ties 8 x 8 inches and 8 feet long brought forty cents a piece if they were white oak. No other species was acceptable for sleepers. The land about Litchfield was mainly native prairie, with forest largely confined to stream valleys.)

Pehr came home to his family—proud, happy, tired, and very hungry! Anna regaled him with one of his choice dishes—pork-rib roast. To salve over the extravagance, she said: "When you stayed away at lunch, I knew you had been hired. And if they hired you, I knew they would pay you well. A good man deserves good pay and good food. Say the prayer before meal, girls—be so kind." This was their happiest evening since they departed Sweden.

Next day, as Nils and Pehr sat eating their lunch, Karl sauntered up the slope to make them an offer of Sunday duty.

"The security people need special Sunday guards to keep kids off our machinery and away from our work areas on the line. If one of the kids got hurt, the construction contractor could be held liable under a legal thing called "attractive nuisance". I'm authorized to name two men from my crew. The pay is two dollars. Would either, or both of you, be interested?"

"Thank you, " said Pehr, "but unless it be an emergency, I prefer not to work for hire on the sabbath. It's not a matter of religion entirely; my family and I are accustomed to sharing one day a week. I could not lightly break the habit."

"And you, Nils?" said Karl.

"If this is for one day only I'll take a crack at it; but please don't commit me further. I may not relish the job."

"I'll put your name down, then. No obligation beyond next Sunday. You should be at the security building by eight, Sunday morning, and you must stay on duty until dark—unless the man in charge relieves you earlier. You will carry no sort of weapon."

As Karl turned to go, his glance caught Pehr in the act of honing his axe bit with a sizeable whetstone.

"You lay great store by your axe, Pehr. Is it out of the ordinary?"

"Well, yes," answered Pehr, "it is special in a way. It was a very ordinary, heavy (5 lb.) axe; but I had a good Swedish blacksmith take the bulge off it and draw it out, straight from the eye to the bit. It is much better to chop with than a regular axe, but not much good for splitting. Would you like to try it?"

Karl grasped the helve proffered him by Pehr and took a chopper's stance by the nearest oak. He took four or five hefty swings; then stopped to examine the axe closely.

"It certainly goes into the wood remarkably, but it sort of sticks, doesn't it?" questioned Karl.

"Yes, it does sort of hang in the cut, but a short, quick snap of the wrist after each swing releases it. The little flick becomes automatic with practice. I'm at a loss with another kind of axe," said Pehr.

Half to himself, Karl said, "I should like to borrow it sometime and show it to our blacksmith. He might improve our choppers' efficiency and save us money."

"You are welcome to borrow it any evening, or on Sunday," asserted Pehr. And then he addressed himself to his next oaken victim.

Sunday morning, 6 June, the family went to church and offered devout thanks for safe arrival and their blessings thus far in a new strange land. Pehr was over-joyed to see his wife apparently happy, and he hoped that her cheerful outlook might endure.

Pehr took a luxurious nap after Sunday dinner, and during the afternoon, the girls entertained the two Jönson boys and a little girl from next door. All of them spoke Swedish, and the girls seemed as much at home as had they been in Skåne. Pehr observed, and was amazed, that the young could so much more readily adapt to a new situation than could their elders. America, he concluded, is a land for young people, and he was glad that he had come before he grew older.

Days and weeks became quite routine. Time and again logging was interrupted by rain showers, but no wages docked!

Whenever Karl suspended operations for a half day, Pehr—sometimes with Anna—scouted the town to ascertain just where they might purchase homesteading needs when the time came to buy them.

One rainy afternoon he and Nils rode the stage to Greenleaf and spent hours in the Land Office, much of the time talking with a friendly Swedish-speaking clerk from Massachusetts. They must learn how the land was surveyed and marked so that they

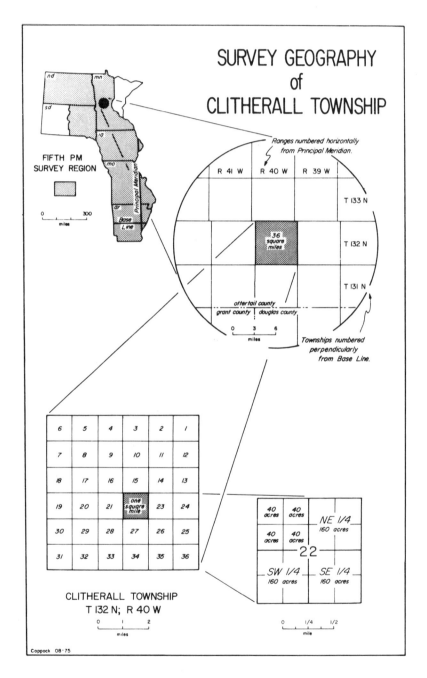

Figure 2.1. Map: Survey Geography of Clitherall Township, Otter Tail County, Minnesota. (Self-explanatory).

might go and select a quarter section and surely return with the right data for filing a claim.

Here's how the young clerk explained the land survey and the procedure for filing:

"The land survey with which you will be involved stems from a federal ordinance of 20 May 1785, which provided for a rectangular system of survey of the public lands, and a more definitive Act of Congress, 1796.

"Basic to the entire system are geographic reference lines—meridians, which run north-south, and ranges which run east-west. These you needn't worry about, but be sure you note the range number *(Figure 2.1)*. It's indicated on the survey posts by a capital R followed by the numeral. Next to note is the township number, indicated by a capital T followed by the numeral. You needn't tell us whether the township is north or south of the base line; we can determine that here in the office. But note down the township number.

"Now! This you need to know and note exactly! Each township has thirty-six sections, numbered this way." He drew a sketch *(Figure 2.1)*. "On our maps, a section is identified by a capital S followed by the numeral.

"Don't file on section 16 or section 36; those were given to the state for the support of public schools. They will be sold by the state in due course.

"The surveyors set posts at all section corners, turned diagonally to the section lines, so that each flat face is toward a section corner. One face has gouged into the raw wood an S followed by the section number, a T followed by the township number, and an R followed by the range number. Like this, let's say: S 25; T 100 (N or S); R 40 (E or W); *(Figure 2.2)*. The other three faces have only section numbers, thus S 25; he wrote these out. "Take down all this from the corner of the section in which you wish to choose your four forties."

"Now—and this is the nitty-gritty, there's a post at the midpoint on every section line, to identify quarter sections. These posts are set on the diagonal, same as the others, but they identify only the quarter section corners in any section. They're inscribed this way on all four flat faces: ¼ S.

"Now, since each quarter section has four forties, 160 acres—if you choose the square, all you need to tell us then is which quarter of which section, township so-and-so, and range so-and-so. On the other hand, if you choose forties from two quarters or from two sections you have to spell out each one, like this: SE¼ of NW¼ of S 20, T 100, R 40. You have to estimate on the ground where forties corner, because those corners were not established by the surveyors."

"Would you like me to go over it again, or do you think you have it?"

"I shall have to study it some more, to be sure that I make no mistake. May I have those sketches you made, so I can study them at home?" asked Pehr.

"By all means," said the patient young clerk. "I made them for your use. If they confuse you come back in again some day and I will set you straight."

The Swedes thanked the young man over and over again, while pumping his hand strenuously. They heard much about filing a claim, and now they thought they knew how to do it. As Nils was opening the office door to go, the young clerk called to the land seekers: "You will get more help at the Alexandria Office. You'll have to pass right by it in order to reach the Otter Tail Country, where the nearest good open land remains to be claimed. You'll want to go some distance north into Otter Tail County. I'm told there is some beautiful prairie. Good luck!"

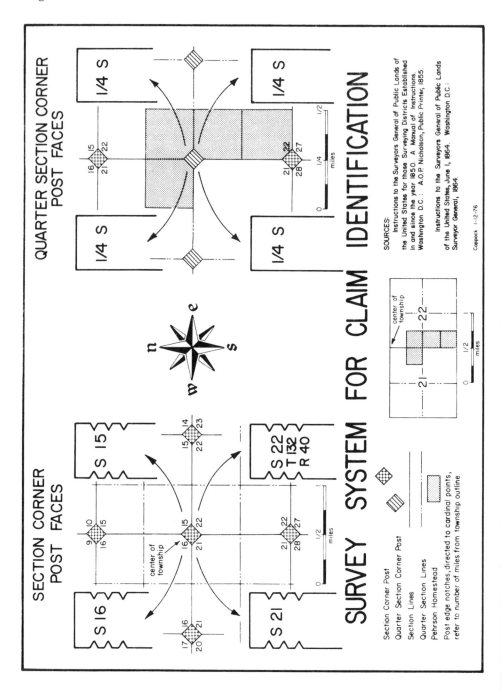

Figure 2.2. Diagram: Survey system of setting and marking posts to identify land units. (Also explained in text.) Tops of posts were cut at a 45° angle, the better to shed rain and snow.

After the return stage-coach ride, Pehr hurried home to tell Anna and explain the system to her. If she were not interested, at least he would get some practice.

On Monday, 14 June, Pehr was taken off what he considered logging, and set to work splitting out and hewing to size the sleepers he and Nils had felled and bucked to length during the past two weeks. Nils had asserted that he was no good at hewing a large piece of round wood to a flat surface; but rather than logging with unskilled partners, he elected to join an earth-moving crew at a dollar a day.

Pehr was quite as expert at splitting and shaping as at felling and trimming, so he welcomed the change of work, but he regretted the sundering of his congenial partnership with Nils. They would remain fast friends despite any circumstances.

The first morning on the new job, Pehr stood before the gigantic stack of sleeper-length logs. There were, he knew, some three thousand pieces; and of these, he and Nils had cut a large share. Nor did he stand and reflect very long; he had much work to do.

With maul and wedges he attacked one of the largest logs—large enough to yield four crossties. He split it in half, and then split the halves in two. Next he selected a log not quite sufficient in girth to yield four ties, laid it flat on the ground; and into it, at midpoint, he chopped out a deep "V" notch. Into this notch he laid one end of the timber to be squared with the adz and broadaxe. Then he laid another log parallel to the one he had notched, just clear from the low end of the timber he was to work. This would keep the log being squared from slipping backward as he hewed it. Behind this barrier log he drove into the ground two sturdy stakes garnered from a sapling disdained by loggers. He straddled the piece, hacked and hewed with a downward swing and kept the bit of his tool clear of the ground. One side squared to the midpoint, he over-ended the piece and did the other half of the length in like manner. In this way he squared the three sides with bark on them, throwing off sizeable slabs. The fourth side, raw-split, was easily shorn of slivers and hewed flat and true. When he had wrought the first crosstie, he examined it critically and then laid it down, well to one side, where he would stack the others as he completed them. He kicked aside the considerable heap of chips and slabs from the first unit and fitted another quarter into the groove. He straightened and stretched his back, and commenced anew.

He worked steadily until he had squared and stacked all four quarters from the large log. Then he sat down on the little stack, and consulted his watch, while still puffing from sustained exertion. For him to split out and square up four railroad sleepers had taken almost an hour and a half. Could that be an acceptable rate of production? Perhaps he could work faster with the Company's adz and broadaxe!

Next he squared from the round, a log only large enough to make one crosstie. This sort would require even more hacking and hewing than did a split-out quarter; but after squaring only one side, he wedged the other slabs off before wielding the axe. This facilitated his work substantially; but he was well aware that slabbing with wedges could be done satisfactorily only on straight-grained timber, such as the oaks he had just worked. Now he smoothed top and bottom with the adz.

At noon-lunch-time he had a dozen finished sleepers in the growing stack on which he sat to eat. Karl came by to check on his progress. He examined critically Pehr's little stack and then sat down beside his master woodsman.

"Pehr," he said, "you have laid up a record half-day's work, and I have no fault to find. You have worked diligently, that is obvious. I am not criticizing, but you may be a bit too meticulous. You can spare yourself considerable work if you leave rounded corners instead of squaring them out to an edge. Those you have done here are squared more precisely than necessary. I know that your output will be abundantly adequate; but I suggest you make a little less work out of it. I must tell you that you may do this on piece work if you wish. We pay ten cents for hewing out a tie. At the rate you appear to be going you could earn two dollars a day—for 20 ties."

"Thanks," answered Pehr, "I shall do piece work then, and I will heed your instruction. I am out of practice and have not yet regained my knack for hewing square timbers. When I get back into the swing of it, alternating between adz and axe, my squaring of corners will come with ease. I want the track-laying crew to appreciate my workmanship. I would like to know whether we are sitting on a fair half-day's work? Am I slow?"

Said Karl, "As I said, you have done a very good half-day's work—the best I have seen. You are certainly not slow; don't be concerned on that score. Just don't work too hard; this is monotonous, backbreaking work. Take time to rest and get your wind between timbers. I see you have sharpened the broad axe and adz; our tools get rough treatment."

"Yes," said Pehr, "they were badly in need of sharpening."

"Say, Karl," he went on, "I've been wondering how long white oak sleepers, laid in green, can be expected to hold up?"

"Shoo! They won't last more than four or five years," answered Karl with disgust. "If they were seasoned a year before laying, they would be good for eight years or more, if laid on gravel or cracked stone ballast, untreated. Many are laid flat on the ground without any stone under them; those will probably rot in a few years. I have seen considerable stretches of track laid right on mucky earth fill. The sleepers sink half way in before fishplates can be laid and spikes driven into them. That's a terrible waste of timber!" With that, Karl arose and commenced walking off. Then he turned and called to Pehr: "Nils sends you greetings. I saw him in the earth-moving crew this morning."

When Karl came again on Wednesday, Pehr regretfully informed him that Friday would be his last day on the job. Saturday he must go to Forest City District Court for his first naturalization papers *(Figure 2.3)* Then on Monday he would go land seeking. Karl expressed genuine regret that Pehr was quitting. He returned Friday at the work-day's end, counted up Pehr's ties and paid him ten dollars. Pehr had hewed 20 ties a day for 5 days. Pehr handed Karl the company's adz and broad axe, fresh sharpened. The men shook hands sadly; Pehr shouldered his trusty axe as they parted.

Pehr came home to a family in a state of panic. All rushed to meet him the instant he stepped in the door. Anna threw her arms about his neck and pulled him to her. The girls stared in fright.

"What *is* the matter?" he asked loudly. "Calm yourself, and tell me what's wrong."

"The Indians," said Hanna.

"Yes, the Sioux Indians," said Elna.

"Have they been here," asked Pehr. "I've been told that the Sioux were driven out of this state several years ago."

"Mrs. Jönson told us about the massacres in 1862," said Anna, haltingly. "They

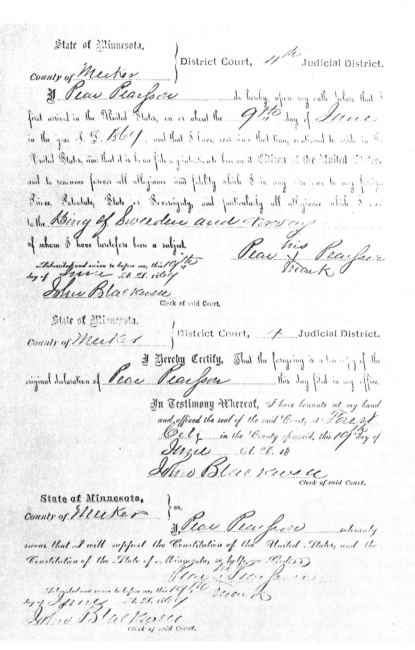

Figure 2.3. Facsimile of Pehr's Application for Citizenship, Fourth Judicial District, Forest City, Meeker County, 9 June 1869. (This and other legal papers relating to homesteading and naturalization (except the government's copy of the land grant Patent in the Bureau of Land Management files) are from originals in the National Archives of the United States.
All were reduced to convenient size by Photos, Inc. Minneapolis, Minnesota.

killed and burned whole towns near here, a place called New Ulm was almost completely destroyed. We are scared to death that we will run into the savages when we go north to settle. Perhaps we should go back home."

"You are unnecessarily upset," Pehr assured them. "If we see any Indians up-country, they will be friendly Chippewas. Some of those may be there; I was told about them in the Land Office. They will hurt no one unless he hurts them first, and this we will not do. The Chippewa Indians have actually helped white settlers time and again. I only wish I could talk their language, or they could talk ours. But we shall make do with signs and gestures. We shall be kind, and we can expect kindness in return. Now! Put aside your fears and get ready for supper! I must wash off my sweat and grime before I can eat."

The family was, outwardly, reassured; though some secret fears remained.

Saturday morning at eight o'clock, Pehr and seven other newcomer Swedes crowded into a stagecoach bound for Forest City. Hans Mattson had made arrangements with the Judge for those Swedes he could contact. With an over-full coach, he got from the stage operator a special rate—50 cents a piece, for a five mile trip and return. He rode atop the vehicle with the driver.

The eight Swedes were brought before the judge, and Hans Mattson vouched for their worthiness to become American citizens. The judge then ordered them to stand (Hans prompted them) and raise their right hands. They then swore, repeating after the judge, renouncing any allegiance to a sovereignty other than the United States of America, to defend the constitution and the nation *(Figure 2.3)*. (Be reminded that Norway was part of Sweden in 1869; indeed, until 1905.)

Pehr got home in time to tell his family about the entire legal adventure before supper. He would be eligible for final papers (full citizenship) after five years. And his citizenship would confer citizenship also on his wife and daughters.

So many newcomer Swedes labored at railroad construction across the Middle West that the borrow pits whence had come the spoil for grades and fills became facetiously identified as "Swede Holes."

Contributed by Dr. Lewis G. Wixon
Geographer, at Saint Cloud State University.

Chapter 3

THE LAND SEARCH

By pre-arrangement, Nils Johnson came to Pehr's lodgings at three o'clock Sunday morning, bringing with him two additional newcomer Swedes — Sven Person and Nils Anderson. Sven was almost as rangy of frame as Johnson, but with blond rather than dark hair, and a retiring nature, whereas Johnson was brusque and loud in his speech and behavior. Anderson was a younger man—not yet 21, with a head of thick jet-black hair and a large goatee to match. He was notably well-met, with a "don't give a damn" attitude, to which he lent expression at the least provocation.

All were bachelors except Pehr, thus his invitation to breakfast before departure. All except Anderson were tall and lanky; but he was short and stocky, and soon became identified as "Short Nils" to distinguish him from Nils Johnson in conversation.

All were from Skåne (southern Sweden), and spoke the gutteral Skåning dialect. They were young men so well endowed with stamina, courage, determination, and wit, that they might defy and defeat a wilderness.

Anderson would contribute to the party the refreshing frivolity and jocundity of youth, which admitted of less strain and frustration than actually felt. He was of that brunette strain of Swede said to be evolved by adventuring Normans who regarded the soft, blond, warm maidens of Sweden their most delectable objects of romance.

Nils Johnson and Sven Person were several years older than Anderson, but considerably younger than Pehr. Sven, as previously intimated, was quiet and soft spoken, Johnson boisterous and vociferous. Sven was quietly very religious; Johnson, profane and vulgar in almost equal measure.

All were honest self-confident men; none of any considerable property, but neither with any material debt. Each accepted every other in the group as neither more nor less than his equal. However, Pehr, by dint of seniority and unique necessity of purpose, and quite as much because he exercised a deliberate mature judgement in the resolution of any issue, elicited a certain deference. By neither election nor appointment, but by unspoken acknowledgement, he became leader of the group. He, himself, never made a point of it.

Each man carried a bundle of food in his blanket roll, the main staples being salt pork, cheese, and meal. The meal, after addition of a little water, could be worked into a firm cake, which held over an open fire or buried in hot ashes, quickly became highly palatable, though hard and dry. Each carried a small pouch of ground coffee and an earthen mug in which he might steep it.

Anderson carried half a flour-sack full of food—provisions intended to last a week; the others carried only what they considered emergency rations. Anderson's landlady, with whom his jovial good humor had made him a favorite, furnished him his generous bundle of food without charge. Johnson's landlady furnished him, in lieu of the regular meals he would miss. Sven had bought and wrapped his food articles at the grocery store. He carried the largest supply of cheese—a huge wedge of sharp cheddar. Anna prepared Pehr's generous bundle, the only one containing hard bread, hard boiled eggs, and a pair of salt and pepper shakers.

As insurance against possible hunger, Pehr carried his Swedish double-barreled musket, one barrel loaded with a ball, the other with shot. His powder horn hung at his right side, suspended from a leather strap over his left shoulder. He was the only one with a compass. Sven carried a small hatchet for use in preparing fire wood, and every man had the indispensable pioneer tool—a sturdy sharp pocketknife.

Long before full light, Anna served the party a working man's breakfast of bacon, fried eggs and potatoes, bread, butter, and coffee. The bachelors complimented Anna on the delicious meal and thanked her several times over.

Pehr looked in on his precious sleeping daughters and hugged and kissed his wife so she blushed before the witnesses. Then the land seekers, stimulated by the cool morning air of 27 June, struck out in a northwesterly direction with the practiced deliberate strides of those accustomed to distance walking. Before the sun rose above the horizon they were a Swedish mile from Litchfield.

They held to a northwesterly course, as Nils J. and Pehr had been instructed by the clerk in the Greenleaf Land Office. Pehr carried a map that the young man had helped him prepare. It showed how Alexandria, Fergus Falls (mere villages), and Fargo lay almost on a direct line from Litchfield. On a bee-line, Fargo lay only about 160 miles from Litchfield; but when one bent his path about lakes, marshes, and thick woods, his distance to Fargo approximated more nearly 200 miles. Pehr had noted that the master map on the Land Office wall showed open (unclaimed) land a short distance north of Lake Christina, and that lake they should reach by nightfall of their second day out—80 American miles. But first they must reach Alexandria and consult with the Land Office people there. (This must be done tomorrow morning) (*Figure 3.1*).

During the first day they came in view of numerous cabins and chimney smokes; the land was largely occupied, with here and there small fields of grain enclosed by rail fences. The fields lay emerald green, in sharp contrast with adjacent areas of grubland and gray-green prairie.

As dusk deepened, slowly ending the long twilight characteristic of high latitudes, Short Nils was moved to say: "That quick lunch we ate about a week ago seems to have disappeared. I think we should stop and eat while we have enough light to gather dry wood." Pehr's big watch showed nine o'clock, and he too thought it best that they stop to eat and bed down for the night. Before he could express his

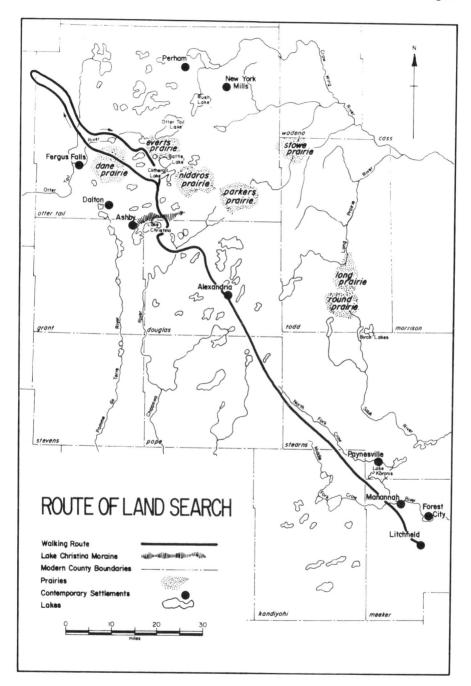

Figure 3.1. Map: Route walked by four Swedish friends seeking desirable land on which to file homestead claims.

thoughts they stood in the edge of a clearing, and all agreed that they would stay here the night. (Stocky short-legged Anderson was particularly pleased to stop; for, though pride forbade his showing it, he was near exhaustion.)

Light came from a habitation in the clearing, but they would not ask for lodging: the weather was fair and warm, the sky without a cloud. However, both supper, lodging, and breakfast would be thrust upon them. The settler had heard them arrive, and himself a Swede had overheard their talking. He came hurriedly to meet them, and hailed them in a midland Swedish dialect. He rejoiced in company, after many weeks of isolation. Nor was his warm invitation out of the ordinary or uncommonly noble: It was custom on the frontier of settlement that the traveler be afforded food and shelter wherever night overtook him. Rarely was true hospitality compromised, however simple and crude the accommodations.

After introductions and handshakes all round, he led the party to his log cabin, and introduced his pretty young wife. She appeared even more pleased than her husband; and after smiling at each traveler as he was introduced, she busied herself at stove and cupboard.

Soon the hungry tired party was feasting on venison steaks at the settler's table, seated on split-log benches, nicely planed on top. Oskar Vedeen, their host, sat at one end of the table on a stool attempting to converse with his guests while they wolfed his food.

After gorging themselves, each insisted on pouring from his sack a measure of meal, and Mrs. Vedeen reluctantly held a pan into which they poured. Short Nils forced upon her a generous slice of his delicious cheese.

Pehr asked how far they were away from Alexandria, and Oskar replied that there was near at hand a trail that led to the town in only about four American miles. He had never been far beyond Alexandria, so he knew little about the land to the north. "But they can tell you all about it in the Land Office," he assured them.

Pehr stifled a yawn with the back of his hand, rose deliberately and made for the door, his purpose obvious to everyone; and all the others, including Oskar, followed.

On returning indoors, at Oskar's insistence, they shoved table and benches to the walls, removed their boots, and rolled up in their blankets at the end of the room opposite the bed. The young wife proffered such bundles of clothes as might serve for pillows. After all were settled in their places, she snuffed out the candle and undressed in the dark.

Pehr called to the young couple: "We will be quiet when we leave in the morning. We must depart before dawn in order to attain our goal for tomorrow night—the vicinity of Christina Lake." *(Figure 3.1)*

"You will not leave my house without food in your bellies! We shall be up when you are and you shall have breakfast before first light. My Manda has a built-in waking device she can set for any hour."

Early next morning the young wife fried side meat and pancakes for all hands, and they did her proud—although, to be polite, the travelers ate somewhat less than they might. When done, they each proffered to Manda a dollar for their kind accommodations; but a glance from Oskar caused rejection of every offer.

He said, "We have no board or room for hire. We do only as we would be done by."

So the party departed their first hosts on their long walk, amid vigorous handshakings and many genuine expressions of gratitude to persons who a few hours before had been utter strangers.

The hike resumed and the Vedeens stood together at their door and watched the party's departure in the dim light of dawning. Before entering the open woods before them, the travelers turned and waved to their hosts and saw their waves acknowledged.

When the government agent came to open the Land Office door in Alexandria on Monday, 28 June 1869, four men stood eagerly awaiting his arrival. He unlocked the door, walked in, and held the door open to the men, saying, "Come in, gentlemen. What can we do for you?"

Short Nils replied, "Good, open, Otter Tail land we want to see."

"Location of such land I can show you very quickly, you are only about forty miles from some of it. If you will line up at the counter, I'll show you all at one time." He drew out a map and laid it on the counter, its bottom toward the men. Then he pointed out places on the map: "This is Alexandria, where we are. This is Christina Lake. Go round it on the east side, then straight north. After crossing rough and stoney country, you will come to splendid prairie interspersed with lakes and broadleaf forest. That's open land, but it surely won't be so very long. Do you know how to interpret survey marks?"

"Ya" said Pehr, "we visit Swede man in Greenleaf, Meeker County."

"O.K.," continued the agent, "look for the marks T132 R40—Clitherall Township in Otter Tail County. Notice that full identify of a section is on the southeast face. That's because the surveyors worked northward and westward *(Figure 2.2)*. Now, do you know where to go?"

"I think so," said Short Nils, the English expert.

"O.K. then, take this map with you as a guide. It may help you considerably. I'll expect you back here in a few days to file your intention to homestead certain forties. Remember, each of your forties you choose must join at least one of your other choices along one side. Do you have questions?"

"Nej," said Pehr, lapsing into Swedish.

The eager party struck out again, at a clip that would have winded a man less fit.

The sun was touching the western horizon when they observed from the vantage point of a considerable hill, a large sheet of gold-tinted water some miles north of them, which they assumed, quite correctly, to be Christina Lake *(Figure 3.1)*. Their instructions were to skirt the lake on the east, and they deviated from compass bearing to do so. Twilight was deepening when they reached the southeast shore. Every man squatted at the water's edge and scooped with his hand to drink; no one carried a canteen since their journey was mainly through country studded with fresh clean lakes *(Figure 3.2)*.

Here they would spend the night. The sky was clear, though the sun set in a fiery glow; and the air felt warmer than the evening before. Had the wind been westerly, off the lake, they might well have sought shelter in the woods away from the water. But a balmy breeze blew from the southeast, so they could afford the convenience of nearness to water.

Quickly Sven built a blazing campfire with dry poplar and willow gleaned from the sand ridge that rimmed the lake. Only Johnson was determined to have something hot for supper; he broke out from his gear a small frying pan and commenced slicing salt side meat to go with his bread. The others munched

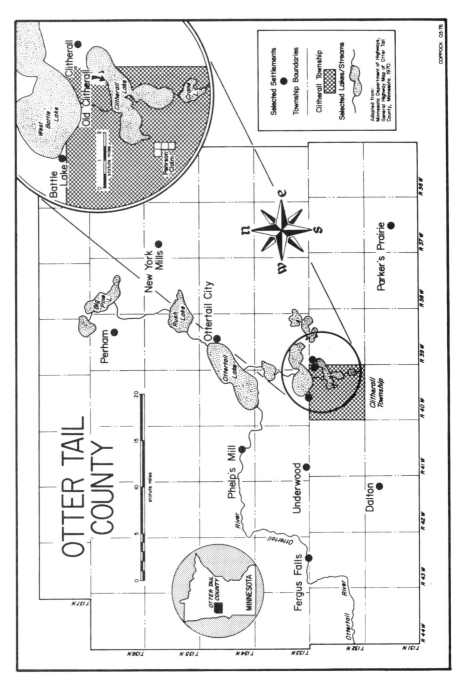

Figure 3.2. Map: Otter Tail County, Minnesota, showing places of early interest to Pehr and neighbors.

disheartedly on hard bread and cheese until one delicious whiff of frying pork sent each to his bundle to take out a slice or two of his own. Each borrowed Johnson's little skillet in turn, and everyone enjoyed a semi-hot supper. Sven, the last to cook, scrubbed the pan with sand and grass, and rinsed it in the lake. Then he wrapped a clean wool sock about the handle and held the prized utensil over the fire until both water and fat evaporated from it. "Rust prevention," he mumbled. He returned a sterilized frying pan to its owner.

As they were bedding down for the night, Nils Johnson asked of Short Nils: "Do you sleep with your mouth open?"

To which Anderson replied, "I don't know, I'm never awake to see. Why?"

"Because if you do, a peculiar kind of Minnesota snake may crawl in you and eat so much food he'll starve you. I heard tell of one fellow who got a snake in him, and quit eating to starve the snake. Damn, if the snake didn't stick his head right up in the man's mouth looking for food. If you're not sure you keep your mouth shut when you sleep, you'd better shove something in it—an old sock, or something."

Short Nils, half asleep, mumbled some obscenity, unintelligibly, and commenced snoring with his mouth open.

The morning of their third day broke slowly under a heavy sky, threatening rain. Sven re-built the fire, and each man steeped coffee in his mug, dunked and ate a chunk of hard bread, and that was breakfast. They rinsed their mugs in the lake, tramped out the fire, and then commenced their third day of walking.

They had gone only a short distance, to about the midpoint of the lake's easterly curve when a barking dog met them and unintentionally led them into a large clearing, in which stood a trim log cabin and a sizeable stable to match.

A large red-bearded man emerged from the house and strode out to meet them.

"And whom do I thank for this company?" he asked in middle Swedish. "We have few visitors. You must come in for breakfast."

"We are land seekers," answered Pehr, "on our way to the Otter Tail Country to file homestead claims. We slept on your lake shore last night."

Handshakes and introductions all accomplished, the burly Swede insisted that the party come in for a hot breakfast. "If you're to walk all day, you need a solid breakfast," he proclaimed.

"What we had was solid enough," quipped Short Nils, "hard bread dunked in black coffee. I could feel mine when it struck the bottom of my stomach."

Half shoved by Eric Swenson, the party crowded into the cabin. There Eric introduced his buxom wife, Eva, who immediately seated the travelers to table and commenced frying bacon and eggs in two over-sized skillets. With these came fresh bread and newly churned butter. The travelers ate enough for a full day's walking. Eva beamed, though flushed by the hot stove, and Eric talked earnestly with Pehr, instructing him about open land to the north. "I'll tell you the truth, I made a mistake. I chose the lake shore and woods, with open prairie hills; but the lake is too shoal to be much good, and the prairie hills are the devil to work: they're so steep-sided. You are wise to scout the Otter Tail country. Do stop and tell me about your luck on your way back to Alexandria."

"That I promise you we will," said Pehr, "but not to eat you out of house and home again."

"We have plenty, never fear," Eric assured him. "Our only son, Axel, there, and our daughter, Freda, almost strong as her mother, help us a great deal. We couldn't make it alone."

"Come, children and shake hands with these men. You shall see them again."

At last, having killed an hour eating delicious food and visiting genuine folks hungry for company, the party shook hands and expressed profound thanks all round, (Short Nils held Freda's hand a bit longer than necessary. She blushed.)

Pehr consulted his compass, and guided the party straight north as he had been instructed. North of the lake they encountered hills so high, steep, and stoney that they debated a change of direction. (They saw northwest of the lake the forward slope of a magnificent frontal moraine deposited by glacial ice melt some ten thousand years before.) No wonder they saw no cabins in this jumbled country; what fool would lay claim to such land?!

Pehr remained adamant: "The young man said straight north from Christina Lake. We are deriding what we have not yet seen. We must go beyond these hills to find open land of such quality as we seek." And in less than an hour, Pehr's prediction materialized—just as the morning's murk fully dissipated and the sun shone brilliantly between white woolly clouds (fair weather cumulus humilis).

The men quickened their pace, as if drawn forward by the improving prospect. They had learned to follow ridge crests whenever possible, the better to view the country from high, often open, viewpoints which also facilitated their progress. They were thus wending their way along a grassy ridge top and had just ascended through a thin fringe of woods when they emerged on the brow of a hill that would render this day memorable to them throughout their remaining lives *(Figure 3.3 and Frontispiece)*.

Figure 3.3. Contemporary view toward the northwest from Discovery Hill (later called May Flower Hill).   *Photo by author's wife, Mary Louise.*

Pehr was first to see the panorama that lay before them; then each of his fellows in turn came up with him, and, as if on command, stopped on impact of the view. There below them, to the west and northwest stretched the prairie, swell after swell far as the eye could reach. A brisk breeze from the southwest stirred the grass into waves as if on water, and the cloud shadows driving across the whole appeared as at sea a long ground swell reminds one of a storm that has passed. The alternate moving light and shadow, caused both by drifting clouds and the changing exposure of the wind-blown grass, seemed to stir the entire scene into animation, changing its hues from a blue-green sheen to a darker gray-brown dullness as grass and cloud shifted the light reflection. It was hypnotic to gaze upon; Sven observed later that he grew almost dizzy staring at it *(Figure 3.3 and Frontispiece).*

For a time the four men stood still and silent as if struck dumb by the view. Then they met each other's eyes, and the eyes were saying: "This is what we have sought." They relaxed then and appraised the landscape more prosaically. There in the north lay a sheet of lead-colored water that must be part of the large lake that they had skirted about its south end—where they had noted deep wagon ruts crossing the little creek entering the lake. They had followed those tracks to this very spot, and they were, indeed, standing amid the deep prints of sharp-shod hooves in the sod, and the long slashes of wheels heavily laden. These were not tracks made by land seekers such as themselves, whose total aggregate possessions would not make one moderately heavy wagon load.

Could it be that this beautiful promising land lay unclaimed? They scanned the scene systematically to the distant horizon, and saw no sign of human occupance— neither a cabin nor a curl of smoke—no sign of human habitation.

Pehr spoke the minds of all except Johnson: "If no one has filed on this, it's because no one has seen it."

Sven and Anderson assented, but Johnson said: "I want all prairie if I can find it. I've grubbed and struggled with trees and stones my whole life, and I'll certainly not continue such slavery of my own choice. There in the distance to the northwest appears to be what I'm looking for. But in case this is not claimed, and you fellows want it, let's find some survey posts so we can see how the sections and fractions lie."

They fanned out as "deployed skirmishers" in the infantry, and advanced through the tall thick prairie toward the northwest. Close at hand they could detect two components of the grassland: the dry sere mat of last year's growth, and the new lush growth, in places more than hip high. It was heavy to walk through, except in places where snow drifts had pressed the old growth to the very ground.

From instructions at the Land Offices they knew, or thought they knew, what they were looking for. They had passed survey posts to the south but had not bothered to decode their markings: "raw wood posts about four inches square on top but sawed off at a slant to shed water, set in earth mounds from which they projected about two feet, to clear most of the prairie vegetation; on the sides of which, diagonal to survey lines, near the top were gouged out with a chisel-like tool the numbers and letters identifying the land in four directions—northwest, northeast, southwest, and southeast." (From surveyors' instructions.)

In a few minutes Sven and Pehr, the middle men, called to each other and pointed to a post just over the crest of the first hill they had climbed. The party assembled to examine the marker, and it was as they had been told—but it was a mid-section line post, each side marked simply "¼ S." They studied Pehr's compass and sighted with it. The post was, indeed, turned on a diagonal to the land lines.

Said Pehr quietly: "If I may have my choice, I'll claim these three forties cornering on this post and the wooded forty south of the two easterly ones (he pointed)." Everyone saw the merits of his selection and no one raised the least objection.

"Let's find the section corner post, there on the hill to the north someplace, if we can; and then mark the identifying landscape features about, so we may readily find this spot again. Nils Johnson wishes to seek further, but I may wish to come back to this."

The section corner post stood on the brow of the hill, in clear view soon as they ascended far enough to see it. Here were the key symbols to Pehr's prospective claim: on the southeast face: "S22, T132, R40" and on the southwest face—"S.21." From these data he could figure out the rest, should they fail to come back. He jotted down the identifications on a slip of brown wrapping paper he had carried for the purpose. The paper shook, and tears ran down his cheeks as he wrote. The thought of once owning all this beautiful land was overwhelming. The others looked away, to spare him embarrassment. The notes tucked into his inner pocket, he struck out hastily toward the northwest, thinking to hide his emotions; but in this he had failed. The company walked in silence for a considerable time. Johnson pondered his likely reaction, should he find what he envisioned; he might be no less moved than Pehr.

The prairie became flatter and broader, almost treeless, as they progressed. Soon it was Johnson's turn to call a halt: "This is so nearly what I had in mind that I shall probably find nothing more suitable. This is near Pehr's so we'll come back this way. I'll read the post markings then. If no one objects, I should like to see the land a little farther west and north. I've been told that there is flat black land some distance north of Fergus Falls village. I should like to go and see."

Everyone was agreeable, and off they went, this time in a direction more westerly than northerly. In less than an hour they came to a sizeable, swift stream (Otter Tail River), and finding no suitable place to cross it, they followed its course almost to Fergus Falls. *(Figure 3.2)*. There, about a mile above the falls, they crossed, albeit even here the stream was deep and swift—but narrow, with firm banks. They removed all their clothes and tied them up with the shirt sleeves. Then, holding clothes and all other gear atop their heads, they waded across. So swift was the main current that they were hard put to keep their feet. Short Nils was so nearly submerged that his goatee got wet *(Figure 3.1)*.

The strenuous river crossing persuaded everyone of his fatigue. Short Nils put it in words: "It seems to me that we have walked farther today than in any day before. I suggest that we camp here on the river bank, eat supper, and bed down for the night." He was fully dressed again, as were they all.

Everyone agreed that it was time to stop; and everyone helped Sven gather a supply of firewood. After a supper of fried side pork, bread and cheese, and hot coffee, they rolled up in their blankets and were almost instantly asleep. Late in the night a dog from the nearby village came sniffing about, and Sven threw rocks at him until he went away. No one else awakened, and Sven suggested in the morning that someone could steal the others blind without their knowing it. "Shucks!"

exploded Short Nils, "How could anyone steal my bundle when I sleep with my head on it."

"Nor my musket," said Pehr, "primed and wrapped into my blanket beside me!"

"Alright," concluded Sven, "the cur got nothing, but a human predator bent on mischief might do us harm. I shall not sleep far from Pehr and his musket!" Sven got a ripple of laughter.

After a quick breakfast they walked almost twenty English miles northwestward and came, indeed, to black almost level ground, as Johnson had anticipated. But he was not excited: "This land is richer than any other we have seen; but I'm afraid that it is wet every spring, and it cannot be worked when it's wet. I believe I'd prefer the lighter, higher prairie land we looked at earlier." *(Note Figure 3.2 for frequent reference in connection with future events.)*

The party turned about, recrossed the river as before, just at dusk, and commenced looking for a likely shelter in which to spend the night. The cumulus clouds had passed, and the sky was darkening in the west, abbreviating twilight and hastening darkness. Rain would probably come before morning.

A few miles to the southeast they came to a shack occupied by a young Danish bachelor. They came on him as he stood on his porch washing his hands and face after his day's labors. Quickly he dried himself on a dirty towel and hung it back on its nail. Then he shook hands and introduced himself to everyone, and invited the party to be his guests for supper and the night. Then he swished the washdish clean with a dipper of water, placed in it a dozen middle-sized potatoes, added water, and set the pan over a stove eye to boil. At this bizarre procedure Pehr's notions of sanitation revolted, and he spoke for all: "We thank you most kindly, but we have too much distance before us to stop this early, Is there another settler some four or five miles east of here?"

"Indeed there is," replied the disappointed young bachelor. "Follow the wagon spor, and you will soon find another settler, Good luck on your journey."

On the trail again, the group thanked Pehr for sparing them from potatoes boiled in a dirty wash-dish. In an hour they stood before another settler's cabin, this one also Danish, but with a brisk yellow-haired wife and two small children. Here, with the Rasmussens, they enjoyed a delicious supper of fried pork and baked potatoes, and a comfortable night on the cabin floor. They slept to the tune of a driving rain against the shake roof, and wakened early and much refreshed.

For breakfast the bustling young wife served them delicious sweet rolls with butter and coffee. The travelers offered pay for their accommodations but were sternly rebuked. Said the housewife: "We have done no more for you than one of you would do for us. We are proud to have had you as guests in our home!"

The travelers shook hands with husband and wife, and thanked them over and over. Pehr said, "hug the little ones for me when they wake up. I have two about their size at home."

"That we will," said the wife, smiling.

Now they headed for the land about which Johnson had speculated day before yesterday. They were there in two hours. They quickly located the corner post of sections 8, 9, 16 and 17. Johnson simply noted down: SW quarter of Section 9, Clitherall Township, and that was that *(Figure 2.2)*. He stuck the precious slip of paper in his shirt pocket. "I'll come and steal stove wood from you," he said jokingly to Pehr; to which Pehr replied, "And you will be welcome to it."

They walked southeastward to a shady oak woods and sat down on a large fallen tree to eat lunch. Short Nils surprised the company with a fresh supply of cheese and buns that he had procured in the Fergus Falls saloon after the others were asleep. The food was good, but everyone ate sparingly; tonight, the good Lord willing, they would eat hot food at the Swensons.

After their quick lunch they walked rapidly southeastward, Pehr setting the pace. After about twenty minutes he stopped abruptly atop a rise and turned to his fellows, "See there," he pointed, "that's the hill from which I first cast eyes on the land I want. I shall call it Discovery Hill. We shall have my specifications in a little while; and then, if Sven will honor me as a neighbor, we can get his post marks almost as quickly. We must now locate all the survey posts that identify my claim."

He led off southeastward, and, after a few minutes, struck out at a run; he had spotted the first post they had critically examined on their way out. There it was with each side marked simply "$\frac{1}{4}$ S."

Said Pehr, "this is as we thought—the halfway post between section corners. Let me run back up that hill and make sure that the notes I took down are right." He ran the entire distance, squatted down by the post and checked its markings against those drawn from his pocket. They corresponded exactly, but he noted for the first time that the post symbols had been traced over with a red chalk. He noted also that each corner of the post had three neat notches cut into it, the meaning of which he knew not. (In fact, the notches indicated the shortest distance to the township line (one notch = one mile). He was standing by the center post of the township.)

He quickly returned to his fellows waiting at the mid-section line post. He looked about—to the south, southeast, and southwest; and then announced: "I should like to have the two forties cornering on this post, one to the west and the other to the east, north of the post—one on each side of the section line. You, Short Nils, you are quickwitted! How would you legally describe them? Remember that the forty is the basic unit."

Short Nils furrowed his brow, tugged at his shiny black beard a time or two, and then gazed intently at the land. He stood so a minute or two before speaking. Then he said: "We are here standing at the midpoint between sections 21 and 22. The forty north of and cornering on the post would then be the southeast quarter of the northeast quarter of section 21. By the same reasoning, the forty you want east of the section line would be the southwest quarter of the northwest quarter of section 22." Everyone listened intently until Short Nils had spoken his piece. No one had anything to say when he had done. "Now, you think that over and see if I'm right!"

Pehr and the others did some mumbling and whispering to themselves, poking a finger here and there at the land as they ruminated. Pehr did some crude sketching of squares inside squares on a pocket-worn piece of paper.

Nils Johnson spoke out first: "I think that must be right."

"I agree," said Sven.

"So be it," said Pehr, "I see it the same way. Four poor dumb Swedes from Skåne can now interpret the coded posts set by American surveyors. Please wait while I hurry up to the section corner stake and make sure it matches what I wrote down before."

He returned down the hill, almost at a run, and called out as he approached the three waiting: "That's the stake and I have it correctly written down. Now! south of this second forty on the east of the section line, I want the two forties running south of it; the southerly one wooded. That woods forty should be in the southwest corner of section 22. That corner is in the woods and may be hard to find. Will you all kindly come and help me?"

The group struck out without a word. When they reached the edge of the oak woods, short Nils stopped and said: "Pehr, I warn you, if the square quarter section there (he pointed) across from your south eighty has not been filed on before we reach Alexandria, and it remains open until I am twenty-one, you will have a whiskey-drinking, skirt-chasing Swede with black beard as your nearest neighbor—just across the section line road that will come."

"Nothing could suit me better," said Pehr laughingly. "I almost wish I were disposed to share both whiskey and skirts."

"This rough land will be of little worth except for wood and pasture," said Pehr, half apologizing for the land, "but that is exactly what I want it for." He consulted his compass from the vantage-point of a sharp little ridge running east-west between two deep sloughs (geologically speaking, a kame and kettle topography).

"The post should be right down there in the west edge of that slough. We may have to swing a little west to keep our feet dry." But he plunged straight through the thick tall marsh grass. He stood an instant where he thought the post should be, and then called out excitedly to his friends beating the brush about him. "Come here. Here are the markings, but not on a post. They're on a ten-inch ash tree."

They gathered around to view the singular corner tree (rarely did a tree stand so exactly where a post would have been set that the tree could be used in lieu of a post). About three feet off the ground the tree had been blazed (hewn flat) on four sides, simulating a post. On the northeast side, facing outward from the deep woods behind, was the full legend: "S22, R4OW, T132N" On the other sides were the simple identities: "S21, S27, and S28." Pehr had all the specifications with which to file a claim—carefully noted in pencil on a stiff piece of paper, which he tucked into his inside pocket. He beamed with pride and happiness. Excitedly, he shook hands with each of his companions and thanked him for his help. None felt particularly noble!

Now Sven spoke out: "I decided some days ago to take land adjoining Pehr's, but I didn't wish to interfere with his selection and search. Now will you help me choose and identify four forties east of Pehr's?"

"Indeed we will," and off they went, proceeding as they had in orienting Pehr.

Sven rejected Discovery Hill as too steep and stony, and also the forty adjoining on the east Pehr's northeast one. It had a large willow slough in the northwest part and a sandy hill occupying much of the eastern half. He selected the forty lying east of Pehr's middle one. Although it had a large slough in the northwest corner (also extending over on Pehr's). Then he selected a north-south row of three forties to the east, the southerly one adjoining on the east the one first chosen (next to Pehr's). The land was hilly, and some of the hills were sandy or gravelly, but it also included flats of splendid black land. It was devoid of trees but for a few slough borders.

When Sven's data had been properly noted down, everyone of the land seekers was happy, but very tired. (For all above selections see Plat Map. *(Figure 12.10).*)

When the party was ready to head southward from Sven's southeastern corner, Pehr spoke up inquiringly: "If you will continue so (he threw his arm out to indicate a southeasterly direction) following the wagon spor, I will join you beyond the woods before dark. I wish to walk over my Discovery Hill again and see whether the tracks have been worn since we first saw them. I intend to come this way with Anna and the girls when we arrive by wagon, so they can view our claim as I first saw it."

"Don't get lost," chided Short Nils. "If you don't catch us beyond the woods, we'll stop and call to you. In any event, we will stop where the wagon trail skirts the south tip of the lake and crosses the little creek. Do you remember the place?"

"I recall it well," replied Pehr, "and I shall be there almost as soon as you will."

Pehr walked to the crest of his Discovery Hill, and virtually drank in the view to the west and northwest—the beautiful land that might one day be his. The gently rolling hills lay golden under the lowering sun, and that picture remained one of his secret treasures throughout his long life. A few moments to absorb the beauty, and he turned his back on the scene and walked briskly southeastward along the wagon trail. He overtook his friends just as they were about to wade the little creek, and he called to them as he approached: "Don't cross the creek. We must go west of the little lake south of here, and then head for the east end of Christina Lake. Don't you remember? If we hurry, perhaps we can sup and sleep with the Swensons, as we did on our way out."

"And don't you attempt to roll Freda in the hay or bushes!" said Johnson sternly to Short Nils.

"No such thought ever entered by head," averred Short Nils; but indeed it had. He thought: (She must be at least eighteen, and built as a Venus with arms.)

They walked the lakeshore southward and then turned southwestward on high ground. Soon they sensed acquaintance with their surroundings; though, as they well knew, a vista seen from one aspect may be difficult to recognize from another point of view.

"Here we are," burst out Short Nils. "The waters there to the west are Lake Christina, and there in front of us I think I see a glimmer of light that may well come from Swenson's."

Right he was, and they were soon in jovial conversation with their kind hosts of several days ago.

Said Mrs. Swenson: "You are so late that you may have to make your supper mainly of left-overs, and no abundance of them either. But we'll fill you somehow." She commenced slicing ham and Freda sliced a large plate heaped with bread. She also placed on the table a large dish of butter. "By the time you all get washed up, Freda and I will have something hot for you to eat. You remember where the washstand is on the porch?" To her husky half-grown son she said: "Axel, go fill the pail with fresh water from the well!" He took the bucket, and hurried to complete the errand.

They ate the delicious food as politely as they could, hungry as they were, alternating mouthfuls with slurps of coffee from man-sized cups. Short Nils kept viewing Freda slyly, and knew her every measurement before the meal was over.

When they had risen from the table, Pehr announced: "This is Thursday night. I propose to be in Alexandria tomorrow night and be at the Land Office when it opens on Saturday morning. Are you all agreed?"

There was no objection.

Then Swenson told them: "There's new sweet hay in the stable, much softer than this floor. You would sleep more comfortably there, but I must first be assured that you will not carry matches into the hayloft or smoke there. Such articles I beg you to leave here on the table until morning. Every land seeker dug a few matches out of his pockets, and Short Nils hauled out his pipe. The entire collection was laid on the table.

The company conversed only briefly, mostly thanking Eva and Freda for their sumptuous supper. They tarried but briefly before making for the stable to bed down. Eric lighted their way and waited until each had relieved himself outside and found his place on the hay. Then he bade them, "Good night, see you for breakfast," and closed the door as he went out.

Only Short Nils failed to fall asleep immediately. He had visions of Freda with him in the hay, and such thoughts do not induce sleep.

For him the entire excursion was a lark—for possible future reference. The youngster of the group, he thought more about willing women than about virgin land. He lay a long time half asleep and half in reverie. Why settle down alone on a quarter section when he could be ranging about among daring young men and voluptuous young women?! Hell, he was too young to file a claim without lying about his age, which he would do for no amount of wealth. That must wait until he'd sown many more bushels of wild oats. Railroad construction and logging camps had their following of women; never mind whether looseness be their main virtue. They were accomplished in their art, and that a vigorous young man could appreciate. Wonder where that hot little Italian bitch might be now—the one who stole Frank Nelson's watch and folding money while he was sleeping off a night of drinking and jousting. "She could do more tricks than I could pay for," Frank said. "Wonder," thought Nils, "whether Helga, the big statuesque Norwegian will be at her own place Sunday night when we get back to Litchfield. I've heard tell that the saloon is not her only place of business."

Then his reverie turned to less exciting thoughts: Pehr and Sven would be splendid neighbors, with both of whom one could be both pleased and proud. We shall see!

(As a matter of fact, Anderson became Pehr's nearest neighbor, their houses only about an eighth of a mile apart. By shouting they could converse between their respective doorsteps, unless a wind frustrated them. Long after the advent of the telephone, they disdained the party line in any case of real urgency or provocation. So long as both lived, they quarreled repeatedly about the position of the section line between them. Between the quarrels, which never became violent except vocally and never lasted more than a week or two, they were good and helpful neighbors. Quarreling broke out anew each time one or the other repaired any part of his fence fronting the section line. Neither lived to see how, when the section line road became State Highway 78, the engineers took both sides far into the fields, beyond where the provoking fences once stood.)

Early next morning they took turns washing their faces on Eva's porch. For breakfast, the wife and daughter served their transient guests fried smoked sausage and potatoes with bread and butter and abundant coffee.

Before they ate, all bowed their heads while Eric said grace. The food was most delicious, and every guest praised the cooks.

On arising from the table preparatory to departing, Pehr announced, "We shall probably meet again, 'ere long; three of us hope to settle on claims only about ten to twelve miles north of here. You have a standing invitation to come and visit me and my good wife, Anna, soon as we are settled in. I should have our cabin built by about the middle of August. We will be disappointed if you don't come."

"We'll come," said Eric, "You can count on it." And laughingly, "We'll eat your groceries next time." (But they never came.)

The travelers shook hands again, all round, and Short Nils held Freda's hand even longer than the first time. (She blushed prettily, in gratitude.)

Once again on the trail, each of the group walked in silence, every individual with his own daydream. Everyone thought about sleeping on a bed in Alexandria, after shaving, washing, and putting on the clean clothes in his blanket roll. Other day dreams were peculiar to each of the elder members. The "juvenile" had done his dreaming last night.

Nils Johnson walked along thinking to himself: "Praise be! I've grubbed my last stump and sawed my last big log. Who the hell would want more trees after digging out half the alder and juniper brush in Sweden?! Not I! I didn't cross an ocean for the privilege of grubbing trees or brush. Because a man grew up among trees, must he be enslaved by them? Hell, no! A Swede can come out of the woods! The forest is shelter for foxes, wolves, and all manner of vermin that steal and destroy. I'll be well rid of them." (Johnson was soon to learn that the coyote, then extremely numerous in Minnesota, was more at home on the open prairie than in the forest.)

Sven's reverie was more placid: "I believe Pehr is my kind of man. He should make an ideal neighbor—helpful without meddling, candid without being unkind. I shall build on the forty adjoining his." (These two quiet reserved pioneers became almost life-long friends and neighbors, and brothers-in-law to boot. Sven spent his waning years near Henning, Minn. where two of his daughters had settled. He also moved to join the Baptist Church, it was said.) Throughout several decades, Pehr and Sven, and later their sons Nels and August, maintained between their houses a well-worn wagon trail, across which was no impediment other than wire gates (gaps) when pasture arrangement required them.

Pehr's sober reflections as he walked pertained to his new-found land: "How could any sane man hold any material thing more dear than good land? And he was about (he hoped) to claim an ideal spread of it. The southerly forty, the wooded one southwest of Discovery Hill, would furnish fuel for heating and cooking, and material for many articles essential to the establishment and maintenance of a home and development of a farm. True, this forty was rough and hilly with several sloughs (kettle holes, geologically) in it; but those sloughs would furnish water until he could sink a well, and the hills and slough edges would be good long-season pasture." Actually, the mammoth white oaks and magnificent paper birches were assets enough for Pehr, whose hands knew well the feel of fine woods. He regretted that there was no beech, a wood familiar and useful in southern Sweden. The two forties running north from the woods were beautiful rolling prairie, all plowable except a steep wooded bluff on the eastern midpoint of the middle forty and a willow draw half-way across the northerly one. Finest of all was the northwest forty, lying west of the section line from the others. This, the "west forty," had only one sharp knoll on it near the northwest corner, and one slough hole southeast of the knoll with a fringe of willow trees along its south side. The land was otherwise gently undulating prairie, with a thick uniform grass cover—evidence of a deep black loam underneath. Little did it matter that the tract lay L-shaped instead of square; it fulfilled all requirements for a self-contained homestead. On this land any man worth his salt could shortly become independent.

At noon they stopped on the shore of a little lake and ate lightly of hard bread and cheese, washed down with coffee steeped in lake water—as so many times before.

Said Short Nils between slurps of coffee: "I believe we are more than half-way to Alexandria. We can be there while the sun is still high. I'll wager anyone that we'll be there before five o'clock." He got no takers. He thought to himself: "I'll have time for a haircut, shave and bath in the barbershop. Then I'll buy a few clean clothes and, after supper with my companions, have a night on the town. Perhaps Alexandria has a good substitute for Helga!"

They did, in fact, reach Alexandria before five o'clock, and Short Nils went straight to the barbershop soon as they had registered for rooms at the hotel. Johnson carried his blanket roll upstairs. Short Nils and Johnson would bed down together in one room; Pehr and Sven in another. While Short Nils was beautified and sweetened at the barbershop, the other three men washed and shaved in their rooms. They had worn their change of underwear only two days, so it was not yet pungent.

The hotel rate of a dollar and fifty cents for supper, bed, and breakfast, included all the warm water they wished to carry in the huge ornate porcelain pitcher furnished each room.

The supper of roast beef and mashed potatoes was good, but the cook might have taken lessons from Mrs. Swenson.

After eating, Short Nils excused himself and took off. Johnson called after him, "good luck!" The remaining three took a short walk about the town to settle their heavy supper, and then returned to the hotel and went to bed.

When Short Nils stumbled in about two o'clock, Johnson wakened enough to inquire, "was it good?," to which Short Nils mumbled an unintelligible reply, peeled off his clothes quickly and crawled into bed. He was asleep instantly.

When the hotel dining room opened next morning at seven o'clock, our travelers were waiting to get in—all shaved, combed, and dressed neatly as possible. Short Nils remained a bit unsteady, and leaned on the back of a chair.

They were served a thresher's breakfast of fried eggs, fried salt side meat, and fried potatoes, with bread, butter, and coffee. They ate heartily, paid their bills at the desk, and in a few minutes stood before the Land Office, awaiting the clerk to open up.

The clerk appeared exactly at eight o'clock, greeted them cheerfully: "Did you find land to your liking?," opened the door and let them in.

The others deferred to Pehr; and he gained the counter in two giant strides, his cardboard square in his hand. He pushed it in front of the clerk, who immediately checked the symbols against a large map on the wall behind him. After only a minute or two he came back to the counter and said to Pehr: "You're in luck. The land you wish to claim is open and available to you. If it remains your choice, I need only ask you a few questions and then issue you an "Intent to File" paper, to hold the land until you can begin its improvement. Obviously you are past twenty-one, yes?"

"Ja, Ja," said Pehr.

"Married?"

"Ja."

"Children?"

"Two."

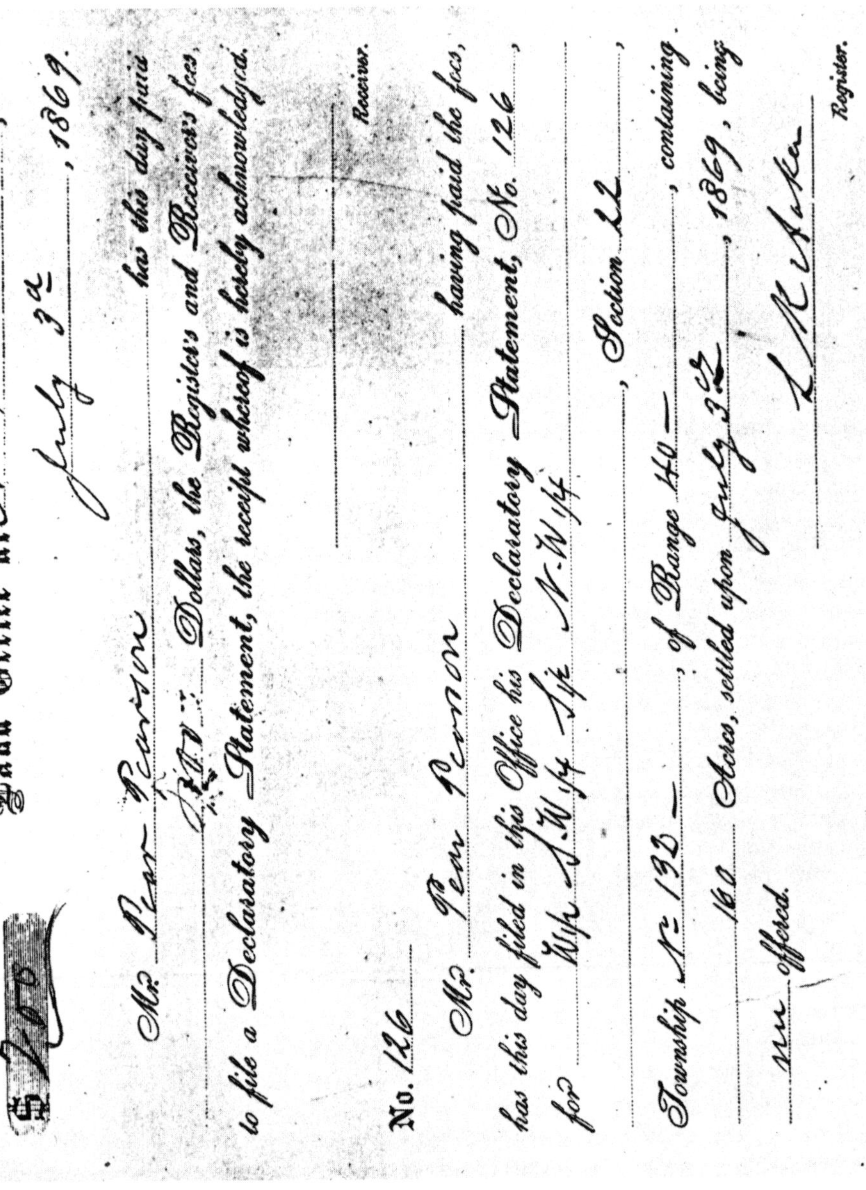

Page 80

Land Office at Alexandria Mines

July 3rd, 1869.

Mr. Peter Renson has this day paid
$2.00 Dollars, the Register's and Receiver's fees
to file a Declaratory Statement, the receipt whereof is hereby acknowledged.

                                                                Receiver.

No. 126

Mr. Peter Renson having paid the fees,
has this day filed in this Office his Declaratory Statement, No. 126,
for W½ S.W.¼ S½ N.W.¼, Section 22,
Township No. 135, of Range 40, containing
160 Acres, settled upon July 3rd, 1869, being
not offered.

                                                L.M. Aiken
                                                                Register.

Figure 3.4. Facsimile of Declaratory Statement of intent to file and receipt for two dollar fee.

"Do you intend to become an American citizen?"

"Ja! Ja!" said Pehr again, and took from his wallet the piece of paper given him in the court at Forest City, his first paper.

"That's all I need," said the clerk. "I shall issue you what we call a Declaratory Statement that will hold for you the land you selected until you can begin improvement on it—build a house and such. Do this within a year and come back and tell us you have built or plowed a little, and we will then issue you a real filing application." He was busily completing a blank as he spoke, and in a moment he pushed it across to Pehr. "This costs you two dollars and serves you as a receipt *(Figure 3.4)*. Try not to lose it, although we keep a copy." Again Pehr went for his wallet and extracted from it two dollar bills, which he handed to the clerk.

"Now you are all set," said the clerk, as he handed him the paper. *(See facsimile, Figure 3.4.)* "When you come to file the main application, within the year, I must charge you fourteen dollars. I mention this so you will know the cost. Good luck, Mr. Pehrson." He shook his hand! "I shall probably see you again soon." Pehr wanted to say that he'd be back before year's end, but his English failed him.

Johnson and Sven had also chosen open land, and after the same procedure visited upon Pehr, they also were potential claimants of a homestead.

To each the clerk gave a copy of the legal description of the land he wished to claim, the same copied in a large ledger under their respective names. Pehr's read:

SE ¼ of NE ¼ of Section 21 Township 132N Range 40W

SW ¼ of NW ¼ of Section 22 Township 132N Range 40W

NW ¼ of SW ¼ of Section 22 Township 132N Range 40W

SW ¼ of SW ¼ of Section 22 Township 132N Range 40W

To all three the clerk now said: "These are the legal descriptions of the land you have chosen. Keep them in a safe place and fetch them with you when you come to file your formal application. You must live on your claim and have a small acreage plowed before a year from now; otherwise someone else can come and take it away from you."

Pehr spoke: "I intend to be in my cabin before September and, this fall, have two acres or more plowed for wheat sowing next spring."

The clerk caught the gist of Pehr's speech, having dealt with hundreds of Swedes before, and said again, "Good luck, Mr. Pehrson."

When all the others had transacted their business, Short Nils stepped forward, and begging his pardon, said to the clerk: "The square quarter west of Pehrson's, southeast quarter of Section 21; has that been filed on?

The clerk quickly consulted his master map behind him and said, "A man named Martin Löf filed on that quarter last September. Was no one there?"

"No, we saw no sign of any human on the place. Can one assume that he has lost interest and intends to relinquish his rights?"

"Intentions carry no weight beyond the papers I've given out today. Löf has not made formal application; and should he fail to do so by the end of next September, we can, on evidence, declare the land open and subject to another's claim. The procedure is called 'claim jumping' and has an onus it does not deserve. We have had a great number of cases."

"I shall watch this one," said Anderson; and indeed he did. He "jumped" Löf's claim soon as it fell delinquent, and thus became Pehr's nearest neighbor.

Their business done, the four men began shuffling toward the door, but the clerk hailed them back to the counter. He was examining a large ledger they had not seen before. He riffled the pages until he found those he sought.

"Since no one else is waiting, I have time to tell you something of interest. According to the field notes pertaining to your land, the surveyors rated most of it 'first rate' prairie."

"A Major George B. Clitherall of the United States Army (formerly a Confederate officer) was in charge of the frontier Land Office when your land was surveyed, and for him is named both your Township and the large lake in its middle eastern portion."

"När was the posts set?" asked Pehr, in his brave attempt at Engish.

"He asks when," prompted Short Nils.

"Let me see," mumbled the clerk, as he ran his finger over the open pages, "the posts that identify the sections and quarter sections containing your forties were set on November 7 and 8 in 1866, one on each date. That's only about two and a half years ago. You may be sure that all the open land in the area will be claimed before those posts rot out."

"Suppose a man came along and just pulled up two or three posts and threw them in the nearest slough. What could be done then?" asked Short Nils.

"That has actually happened," replied the clerk, "and we suspect that the Sioux Indians carried off and burned many posts, feeling that they infringed on their land rights. In any case, the surveyors can quite readily find the spot where a post was set by consulting these field notes and then employing compass bearings and distances based on posts remaining in position. Further to facilitate the positioning of a lost post, many were assigned a reference tree at a measured distance and on a specified compass bearing from the original post. Here, for instance, relative to the quarter section post at the midpoint of the section line between sections 21 and 22—one of your posts, Mr. Pehrson—has this notation 'Set post for ¼ section corner from which Burr Oak, 6 inches diameter, bearings north 83½ west, 153 links distant. No other tree near.' If that post alone were lost, its position could be reestablished by a few measurements and sightings."

"This makes me wonder about something else," said Pehr, to no one in particular. "How are corners of forties fixed?" Short Nils explained Pehr's question to the clerk.

"That, I regret to say, is left up to the adjoining landowners," answered the patient clerk. "The government assumes no responsibility for it. As far as I know, most corners have been agreed upon by neighbors without serious controversy; a few owners have filed suit and gotten a court decision."

"I, for one, shall try to avoid any quarrel," retorted Pehr. "The government men have laid out such a remarkable framework that we ought to be able to fill in the lesser detail peaceably." Short Nils rendered an abbreviated translation for the clerk.

Said the clerk, closing the large book: "I am pleased that you appreciate the tremendous task accomplished by the hardy surveyors. Perhaps they well deserve such nominal memorials as bestowed on Major Clitherall."

The prospective land owners thanked and bowed—and departed, each happy with his lot.

They had tarried longer than anticipated, and agreed to buy each a cup of coffee before departing Alexandria.

They would walk late tonight, sleep on the trail (to save both time and money) and be on their way toward Litchfield early tomorrow morning (Sunday).

Indeed, they reached Litchfield just at Sunday sunset (9:00), and went together to Pehr's quarters, there to ascertain whether any article of one had got into another's roll.

Pehr hugged and kissed his little Anna; then he lifted to him his little daughters, one on each arm, and nuzzled them soundly. They were dressed for bed, and when he put them down, they scampered away to sleep.

Anna spoke: "I'll wager that you didn't stop for supper; and THAT I shall remedy, if you will be content with pea soup, bread and butter. I prepared a large pot of it in anticipation of your HUNGRY arrival. I made it yesterday, hoping you would be home then, but it awaits you now."

"None but a fool could refuse such an invitation," said Short Nils, to the surprise of everyone. They expected him to high-tail it toward Helga's house.

The fare was tasty and plentiful, and everyone enjoyed Anna's soup as much as any special treat on the entire expedition. (See again *Figure 3.1, Land Search Walk.*)

After all had eaten themselves uncomfortably full, they rose from the table, shook hands all round, thanked Anna over and over again, and went their separate ways, Pehr remaining, of course.

"I can scarcely wait for you to see our claim," he told Anna when the others had gone. "I found just such land as I sought, just such a combination of prairie and woods. See, here's the paper showing my intentions to file a claim. It cost only two dollars." He went on and on as Anna washed the dishes.

Then she said, "My dearest, I want to hear all about it when you have rested. You are dead on your feet. Let's go to bed and sleep. I've been wakeful during your absence, so I need rest too. I am so happy to have you back, and so fortunate!"

When they were in bed she turned and kissed him, but turned quickly away again. He also turned away and was snoring smoothly in two minutes.

Short Nils, despite a long day's walk, was not ready for sleep. After supper he headed straight for the saloon, which was in business this Sunday evening in celebration of the Fourth of July.

He was so full of pea soup that he felt no need for a drink; but he had need for Helga. He sidled up to the bar and asked the bartender in a half whisper: "Will Helga be in tonight?"

The barkeep answered so loudly that Nils felt like going through the floor: "She's already upstairs with a drummer from Minneapolis. He engaged her for the night. He's had her before."

Short Nils thought briefly of the ecstacies that could not be his, ordered a brandy to soothe his disappointment, paid the barkeep, gulped the brandy, shouldered his bedroll, and walked to his lodgings.

His landlady welcomed him home with a river of questions. He sat and answered her for an hour; then thanked her profoundly for the food she had sent along, stifled a yawn, excused himself, and went upstairs to bed.

He dreamed a beautiful, innocent dream of Freda, and wakened little regretting that he might never know the vaunted techniques that Helga employed in bed.

Chapter 4

PREPARATIONS FOR ISOLATED SUBSISTENCE

Next morning as he was eating breakfast with Anna, long before the girls would be up, Pehr continued his glowing description of the land that would be theirs, almost free.

"I found our land, Anna," he said excitedly, "a whole 160 acres. We shall soon be independent farmers. It's beautiful land, mostly prairie but with abundant woods too. I have the legal description and my two dollar receipt for paying what they call "intent to file" fee.

"After we eat, I shall go to the Swede who deals in cattle and see if I can buy a good pair of steers already broke to pull and haul. It's the place you have seen, Anna, with the high peeled-rail fence around it."

Almost before swallowing his last bite, Pehr was off to the corral to bargain with the big Swede. No language barrier interfered!

"I need a good yoke of oxen," said Pehr, "strong enough to pull a breaking plow and rangy enough for a brisk walk on a wagon."

"Then you will like this pair," said the big Swede, Ola, indicating a large pair of steers he had just yoked together. "They are less than three years old, but already very well trained for driving, plowing, and logging. They're as good a pair of work animals as I have seen. They go when you say 'come' and stop when you say 'wo.' The off ox, the red one, is Buck; the near ox, the red-and-white brindled one, is Bride. Don't ask me how Bride got his name, and don't try to change it! These steers respond beautifully to their names and to standard commands. If you call 'gee' they turn right; 'haw' they turn left. Here, take the whip and try them."

"What's this 'Bride' name anyhow? I can't even pronounce it. The ox may not understand me."

"He understands me, and my Swedish is much the same as yours. You'll see."

"What does it mean, exactly, if it means anything?"

"Ho," chuckled the Big Swede, "it has a very nice meaning. We say 'Bru' in Swedish—a Bride. But I admit it's a hell of a name for a big ox. If you should buy him, you could tell your wife that you're bringing home another 'Bru'. That would 'scramble your eggs' for fair."

"That would be a good joke; and I'll use it—thank you—IF I buy the animal. It would divert her thoughts from Skåne for a moment, at least. She has grieved for Sweden and old associates ever since we departed for America. Sometimes I wish I had stayed at home and contented myself with permanent poverty."

"Never regret that you came to America! I have seen many such as you and your wife, and after two or three years in America they were glad they had come. Settlers here-about who have proved up a homestead were half-rich in just five years. Never say you regret coming to America! Here's the whip."

Pehr took the whip, but he didn't crack it; with the butt end he tapped each ox gently on the back and said "come up, Buck, Bride," and the magnificent steers stepped out as one. Pehr walked alongside Bride across the corral, called out "gee" and the oxen turned right as if automated. He gee'd again and returned to the point of origin, where stood the dealer with a grin of satisfaction on his face.

"Maybe they named the near ox Bride because the white markings down the left side of his face look like a bridal veil?"

"Perhaps so," said the dealer. "Would you like to see them pull a heavy load?"

"Yes," said Pehr, "that I would see!"

"Alright, we'll hitch them to that stoneboat, and you can see how evenly they pull something heavy."

The stoneboat was a solid planked affair with a slight "runner" slant at the front, loaded with several large boulders. The "boat" was about three by eight feet in flat dimensions, and the load must have weighed a ton. The trader kept it for demonstration purposes.

"If they will pull that without jerking or twisting," said Pehr, "I shall be ready to talk price with you. If those steers will put their necks against a heavy dead weight and move it, they are the kind of oxen I need."

The trader hitched the oxen to the stoneboat with a heavy log chain extending from the midpoint of their yoke, back between the animals, to a heavy draw-pin. At his command, the gentle powerful beasts put their massive necks to the yoke without hesitation; and as the muscles in their hind legs flexed, forward came the load with apparent ease. They dragged it across the entire enclosure before the driver called "Wo."

Pehr was most favorably impressed. If he could afford the price, he would have himself a splendid yoke of oxen.

"What is your rock-bottom price on this pair?" he asked the dealer.

"They will easily bring me $300.00 and I consider them a bargain at that price. They can be expected to work for you ten years or more, and they are a gentle faithful pair."

I like these animals very much," said Pehr, "and I may take them at your price, provided you will care for them here a few days while I prepare to go out. I've filed on a Homestead!"

"Surely—I'll do that," said the trader. "I have plenty of hay, but no oats to give them. They will be soft from lack of exercise, so you'll have to go north at a walk. These splendid animals are worth kind treatment."

"They will never be abused in my service," said Pehr, "but they will have to work as hard as I do. Could we yoke them to a wagon and let me see how fast and smoothly they walk without whipping?"

"Certainly, you may see how well they haul a wagon. Here, we can use this one."

The oxen were quickly hitched to the wagon tongue.

"They handle well from up on the seat, if you wish to try them from there."

"Oh no, I'll walk with them. I don't expect to ride very much."

Pehr drove the wagon through the gate and made a wide circle about the entire corral, walking beside Bride and calling commands in a conversational tone. He had to step right out to keep stride with the cattle. He stopped the rig where it had stood before and motioned a thumbs-up sign to the dealer.

"You understand you're buying them naked! You'll have to get your own yoke, bows, and chain."

"I assumed that you furnished no equipment. I am prepared to buy my own. Do you sell cows as well as work animals?"

"Yes I do, but I have none here today. I may have a couple or three tomorrow. I have some promised. Come around tomorrow and see what I have. I've sold you a splendid yoke of oxen, and I will try to suit you as well with a milk cow."

"Speaking of the oxen again: If the long curved horns become a menace, I suggest you saw the tips off. The animals are gentle as can be, but those horns swinging about could be dangerous. They're more than three inches thick at the head; too large for dehorning. Many settlers around here saw off the tips and screw in brass buttons sold in hardware stores. They look nice."

"They shall keep their horns as they are," said Pehr, "and they will probably grow even longer and heavier during the next year or two. The yoke keeps them sufficiently spaced so that their horns clash together only infrequently. I will treat the steers so kindly that they will never attempt to gore me or do me the least injury intentionally. They are gentle, and I will treat them gently!"

Pehr peeled off enough bills for half payment—as earnest money! He had bought his first yoke of American oxen, and he went away pleased with the transaction.

After the trials and demonstrations, Pehr walked home to a light lunch of bread and cheese with coffee. He said to Anna: "I bought us a fine yoke of oxen for $300.00. This afternoon I shall look for hitching equipment and a good lumber wagon. The cattle dealer thinks he may have some cows I may choose from tomorrow. He had none today."

Little Elna, across the table, asked the name of the 'oxes'; but before he could answer her Anna inquired: "Why did you buy oxen and not horses? Oxen will take a week to get to the homestead. Shouldn't you have bought horses?"

"My dear, I would prefer horses, but I can't afford them, nor could I properly stable them next winter. Oxen cost less and can rough it far better than horses. They can work well on hay; and horses must have oats if they are to work much. Oxen are more sure-footed in rough country and can wade across mucky areas more easily. Oxen have several stomachs. They gulp their feed, then belch it up (ruminate) and chew it at their leisure. They waste little time eating and drinking. They also stand heat and sun well. Oxen work with merely a yoke and a chain, whereas horses must be harnessed with expensive leather gear. I really had no choice, Anna; horses will come later. The oxen should get us to the claim in four or five days, so we need spend only three or four nights on the trail." Then he lied: "I sort of look forward to the trip. It could be fun. The girls will enjoy it if you can hide your fright from them. I will not expose you to any real danger, believe me!"

"I will do my best," said Anna, soberly.

Pehr took up his hat, quickly kissed his daughters and his wife, and strode off toward the town. He viewed several sales exhibits of ox yokes, wagons, and plows;

and he stopped where all three kinds of equipment appeared to be offered. A spanking new wagon with fire-red gear and grass-green double-box was just what he wanted (but he feared the price). It had narrow wheels with thick steel tires, the back wheels high and the front ones low enough to permit fairly sharp turning without rubbing on the box. Hooked atop the double box was a wide seat with leaf springs and a low back. (On this Anna and the girls might ride comfortably.)

By the time he had inspected the wagon quite deliberately, appeared the dealer and asked: "How do you like that wagon?"

Pehr waggled his left hand at him and managed: "No English; I Swede."

At this the dealer bawled out: "Lars! Lars! customer for you."

A strapping young man appeared, introduced himself as 'Lars,' and asked whether Pehr was interested in buying a wagon. The conversation was now in Swedish; Pehr said that he was, indeed, interested in such a purchase.

Lars confided, in a soft voice: "This wagon looks new, but it has had some use. I painted it myself. I can tell you that it is very little worn and would last you many years on a farm. The hubs and spokes are of oak; the fellers of hickory. The tongue, boxes, and under gear are oak; the whipple-tree, hickory; and the neck-yoke, ash."

"What are you asking for a second hand outfit such as this?"

"The price is $135.00, including double box, whipple-tree, neck-yoke, and seat. The box is almost tight enough to haul water!"

"I shall be driving oxen, so I have no need for a neck-yoke or whipple-tree. How much are they worth?"

"How much will be knocked off if you don't take them? I'll have to ask." And he disappeared within the establishment. In a minute or two he reappeared and announced that "the boss will knock off $5.00 if you leave the neck-yoke and whipple-tree—with single trees attached, of course."

"Of course! I have no use for single trees until I butcher my first American hog. While I think on this, will you show me your ox yokes and breaking plows?"

"Yes indeed, the plows are over there"—pointing. "The yokes and chain are inside. Let me show you the plows first."

Pehr followed Lars to an assortment of plows, and the young man stopped by an unwieldy affair with a tremendous oaken beam and heavy handles of similar material *(Figure 4.1)*.

Grasping the handles as if ready to plow the entire state of Minnesota, Lars said: "This monster is billed to us as a steel breaking plow and we sell many. Notice the length of the landside and the smooth twist of the mold-board. Each of them is a solid piece, and very strong. Notice also the heavy iron knife sticking down from the beam just forward of the share. It will sever even brush roots. That splits the sod so that the plow turns a clean even furrow. The share comes off by undoing only three bolts—in case it needs sharpening; and we also sell shares separately. The wheel under the front end of the beam helps keep the plow at constant depth. This is the plow most in use among Minnesota settlers. It sells for $17.50 without any hitch."

"Perhaps that's the plow to get, but let me now see your ox yokes. I need one complete with bows and pins."

"Come inside," said Lars, "and I'll show you what we have."

The cumbersome yokes were displayed on a wall, to good advantage. Pehr was attracted to the sturdiest one in the lot. (No light yoke would hold his powerful oxen). He hefted the contraption free of its hooks and inquired: "Is this oak?"

Figure 4.1. A monstrosity such as shown above was Pehr's first American plow. Its working parts were of steel (only recently perfected), with a share removable for sharpening. This was a brush breaker, but it served quite as well for breaking prairie sod. Note the knife, forerunner of the rolling coulter, and the wheel in front to help regulate depth. One yoke of big oxen were scarcely adequate power for this implement; two yoke, in tandem, were preferred, and employed when available.
Photo courtesy Otter Tail County Historical Society

"Yes," said Lars, "every bit of it—yoke, bows, and pins. We have none stronger, but it would be too heavy for young oxen."

"My oxen are old enough and strong enough! What is the price?"

"That yoke, complete, is $4.00. It's supposed to be specially balanced and shaped for heavy pulling. The price is steep, I know; but I can throw in an extra bow and two extra pins."

"That seems fair enough, and I won't haggle," said Pehr; "but I will require a somewhat better deal on the plow and the wagon. For the plow, throw in two clevises for hitching a chain to the beam; on the wagon, give me off ten dollars for the neck yoke and whipple-tree. I want the double box complete with all end gates and rods, and I want the seat that's on it. I will owe you $125.00 for the wagon, $17.50 for the plow, and $4.00 for the yoke."

"Say, now! I must have a goodly length of heavy log chain, say a twelve footer—with a slip hook at one end and a grab hook that fits a link at the other—a regular logging chain. Do you have such a one? I almost forgot."

"We have that, exactly," answered Lars. "See for yourself." He pointed and sauntered toward a corner, in which Pehr saw more chain in one place than he had seen in his whole life before. Lars pulled on a pair of grimy leather gloves before he lifted a section of luster-new chain, but Pehr disdained his offer of a similar pair. Soon they had between them a twelve-foot length with the proper hook at each end. Pehr hauled it to the door for better light, and there systematically inspected the weld on every link. Especially did he scrutinize the end links, each threaded through the eye in the shank of the hook before final crimping to and welding. He found no flaw, gathered up the chain in loose loops on his arm and asked: "How much is it?"

"Heavy chain is awfully dear," answered Lars; "it sells for four cents a link and ten cents for each hook. You are holding about forty pounds of iron and it's worth five dollars. Since you already made a considerable purchase, I think we can knock off fifty cents. The boss has signalled me that your offer for the other items is quite acceptable."

"Alright, then," said Pehr. "Here's a hundred dollar bill. I will come tomorrow to collect the whole lot and pay you the balance. Good day to you!"

Pehr walked happily to the lodgings and greeted his family with hugs all around. He had sufficient money remaining to pay for a good cow and the best stove that Anna might select. Tomorrow he would buy these and necessary sundries, but he would leave himself fifty or sixty dollars to take along up-country.

Anna's shriek interrupted his thoughts. "Those hands! What on earth did you do with them?"

He thrust his hands forward, palms up, and they were, in truth, black as coal. "I forgot. I examined a log chain that I bought. New chain is dirty to handle. Give me some hot water in the wash bowl." He scrubbed with strong soap, but much of the black remained. Now he knew why Lars handled chain gingerly even with gloves on. Next test of the chain would be by the brute strength of his oxen.

Next morning, after gulping his mush and coffee, Pehr asked Anna: "While I go after my purchases of yesterday, will you take the girls and go to the hardware store with the false front and look at their stoves. We need one that will keep a room warm in winter and will also serve for cooking and baking. I will meet you there with the wagon after I have loaded up the other things. Choose the best stove they have; there's enough money for it."

With that, he slapped on his cap and was off. At the implement place he took up the heavy yoke, laid it over his right shoulder, and walked the half mile to the corral. He waved to the big Swede, Ola, as he approached, set the yoke down with a grunt of relief and asked: "May I borrow my oxen?"

"Indeed you may," said the Swede. "They're tied over there under the straw shed. They lead nicely by the rope tied about their horns. I'll help you put them under the yoke. You may be pleased to know that a man offered me three-fifty for those steers after you had bought them."

"I'm proud that you kept our bargain," said Pehr. And then, changing the subject abruptly: "Do I see some cows over on the other side?"

"Yes, they're cows, but none such as you would have. One is so old her teeth are most gone; the other so wild she must be roped from horseback. I offered to sell her for a fellow. Must be fresh from Texas, I think. She's a menace to my animals, and he'll have to take her away from here. Tell you what; if I get in one you might like, I'll hold her until you come and see her. Better come by once a day, at least, until I get what you want. It shouldn't take more than another day or two."

His oxen yoked together, Pehr walked them out the gate, across the open ground, and onto the dirt street leading to the implement dealer's. Lars helped him run the wagon tongue between the brutes and secure its tip to the yoke. Then he removed both end-gates from the back of the wagon and helped lift in the plow. Then, with gloves on, he draped the heavy chain about the plow beam to save floor space. Then he replaced the end gates and tightened the screw rods.

From his wallet and his coin purse, Pehr counted out in Lars' hand exactly the balance owed and was about to start his oxen when Lars intervened.

"You are traveling up-country to a homestead, yes?"

Pehr nodded and grunted, "Ja."

"Then you have forgotten a most important item! You need a wagon cover. We have them ready-made, with tall bows to fit onto your wagon box. They are rain-proof and durable—made of canvas. You need one to keep your goods dry and to shield any passengers from the elements. We get rain storms this time of year, and nights get cool, as you well know."

Pehr knew that the young man was right and sincere; but he feared to ask the price of the recommended wagon cover. Lars sensed his doubts and quickly dispelled them.

"I have a real bargain for you, if you wish it," said he. "We have an unused cover that got a tear in it, so we had to sew on a patch. It's perfectly good, but cannot be sold at full price. It's original price was six dollars but I can sell it for five. You'll thank me for pushing it on you. Most settlers sleep in a covered wagon until they get a shack built."

"I believe you," said Pehr, "and I appreciate the advice. Here's your money. Will you put it on the wagon so I can learn how?"

In a few minutes the wagon became a "Prairie Schooner" and Pehr thought: "It can't come off the stove; it must come from the residual cash I had hoped to carry."

Pehr headed proudly for the hardware store, where Anna and the girls stood waiting. He stopped the oxen, and his three girls came quickly toward him. Anna exclaimed; "You didn't tell us that our wagon had a roof! Now I am much less fearful of the journey. You are resourceful, Pehr!"

Pehr looked sheepish, but said nothing about the manner in which he had chosen the wagon cover. He'd better have a few credits to his account lest his standing be utterly dissipated by the impending travel.

The little girls gaped in amazement. They would go far away, with the wagon as a house and those giant cattle to pull them. Pehr lifted them and introduced the oxen by name, as little hands gingerly stroked their foreheads. (So began a relationship of trust and affection that would endure a decade.) Anna looked on, with both pleasure and apprehension, until both of the young ones were deposited safely upon the boardwalk fronting the store.

They went inside then, and Anna pointed out which she thought the best stove. She repeated to Pehr and showed him, as the clerk had for her previously, the salient features of this stove as superior to those of other design: the grated fire box, the large ash pit with removable container, the damper, the four eyes with removable lids, and, best of all, the large oven in the right side with hot air space about it.

The stove, a sizeable article of cast iron, was newly blackened for sales appeal. Pehr thought it must be the best he had ever seen, but wondered how it would demolish his budget. His hand almost trembling, he turned the price tag and read the astounding figure of $17.50. It was below his expectations. They could afford it, and since this was Anna's main purchase, he would not haggle! Attached to the stove was a four-foot length of pipe, oval at the bottom to fit the stove collar and round at the top to receive additional pipe lengths. About two feet above the stove top was a damper in the pipe, adjustable by a thumb-and-finger grip on the outside. The draft could be controlled, however strong the wind on the roof! Pehr stepped to a side of the store and returned with three three-foot lengths of pipe and laid them on the stove. The clerk understood and added thirty cents to the bill. Anna took the lid-lifting handle and laid it in the oven. Pehr counted out $17.80 and the young salesman helped him put the new acquisition in the wagon. They slid it to the very front of the box and then replaced the end-gates. They had now bought all their major requirements, except a cow.

Pehr lifted Anna so she could put a foot on the hub and climb to the seat. Then he handed up the girls, so excited they could scarcely sit still on the seat—one on each side of their mother. Then he took up his stick, talked to the oxen, and they lumbered away toward the lodgings.

He stopped the wagon in an open space behind the house, helped his family down from the seat, unhitched the wagon tongue from the yoke, and walked the oxen back to the corral. The big Swede greeted him cheerfully and volunteered safe keeping of the yoke until Pehr should need it again. Pehr strolled back to his temporary home light-hearted and grateful to be so nearly ready to complete his long journey from Sweden. Another day or two in which to assemble some minor items of equipment and a goodly supply of foodstuffs, and they would commence the trek up-country. That night, and each night in Litchfield thereafter, he bedded down in the wagon with his musket primed beside him. Land-seeking settlers were generally honest and open-handed; but railroad construction attracted many migrant whiskey-drinking toughs who might readily steal exposed property. He could not risk losing his wagon or its contents; they were almost the sum total of his worldly goods!

Next morning, after a hasty breakfast, he walked hurriedly to the corral; and Ola greeted him with more than his usual good humor. "I think I have your cow for you now," he said. "She was brought in last night soon after you went home. Come and have a look at her."

He led the way to a sheltered corner opposite that where Pehr's steers were tied, and there stood a large red cow, peaceably munching hay from the crude rick. At their approach she turned her head to see them, but without changing the rhythm of her jaws. Pehr walked up to her and stroked her neck and back, and she stopped chewing as if to express her appreciation. She was less receptive when he opened her mouth to inspect her teeth, but she accepted the annoyance without resistance.

"Can you tell the age of a cow by her teeth?" asked the big Swede.

"No, but I can judge it fairly well by how much they are worn. The teeth of cattle do not show age as accurately as do those of horses. However, I would wager this animal to be no more than three or four years old."

"The man I bought her from said that she had dropped her second calf, so your estimate is pretty good. I bought her for a springer, but I can't guarantee it. She doesn't look that far along to me. I milked her this morning, and she gave ten quarts. That's good for a red shorthorn. I'm sorry about the stub horn; she has to be tied around the neck." The cow had a good horn on the right side, a handsome horn that curved forward and then in toward her face. Had not its mate been crumpled she would have been handsome, as cows go.

Pehr loosed her from the rick and led her away by the rope, calling "Come boss, come boss." She followed him without once tightening the rope, and he knew that she would lead with no trouble. This cow would do very well, but he wished he could be sure she was with calf. He said to the Swede: "She has a good barrel on her, but I certainly can't tell whether she has been bred. Grinding away on nothing but hay wouldn't shrink her guts any."

Answered the Swede: "As I say, I can't guarantee it, but I can tell you this: I have dealt with her former owner many times, and I have yet to catch him in a lie."

Every homesteader wanted a cow that would freshen without further service by a bull because bulls were scarce on the outer fringes of settlement. Those born there became oxen. Determined to sell his trade stock, with calf or not, an unscrupulous dealer often resorted to bloating a cow with certain green feeds, salt, and water. Many an unwary buyer paid for twins and got a bag of wind.

"What must you have for her?"

"With two good horns she would have brought $125, but with one stump, I can't get that much. Let's say $110."

"My equipment money is almost gone; and I had figured to get a cow for $100 even. Could you let me have her for that? I would appreciate it!"

"Pehrson, I have talked with you enough to respect your honesty and to wish you well on your homestead. I shall make less profit than I ought to, but you may have the cow for $100. I will also keep her and feed her, until you come for all three animals. You can pay me what you owe me then. You'll have to come and milk her morning and night, because I might be unable to attend to it."

"Thank you, my friend," said Pehr. "I will come and milk her, and I'll pay for her right now," handing the Swede a hundred dollar bill. "I will pay the balance on the oxen tonight when I come for the milking. We should be ready to leave here in about two days."

The men parted with a handskake, and Pehr had walked off several paces when he turned and called: "Does the cow have a name?"

"None that I heard of," shouted Ola in return.

Pehr resumed walking, and thought: "We'll just call her 'Bos.' The girls will call her 'Bossy,' of course. That will be good."

He went to the hardware store and bought, for 35 cents, a three-gallon milk pail that came to a neck at the top, into which fitted a tight lid with a handhold made into it. It was smoothly galvanized and well soldered in the seams.

With the new pail in hand he walked home to his family, there to discuss the necessities remaining to be acquired.

Anna was busy about the house and the girls were playing on the floor, but on his arrival all activity stopped, and questions came in quick succession.

"Did you see Buck and Bride?" "Did they know you?" This from the girls.

He answered them: "The steers are good as ever, but I didn't get near them. I bought us a cow."

"Is she gentle and easy to milk?" asked Anna.

"She is very gentle, and apparently easy to milk. Ola, the big Swede, milked her this morning and got ten quarts. I shall milk her tonight; that's why I bought this pail. She leads without stretching the rope. She must have freshened about two months ago, so she should be with calf, but no one can tell for sure. That's a risk we have to take. You will think her odd looking because she has only one normal horn, a pretty one; the other, the left one, is just a lump. I don't mind in the least, and I got her at a better price because of her shriveled horn. I paid just the $100 I had ear-marked for a cow.

"What's her name?" piped up the younger little girl.

"Apparently she had no name, but I suggest we just call her 'Bos'; will that suit you?"

"Oh, yes," said they in unison. "Now we have four animals to live with us in the country," said Elna. "Now we won't get lonesome." She counted Svarten in, as a test trial! ('Svarten' was Blackie, the stray cat.)

Anna and Pehr talked of remaining purchases to be made. They agreed that Anna should get the provisions and Pehr should get all other necessities for establishing a home on the prairie border. Pehr concluded the discussion: "Today is Thursday. Let's try to procure what we need this afternoon and tomorrow. Saturday is a busy day in town, so we should leave little to be bought then. If all goes well, and the weather is good, we can leave early Monday morning."

"I'll do my best," said Anna, "and the girls can help me carry."

"You will probably have much more than all of you can carry. You get the larger items such as the pork and flour barrel marked and set aside; I'll fetch them with the oxen and wagon toward evening, after I have assembled what I can."

Next day they scoured the town for essential provisions and items of equipment. Demand was great for the articles they needed because there were many others with similar needs. Freight now came by rail almost to Litchfield, but supply could not be constantly maintained. Pehr would have quality goods at a fair price. He bought nothing without first hefting, sounding, or tasting it, according to what he adjudged the surest test of durability or purity. Experience had taught him to buy the best available and on the frontier the best was often none too good.

Anna accumulated in the grocery stores a legion of bags and little wooden boxes containing meal, potatoes, brown beans, dried peas, sugar, salt, black pepper, coffee, rice, onions, dry yeast, and a considerable variety of spices. The potatoes were small and cost her $1.75 for a bushel. The grocer's wife explained: "A striped beetle came last year and ruined most of our potato vines; some they stripped to the ground. I'll give you a few tiny ones in a paper sack—for planting. But you can as well plant peelings if you select lengths with eyes in them. They'll grow as well as cuttings." Anna thanked humbly, for both the marble-sized seed potatoes and the free advice. She bought only five pounds each of coffee and sugar, because each cost 50 cents per pound. She bought and marked a barrel of flour ($10.00). She got vinegar and molasses in earthen gallon jugs, and lard in a wooden pail. She bought a large thick side of fat salt pork, and a small keg of herring in brine. She bought matches and tallow candles, a black iron cook pot, a stone crock and two earthen bowls (each a gallon measure), a coffee mill, and a wooden dasher churn, two wooden wash tubs, and one copper boiler, and many lesser articles.

Pehr concerned himself mainly with farm equipment and wood-working hand tools (of which he already had a well-chosen collection from Sweden). He bought a grass scythe and snath, a square-bottom spade, spare clevises and draw-pins, a grub hoe and a garden hoe, an adz, a broadaxe, two steel wedges, a loud cow bell, a one-man crosscut saw, a crow-bar, a large steel file and a whetstone, several lengths of three-strand Manila rope (half and full inch), a pair of strap hinges and a door latch, two window frames each with four 8 x 8 inch panes, and an assortment of bolts and wood screws—everything selected on the basis of contemplated utility. He bought a tight wooden pail with fitted lid, full of a tallow-tar mixture with which to lubricate the wagon hubs. The pail would hang under the wagon, suspended from the reach pole. He bought, and struck from his list, every entry except nails. Those square-cut blunt stays of destiny were scarce on the frontier. After much diligent searching he had appropriated only two pounds in mixed sizes, and most of them rusty. He did acquire, sort of as consolation prizes, several empty nail kegs—much sought as containers for provisions to be stowed in a wagon.

Pehr drove round with oxen and wagon to gather up all the sizeable articles. The flour barrel he placed "mid-ships" in the wagon, there best sheltered against rain and dew.

At supper, after the girls said grace, he added for the group their abject gratitude for having thus far progressed toward their goal.

Anna remembered that she had seen in one store another residue of little potatoes that she intended to ask for.

"I know they will be given me if I but ask; they would do as well for cutting and planting as would the bigger ones." She did, indeed, go to the store at opening time next morning—and got a little cloth sack full of small potatoes. Now she was abundantly supplied with seed.

"You are welcome to them, Anna," said the grocer's buxom wife. "I hope they grow well for you. You'll have to water them when the weather becomes dry and hot. It'll be late for planting them."

Saturday afternoon Pehr made the rounds of all places that professed to sell nails and inquired as to whether any had arrived since yesterday. He had no success.

At evening he took his pail to the corral to milk his cow. Ola was there. Pehr asked him: "Can I get my oxen and cow just at first light Monday morning?"

"Of course," said Ola. "I'll just lay the latch on, but leave the pad-lock open. You might lock it for me after you are out."

"I will do that, surely," said Pehr, "and thank you for trusting me."

"If all my customers were like you, Pehrson, my business would be a pleasure. I wish you every success on your Homestead. God go with you."

"Thanks, sincerely," said Pehr; and, embarrassed by the compliment, walked off with his milk pail.

Chapter 5

TO THE CLAIM BY COVERED WAGON

After supper on Saturday (10 July 1869) the little family sat together and considered their prospects. A strenuous journey lay before them; a long march into the wilderness, with unknown hazards along the trail, and little hope of help in event of illness or accident. They would go beyond the outer fringe of settlement where few white men had set foot before them. They would go fairly well-equipped for their purposes; but they had remaining of their hard-earned and cautiously expended money, scarcely any reserve with which to counter an emergency. They had become pawns of the frontier.

Anna dreaded the impending journey by wagon and oxen more than she had dreaded the voyage across the Atlantic or the brutal train ride from New York to Minnesota, but she suppressed her fears silently. In her purse were only twelve American dollars. She had given Pehr a hundred, after their money exchange in New York, and she had spent for such luxuries as coffee and sugar much of the thirty-three-dollar residue she had kept for herself. Her little fund she kept secret.

After Pehr had bought and paid for all items deemed essential, he had only a hundred dollars in bills left in his wallet.

July was more than a third gone, and time had become of the essence; if they delayed planting much longer they would have no potatoes for the winter. Frost would harvest them, immature.

But for his uncommon self-restraint and a certain feeling of reverence for the whole undertaking, Pehr would have broken the Sabbath on that second Sunday in July 1869; so eager was he to begin the journey Monday morning. But he could ill afford to trifle with the sacred just when he stood in severe need of divine guidance and protection. The Sabbath would be kept, however frustrating the incidental delay. He didn't yield when he broke open his pail of tar and tallows, a mere flick of the wrist! He didn't yield when he loosened the wagon wheels, one by one, and drew them part way off to see how dry the hubs were. It was no real work to give the axle a dab of lubricant before he eased a wheel back on and tightened the nut. There was no real work to greasing an empty wagon, anyhow. The plow was, indeed, already in the wagon, as was the stove, the chain, the barrel of flour and other items. The plow he snugged back against the end-board and tied it securely, with land-side against the wagon box and handles sticking out beyond the canvas. Thus, his sensitive conscience approved one little task after another until the wagon stood more than half loaded at sundown. Pehr bedded down early and slept well, having kept the Sabbath.

Next morning he wakened before the birds and roused the entire family. This was the great day for which they had waited. They breakfasted by candlelight, and no one ate much. Over his coffee cup, Pehr brightened his little daughters with permission to take Blackie along. Blackie was a stray cat that had come to live with them. When Pehr departed the table and began to lift, carry, and stow, he had two cheerful little helpers. An early passer-by helped him hoist the great chest into the wagon. By himself, he crowded in beside the plow the crude bunk he had fashioned for Anna and the girls. Hay and a comforter in a board frame should be a reasonably comfortable bed. This done, he secured the canvas all around. They were ready to go, but for muscle power. While he fetched oxen and cow, his dutiful wife tucked the last pieces of clothing and bedding under the wagon cover, and set their lodgings in order for new occupants, in event such should appear. Their half-paid benefactors, the Jönsons, had regrettably bade their short-term tenants farewell and Godspeed the night before, so they needn't delay their departure. Anna was saddened and apprehensive at departing even this borrowed semblance of civilization. But, when the ox yoke was hitched to the wagon and the cow tied behind, Pehr's call reassured her:

"Come, now, Anna!"

Before she reached his side, the little ones were safely on the seat, momentarily awed and silenced by their high perch. Blackie was asleep under the canvas. Pehr lifted his little wife and held her in his arms for one tender moment before he set her feet on the hub and steadied her to the seat between her daughters. She smiled down at him, and he returned her smile. Then he started the oxen by name: "Come, Buck and Bride," and walked off in the driver's place beside the near (left) ox, Bride. They were on their way to the land that would give them security and independence! (How great a blessing is our ignorance of the future! The brave, sad little woman who sat half smiling could not foresee that she would be buried in that new land before two years had passed.)

With characteristic caution and foresight, Pehr had determined in advance exactly where to find the main wagon trail leading north. He was not confused by the numerous logging trails that struck out in the same general direction, only to end abruptly at a logging camp, or fade into the forest. He was soon well clear of the settlement; whence the road, if such one might call it, drove a crooked path of least resistance, between the swells, up the valleys, and about the lowlands most heavily wooded.

One might follow this trail even in the dark, if need be, by the sound of the wheels, and it would take him to a road leading northwestward, a few miles out from Litchfield.

The Swedish-speaking young man in the Greenleaf Land Office had instructed Pehr (Nils Johnson had not been concerned), with the aid of a large wall map. He had, indeed, given Pehr a small sketch to aid his memory enroute. Since any mileage estimates were to Pehr highly confusing, the Swedish mile known to him being more than six and one-half times as long as an English (American) mile, the kindly young man had advised him in terms of daily marches. He instructed Pehr to hold to a northerly course until he intersected the Forest City road, a few miles north of Litchfield. He also admonished Pehr to consult his little pocket compass frequently to ensure progress in the right direction. This Pehr did, each time he rested his animals.

Further had advised the young clerk: "A few hours out you will come to a stream called Crow River. Wagon tracks will lead you to a hard, shallow ford. That ford is on the Forest City Road. After crossing, follow the road northwestward to a little settlement called Manannah. There you will cross the Crow again, and then head to the northwest. If you press on steadily, at a leisurely pace but without long stops, you will come to a beautiful lake at about dusk. That will be Lake Koronis, and the trail I know skirts its western shore. Right there might be a good place for you to spend the night if you intend to sleep out. The lake has good water, is easily approached on the west, and the grassy spots should afford adequate grazing for your animals. Keep on going north the second day, following a fairly good trail. If you make good progress, you'll cross the Sauk River before sundown, right there"—he pointed out a place on the sketch. "That stream may be troublesome, because it loops all over the landscape; and it will be high this year, because of so much cool rainy weather. Soon after crossing the Sauk you will strike the main road between St. Cloud and Alexandria. If I were you, I'd drive the road to Alexandria and from there strike out north to the Otter Tail country. I can't direct you beyond Alexandria, because that's as far north as I have been in Minnesota." *(Figure 5.1)*

The topography north of Litchfield was flat enough to recall parts of southern Sweden known to Pehr and Anna—broad level valleys with low undulating uplands between them. Over such terrain the cattle could probably walk four or more Swedish miles between dawn and dusk. This was near mid-July; not far beyond the longest day in the year. If push came to shove, they could march fifteen or sixteen hours a day. Twilight was long at both ends; but the moon was dark, so they dared not go far after sunset.

They were several miles out before they topped a considerable rise, and looked down a long slope they must next negotiate. Pehr knew he'd better brake the wagon to descend safely, and conventional brakes he had none. But he could simulate brakes by tying a rear wheel so it could not turn. Those less conservative than Pehr simply thrust a rail or a post through the wheel to stop it, but Pehr hadn't the heart to abuse his wagon so; the spokes soon lost their paint and became scarred and bruised. He had a better way, and he was prepared for the eventuality. He had in the wagon two short lengths of half-inch rope; and with these he could hold both hind wheels if necessary—this became necessary several times during the journey, although the wagon carried a relatively moderate load. In this first instance, Pehr tied the left hind wheel; he tied his rope about the rim and tire just behind a forward spoke, and then secured the other end to the bracket holding the step attached to the bottom of the wagon box. He deemed the bracket strong enough, and it proved to be so.

During this procedure he kept wishing to himself that he had horses instead of oxen. Horses in harness with breeching could hold back a heavy load, but oxen in a yoke could not. If the wagon ran forward, the yoke slipped forward to their horns, in which position, if the beasts were sufficiently tolerant and steady, they could hold back a light load. But many oxen became unmanageable when the yoke pushed forward on them; they bawled and took off, tails in the air, frightened by the

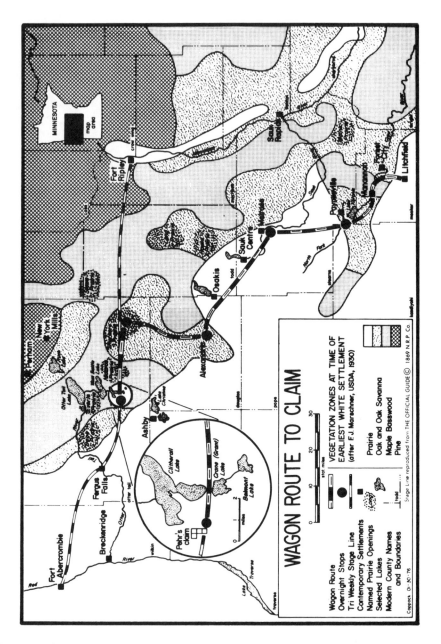

Figure 5.1. Map: Route to Pehr's claim by covered wagon. This was a strenuous trip for all, particularly the cow. In less than five full days of marching, they traversed hardwood forest, some thick, some open or scattered, and broad stretches of open prairie. At no point did they enter the great pine forest, which lay to the northeast. Note: Belmont Lake is, in its vicinity, the uppermost water body with drainage northward.

wagon bearing down on them. Pehr would not risk a wreck for failure to stop a wheel, but he pondered the possibility of putting breeching on an ox. He consoled himself that the frequent wheel tying took little time inasmuch as he did it while the animals got their wind. He begrudged the halt at the bottom of the hill to untie the wheel, but this soon became a routine of mere seconds; he left the rope secured to the step bracket and loosened only the end tied to the wheel.

The plodding oxen were soft and short-winded from weeks of idleness, and could not be driven hard; nor was it wise to lead the cow faster than an easy walk. Trudging alongside his steers, Pehr could easily gage their need for rest. He stopped often to wind the animals, sometimes in cool shady places, but more often after gaining the airy tops of long inclines. Progress was slow but steady. The day was clear and pleasantly cool, reminiscent of Skåne at the same time of year.

At noon, having just passed the village of Manannah and crossed the Crow River a second time, they turned off the trail on a grassy rise next the river. Pehr had given his animals adequate time to drink when they had forded the stream. Now he herded them out to graze while his wife made lunch ready. They sat on the grass and ate sparingly. After eating, the girls climbed the grassy knoll to gather flowers, of which they found a considerable variety—some familiar and others foreign to them. Their parents sat and talked quietly—about their good fortune in having a well-worn trail to follow; about the country they had traversed and the miles that lay ahead; about fuel with which to cook supper; about the desirability of keeping a campfire burning at night; and about much else of common interest and concern. Anna concluded the conversation with an admonition that Pehr henceforth ride the wagon when fording streams. "No need to risk damage both to your boots and to yourself, when you can as readily keep your feet dry!"

Pehr was glad that his wife seemed more cheerful and confident and less frightened and apprehensive. She was learning that the wilds are neither hostile nor vicious, but simply untamed and misunderstood. Pehr herded the cattle onto a notably lush patch of grass, but they got little of it; in a few minutes he led them to the river for another drink and once more hitched them to the wagon. Their driver was not ignorant of ruminants. They could gulp their food and chew it later. No need to waste hours of daylight for feeding; the animals could lie and chew their cuds all night if they wanted to. There'd be time for it then.

"Come up, Buck, Bride."

The wheels had barely commenced turning when a shower of flowers erupted from the wagon. The girls had discovered plant lice in the blooms.

During the afternoon, mother and daughters elected to walk behind and stretch their legs rather than jouncing on the seat. They talked and laughed happily as they walked. Pehr rode the seat for awhile, resting his wet feet, lest he blister them. He had many miles to walk, and could ill-afford sore feet.

Just as the sun began to set and the long, high-latitude twilight began, Pehr glimpsed a large body of water some distance ahead. They reached their day's destination well before dark and selected a splendid camping spot in a grassy glade near the lake. It must be Lake Koronis—fringed with elm, oak, ash and birch, with here and there quaking aspen bordering grassy openings *(Figure 5.1)*.

Only a short distance back they had passed a tangle of aspen on the ground, wind-thrown and dry, superb fuel for a quick hot fire. Pehr hauled his axe from under the plow, removed the wooden guard he had tied over the bit, and headed for the wind-fall. He returned in a few minutes with an armful of dry wood and three stout stakes with which to tether his animals. After watering the livestock in the lake he tethered them on grass, sufficiently far apart to prevent any tangling of ropes. He drove the stakes almost flush with the ground so that no animal could wind its rope about one and strangle itself. (He saved these stakes, and they served for the entire journey).

Always cautious and provident, Pehr fetched one armful of dry wood that he stuck under the wagon (for cooking breakfast) and another that he stowed in the wagon against a rainy day. The sun was setting with a glorious flare of light reflected from cirrus clouds in the west—which he interpreted as harbingers of rain tomorrow. Of these thoughts he said nothing to his family.

The girls fetched water from the lake, and the mother took her stew pot and a hard flat loaf of bread from the wagon. The pot was half full of thick meat-and-potato stew, sealed over with fat. From it she would give her family hot suppers every night of the journey, or at least until it soured. Of the round nourishing loaves she had more than they could eat in a week. The stew tasted good to everyone, including the cat, and they ate heartily. After supper, Pehr had just time to milk the cow before dark. He gave the cat a plate of the warm milk, then covered the bucket and set it up on the seat where the night breeze could strike it. In the morning there'd be cream for the coffee and cool sweet milk for the mush.

While there was still light enough to see by without a candle, he helped his little family bed down in the wagon. Mother and younger daughter shared the bunk he had made for them; the elder and Blackie shared a heavy wool comforter on the floor. He tucked them in and kissed each one good-night—except Blackie. From the family he turned his attention to the animals. The oxen had lain down, as near to each other as their ties would permit, but the foolish cow was ambling about restlessly. He pulled her stake, and tied her nearer the wagon. Then he spread the dying fire and crushed the embers. He ridiculed the notion that a fire kept wolves away, but he knew that a spark could ignite the wagon cover. Satisfied that all was safe and secure, he pulled off his boots and rolled up in his blanket under the wagon, his musket beside him, primed and ready.

A night hawk called. An owl hooted from a near-by tree. The cow lay down. And he fell asleep to the dull grinding and rumbling of his oxen as they chewed their cuds.

When he awakened, his wife stood stirring the mush, and the girls sat watching her. He must have over-slept. He called a cheery "good morning" as he reached for his boots. It startled the trio, but they turned their faces and replied. The girls were bright and lively, but the woman was obviously wan and tired. He walked over and laid a gentle hand on her shoulder. She turned and buried her face against his chest, sobbing audibly. He patted her head and asked tenderly:

"What's the matter, my little woman?"

And, between tears and sobs, he learned. She had spent a miserable night. The ominous stillness and heavy darkness had frightened her, and she had lain awake. Coyotes had howled hungrily; first in the distance, then closer by. She was terrified, expecting them to attack. She had called to her husband in frantic half-whispers, but he hadn't heard.

She had risen and stood guard over the sleeping children, watching the darkness through the rear of the wagon. At the first trace of light, she had quitted the wagon and rekindled the fire.

"I'm sorry to be a scared rabbit, but I can't help it," she apologized.

Pehr promised her that she would not spend another night on the trail if he could possibly arrange otherwise. The woman must have rest; there'd be hardship enough without meeting it fatigued!

(The next night of the journey was spent at a homesteader's establishment. The animals got sweet wild hay and the settler treated each of them to a measure of oats from his first harvest. Pehr slept under the precious wagon with the cattle staked nearby, but his family slept indoors.)

The second day was gloomy and rainy, as Pehr had feared it would be. The morning was sultry, and before noon the travelers stopped for a quick lunch. (Better be on the trail in event of rain.) The northwestern sky darkened ominously, and before mid-afternoon a violent thunderstorm broke over them. Mother and daughters took refuge back under the canvas, but Pehr, on foot, was drenched by the down-pour. Fortunately, no hail fell, and the animals kept going quite as if they enjoyed the cooling rain. For fear of lightning, Pehr dared not take shelter under trees, but remained exposed to other of the elements.

The storm struck and departed in less than an hour's time, but it left the ground muddy and slippery, severely retarding progress. For descending even slight inclines, Pehr tied the wheel, lest the oxen, slipping and sliding, be caused to fall and become entangled. Such an accident, often as not, split the yoke and broke the wagon tongue.

Before twilight, they had crossed the Sauk River, gained the main road, and were traveling northwestward as darkness overtook them. They saw a dim light off the road to the right, and Pehr steered his oxen toward it. Soon they came to a large log cabin and were greeted joyously by a Swedish settler and his matronly wife. Of course the travelers must stay the night; visitors, especially Swedes, were a welcome treat. The children rarely had playmates other than their own siblings. All could be bedded comfortably, and the hosts would be honored. So, stay they would *(Figure 5.1)*.

Anna insisted that all must share her stew, so Pehr fetched the pot from the wagon. It remained delicious, but might have gone bad in one more day, had the weather turned hot.

Before eating, Pehr and his new-found friend, Hans Jakobson, stabled and fed the oxen and the cow. Pehr did his milking and brought the milk into the house. The girls and three Jakobson children played together until the outdoors was pitch dark. Their parents discussed problems entailed in the building of a home and in breaking and sowing prairie. Soon after dark the kind matron, candle in hand, guided her guests to thick pallets on the floor where they would sleep. Then she went to her bed and extinguished the candle. Everyone undressed in the dark. Anna had earlier put her girls to bed in the loft with the other children.

All were awake and stirring at first light next morning. They breakfasted heartily on white bread and butter, fried potatoes, and fat salt side meat. During the meal, Mrs. Jakobson advised Anna about vegetable growing on the claim. She must get her potatoes planted just as soon as possible; otherwise the tubers would not mature sufficiently to keep through the winter. Night frosts might commence early in September, if not in late August. The potatoes must be dug before frost went deep enough to damage them.

Although their Swedish origins were distant one from the other, dialects imposed no obstacle. They asked so much about "home" that Anna waxed sad and silent with longing.

In good time the travelers were on the road, heading northwestward at a good pace. Almost immediately they came to a considerable town (Sauk Centre), through which the road lay. The country was almost flat, necessitating few rest stops and no wheel tying. Despite the delay by the rainstorm yesterday, Pehr figured to be in Alexandria before nightfall. He would bed his family in the hotel and stable his cattle in the livery barn. He did not speak his mind; Anna would be pleasantly surprised.

At lunch time Pehr tethered the cattle to graze and fetched each a pail of water from a nearby slough. Gratified to be so well on the schedule laid out for him in the Land Office, he relaxed with his family; and they lingered over their picnic lunch.

They spent the night in Alexandria, as Pehr had envisioned: $1.50 for supper, bed, and breakfast for each adult and 50 cents each for the little children; 25 cents per head of livestock, for stall, hay, and a measure of oats night and morning. The stop cost Pehr a total of $4.75, but he deemed the comforts well worth the price. With the residual of a five dollar bill he bought 5 cents worth of candy for the girls and a small wedge of cheese for Anna and himself.

When Pehr came to milk Bos, the Swedish stable boss engaged him in conversation about things at "home," the improved accommodations aboard ship, the speed of steam compared with sail (often exaggerated) etc. etc. He was amazed to learn that the steamship *France* had at times carried a very considerable spread of square sails, although she was powered mainly by steam. When came Pehr's turn to be inquisitive, he asked about trails running north from Alexandria. The stable boss assured him that there was a good trail running due north to a little place called Parkers Prairie, about twenty miles away, and explained how he should go out of town to get on it *(Figure 5.1)*.

"Do you know where there is an east-west wagon trail north of here?" inquired Pehr.

"Yes, there is one," replied the new acquaintance, "but I don't know whether it runs north or south of Parkers Prairie. It's a stage coach route, as well as an Army freight route, so it should be quite good."

Pehr thanked for the information, took up his milk pail and delivered the milk to the hotel kitchen. The cook thanked him "ever so much."

"May I have a dish full for my daughters' cat?" asked Pehr. "I'll take it to him in the wagon and return your dish."

"Yes, indeed," said the cook, handing him a saucer. He walked off with a dab of milk in the pail and an empty dish. When he returned with dish and pail the cook said: "If you'll wait a minute, I'll wash your pail for you so you can take it along."

While she scrubbed and scalded, Pehr stood with a wry smile on his face, thinking how he would regale Anna with a view of the claim from Discovery Hill. It would be worth a few extra miles, and this way he would avoid the rough stony country in the vicinity of Christina Lake. He would go north, and then west, making a right angle turn where he might have gone in a straight line but for intervening lakes and marshes. He would break about even on time, and Anna's pleasure at seeing the view would be worth a few extra miles of travel. In two more days they should arrive at the claim, and he must reach Discovery Hill well before dark. He awoke from his reverie only when the cook shoved his scoured pail at him. "Thank you," he said and stalked to his room with his pail.

They were on their way next morning a bit later than usual, but they would easily make good Pehr's self-imposed schedule for the two remaining days of travel. Pehr thought to himself: so much as we go beyond twenty miles today, so much less than twenty miles will be left for tomorrow.

After passing several lakes that compelled the trail to swing about considerably, they came onto a stretch that ran straight north far as the eye could see. Here was open prairie, with only a scattering of wooded areas—of oak, aspen, elm, maple, ash, birch, and other deciduous broadleaf species. Nor did they see many settlers' homes. They were on the very fringe of settlement and would probably sleep out their last night on the trail.

Perhaps open prairie would strike less fear in Anna than had the dark woods their first night out. The moon was now almost at first quarter, so nights would become progressively brighter except as cloudiness might intervene. The ground was now firm and dry under foot.

As the day waned he became increasingly apprehensive about the prospect of stopping for the night on a dry camp site, but fortunes of the little company held, and as twilight deepened they came upon a large firm-bottomed slough with water acceptable for watering the stock and boiling for coffee. They saw no sign of settlement *(Figure 5.1)*. (Indeed, they made camp less than a mile south of Parkers Prairie, and were amazed when lights began to show in the distance, after Pehr had made camp. They would sleep out.)

Before he commenced the camp chores, Pehr expressed to Anna his regrets that no lodging had come into view. She replied cheerfully that she had half hoped that they would have to sleep in the open so that she might display more courage than she had their first night out. She said, "I expect to sleep out tomorrow night too, but I do not intend to be afraid."

"I'm proud of you," said Pehr. "I will build the fire some distance away and down-wind from the wagon. You'll be able to see it through the rear flap of the canvas. I will keep it going as long as my wood lasts; I took all I had stored in the wagon. Tomorrow we must collect some dry fuel enroute to ensure a fire tomorrow night. We shall have to eat a cold breakfast tomorrow morning. We can drink the fresh milk rather than letting it sour during the day. When you skim off the cream in the morning, why don't you put it in a jug and hang it on Bride's end of the yoke? We might churn our own butter as we travel." Anna enjoyed the humor, and determined to search for a suitable container. (Bride did, indeed, churn butter.)

During the night, coyotes howled in the distance intermittently, and noctural insects sang a continuous chorus. In the gray of dawning, a skunk ambled up from the slough edge and was busily digging grubs about Buck's tether. Buck's curiosity arroused, the ox rose up to investigate, and the short-sighted skunk sprayed him full in the face. Buck let out a bellow that could have been heard a mile off, lunged for the slough, jerking his stake out of the ground, and stood for some time splashing his massive head about in the water. Fortunately, he had been staked out between the wagon and the slough, so he damaged only his oxen pride.

The commotion waked everyone. Pehr hastened to Buck, waded out beside him and splashed his face vigorously for several minutes. The ox quieted and came obediently to the yoke. Pehr quickly yoked the oxen and tied the cow in her place.

He told Anna to stay under cover with the girls until he could get away from the over-powering scent. He poked the oxen a bit more severely than usual and they set out at a brisk walk. A northwesterly wind might have refreshed them, but poor Buck, still heavily perfumed, walked up-wind from the wagon. (He would carry the scent for several days.) In less than an hour, some distance north of Parkers Prairie, they came to a pretty little lake bordered by willows and cottonwoods. Here were both fuel and water ready to hand; a good place in which to milk the cow, let the cattle graze, and eat a hot breakfast. Despite the disgusting odor that hung about, the girls enjoyed the entire comedy.

After milking Bos, Pehr poured the customary saucer-full for Blackie, but Blackie failed to appear.

"Girls, have you seen your cat about? Is he away hunting, or did the skunk get him?"

"No Papa," said Hanna. "I haven't seen him since we stopped last night. He must be in the wagon."

Pehr lifted the girls into the wagon to search for their cat, and almost instantly their shrieks and exclamations startled their parents.

"Svarten has five kittens," called Elna, sticking her head out the rear flap.

"That's fine," said Pehr. "We may need several catchers of rats and mice. But, say, you'll have to change her name from 'Svarten' (black male) to 'Svartan' (black female). Here, give her the milk where she is; she'll come out and eat tomorrow."

The girls left Blackie reluctantly and were lifted down for breakfast. In their excitement they reached for bread and cheese without ceremony.

Anna interrupted: "Girls, you will pray before meat, as usual!"

"There is no meat," countered Elna. "The last was in the stew. Remember?"

Pehr almost burst out laughing, but he knew that would be wrong. He stifled the laugh and turned his head away.

"Say your prayer—and we may have meat tomorrow," he concluded.

The girls recited their short grace in unison, as they were accustomed to do. All sat with bowed heads.

A quick breakfast eaten, Pehr was soon smearing the wagon hubs ('for the last time on the journey,' he thought to himself.) He had smeared those axles every morning, to spare wagon and oxen alike.

Anna washed and stacked the dishes away and came to sit a moment with Pehr by what might be their last campfire on the journey. Pehr appreciated her gesture.

"I believe, Anna," he said, "that we are little more than half a day's march from our claim. We should be on it before dark, at least. I pray that you will see in it as much beauty and security as I did when first I saw it; that you will be truly happy to have come."

"Dearest Pehr," replied Anna, "I will love and admire what you love and admire, be it here or anywhere else, but I cannot quit my thoughts of home. I must simply learn to recall the past happily instead of with regrets. I am trying."

"You will do it, Anna," said Pehr, "You're a fine, smart woman and a good wife. I shall always be proud of you. Your happiness means all to me. But now—we'd better hitch up and be on our way."

A few miles of open prairie, with only gentle swells and swales, and they arrived at the rutted wagon trail that Pehr had waited to see. They turned west on it and continued the march without hesitation. The heavy dew was rapidly evaporating from the tall, thick grass, but Pehr was soaked above his boot tops.

An hour later, when Pehr had stopped the rig on a low crest of land, Anna called to him from the seat: "What are the large birds we're seeing now and again?"

"They look a little like chickens," prompted Hanna.

"They are chickens," asserted Pehr, "wild chickens, prairie chickens. The young are probably just beginning to fly. In autumn they congregate in large flocks, I'm told. They're said to be easy to shoot or trap and delicious to eat. After the young are full-grown, we shall try them. We're in the New World, my girls, where the bounties of Nature remain unspoiled."

"Is the grass dry enough for us to get down and walk a little?" asked Anna.

"Yes," replied Pehr, "I'll help you down." The mother and daughters walked some distance, but they soon fell behind the long-striding cattle, so Pehr had to stop and wait for them. After several repetitions of this routine, Pehr stopped and called on them to hurry. He would help them to the seat, lest they be too much delayed. Running toward the wagon in front of her mother and sister, Elna came on a snake which so frightened her that she stood and screamed. Anna quickly caught up with her, held her close and calmed her, assuring her that Minnesota had no poisonous snakes, so they need not be feared.

They stopped early for lunch, more for the sake of the animals than for the humans; they had been on the trail since before daylight. Pehr tethered his cattle and brought them water from the slough at which he had elected to stop. Then he sat down to his cold lunch. He sat musing, half gloating over their good fortune thus far, so near the end of their journey. As he gazed about the landscape, his ears caught a small metallic sound, far distant to the east.

"I believe I hear something coming," he said, and all eyes looked in the same direction as his. The moving sound grew louder and louder, until there emerged from the haze a tremendous team and wagon rig.

"It's an Army freighter," said Pehr. "We'll ask the drivers about their route to the west."

As the six-mule team and monstrous wagon drew near, Pehr stood up and signalled the driver to stop. When all the commands and jangling subsided, he asked, in Swedish, about the trail westward. The man riding shotgun and brake-man on the high seat sat silent. The mule skinner astride the left wheel mule said something in English that Pehr could not understand. Then he motioned toward the west, and with both hands spread before him, a black-snake in one and a jerk-line in the other, palms down, indicated almost as well as he might have vocally that the trail was good—gentle, firm, and fast *(Figure 5.1)*. Then he called sharply to the lead mules, cracked his long whip; and the rig took off, the mules flat out, at what seemed a reckless speed. Both men waved as they hauled away.

The little immigrant family stood silently and watched the great wagon recede into the distance and disappear among the trees. Pehr reflected happily that the remainder of their journey might be the easiest part, soon to be completed. He hoped that his surmise was correct, that this wagon trail ran over his Discovery Hill whence he had first seen and admired his claim. He would know in a few hours.

(The freighters and stage coaches did, indeed, go over THE hill and across Pehr's claim, hard by the spot on which he would build his house. The great mule teams and wagons hauled military supplies and equipment between Fort Ripley in Central

Minnesota and Fort Abercrombie, just across the Minnesota line in Dakota (some distance north of the Breckenridge-Wahpeton vicinity) *(Figure 5.1)*. This trail also served a tri-weekly stage coach service between the two terminals. Partly by reconnaissance survey and partly by trial and error, the route swung north of rough stony country and crossed the lake-spattered region between the groups of lakes wherein one might easily be trapped by marsh or swamp. The high-wheeled, heavy-laden Army wagons had cut and creased and worn the sod, and the sharp-shod hooves of six-mule teams had trampled and inflamed the wounds. The road, so-called, kept to high ground for the most part, swinging wide with ridges and saddles on the open prairie, twisting and turning where dense stands of forest, rocks, or sharp declivities interposed. It was an ideal road for oxen, most of the ups and downs having been circumvented; and although apparently circuitous in places, it spared one from dead-ending in marsh or swamp.)

Where the winding green-brown ribbon swung wide on the curves, Pehr cut the loops short; wherever it narrowed to a single pair of ruts he learned that the constriction was necessary, so he followed the ruts.

They finished lunching quickly. Anna gathered up the lunch things and put them in the wagon. Pehr yoked and hitched his oxen, tied the cow behind, and helped his family to their seats. Then they marched again.

They had now traversed almost flat country, devoid of timber, for most of two days; but they would soon be across the flats and into hilly country. Pehr began to glimpse sun-lit wooded hills to the west.

The very first hill they crested was so steep on the west side that Pehr tied both hind wheels, and the wagon almost over-ran the oxen even so. At the bottom, as he loosed the wheels again, he looked up to Anna and joked: "Had this been rime frost instead of slippery prairie grass, I should have needed five wheels to tie." She missed the joke, but laughed to be polite.

Pehr could scarcely confine himself to a walk any longer, so eager was he to show Anna and the girls the view from Discovery Hill. He scanned every vista of prairie, hills, and woods, fearing that he might not recognize the over-look when approached from the east.

But, lo! In late afternoon he recognized the swells of land that rolled on to the crest he sought; and then there it was. There they were, viewing the undulating prairie that stretched northwestward as far as the eye could see.

He halted the oxen, helped Anna and the girls down from their seat, and swinging his arm west to north, proclaimed:

"There you see it. Isn't it beautiful? There (he pointed) the south forty has splendid stands of white oak, paper birch, and other good trees; three or four perennial sloughs from which cattle can drink; and beautiful prairie knolls. This shall be pasture. There (he pointed straight west), in the north edge of that oak grove I propose to raise my buildings. We will drive through it in a minute. The north, middle, and west forties are almost entirely open prairie. Man need only plow, harrow, and sow them to produce an abundance of grain."

Anna stood silent, but with tears streaming down her cheeks. Pehr noted her emotion, but made no comment about it. He lifted each girl in turn and repeated the pointing and explanation for her. They seemed awed by the bigness of the country that would be their home.

His long-awaited ceremony over, Pehr tied a wheel for safe descent; the mother and daughters walked beside him until they stood in the oak glade wherein their house would be. They stood, and silently gazed all about them, seeking to appreciate every feature.

Pehr broke the silence: "I saw a smoke about two forty lines west of here. We saw no sign of habitation when we came to select land. I suggest we go and see who lives there."

"Oh yes," said Anna, "let's go see whom our neighbors might be. I'll wager that neighbors are nowhere else so highly valued as on the frontier." So, off they went.

The smoke came from a cellar and sod home, in which lived a young Norwegian widow and her half-grown son. They welcomed the travelers with obvious pleasure.

"My husband died in the terrible war, and this quarter section was granted to me as a soldier's widow. Tollef, here, and I hope to make it productive in time."

Indicating Anna and the girls, the kind woman said: "You must stay here with us until Mister can build a house for you. If you can sleep in the wagon, we can cook and wash and work together in the daytime. We would be ever so pleased to have you, although, as you see, our room is too small for all to sleep."

Standing together to one side, the children conversed among themselves, albeit with some difficulty. The boy managed to be understood when he asked Elna: "Did you drive over a skunk?"

"Oh, no," she replied, "one squirted Buck, the red ox. I can't smell it anymore."

"Did you see the animal do it?" asked Tollef.

"No, it was too dark," replied Elna.

"I've seen a skunk," bragged Tollef. "Ma said they live only in America."

"Papa said we didn't have any skunks in Sweden," added Elna, not to be outdone.

"You are kind, and we are grateful," said Pehr. "I will see that there is food for all."

"I will help with everything the best I can," said Anna, "but I have no knowledge of this kind of living; I have much to learn."

"You are not alone," said the kind widow. "We shall have to learn together. This much I know: hardships bear down worst during the first year; after that things become easier. You'll see."

Pehr unyoked the oxen, untied the cow, and turned all three loose. He knew that the cow could be called for her milking; and if the steers strayed off, he could certainly find them tomorrow.

Thus, the little family of Swedes became pseudo-guests of a Norwegian widow—all of them an entire ocean and half a continent away from their native homes.

For supper the group ate freshly baked bread and milk, which delighted the girls especially.

The little sod-cellar house was indeed small, and crowded with six persons; so all returned outdoors after eating.

Pehr called Bos for her milking, and in a few minutes she came to him and stood. He set a heavy stick of firewood on end to serve him as milk stool. Bos let her milk down more freely than usual, as if she sensed that her arduous travel was ended.

High-piled clouds in the west were now threatening, and Pehr became concerned about a dry place in which to sleep. He whispered, unseen, to Anna: "Might you sleep with Mrs. Lien on her bed so I could crawl in the wagon?"

Anna violated the secret: "Mrs. Lien, might I sleep with you tonight? I would so much like to sleep indoors just one night. I noticed that your son sleeps on a floor pallet."

"Of course, you shall share my bed," said the good widow. "I should have thought to ask you."

"Thanks," began Anna, but Pehr cut in: "It was my idea to ask, Mrs. You see I've lived in these clothes and slept under the wagon, but I fear I would get wet under there tonight. I would also like to get out of these strong dirty clothes before I lie down to sleep. Anna, can you dig out a clean suit of underwear and a clean shirt for me?"

She stepped to the rear of the wagon. He quickly removed both end gates and helped her up. In a moment she emerged with his clean clothes on her arm.

"Just wait there a minute," said Pehr. "Now that we're so near the claim, I'll unload the plow to make a little more room." He pulled the plow back, eased it down and out until the handles rested on the ground and the beam rested on the end of the wagon floor. Then he grasped the beam as far forward as he could reach from the ground and swung the plow out and down. The women, each to a handle, helped him carry it aside. There he up-ended it so that the share and other business parts were off the ground and less subject to rust. He would smear it with tar and tallow tomorrow.

The storm broke before midnight, with violent winds, sharp thunder and lightening, and torrential rain; but thereafter everyone slept—dry and comfortable. Before Pehr slept, he thanked his gracious Lord for their safe arrival. He prayed, not vocally but mentally, as was his wont.

Chapter 6

HOME ON THE PRAIRIE BORDER

Next day was a busy one for everybody. It was Saturday, and tomorrow they would rest. By the grace of the Lord and a yoke of sturdy oxen they had arrived safely at their destination. On the Sabbath they would honor the Lord and let the cattle roam at will.

Pehr cupped his hands about his mouth and called to his bovines: "Come Bos, come Buck, come Bride." Then he waited a few moments and called again.

"They have gone to the slough to drink," offered Mrs. Lien. "It's about a quarter mile away, but they should be able to hear you."

Pehr kept calling, his voice booming out over the nearby woods; and directly, quite to his surprise, came the cattle out of the hazel brush that edged the forest—Bos leading and the oxen in single-file behind her. Pehr was delighted, and announced so all could hear: "See those animals come! They are not wanderers. They like our company." To himself he thought: "But, I'll bell the cow, in case she does stray. I hope my bell has a distinctive tone that I can recognize at a distance."

Anna came with the pail and suggested that she milk Bos and get acquainted. It would be her chore to do, soon as Pehr became preoccupied with building, haying, and all the other work he must do. Bos stood as if pleased with the gentler touch of Anna's hands.

Pehr fetched the bell from the wagon, holding the clapper mute, lest he startle the cow, and Anna too. When Anna rose from her task, he strapped the bell around Bos' neck and tapped it to make it ring. Bos shook her head, causing the bell to ring more loudly; but she made no further protest. Pehr suspected that she had carried a bell before he bought her and was accustomed to a constant tinkling when she grazed. The steers would probably become drawn to the bell and never stray far from it. The thought was comforting to Pehr. He knew that herding animals often follow a bell, so that a herd or flock does not become widely dispersed.

But this day was not one for contemplating any sentiment or logic appertaining to animal herding; this was a day for unloading, sorting, and stowing their goods and equipment for readiness as needs should arise. All the paraphernalia of homesteading must be arranged under necessary shelter in inverse order of their anticipated use. One dare not bury Pehr's building tools under a complex of dry beans, jugs, and salt pork! There must be system in the project.

First, all wagon contents were unloaded and set on the ground. (The chest was emptied before Pehr dragged it out and set it down.) The flour barrel he laid over on its belly and eased it down a ramp of two stout rails. Articles vulnerable to the elements, such as foods, seed, etc. went into a crowded corner of the widow's cellar home; those more durable went into a rail-sod shed erected to shelter her cattle during severe winter weather.

Now man and women together pulled the wagon into the shelter of the broad-crowned burr-oak near the cellar entrance, where it would be in afternoon shade. Pehr knew that he needed an able-bodied man to help him lift the double-box off the wagon gear, but such help he was denied. Two men could have lifted the heavy box over the wheels, one end at a time, and eased it to the ground; but since adequate brawn was not available, more subtle tactics must be employed. Pehr stacked lengths of stove wood under both axles on one side; then as he lifted each wheel in turn, Anna shoved another stick under until both wheels were off the ground. Then he unscrewed the large nuts in the hubs and pulled the wheels off their axles. With wheels out of the way, he easily lifted the rear end of the box onto the bolster standard, then off to the ground, the front bolster turning with the box. More difficult was lifting the front end clear of the bolster because the standards tended to bind against the box; but with considerable grunting and jolting, it too came clear and was lowered to the ground.

Pehr set the box on two stout rails laid down to receive it. They would hold the box off the ground, thus inhibiting rot and facilitating drainage. He faced the open(rear) end toward the east, alee of prevailing winds. There it was, his sleeping porch for the summer. Finally, he returned to the protection of the wagon box which covered the chest, the flour barrel, and the stove. Since the kindly young widow had generously offered them the use of her kitchen, he saw no use in leaving the stove out to rust. They would impose on her kindness only until he could erect a house of their own. Then he would make liberal restitution by laying up for her a supply of fuel and hay for the coming winter.

At evening when Anna came with the milk pail, Pehr took it from her, saying: "You'll have enough of milking when I am hard at work. I'll let you begin Monday morning."

While he sat milking he pondered the comparative merits of grass thatch and sod on a roof.

Rain ushered in the Sabbath and continued to fall until evening. For her morning milking, Bos stood dejected, her rump to the wind. Rain trickled down her flank and dripped into the pail.

The girls and their new friend, Tollef, spent much of the day in the wagon playing with Blackie and her kittens. Pehr sat in the cellar and talked with the women. After dinner he usurped the wagon for a good nap. Before dusk the rain had passed, and Pehr milked the cow without polluting the milk.

Monday broke clear, fresh, and beautiful; so beautiful that stoic Pehr determined to use the day for planning instead of laboring. He would take Anna with him to his proposed farmstead site, and together they would plan its temporary—and continuing arrangement. She would become no less part of it than he; she should therefore have equal voice in its conception.

"Dear you," he addressed her at breakfast, "I should have milked the cow this morning, because I don't intend to work today. Will you come with me to the home site I proposed and see whether you agree with my choice; and on whatever choice of site we finally select, help me decide the arrangement, or layout, according to which I shall build?"

"I am proud that you asked me," replied Anna. "I will be ready soon as I help Mrs. Lien with the dishes."

"You two go on," spoke up Mrs. Lien. "Elna and I will do the dishes. I'll see after the children for you. Take a lunch with you so you can have time to see all about the claim."

"Thank you ever so much," said Pehr. "We can go whenever you're ready, Anna. There was little, if any, dew last night, and the southwesterly breeze has quite well dried off the grass."

Soon they were off, Pehr shouldering his axe and carrying his grubhoe in the other hand, Anna carrying a bundle of food tied in a white cloth. She would spread their lunch exactly where the house would stand. They walked briskly into the warm morning sun.

On the high broad hill overlooking their claim from the west they stopped to view it from this new standpoint. Pehr once again traced out the four forties with a slow sweep of his axe helve, to orient his pretty partner anew. Then he set down the axe and inclined his shoulder to her eye level, so she would sight along his arm.

"See that hill, that one with the tall oaks on its northerly flank? We stood just southeast of that grove last Friday. See how nearly that grove defines the boundary between forest and prairie. That hill is on the line between our south and middle forties and just east of the section line. North of it lies a stretch of smooth prairie devoid of any obstruction to its plowing; south of it stands good timber, whence shall come our fuel-wood and materials for a hundred useful purposes. Whenever it comes, the public road will lie on the section line. That seems to be the ideal spot for our farmstead. Come, let me show you better; we viewed it too hurriedly last Friday."

She had no cause to doubt the wisdom of his choice, especially since his mind was so clearly made up. Nor did she have time to object before he had her by the hand, fairly dragging her down the grassy slope. His inspiration was her obligation.

He made straight for the designated hill flat; and in a few minutes they stood upon it—in a grassy opening almost arched over from the north side by towering white oaks. Truly, his enthusiasm was justified. Anna was breathless with exertion and wonder, but she smiled her hearty approval. Pehr pushed back her bonnet and kissed her; a surprise to both of them because they were in broad daylight and saying neither "hello" nor "goodby." Both blushed with emotion and embarrassment. Pehr laid down his tools and hugged and kissed his wife quite thoroughly. They might have imagined it night and made love in the grass, but both remembered Anna's sworn abstinence. She had bedded apart from her husband since he had proclaimed his determination to seek his fortune on the American frontier. So frightening and revolting to Anna was the prospect of bearing a child in the wilderness that she quite simply discontinued their previously normal sex relations. Pehr awaited the day when she might feel sufficiently secure to end his enforced celibacy, already of more than a year's duration.

They walked happily together through their woods, exploring every hill and hollow that they deemed part of the south forty. The deep forest duff was as a fragrant cushion to their feet; and Pehr wondered silently how long it might endure against grazing cattle. Rabbits darted in and out among thickly leafed bushes. Gray squirrels scolded as if the intruders were to blame for the poor concealment afforded by the oak leaves. Chipmunks chirped their annoyance from half-hidden ambush. Birds sang among the trees, happy with their progress in the rearing of new families. A ruffed grouse observed from a wind-thrown log, unseen until the intruders approached too near and he whirred noisily away, startling both man and woman to a sudden stop. A family of mallards on the last (southeast "corner") slough, paddled to the far shore and gossiped about the strange visitors.

Pehr thought how tasty wild fowl might be for supper, but he knew that every living creature was safe from him this day and this season. The day was memorable, almost hallowed, and must not be marred by killing. The season was for reproduction and family-rearing, during which all creatures should be spared. If his own young were hungry, Pehr would take fledglings or their parents to feed his children, but he would do so under no other circumstance. In autumn and winter he would hunt and kill for the table without self-incrimination.

The sun had passed the zenith when the newcomers returned to the grassy glade on the hill and seated themselves exactly where their house would stand. They sat near the southeastern edge of the grove, in which, to the north, stood tremendous white oaks with massive straight boles and expansive crowns. The site was obvious, and their choice of it spontaneous when they came to it; but they had walked about the entire hill flat and contemplated it from several directions before they found the place that seemed designed for them by Nature. The majestic oaks to the north stood as a legion to protect against the icy northerly blasts of winter. The lesser trees to the south would shield against the searing heat of summer sun.

Their sandwiches took longer than a four-course dinner, because they planned out the entire farmstead between mouthfuls.

"If I grub out that cherry and those three young aspens west of the house site, we can have a good-sized rectangle cleared for a garden. It will be large enough for this year, at least; the season is too far advanced for the planting of most garden varieties," thought Pehr aloud.

"Can we grow enough potatoes?" asked Anna, with apparent concern.

"Umn!" grunted Pehr, "pretty late to plant any, but we'll try it. We should have edible tubers by October, but they will probably not be sufficiently mature for winter storage. We'll have to beg, buy, or borrow some. Next year I promise you an abundance; I'll plant a large patch out on the open prairie. Incidentally, I'm still wondering whether grass sod can produce richer soil than a forest duff. If the soil be so fertile, why do not the trees occupy the land? Can grasses prevail against trees?"

Anna answered dubiously: "Maybe the squirrels and other animals eat all the acorns? Or, maybe the acorns cannot take root in the thick grassland mulch and sod?"

Pehr ignored her foolish ideas, and changed the subject: "Over there (pointing), on the south facing slope I'll set a stable for the cattle just below the break of the hill so that I may remove the manure down-grade, out of sight and smell. I shall, even so, be ashamed to taint this sweet prairie air with vapors from a dung heap." He sniffed and inhaled deeply, as if to make his point.

Anna disagreed with his thoughts, but remained silent. She reflected that the homey smell of stable and animals would, in its own peculiar way, help tame the wilderness. But her reflection recalled barnyards and firesides far away, and she dismissed it. This was no time to be homesick. She seized the lull in conversation to observe that they had sat long enough, that it was time they resume their exploration so they might complete it and regain their borrowed refuge before dark.

"I wish to complete supper before my Minnesota lamp goes down," she said jokingly.

Both laughed, and Pehr observed: "I've noted that your lamp gives good light when it's lit. And it takes not a drop of coal oil or tallow."

He laid the grub hoe beside one of the aspens, where he would recover it for work tomorrow. He shouldered his axe, and they resumed their expedition.

They now headed northward on the open prairie, where walking was easier and faster than in the woods. They viewed the three northerly forties from two vantage-points; one the first hill-top north of the chosen home site, the other one near the south side of the west forty. They stood for some time at each place and quite deliberately appreciated the landscape in all directions about. Now Pehr had acquainted his helpmate with their entire domain.

He took care not to point out the numerous large animal skulls that lay bleached white on the prairie slopes surrounding the middle slough of the north forty. They showed vaguely through the thick grass. He should have to gather and remove them later.

They turned their steps toward the widow's cellar, and assumed a more leisurely pace. They scared up a handsome jack rabbit in one place and a pair of prairie chickens in another; and they marvelled, as before, at the size of beast and fowl in America. Truly, this must be a wonderful land!

As they approached the cellar and wagon, Tollef and the girls came running to meet them. Hanna took her father's free hand and walked beside him. Anna related some of their observations, and Elna begged that she, Hanna, and Tollef be shown them tomorrow. Anna could do aught else but promise to guide them.

Anna thanked the widow profusely for monitoring the children. Then the elders fell into animated conversation about the claim and all its virtues. Mrs. Lien could verify most of Anna's and Pehr's suspicions and assumptions.

In reference to the fertility of grassland she said: "The prairie soil is rich and produces heavy yields of grain. It is better for wheat than for potatoes, though it gives good crops of the tubers as well. The hill tops and knolls can be deceptive. Some have brown clay or marl under the sod; others have sand and gravel. Early drought may burn the sandy ones and curtail their yield; those with clay resist drought quite well. Pehr, you need plow only deep enough to turn the sod well over; to go deeper is a waste of ox muscle. When we manure this land it should become a veritable garden!"

Elna dreamed that night—of exploration and discovery; and next afternoon her mother and Mrs. Lien led the children on a considerable expedition. The young did, indeed, prove themselves more observant, in their way, than their elders. They asked questions by the score; about tree and animal species, bird songs of wood and prairie, kinds of prairie grasses and flowers; and many went without satisfactory answers. The mothers determined to inform themselves at every opportunity. In time, they would be conversant with their new environment.

After grubbing out the cherry and aspens in the garden space, Pehr spent the entire day, Tuesday, cruising the large forest that extended eastward from his claim all the way to the lake. He sought the best available timber for house construction, furniture making, and for shaping into a variety of useful, even essential, articles for the home and the embryonic farm. Somewhat west of the southerly lake lobe and on the broad base of a peninsula extending into the lake from the southwest he found splendid stands of white oak superbly suited for house logs. Hard by the lake he found clumps of large paper birches and even larger linden (basswood). He found also a goodly scattering of sugar maple, green ash, elm, and hophornbeam (ironwood). Every species would be useful to him eventually; and he made mental note where stood the best of each kind.

He would have commenced chopping and hauling logs at once had not Anna pleaded that their potatoes and rutabagas should be planted first. He knew she was right, and he rescheduled his work accordingly. Shelter would be useless without food. The moon phase was shifting from dark to light. He told Anna, "I will have the ground ready tomorrow. Root crops, such as our rutabagas, carrots, and potatoes, we must plant immediately, before the next light of the moon. I will help you plant the potatoes. You can sow the carrot and rutabaga seed without my help. I hope all three mature enough during the remainder of summer to keep in the cellar through most of the winter. Never before have we planted any one of them quite so late."

Anna heard him out, and then she made a request that both amazed and delighted him. She asked that he delay his departure with the plow next day until the girls should awaken and have their breakfast. She wished for herself and her daughters to witness the first breaking of the sod on their claim. Of course he could wait! It would take him some time to lay a loose bed of rails on the wagon gear, load the monstrous plow onto them and secure it with chain. (Men less frugal and cautious than Pehr would have simply hitched the oxen to the plow and dragged it on its landside the mile cross-country to the claim. But the austere Pehr would not so foolishly wear a costly implement.)

The historic sod-breaking party departed about eight o'clock, the little girls still a bit groggy from early wakening. Tollef almost wept to go along and was warmly invited when Anna sensed his feelings. She apologized to his mother for having been callous. She asked Mrs. Lien to come along as well, which she did.

Everyone walked; Pehr deemed it dangerous for anyone to ride beside the plow, bumping along on a collection of loose rails. Indeed, he doubted that the plow would remain on the wagon for the entire mile-long haul. He stopped several times, to push it into a more secure position. On arrival, he motioned everyone to stand well clear while he wrestled the implement to the ground. He had stopped the wagon at the southwest corner of the glade, where it would be in shade most of the day. In about the time it takes to tell it, Pehr unhitched the wagon tongue from the yoke and attached instead the end of a log chain, maneuvered the oxen into position, and secured the other end of the chain to the draw-bar on the plow. The moment of truth had come!

Pehr raised the plow to its upright position, lifted on the handles so that the nose of the share was hard against the turf (facing east), and called to his oxen: "Come! Buck, Bride." They stepped off in unison, as was their wont; the plow took hold, and a black, shiny furrow commenced turning up and over against the long, twisted mold-board. The witnesses waxed so noisy with excitement that they almost frightened the oxen. The sod was so fibrous and tough that the new-turned furrow lay unbroken half the length of the clearing—until the nose of the share became snagged in a root. Pehr, then had to twist and turn the heavy implement to free it; then haul it back for a fresh bite, clear of the root. Pehr thought he knew the sweat and muscle entailed in breaking new ground, but the first round about the clearing was even more strenuous than he had anticipated. Before he came back to the corner whence he had begun, he had struck and cleared at least two dozen roots too stout for the plow to sever. Several he had chopped out with the grub hoe and thrown aside. At the corner he stopped, dragged the plow round as he "hawed" the oxen, eased the share under a second furrow, and stopped to rest. Perhaps he should have plowed in a smaller rectangle and avoided most of the roots. Ah, well, the first (outer) furrow must have been the worst; he would strike fewer and smaller roots as he came nearer and nearer the middle of the glade. Round by round, his assumption became realized; the work became less laborious, both for him and for the oxen. Yet he persisted in "winding" his animals and himself at the end of each round. He had furrowed-in a rectangle about forty meters long (east-west) and thirty meters wide (north-south) so each round was of considerable length.

When about half the rectangle lay black, his admirers stood awaiting him at the "home" corner. Anna stepped up to him and admonished him to take more time and rest from his task more frequently.

"You will exhaust yourself and the oxen if you persist as you are doing. The gardening is of less consequence than the continuing well-being of yourself and the animals. Remember your rupture."

"Don't fret yourself, my dear," answered Pehr, between breaths. "The worst has been done. That was more like brush-breaking than prairie-breaking. We shall be alright now. I shall have this dead-furrowed about noon, and join you for dinner at the cellar. I'll bring the oxen and the wagon, and then turn the animals loose. I'll come back here this afternoon with my scythe, and clear the brush back from the edges of the plowing. I'll have to use my axe on most of it. I'll also chop off all the roots you see sticking out, and pick off the stones I plowed up. Tomorrow I'll come back with the oxen and the log chain. I think I can contrive a sort of drag with the aspens I chopped down, and smooth out this breaking fairly well. You might return with me tomorrow, and bring the seeds and potatoes so they'll be put in the ground during the dark of the moon. Underground stuff must be planted during the dark moon; otherwise it yields poorly! We can have the garden planted by tomorrow noon, if we cut the potatoes tonight. Are you agreeable."

"Certainly, I'm agreeable," replied Anna. "I'll sort out the seeds this afternoon. I only wish it was early enough in the season to plant a greater variety. I'll go now and have dinner ready for you when you come."

"Come! Buck, Bride!" called Pehr to the oxen, and they turned another round. By noon the entire rectangle lay black. Pehr drove the oxen, dragging the plow, to the corner where the wagon stood. There he turned the implement up on its handles, well clear of the plowing, in the edge of the hazel-nut bushes. Tomorrow he would smear it with tar and tallow to protect it against rust until he should use it again.

After supper the women and Pehr cut seed potatoes by candle-light. Pehr insisted that they first whack off the bud-end of a potato, and then make of the remainder as many pieces as possible, each cutting to have only one or two uninjured eyes. The cutting done, they had enough pieces with eyes to plant more than three hundred hills. Anna brought out her root seeds: rutabaga, turnip, carrot, and onion. It was late in the season for all these kinds; but the risk was not great—a few seeds, readily replaceable next year.

On Thursday, 22 July, Anna and Pehr planted potatoes, he digging and covering and she dropping the cuttings—just as they had done together many times before at home in Sweden, but never so late in the year. The potato planting was so quickly done that Pehr volunteered to help his good wife sow the root-crop seeds, as well. He grooved rows into the breaking with vigorous sweeps of his hoe handle. She sprinkled the seeds into the grooves, and he covered and packed the soil over the rows by treading them with his boots. They had the work all done, and walked home to Mrs. Lien's in time for supper.

The urgency of garden planting dispensed with, Pehr turned all his thought and energy to the construction of a log cabin adequate for housing his family. After considerable deliberation between husband and wife, Anna conceded that they might live, albeit crowded, in a room with floor space of five by eight meters.

Pehr determined to cheat a little, secretly, to simplify his measuring in the woods. He would cut the logs for the walls sixteen and twenty-four feet long, thus making those measurements the outside dimensions of the structure. He would use the yardstick given him by the hardware dealer in Litchfield, from whom he had bought his scythe, spade, hoe, grub hoe, and other tools. It was as well that he learn soon as possible the American system of measurement! He had, during many weeks past, given much thought to structural design and materials. He had inquired of several experienced pioneers, and gotten many helpful answers. He knew well how to go about the project. (Had not the Swedes invented the log house!) He also knew well that it would be difficult to accomplish without another strong man to help lift the logs into place as the walls went up. (Customarily, a log structure was laid up by four men; one at each corner.) He would have to show the two young women how to do one man's work.

Denied adequate help, he knew that he ought to settle for a simple shed-roof affair, but he could not so degrade a Swedish invention. He would build a gabled house, with a roof pitch of forty degrees—steep enough to shed rain and snow fairly well; flat enough so that sod would not slide off. He would run the long walls north-south, sighted with his compass. The door and one window would face east toward Discovery Hill. The other window would be in the west wall, opposite the one facing east. The house must stand on the very highest part of the flat hill, so that water would drain away from it in all directions.

Over and over he had visualized and mentally counted out the materials he should need. The walls would be of white oak, twelve twenty-four foot logs for each long wall, thirteen sixteen-foot logs for each end, and eight or nine for each gable, graduated in length from about fifteen feet to one foot, and sloped on the ends to fit the outer rafters in the gables. He would need seven rafters twelve feet long and notched half-way through and four inches from the end to receive their shorter opposites—eleven feet eight inches long. He would flatten the rafters on top, the better to fit a roof onto them. So well supported, at intervals of only four feet, his roof would never sag. Nearly as possible, rafters would be five inches in diameter at the ridge, the smaller end of the log. All main logs of white oak must be of such diameter that he might peel and flatten them slightly on top and bottom, so they would lie tight to each other, and so that each course would raise the wall eight inches. To support the loft floor he would need five sixteen-foot logs nine to ten inches in diameter, flattened considerably on top to receive the floor, and dove-tailed into the tenth log in each long wall—to serve both as floor joists and tie-beams. At the gables he would support the floor with cleats fastened to the logs.

The roof must project at least a foot beyond the walls all around, the better to protect the structure, and for this his measurements would allow.

He speculated that he might need willow withes, and perhaps some hay, laid on the roof under the turfs. Better still, he might lay on a birch-bark cover, beginning at the eaves and over-lapping the sheets as one would shakes or shingles. He had never before constructed a sod roof.

After eating quickly Thursday noon, Pehr shouldered his trusty axe and struck out for the woods, the one-man crosscut saw under his left arm. He walked due east from his cabin site, about a mile (English) to a beautiful, almost pure, stand of straight, clean-boled white oaks of the size he required. They stood on a north-facing slope, so their wood should be tough and strong, having grown under relatively moist, cool conditions. Assuming that each tree he took down yielded one or two lengths suitable for use in some part of his building, he would need at least fifty stems; there were many more than that, so he could choose carefully.

He leaned his saw against a maverick green ash and commenced chopping a fine white oak standing near. He felled, trimmed, and sawed into useable lengths, half a dozen, well before sunset. He saved for fuel and stacked separately all limbs and tops more than two inches in diameter. The fuel took about as much time as the logs, but fuel they would need in abundance, and he would waste none in the woods. He piled all small trimmings and brush in neat piles, and left no considerable slash to corrupt the woods. He hewed to eight-inch thickness and peeled entirely free of bark the logs he felled, but he left them, helter-skelter, where they lay, too tired to lift and carry them out into a pile. He stuck the saw deep into a brush pile where it might be free of dew and rust, shouldered his axe and plodded toward home. (He would sharpen the axe after supper.) Twilight deepened as he went.

On Friday, his work facilitated by both adz and broad-axe, he turned out a dozen logs, twice the number done on Thursday. He thought to snake them out and haul them in on Saturday, but rain intervened. Showers commenced Friday night and continued until Saturday noon. After dinner on Saturday he walked to the woods, and turned out four logs before dark. Now he had sixteen, more than a third of his requirement.

Monday he would have hauled these, but the ground remained so wet and soft that he feared miring the wagon in one of the low swales he had to cross. However, he must now establish some semblance of order in his little woods clearing. The white, fresh-peeled logs scattered about were becoming a hindrance to further work; they must be snaked out and stacked at the edge of the clearing where he might approach them with the wagon. So, on Monday morning he yoked the oxen, each with his tethering rope about his horns, looped the log chain around the middle of the yoke, and, shouldering his axe, made for the woods. Ox muscle made quick work of assembling the logs where he wished them, and then he tethered the beasts on good grass, in view of his cutting. At noon, before eating his lunch, he led the sturdy animals to water in a slough just below the logging site. Before dusk he had made six more twenty-four foot logs, and snaked them to the pile. He walked home with his oxen, pleased with the progress of his work. Now he had twenty-eight logs ready to haul home; he needed only twenty more. Weather favoring him, he would have them laid down and ready before Sunday. In three or four days of next week he could have them, together with all the fuel-wood he had salvaged, stacked at the cabin site.

On Saturday night, the last day of July, Pehr came home after dark—so late that Anna had commenced worrying about him. But her fears turned to joy when Pehr walked in and announced that all the cabin logs now lay ready for hauling. The girls and the boy were in bed asleep, but the women had waited to sup with their man. They ate by candle-light, and the cellar took on a festive glow, in celebration of accomplishment. Pehr blushed at admiring words and glances, and was glad the light was dim. Mrs. Lien envied Anna her kind sturdy husband, and had told her so often. For Pehr, the handsome, voluptuous young widow had taken such fancy that she waged with herself a constant secret struggle against her possessive inclination. More than once she chided Anna, slyly, for sleeping apart from him. Had she such a man, yearning to have her, she would "lie with him every night, and sometimes by day!" Anna pondered, but remained firm in her discipline.

Pehr's log hauling was impeded by more rain Monday morning; but when the sky cleared soon after dinner-time, he yoked and hitched his oxen to the wagon. He removed the rails and laid them aside. He took along two short lengths of half-inch rope for tying down the load. Even empty, the wagon cut in quite deeply across low places; he dared not load it heavily. Having stopped the rig alongside his pile of logs, he extended the wagon gear to the very last bolt-hole in the reach-pole, to guard against over-balancing the load with long ends over-reaching the rear wagon bunk. For further insurance, he loaded the logs well forward, heaving them over the side standards one end at a time. He laid one tier of logs the width of the bolsters (five logs) and then piled atop these the random lengths of fuel-wood until the load was about two feet deep. Then, threading the rope through the iron loops outside the standards, he tied the load down over each bolster. The wagon almost mired down in the deepest draw he must cross, but the trusty oxen kept it moving and hauled it through. (He would load a little less next time.) He made two trips before dark; ten logs and a respectable pile of fuel lay on the cabin site. In the next two days he delivered all the logs and made three additional trips to complete the hauling of the fire-wood. The last load he gave to the widow Lien; (he would fetch her much more later on). She was grateful and thanked him profusely.

Next morning (Thursday) at breakfast he announced that he would carry no lunch. He was going to the young big-leaf aspen grove in the north-east corner of the middle forty. He wanted ninety-two straight saplings. He could whack these down, lop them off fourteen feet long, and stack them up before noon. These would go on the rafters, only six inches apart at the small end, to hold the willow withes, grass, and sod. They would be laid large end out, a foot over the gable end and overlapped one foot over the middle rafters. He would have dinner with the family, then yoke and hitch the oxen to the wagon gear and fetch the whole lot in three short quick trips. The loads of green sappy aspen would be heavy, but he would be on high ground all the way, and mostly down-slope.

He walked home an hour late for dinner, his pile of rails still considerably short of the ninety-two he required. He would eat quickly, fetch the oxen and haul one load. Then, while his animals rested in the aspen grove between loads, he would complete his chopping. There would be no slashings worth saving for fuel.

That day, despite some time lost in calling up the oxen at noon, he completed his self-assigned task early, and enjoyed a long pleasant evening with his family and their esteemed new friends.

Friday morning Pehr shouldered his axe and lunch bundle as before, but with another destination. This day he blazed and cleared a suitable wagon trail to the best scattering of straight ironwoods that he had found during his search. They were on the Clitherall Lake peninsula, not far beyond its base. They stood just as he recalled them in his mind's eye—tall, straight, unusually thin, and with minimum taper. They grew amid a generous mixture of other deciduous trees, dominantly basswoods, but the ironwoods were so small that he need have no fear of tangling them in other trees when he felled them. He could whack one off free of its stump and let it fall where it would; he need merely grasp it by the butt end and drag it free. He measured the first one he chopped off and cut it eighteen feet long. This would be his gauge for the others. Branches and tops were of no moment; he would leave them where they fell. The wood was not called ironwood for nothing; it was hard as bone even in this the season of high sap content. But Pehr and his heavy axe persevered; by noon he had seventeen eighteen-foot rails piled by his marked wagon trail; his cutting made room for a turn-around. He sat on the pile and ate his lunch, taking time to appreciate the smells, sounds, and curious creatures of the deep woods. He reflected hopefully that these woods might never be entirely cleared away, but merely thinned from time-to-time and place-to-place so that the wild creatures might retain their native habitat. The sun was still high when he pitched onto the pile his twenty-fifth rail—all the rafters he needed for a shed-roofed stable. He departed the woods at a leisurely pace and in light mood, retracing the route by which he would bring in the oxen and wagon.

Next day, Saturday, 7 August 1869, before noon, he had twenty-six ironwood "rafters" stacked at the site chosen for the stable. He headed homeward, but had come only a short distance west of his claim when he saw and heard the young widow running to meet him. She appeared greatly agitated, and he called to her from a distance, walking forward of the oxen: "What on earth is the matter, Anna?" (He had never used her given name before.)

"Oh, Pehr," she fairly cried, as she came near, "the girls are lost." She fell against him, trembling, and buried her face under his chin. Between sobs she explained that Anna had gone in search of the young ones, while she had remained at the cellar to intercept them, should they return of their own accord. Tollef was not with them either.

"Now, Now," said Pehr, soothingly, taking her gently by the shoulders and holding her off. "We'll find them, never fear! Come, we'll go and see."

She took his arm as if for assurance, and he started the oxen anew. Despite his concern for the children's safety, he had been so roused by the furious press of her warm soft body against his that he dared not stay his head-long march toward their abode. Both were quite composed when they reached the cellar, and no one else would ever know what might have lain between them.

Anna and the children greeted them happily. The girls had not been lost, but they had wandered so far that they were beyond the range of their mother's calls.

Said Mrs. Lien to Anna: "Seems that we have now shared enough of good and ill so that you should no longer call me Mrs. Lien, as if we were strangers. Please call me Anna, just as I have been calling you Anna. Will you kindly do that?"

"It will be our pleasure," replied Pehr's Anna, and Pehr nodded his approval. Then he had second thoughts:

"If I have two Anna's responding to my call, how shall I distinguish between them and avoid confusion? Shall I call one 'little Anna' and the other 'big Anna', perhaps?"

"No, you won't," said Anna Lien. "Don't call me big, even if I am bigger than your little wife. Why don't you call her little Anna or MY Anna and just call me Anna? I think you'll manage not to get us confused," and she laughed.

"So be it," concluded Pehr, "I'm happy to have two Annas, both young, pretty, and diligent, and kindly disposed toward me. I love you both as much as is proper!"

The seventh day of August 1869, became for the settlers a frightening experience. As they rose from the dinner table, the daylight failed rapidly until they stood in darkness at mid-day. All the children and their mothers were frightened almost to the point of screaming. Pehr thought the end of the world had come, and all his hard work would be wasted. Then, before Anna could find and light a candle, light commenced returning, and everyone stepped outside to observe the sun emerging from the shadow. They had observed, as they learned later, a rare phenomenon, a total eclipse of the sun.

Pehr had fifty-three logs on the cabin site that must be dove-tailed on both ends, and numerous others that must be measured and beveled for the gables—hours and hours with axe and saw. But he remained with his family that work-day afternoon, apparently shaken by the eclipse. No one asked, however; and he did not explain. In any case, women and children appreciated his staying. Had he returned to work, they would have accompanied him. Their fright had been greater than his.

On the Sabbath Pehr did no work; the women, only enough to keep the cows milked and the family fed. (Anna Lien's cow, Daisy, wore no bell, but she grazed with Bos every day and followed her wherever she went.) Pehr took enough liberty with the day of rest to put a razor edge on his axe and adz, and he did much secret speculating about the week's work ahead of him. Where might he find the best sod for a roof? Where the best willow switches and slough grass for laying under the turfs? He would have preferred birch bark under the sod; but well he knew from experience that birch bark was too tight in August to be removed from the tree in un-broken sheets such as he needed. After Sunday dinner he stole away to the birch clump on the steep bank south of the first slough and tried the bark on a twelve-inch tree. It would not peel and come off whole, as it might have in April. His surmise was accurate. And it was just as well; he should have had to mutilate a hundred large trees to get the bark necessary to cover the house. He was building five months too late, but it spared his birches for better use later on.

After he returned to the cellar, he crawled into the wagon and slept so soundly that the children playing without, laughed at his snoring.

On Monday, Pehr, with spade and grub hoe, leveled and smoothed the space on which the cabin would be built. He dug away grass and sod so that the bottom logs would lie slightly into the earth, two feet in from the northwest corner, he then dug a four-by-four-foot hole about five feet deep, for winter root storage. He struck fine-grained sand only two feet down, so digging was easy. Later he would cover the hole with basswood planks laid into the ground flush with the floor and extending well beyond the hole on all sides. Such niceties as a wooden floor and a trap door to the cellar hole would come another year.

Now, with adjustable square, axe, and hand saw, he commenced cutting dove-tail notches into the wall logs. So fitted at the corners and fixed in place atop each other with stout dowel pins at both sides of openings, the logs could not give in any direction *(Figure 6.1)*. After notching two twenty-four-footers, on top side only, he laid them in place and notched two sixteen footers for the end walls. When he had laid in place these sixteen-footers, he had the bottom course of the log cabin completed (or so he thought, momentarily). But he could clearly see that the gable-end logs lay some three or four inches clear of the ground, and this gap he must fill with logs dug half-way into the earth. He would have to fetch two additional oak logs, each exactly fourteen feet six inches long, because he had overlooked this little quirk in building with logs. But he would postpone the hauling until another day; he wished to see walls rising before evening. Now, the notched end logs laid in place, he had, indeed, the bottom tier securely in place. He applied his long wooden level at numerous points, notably across the corners, dug dirt away or filled it under, as needed, until the entire rectangle lay accurately leveled and firmly in place. Soon he had another course notched and laid in place atop the first. They lay so well together that there would be very little need for chinking. Now he must bore inch-and-a-half holes about six inches in from the door opening, on both sides, through the second tier of logs and half-way through the first, to receive dowel pins that would hold the logs in place after he sawed out the opening for the door.

But he had forgotten another essential material—oak from which to fashion dowel pins. He'd better make a list of his additional needs from the woods: two fourteen-and-a-half-foot oak logs, several short bolts of oak for dowel pins, some sizeable basswood lengths for splitting and hewing into planks, and additional

Figure 6.1. Logs joined with dove-tailed corners as shown here lay secured against shifting in any direction. Notching logs in such manner required considerable skill and entailed much labor.

Photo by author, southeast corner of barn, 1974.

basswood for table, stools, and benches. He would take oxen and wagon tomorrow and fetch all these materials from the woods. He could be back at noon. Today he would go home and eat his dinner; then go, with scythe and axe, in search of willow and coarse slough grass for the roof. He found both in and about the slough in the southeast part of the north forty. He mowed with the scythe several long swaths of the rank slough grass, and left it to dry. He cut many armfuls of willow withes with his pocket knife and laid them out on high dry ground. Of the axe he made no use. He was home well before supper time, a good day's work done, though not quite as he had planned it.

At supper, he suggested to his family and their hosts that they might accompany him tomorrow and see whence came the timbers for the cabin. His day would be leisurely, and they would visit both of the main cutting sites. They could be home for dinner. His invitation evoked enthusiastic acceptance by everyone concerned. After supper, he relaid the bed of rails on the wagon gear, so that his guests for half a day might ride to the woods. He himself might even ride, for a change.

Guest day in the woods was instructive and memorable for mothers and children alike. Pehr acquainted them with the dominant tree species, particularly those of which he had taken for his use: "This is hop-hornbeam or ironwood, of which I have cut stable rafters. This is basswood, almost identical to our linden in Sweden, with the soft white wood so easy to work. We shall use this for furniture. At the other logging site I'll show you the white oak stand whence I took the logs for the cabin walls. White oak here is not unlike that in western Europe. It is tremendously strong and durable, my favorite wood, I guess. Anna Lien, you had linden and oak in southern Norway, didn't you?"

"Oh, yes," replied Anna, "but I really knew nothing about them beyond their identity."

Pehr took down a large basswood and loaded onto the wagon two twelve-foot lengths, leaving just enough space between the bolster standards for the oak logs he would cut on the way home. He would not take time to hew them and peel them, but would do that at home. At the second logging site the women viewed with amazement the numerous stumps and piles of slash and trimmings left from Pehr's labors. They had not imagined that so vast a volume of timber could go into a simple little one-room house. At each site the mothers and children roamed the woods while Pehr worked. They admired the profusion of autumn flowers in bloom, and here-and-there a tree beginning to display its autumn dress.

Well before dinner time the party went homeward. Pehr unloaded the logs at the construction site, while the women admired the accuracy with which he had shaped the dove-tailed corners of the logs already in place.

Anna Lien said to Anna, "You will have a comfortable, roomy house when it is completed. It will put my sod-cellar to shame. I guess you know how fortunate you are?"

"Yes, I am fortunate," replied Anna, "considering our distance from civilization, but it will be dreary to live twenty-four hours a day in a single room—with a dirt floor."

"You can divide it into two rooms with part of the wagon cover, which you won't need outside after you move into the house. I'll help you hang it up. You can be happy here, Anna, but you must be cheerful and optimistic!" Anna Lien was secretly disgusted with Anna's apprehensive morbid outlook.

Over their dinner, everyone thanked Pehr for the outing. All expressed wonder at the tremendous tree size, density, and areal expanse of the great forest they had visited. Pehr was pleased with their impressions because they evinced achievement of his purpose in their woods visit.

That afternoon he plied broad axe and adz on the newly collected timbers, then notched and laid up three additional courses of logs, doweling each tier to the one below it on both sides of the space he would saw out for a door. In due time he would similarly dowel both sides of the windows. The bottom log and three upper logs would be left whole, the bottom one to serve as threshold and the third from the top as header for a double-battened door. He would set the door frame half-way into the bottom log, and flatten the header above the frame. When the upper log lay at eye level, he would saw out three courses for window openings—one in the east wall north of the door, and the other opposite in the west wall. Before they laid the three upper courses in place, he would saw out the door opening.

Next day he notched and laid out, in separate series, on the ground about the site, all the remaining wall logs; and on the day following the women came to help lift them into place. He quickly built two ten-foot ladders of spare rails, bored through with a one-inch bit and driven onto fifteen-inch rungs of white oak, tapered to fit the holes at each end, and left thicker between for more comfort while standing on them. The women used one and Pehr the other, at opposite ends of each wall in turn, as the laying-up progressed. By evening the log walls stood completed, and everyone admired their handiwork.

Before Saturday night Pehr had completed the sloping end walls (gables), notched in and laid up the floor joists (tie beams), notched, bored, and doweled together at the peak the seven pairs of rafters, and cut a V-notch in each where it would rest on the top log. These points, too, he would secure to the wall with dowel pins.

With the help of the women, who stood on planks he had hewed and laid on the joists, Pehr raised the rafters and secured them in place, properly spaced with one line of rails on each roof shed at midpoint, and a rail at each end braced against the gable peak from the middle joist. He was ready to begin the roof. He had also laid on and doweled in place on the rafters with small oak pins all the length-wise aspen rails. These pins he left sticking out two inches or more, to help hold the sod. His week's accomplishment seemed the greatest thus far, thanks to the helpful women. He went to a late supper, both gratified and proud. He thanked "his girls" over and over again and made light conversation during the meal, into which everyone entered happily. Pehr was rarely so jovial and talkative.

Sunday morning dawned clear and warm, but by noon the sky was well festooned with cirrus veils, harbingers of rain to come.

A drizzling rain commenced Monday morning, and continued, intermittently, through Tuesday. Denied adequate sheltered space in which to work, Pehr resigned himself to enforced idleness and enjoyed the leisure time with his family and their hosts. The time of parting was now imminent, and though everyone sensed a mixture of sadness and cheer at the prospect, no one mentioned it aloud.

Wednesday was fair and breezy, but Pehr's willow and slough grass lay too wet to handle. However, he put the day to good use. First he fashioned a wooden hand-rake, its back of basswood and its teeth and handle of oak. Then he sawed off a five-foot length from a large basswood log, wedged off four thick slices, and planed them smooth on one side. Two of these he fitted snugly flat against each other, pegged them together with cross-wise slabs underneath, and he had a table top—five feet long and about thirty inches wide. He bored one-inch holes six inches in from the corners, each slanted at a measured angle. Into the holes he drove oaken legs, shaped and sized to fit, sawed flush the protrusions atop, and sawed the legs off level—and he had made a table! In similar fashion he made two five-foot benches of the other slabs. Some time still remaining to him before supper-time, he made two square-topped stools in the same way. After supper he sharpened his scythe and all his building tools.

Thursday morning he scythed hay, cutting with his scythe several broad swaths about the head of the northeast slough, somewhat above the level at which lay his roofing materials. Near dinner-time he examined the willow switches and slough grass, and determined that they were dry enough to haul and lay on. He shouldered the scythe, felt for his whetstone in a back pocket, and walked briskly homeward, Enroute he crossed a prairie flat just north of the cabin and woods that appeared to have a dense thick sod cover. He laid down the scythe and squatted to examine it at the base of the grass. It would serve well for a roof, but should he, on even so small a patch as he needed, mutilate this beautiful virgin land? Apparent necessity salved his conscience; he would take, right here, enough sod for his roof!

At table with the women and children he complimented them on their meticulous weeding and tending of the garden. With their diligence they would soon have certain vegetables they might take and cook. The children would learn that work brings its rewards!

"Would you like to help me this afternoon?" he asked the children.

"Oh, yes," came back an enthusiastic chorus.

"Well then," said Pehr, "Soon as I can call up and hitch the oxen, we go. You can ride on the rails as before."

They loaded grass at one end of the wagon bed and willow at the other. Pehr raked the materials together and the children loaded them, as he showed them, crosswise of the wagon bed. When they had considerable heaps fore and aft, Pehr lifted the youngsters onto the piles and walked his oxen to the cabin.

He lifted the children down; and they began walking the length of the remaining basswood logs, and were soon competing to see who could make the greatest number of turns without stepping off to the ground.

Pehr tried, in turn, a double handful of willow and one of the dry grass laid perpendicular to the aspen rails. This, he decided, would not be good; the roof would come apart when he crawled or stood on it to push the sods tightly together. He elected to lay a mixture of willow and grass parallel to the aspen saplings, filling the three to four inch gap between them. Only over the end eaves would he lay them parallel to the pitch of the roof. Over the gable ends he could use short willow switches; on the main roof he could use none less than about six feet long, to ensure that they would not sag unduly between the rafters. In a matter of minutes he had the first load in place on the roof; and, with his "gang," returned to the slough for another. To lay the second load he must crawl onto the roof with each bundle; so he employed one of his crude ladders again. Before seven-thirty all of the willow and grass foundation was on the roof, ready for sodding. He and his gang were home well before eight o'clock, their customary supper-time.

Next day he broke sod with the plow at the chosen site, chopped it off with his square spade into lengths about two feet long, and loaded these carefully onto the wagon bed. On his first trip he hauled only one layer of sod, but, since this seemed a light load for the oxen, he loaded two layers each trip subsequently. To lay them onto the roof without treading any to pieces, he commenced on the upper side, flush with the last aspen rail, laying the sods lengthwise with the pitch of the roof and packing them tightly together as he went. The first course on each side of the top he laid perpendicular to the pitch, then draped over the ridge and onto the first courses an entire course of sods cut twenty-four inches long. The ridge he had laid of stout rails, notched onto the rafter peaks. When he had three courses in place he smoothed the growing grass on them down-pitch; perhaps, combed this way, it would shed some water off the top. The sods were eight inches thick, and only a rain of several day's duration would ever soak all the way through them and drip on the floor. The sod showed a rippling over the aspens, ensuring that it would not slide off.

Pehr slaved with the heavy sod all day, breaking, chopping, loading, lifting and laying, but at seven-thirty about a course and a half yet remained to be done on the west side. He plowed the necessary length of furrow, lifted the plow onto the wagon-bed, and rode home behind the oxen. He swung past the cabin and deposited the plow where it had stood upended before. Tomorrow he would smear it with tallow and tar again. That night he was too weary to make much conversation over supper. He was abed in the wagon box before dark.

Next morning, at breakfast with Anna and Anna Lien, he announced that Monday would be moving day. Tears came to Anna's eyes, and Anna Lien's mouth and lip muscles twitched and trembled. Pehr took quick note of the tension and remarked, pretending cheer: "It's not as if you were parting a long distance or forever. You will probably visit each other almost daily. I wish you would think happily about our considerable progress on the homestead in only the first few weeks. To you, Mrs. Lien, we will always be grateful for your taking us in when we were without adequate shelter. If ever you want for anything within our means to provide, you need only ask. I will, as I promised, keep you supplied with fuel wood, but I can't promise to buck or split it for you. You and Tollef will have to do most of that."

Anna Lien nodded her thanks, but did not attempt to speak; her tears now flowed faster than Anna's.

Pehr hastened away, lest he, too, commence blubbering. He quickly completed the sodding of the roof, and turned the oxen loose. They headed for the nearest slough to drink. He turned to the task of installing the door and the windows. His newly-made table became a work-bench and his benches, though too low for comfort, became temporary saw-horses. Casings for door and windows he hewed and planed to a thickness of little more than an inch. The door he battened of two plank layers, one crosswise of the other, doweled together at two dozen crucial points and also attached to each other with a few dozen of his precious nails. All except the oak pegs was of basswood, so the work was not strenuous. He hung the door with the large strap hinges bought in Litchfield. These and the latch he secured with heavy wood-screws. When the job was completed, the door swung freely and without the least squeaky complaint from the hinges. It closed so snuggly against the door frame all around that not even flies or mosquitos would get in when it was closed and hasped.

The handsome little cabin stood ready for occupancy by mid-afternoon. Pehr cleared away all shavings, chips, and splinters, and hurried to his loved ones; they must come and see the new house at once. Monday they would move into it, well enough, but see it as it stood completed they MUST today *(Figure 6.2)*.

They had afternoon lunch together, and then all returned with Pehr to admire the new house. He stood proudly, quietly by until Elna asked:

"Where is the chimney, Papa. Won't we need a stove and fire?"

"Indeed we shall need a stove and fire," replied Pehr. "We will run the stove pipe right through the roof, first cutting away enough wood and grass so nothing will take fire. I'll pack enough sod and clay around the pipe so there should be no leaking on the stove. I'll do it Monday."

"I want to see the first smoke come out," exclaimed little Hanna.

"We will light a fire in the stove soon as we get it set up," promised Anna. "You shall see the first smoke that comes out, Hanna, but you may not be watching alone."

About midnight a violent thundertsorm raged across the land, accompanied by driving rain. The storm wakened everyone, and Pehr lay wondering about his new roof. In less than an hour the rain ceased falling, the stillness of night resumed, and all returned to sleep.

Next morning Pehr could scarcely wait to eat breakfast before he went, by long strides, to see how the cabin had weathered the storm. To his profound relief and satisfaction, he found only one spot on the dirt floor where drips from the roof had made a mark. He searched as best he could in the half-gloom of the interior, but found no other sign of leakage; the floor had quickly absorbed the drops that came

Figure 6.2. Pehr's original homestead cabin, depicted here, housed his family from 1869 until 1882. The leaky sod roof was replaced with aspen shingles in 1873.
        Artist's conception sketched in charcoal by Julie Wolters.

through. Pehr hurried back to report, happily, that the house stood dry and undamaged. It would quite adequately protect them against the elements, however violent or extreme they might be.

During Sunday the children played together as usual, but their elders conversed more soberly than they were wont to do. They exchanged sentiments and confidences without reservation, and spoke thoughts never before expressed between or among them. Pehr spoke little, as usual; but when he was out of hearing, the women discussed intimacies peculiar to their sex. When Pehr went to admire Anna Lien's luxuriant garden, in the tending of which all had participated, Anna Lien grasped the opportunity to lecture Anna Olsdotter, gently but firmly, relative to her impending obligations as help-mate to her husband in a new home. Said she:

"You will, I trust, be a proper wife to your husband when you move into the new house. Your protracted denial of Pehr seems to me a cruel shame. I saw in the new house only one bed frame for adults, so I hope I can assume that you shall sleep together. Is that right, Anna?"

"We shall sleep together, yes! But we have slept together many nights before without making love. We began our abstention when I agreed to depart Sweden a year ago. Before I consented to come, Pehr made me a solemn promise that he would not take me again before I felt myself sufficiently safe and secure to resume our normal sexual activity. He has kept his word, and I have thus far resisted temptation. Please don't think me mean and heartless; perhaps I feel the strain no less than he. When I yield, you shall be the THIRD person to know. Meanwhile, please do not fret yourself on our account."

They changed the subject as Pehr rejoined them. Anna admired the young man and wife who could maintain such determined reserve, but she also thought them foolish. Didn't Anna know that she was immune against fertilization at least two days in a month? Maybe she withheld herself entirely because she feared that a little yielding would lead to complete abandon. Perhaps she was right!

Everyone commenced hauling and loading immediately after breakfast Monday morning. Before he sat to the table, Pehr had removed the rails from the wagon and restacked them whence he borrowed them, he had emptied the wagon box as before, slipped off two wheels as before and lifted the double box, with canvas attached, onto the gear, one end at a time. After eating, he loaded the flour barrel while the women did the dishes; then they helped him with the stove. The children helped with the numerous small items, and the little girls took special care to see that "Svartan" and her young brood were aboard. Amid a few tears and many endearing exchanges, they gave one kitten to Tollef.

During the loading, Anna Lien kept reminding Anna that there need be no fear of forgetting a few items. They were not crossing an ocean but were moving a mere American mile away. There would be ample opportunity to retrieve articles left behind.

Pehr called up the cattle, yoked and hitched the oxen; and they were off. Everyone elected to walk together rather than climbing to the high seat. Anna led Bos by a short length of light rope. Daisy followed as did Mrs. Lien, Tollef, and the girls.

In front of the new cabin Pehr unhitched the oxen and lifted off the yoke. Anna untied the rope from the cow. The animals shuffled off, grazing as they went.

Pehr made a few considered suggestions on organization of the floor space: "The stove should be in the northwest corner where the cold winter's winds will strike the hardest. Since the door swings inward, hinged on the south side, our sleeping places would be at the south end, sort-of behind the door, less exposed to view and cold blasts. We shall have to keep each other warm, you and I, Anna," he concluded slyly·

The great chest went against the west wall, across from the door; table and benches in the northeast area, opposite the stove. The arrangement seemed functional and convenient. The stove stood three feet from the walls, so it should create no fire hazard. The girls' sleeping pallet would lie against the north wall until the loft could be floored.

Pehr stuck a sharpened stick through the roof where the stove-pipe would go. Then he leaned a ladder against the west eaves, climbed atop the roof, dug and lifted the turf aside with his hands, and sawed out foot-long lengths of two aspen rails where the stick stuck out. He called through the hole to Anna, and she handed up the longest length of pipe. Pehr replaced and packed the turfs around it. (Later he would lay two or three additional layers of sod around that pipe, to steady it in place and reduce leakage.) He climbed down, and quickly assembled the remaining pipe segments and connected the stove.

"Hanna," called Anna, "you bring Papa some shavings and dry twigs, and you shall soon see the first smoke."

All the children ran to collect kindling and firewood. Pehr laid a fire and lit it with one of Anna's matches. Everyone went outside and stood silently, observing the white smoke curling upward into the air.

"Now the new house looks like home," cried Hanna excitedly, clapping her hands. Everyone agreed, but no one commented. The elders resumed their work, but the children stood for some time, fascinated by the smoke column.

Anna called to Pehr's attention the need for places to hang up garments and kitchen equipment. Pehr saw that the need was immediate.

"For shelving, you will have to wait until I can build what you wish. As for pegs on which to hang things, just show me exactly where you want them, and I'll have them up in a little while."

Anna showed him, and he marked the places with his knife. Then he bored holes into the logs at the marks, slanting the auger slightly downward. He whittled basswood pegs, drove them into the holes, and sawed them off to lengths specified by Anna. All protruded from the wall with an upward angle so anything hung on them would not slip off. Several were low, for use by the little girls.

They were settled in before noon, and Anna heated soup on the new stove for dinner. Everyone sat down at the new table to eat—a festive, memorable event. All said grace together. Before rising from the table, Pehr announced that he would today commence haying in earnest. He would need several tons of hay to carry the livestock through winter; and the upland grasses were already a bit over-ripe. The needle grasses had already shed their needles. He would resume mowing where he had begun, about the vicinity of the northeast slough. He would come home for afternoon coffee. He went out, took his scythe down from the tree branch over which he had hung it, pocketed his whetstone and shouldered the scythe, and was off.

For the remainder of the week, Pehr mowed prairie with his scythe every day, dawn to dusk, except during a few rain showers that drove him home to shelter. His

Page 131

broad swaths lay round and about both the northeast slough and the smaller pot-hole in the middle of the north forty. He was confident that he had laid down enough hay to keep his cattle all winter. Much of it lay on high ground; and he had heard that such grass was remarkably nutritious. And well it should be, because its cutting required a razor edge on the scythe, so that one must stop and stroke the blade frequently.

Now when it was well dried, he must gather it up, haul it home, and stack it near the site on which he would build a stable. For these tasks he was ill equipped, but he devised the means of coping with them. Lacking a pitch fork, he simply sought out a forked oak limb, which when cut to size, peeled, and dried in the shade served him through the entire harvest and a year thereafter. For a hay rack in which to haul the hay he devised a rude rick of peeled aspen saplings that fitted into the bottom wagon box and extended some eight feet up and out therefrom, clearing the wheels. The contrivance took an entire day of skilled labor for its construction; and, being of raw sappy aspens, it was so heavy that he had difficulty lifting it into place, even with Anna's considerable help. (It became much lighter in weight as the saplings dried out, and it served him several years.)

Before the first Sunday in September he had four long narrow stacks of hay on the place, built as high as he could reach with his improvised pitchfork. With his wooden rake he combed the stacks down on all sides; and with a final topping of rank slough grass, they stood whole and good until he fed them to the animals. (They contained more hay than needed; half of one stack remained when he loosed the cattle to graze new grass the following spring.)

Next project? A stable to shelter the cattle against the wintry blasts that would surely come. Its siting and construction Pehr had long since decided for himself. It would be dug into the south-facing slope of the "home" hill; away from the cabin, just beyond the hay stacks, which stood on the flat southwest of the house. Pehr spent a half day with oxen and plow to excavate out of the hill a sufficient cut and make a platform large enough to accommodate a structure the same size as the cabin. The west half would stall the animals; the east would serve as woodworking shop. He threw the furrows down-slope, and drove the oxen round and round, furrow after furrow, until he had the flat space required and an excavation about twenty-six feet long. The upper (north) side of the cut was now about three feet below original ground level; the structure would be a so-called "basement" affair. He half-wished that he had built the cabin the same way; it would have been warmer in winter and cooler in summer. But hindsight was aught to worry about!

Materials for the main structure of the stable came from the same places whence those in the cabin, but he used smaller timbers. He used logs with a diameter of only about six to eight inches at the butt end, and he left the bark on them. He spared himself the time and muscle to dove-tail the corners; he simply over-lapped the logs at the corners, saddle grooving them deeply enough so that they lay snuggly together the length of the walls. Log ends protruded beyond the corners. He laid the bottom five courses with oak, since most of these logs would be partially or wholly below ground level, and oak was least subject to rot. Above these he used a mixture of basswood, ash, and elm, now more readily available about his clearings in the woods.

He built a shed structure with a middle supporting beam lengthwise. He pitched the roof, laid the ironwood rafters on loose, about a foot apart, and laid on a thick thatched roof of dried slough grass, combing down the slope of the roof with his rake. He fashioned wooden hinges of oak, and hung a battened plank door four feet wide, opening out. For a latch he carved a piece of oak about three by ten inches and one inch thick. He bored a hole through it at its mid-point and pegged it onto a hand-shaped dowel. This he stuck into a one-inch hole bored through a wall log at breast height. On the inside, he pegged onto the dowel a square of oak almost snug up to the log. On the outside of the door he fitted a wedge-shaped piece of oak onto which the latch fell, holding the door securely and snugly against the frame. The simple little closing devise was operable from either inside or outside. He filled with earth the trench about the basement portion, and heaped earth against the north wall so that the eaves-drip would surely drain away from the building. All visible cracks between the logs he packed with hay and plastered them over with animal dung of mortar consistency. The door he placed at mid-point in the south wall, so he built a manger for the animals at the north, from the west side, half-way across and open-ended at its east end, so he might walk in front of the "critters" to feed them. The rude structure stood ready by the second Sunday in September. Pehr and his girls took almost as much pride in it as in their own quarters *(Figure 6.3)*. The east end became Pehr's private sanctuary, from which would come a variety of useful wooden articles. He soon installed a rough workbench there and stood numerous lengths and species of wood about the walls to season for future use. Soon he would get glass and cut in a window.

Figure 6.3. Pehr's first American stable, shown above, was hastily and crudely constructed, with a roof of prairie and slough grasses. It served adequately from 1869 until replaced by a large barn in 1883. It was a sheep pen for several additional years.
Artist's conception sketched in charcoal by Julie Wolters.

Now that the main essentials of the farmstead stood ready, Pehr relaxed his constant drive of the several weeks past and moved at a more leisurely pace. He confided to Anna that he was a bit weary, though happily weary, and that he would now take time to more thoroughly acquaint himself with their homestead. He spent two days tramping over the land and admiring its splendid qualities. On several hikes Anna and the girls accompanied him; and they came to know the reverence with which he viewed the good earth of which they would be possessed. It was during a family appreciation of the southern (woodland) forty that Elna discovered a bubbling spring just above the north side of the "middle" slough, not more than an eighth of a mile southwest of the farmstead. Pehr returned to it next day, and with grub hoe and spade, dug a neat circular depression below the point whence the water issued. In a matter of minutes the depression held a pool of clear cool water, from which one might dip with a pail. This spring supplied the family with good water for many, many years, requiring only a little dredging now and then. In winter it froze up, but then there was ice or snow to melt on the stove. They even melted enough for the cattle, rather than letting them drink freezing-cold water from a hole chopped through thick ice on the slough. In mid-winter the slough froze too deeply for watering.

Despite the heat and drought of mid-September, Pehr, with his sturdy oxen, broke several acres of prairie immediately north of the farmstead oak grove. Here the land sloped ever so gently toward the south; and the prairie grasses stood tall, thick, and luxuriant. Even in the dry season, the soil remained sufficiently moist to turn from the plow pitch-black and shiny. He turned up numerous small stones the size of one or two clenched fists; these he picked up as they came to view and deposited them on the periphery of the plowing. He struck a few boulders so large that he took them out with a stout wooden prize-bar and the spade. These he rolled out of the furrow, onto the newly-plowed earth; where they lay, conspicuously, awaiting later removal.

The plowing done, he one day built himself a sturdy stone-boat of oak planks, onto which he rolled the boulders and hauled them to the edge of the little field. Near the middle of the field lay one deeply earth-bound glacial erratic so large that its removal defied his means. This he buried below plow depth by digging a great deep hole beside it, undermining it as much as he dared, and then nudging it into the excavation with oxen and chain. This maneuver almost ended in catastrophe, because Pehr slipped and fell just as the big rock yielded, and he got one leg pinned under it. But the obedient oxen spared him from crippling injury: they stopped instantly at his command and stood still. He examined his precarious predicament and determined that a heave on the chain sharply to the left might release his limb. He called to his animals: "Buck, Bride, Haw off," but they pulled the chain too taut before turning. He "Wo'd" them with a shout. Now he analyzed the situation more carefully. If he could back the oxen toward him just two or three paces, take up the slack in the chain as they backed, and "Gee" them off from a standing start, they would, sort of, twist the stone off his leg. It should work, but he must keep his voice calm, lest he excite the animals. Quietly he commanded: "Buck, Bride, back, back, back." He gathered in the chain: "Wo now, good boys."

He waited a moment, and commanded: "Now Buck and Bride, Gee, Gee." They turned before they stretched the chain, and as they put their great shoulders to the yoke, the stone yielded and Pehr's leg came free. "Wo" he called; then "back." The chain went slack, and he pulled it clear. Then he went and almost caressed his trusty beasts. He stroked them along their backs, on their necks and their faces; and he told them how they had certainly saved him from serious injury. Then he rubbed his half-numb leg to restore the circulation.

Pehr was more fortunate than some settlers who undermined and buried huge rocks in their fields. Not many years later one of Pehr's neighbors died that way, crushed to death and buried in his own excavation. Pehr and several other neighboring settlers worked half a day to recover the body for proper burial. One pragmatic heretic in the crew contended that the body should be left in peace beneath the rock and appropriate rites said above it; but since no one seemed to agree with him, he assisted with the digging.

Earth-fast rocks were a unique risk to the farmer before plows became equipped with break-pins that permitted the plow to yield and roll under when it stuck an unyielding obstruction. Those erratics that stuck some distance out of the ground remained a menace to harvesting machinery, especially the platform binder; and most of them were eventually removed from the fields. In later years it became standard practice to drill a hole in such a rock, pack it with dynamite, and blow the monster to pieces. The pieces could then be taken out and dumped in a slough edge too wet for cultivation.

The annual stone "crop" gathered off the eroding uplands and thrown or dumped into a nearby slough, eventually ruined many a mallard habitat in the pot-hole region of Minnesota and the Dakotas.

Pehr never mentioned to Anna his unnerving brush with disaster. But, for himself, he never forgot that his limb, and perhaps his life, would have been forfeit had not his oxen instantly obeyed his every command. He always believed that his animals had saved him in return for his kindness to them. He never abused them!

Chapter 7

FIRST WINTER IN THE WILDERNESS

As the month of September drew toward its close, and the chilly nights forewarned of colder ones to come, Pehr turned his thoughts to the approaching winter and the spring that would follow. His impending requirements of seed and plant materials had slipped his mind during his feverish construction of house and stable. He'd better see to these needs without delay. Above all else he must procure a sufficient quantity of seed wheat and potatoes to ensure so large a harvest of each a year hence that there would be a considerable surplus beyond household needs that he might sell. His total cash reserve was now only some ninety-six dollars and a few cents, much of which would go for seed; he would be desperately in need of money before he could bring in his first crop. His family could not long subsist on wild meat alone; they must have enough vegetable matter in their diet to prevent scurvy! If he failed to provide it, they would all sicken; and the entire homesteading project would fail before well begun. So silent and morose did Pehr become, at table with the family and between times, that Anna became irked and one day chastened him:

"Pehr, not in a week or more have you smiled or spoken cheerfully to anyone. You are obviously worried about something; and I believe I have the right to share the problem with you! What is it?"

Pehr unburdened himself to his good wife; and her retort so amazed him that he stood with open mouth and stared at her:

"We have been beaten by no obstacle thus far, and we shall not be beaten henceforth! You, my husband, will so well provide for our needs that we shall never be hungry or ill-nourished! In your care, I, your wife, have no fear of ever knowing such hunger or cold as I cannot endure. And I speak for your daughters as well. So, for our sake, please shed your worry and gloom, and be confident that we shall prevail against all obstacles!"

Pehr stood momentarily as a veritable statue. Then he threw his arms about her and held her tightly to himself for several minutes. Without a word, he released her and shuffled out the door.

That night before sleep, he drew Anna to him tenderly and thanked her, in half whispers, for her reassurance. She listened, and snuggled to him for one delicious moment. Then she pushed away from him, lest passion overwhelm cautious judgement. She whispered:

"I dare not trust myself farther, Pehr."

And he whispered in reply:

"Have no fear, my dearest. I will not take you again unless you invite me beforehand."

Before they slept he whispered again: "Tomorrow I commence searching for seed wheat. The harvest must now be in, and settlers that came two or three years ago must have grain to sell." He slapped her goodnight on her round buttocks and turned on his other side. They slept without further disturbing each other.

After breakfast they sat debating in which direction might be the nearest fields of wheat stubble. They had seen no wheat field nearby when they came up country. Pehr had seen none to the north or west nearer than about twenty American miles, nor had he seen any directly to the south at shorter distance. He must seek seed-wheat somewhere to the southwest or the northeast. The issue was almost settled when Mrs. Lien and Tollef stuck their heads through the door and came in.

Anna Lien was so obviously agitated that Anna asked at once:

"What IS the trouble, Anna? You look as if you had just escaped from the devil incarnate. Sit you down and tell us."

"It's the cow! We can't call her up, and we can't find her. The damn fool has gotten lost from Bos. We located Bos by her bell, but Daisy was not with her."

"Now, now, my dear!" said Pehr. "You should know about these things! Your cow has been heavy with calf for some time. I'll bet she dropped that calf in a well-hidden place and remains silent in secrecy. She was plumb dry, wasn't she? Let's all go to the woods together, spread out, but within view of each other, and I'll bet we find her. Whoever makes the discovery, please come and show me at once. Unless we sneak up on the calf, clap our hands and holler to scare him, he won't rise up and go with his mother. Then we'll have to carry him home. Pardon me, Anna, for saying 'him.' I hope, for you sake that it's a heifer calf."

The concealed cow and calf were soon found; the frightening noise got the calf to *her* feet; and mother and offspring led the way home.

"Anna Lien," said Pehr enroute, "did you make in Norway new-milk pudding that we call "calf dance" in Sweden?"

"Yes indeed," said Anna; "do you like it, Pehr?"

"I'm very fond of it," replied Pehr. "Anna can help you."

"Oh no," protested Anna Lien. "I shall make it and bring it to you. Is it not the second milking one uses?"

"Yes," prompted Pehr, "the first one is just too thick and sticky."

Everyone returned to the cabin in high good cheer. Mrs. Lien drove her cow home to milk her, the calf staggering along had sucked very little. (A few days later she would teach the calf to drink by giving her the middle finger of her right hand to suck on and then plunging her nose (the calf's) into a quarter-bucket of warm milk. Soon the young animal's instinct to bump her head forcibly against her mother's udder would become less demanding, and the pail a mite easier to hold.)

Pehr virtually loafed until dinner-time, after which he took his musket and struck out in a southwesterly direction.

By his estimate he had walked more than two Swedish miles when he came to a stubble field about six American acres in area. Here must be enough wheat to sow ? section, to say nothing about a five acre patch!

The settler stood before his cabin door and waited as he approached.

"I am Pehr Pehrson," said Pehr in Swedish. "I have a new homestead over near Clitherall Lake." He took the caps off his musket.

"I am Willie Mork," responded the young Swedish settler. "This is my second year. What can I do for you, 'Herre' Pehrson. (Pehr was obviously some ten years his senior, and one showed respect for those older than himself!)

"You may call me Pehr! I'm after enough wheat 'vede' to sow about five acres next spring. Do you have any? I saw your stubble field and thought you might. I figure I need about five bushels (American)?

"Your search is over!" said Mork. "But aren't these American units of measure hell to learn? Acres, bushels, pounds, quarts, rods, miles, inches, feet—It's damned confusing."

"It takes time," said Pehr. "I built a house and stable by American measurements. If you use them, you'll soon master them."

"Come and see my wheat. It's in the house, where it's protected against mice and rats. Do you have a cat, Pehr?"

"I have a whole family," replied Pehr, "and now they will become useful."

Willie motioned Pehr into the cabin, and there they were met by a strikingly beautiful young woman with dark hair, olive skin and a picture-book figure. Pehr was so taken with her beauty that he blushed; but the cabin was murky (as his own) and it went unnoticed.

"This here is my wife, Tilda," said Willie. "Tilda, this is our distant neighbor, Pehr Pehrson, from the Clitherall Lake vicinity, about twelve or thirteen American miles from here. (Tilda curtsied, as Willie talked on.) He wants to buy some seed wheat, and we are ready to sell. Lay an extra place for supper."

"You will stay for supper with us, Pehr?" he asked. "As you see, we have no children yet, although we keep trying. We get a bit lonely at times, and enjoy company."

Pehr accepted the invitation enthusiastically, mainly because it was mid-afternoon and he was already hungry, but also because it would be pleasant to sit and admire the beautiful, busy, young housewife.

"There's my wheat," said Willie, pointing to a corner where stood several canvas sacks such as Pehr had glimpsed before only from a distance—American grain sacks. When full and tied, as these, they stood about three feet tall and more than a foot in diameter. Willie appeared to have about three dozen of them standing full of wheat. "I'll just carry a sack to the door so you can see the wheat in better light." He stooped, grasped a sack in a bear hug, and carried it to the door, which he opened part way. He undid the tie and spread the mouth, and there came to view the plump, reddish kernels of grain. Pehr had never seen better looking wheat.

"You can see that this is good grain, Pehr, and it yielded me fifteen bushels to the acre. It's some sort of flint variety. Bite a kernel and see how hard it is. It makes the very best flour for bread. You can sample it when we eat supper."

"I can see that you have excellent grain, and I should like to sow my land to it. How much must you have a bushel? I need five bushels."

"The traveling cattle buyer was here," said Willie, "and he offered me $2.35 a bushel for all I could spare. I refused his offer, thinking my wheat at least five cents better than the average run. This stuff weighs sixty five pounds to a bushel measure; and, as you probably know, wheat is traded on the basis of sixty pounds to the bushel. My sacks here, packed and tied tight as they are, hold two and a half bushels each, by measure. But we won't quarrel about the weight and measure business. Two of these sacks should give you a good, strong five bushels either way. Do you think they're worth twelve dollars? Let me say this: my wheat has neither cockle nor mustard seed in it. They are bad weeds to get into one's fields. In new prairie one bushel is enough to sow an acre."

Pehr didn't hesitate a moment: "Of course I want the wheat. Will you keep it until I can fetch my oxen and wagon, and carry the money to pay you? If the weather holds fair, I'll come tomorrow."

"You need look no further," answered Willie; "two sacks of wheat are yours; and I'll hold them until you come for them. Will you bring your own sacks?"

"I haven't any good sacks," said Pehr. "Will you kindly sell me the two containing my wheat? I can see that they are new." (Pehr had no sacks at all!)

"I'll sell you the sacks at the same price I paid for them—twenty-two cents each. They tell me they hardly ever wear out unless one lets mice gnaw holes in them." (The seamless canvas grain sack was a recent American invention in 1869; the carrier of our grain crops for more than a half a century.)

"That's a bargain," said Pehr, and they shook hands on it.

Supper was now steaming on the table, and Tilda motioned the men to their seats. She sat down across from them on the side near to the stove. Willie offered a short grace while they bowed their heads. Then they partook of boiled potatoes, cabbage, and fried pork chops, the first Pehr had tasted since departing Litchfield. Pehr ate heartily, the meat and his view both delicious. Tilda sat beaming, proud of her culinary artistry.

Pehr asked, between mouthfuls: "Have you raised your own swine? This is uncommonly good pork."

"Yes," answered Tilda, "we bought four little pigs last spring. We butchered two and saved two gilts for brood sows."

Willie cut in: "I've looked around for a boar to breed the sows this fall, but haven't found one yet. I could take them where I bought them; but there I would risk breeding them to a brother, and this revolts me somehow. Rather than that, I'll have no pigs, but will eat the barren sows instead. I'm going to search farther afield; and if I locate a boar, you can come next April and buy pigs from me. I paid a dollar a-piece for mine at six weeks and I'll sell at the same price. I did my own castrating."

"That interests me," said Pehr. "I'll come and see you later on. If you get your sows bred, I should like to reserve from their litters one gilt and two boars at the price you mention. If you'll figure a date for castrating, I'll come, and hold the pigs while you do the cutting. I would wish you to keep my pigs with their mother for a week after we cut the males."

Willie responded: "That's a good deal! But you needn't bother to come and check on my damn sows. Whether I get them bred, or no, we'll come to see you later on. I'd like to see the country and your buildings; and I'm sure we'd both enjoy meeting your family."

"You are invited," asserted Pehr, "and I speak for my wife and little daughters, too. If you'll come before extreme cold and deep snow, I know we can bed you down quite comfortably, and stable your oxen so they won't stray."

"Oh! we'll come afoot." replied Willie. "Tilda can walk as fast and as far as I can. She's a sturdy wife, as you can see; but we will stay the night, because the round trip would tire us both. Tell me exactly how to find your place!"

Pehr described how he had come, careful to mention all useful landmarks. Then he said: "Would you welcome my wife and daughters when I come for the wheat? We could all get acquainted right then. I believe that Tilda and my wife, Anna, will strike it off immediately."

Now Tilda's dark eyes sparkled even more than before. She said, excitedly: "Do bring your family, Pehr. We would be proud to know them. And you must stay overnight!"

And so was laid the foundation of an esteemed and life-long friendship.

After hearty thanks, farewells, and handshakes, Pehr headed toward home at a clip remarkable even for him. He arrived home after dark, his family awaiting him by candle-light. Anna had kept his supper warm on the back of the stove. While he ate a second supper, Anna bundled the girls to bed and joined him at the table. He told her all about his day's journey: the new-found Swedish friends, the seed-wheat, and the pig prospect. She beamed with interest and satisfaction.

"You see," she remarked sharply, "you needn't have worried about seed-wheat. Do you see how silly was your worry?"

Pehr admitted that he might well have been over concerned. Then he continued: "You and the girls are invited to accompany me to the Mork's when I go to fetch the seed-wheat. We shall go tomorrow, if the weather looks promising. Don't let me forget to take $12.44 with me; that's what I owe for wheat and sacks. We shall stop by Mrs. Lien's and ask her to milk Bos while we're gone. If she's not there, we'll lead the cow with us, so she will be milked."

"It's hard to believe that we shall visit friends from home in this wild country. It will be a special pleasure!"

"The girls will have no playmates, because Tilda remains barren. Willie referred to it jokingly, but I could detect a note of disappointment."

"I'll bet I can tell her how to become pregnant," said Anna, almost laughing. "Of course, I seem to take from merely looking at a nail on which a pair of pants have hung; but even so, I know a few tricks that may help a woman less susceptible. Maybe I can help verify Willie's latent manhood."

"You, my dear, could render a marble statue fertile; and when you see Tilda you'll see that she has no lack of equipment. A more sexy woman I've never seen, unless it be you," said Pehr.

"I shall try to solve her problem; but now let us get to bed and to sleep, if we are to travel tomorrow! I shall have to wake the girls early, but perhaps they will sleep in the wagon."

"While I remove the double-box and set the single one on the wagon gear, you can waken and feed the girls. I must also grease the wagon; we shall make a round trip of thirty miles, or almost. We must stay overnight, lest we offend the good people. Somehow, I feel that we shall become very good friends."

While Pehr was greasing the wagon next morning, Mrs. Lien and Tollef came, she carrying a large baking-pan of "calf-dance" pudding. Despite their hurry to be off and away, Pehr sat down and ate a large bowlful. They explained their haste to Anna Lien, and she was glad for them. She and her young son were soon bound for home; the Pehrsons were enroute to the Morks. Mrs. Lien would milk Bos evening and morning.

Before departing, Anna had suggested that seed-wheat might have been gotten nearer home, from the Mormons on the north side of Clitherall Lake. Pehr had been somewhat taken aback, but had ventured that he might seek his potatoes there instead.

The journey to the Mork's place was without notable event, and they arrived for dinner, though a bit late.

The girls napped after eating; then amused themselves pulling weeds and feeding them to the sows through the rail fence. Willie showed Pehr over his entire homestead. Willie had less open prairie than Pehr, and steeper hills, and was resigned to considerable grubbing of woodland in years to come. Anna and Tilda conversed candidly from the start, and soon became involved in intimate discussion. Soon Anna was dispassionately prescribing for Tilda how she might perform during the sex act to ensure fertilization.''

Tilda listened intently and then blurted out: "But we have tried every conceivable position and every possible trick we can think of. We have often attained climax at the same instant. I can drain Willie several times a week, even when I am most susceptible; and I don't take."

"Then you are trying too hard," assured Anna. "Wait a week between times, and see what happens."

"Believe me," replied Tilda, "we shall try every one of your suggestions; and I hope one of them works."

"You are not afraid of bearing a child in the wilderness?" asked Anna.

"Certainly not," said Tilda, "we want a son, at least, to inherit this homestead. And I know of a highly recommended midwife only a few miles away. I'm strong and healthy, as you can see. Why should I be afraid of having children?"

"I'm glad to hear that you know of a midwife," said Anna. "Perhaps one day I shall terminate my abstinence and have another child myself. I know that Pehr wants a son, just as you do."

For supper they ate two roasted ruffed grouse with all the rich Swedish trimmings.

The girls were put to bed on a soft pallet soon after they had eaten; but the elders sat and talked until ten o'clock. Their hosts insisted that Anna and Pehr sleep on their bed; they bedded down on the floor in the opposite corner.

The travelers were off with their wheat before mid-morning, and were home well before dark. At noon they stopped beside a lake, to which Pehr drove the oxen to drink. The animals grazed while the family ate sandwiches prepared for them by Mrs. Mork.

Pehr squeezed the wheat sacks as tightly as he could into the northeast corner of the cabin. Their tops soon became a favorite napping place for Blackie, and her family. As if in return for their comfort, the cats guarded the sacks against mice and other rodents so diligently that a sack was never holed. In fact nothing in the cabin was destroyed or badly disturbed by such pests. The cats were invaluable boarders and pets.

During September and October (until hard frost) the newcomers enjoyed good, fresh food from the garden. Several times Anna gathered turnip tops and a few carrots and potatoes for soup, cooked on a piece of fat saltpork. Pehr relished such soup and was pleased to eat it twice a week, or more, during the season. Anna ate it with apparent enjoyment, although she disliked it. The girls hated the stuff, but ate of it listlessly, because they were given no other choice.

The garden would have been withered and half-dead during the August dry spells had it not been given water from the spring. Anna carried water in the milk can and the wooden pail. The girls carried in smaller containers. Pehr hauled water in a wooden tub set on the stone-boat and pulled by the oxen; but much of the liquid splashed out enroute. He laid heavy, hewn planks over the tub, but they were only partially effective in reducing the loss of water. But save the garden they did, and it become more productive than they had hoped. Pehr became so confident of getting potatoes and roots to store that he lined the cellar hole with stones gathered from about the garden, from his plowing, and from the prairie. He worked diligently an entire day, gathering, hauling, carrying, and laying in place. Lacking mortar, he sloped the walls enough so that the stones, one atop another, held themselves securely in place by their own weight. He used none less than about eight inches across. Next day he built a short ladder of basswood and stuck it into the cellar hole against one wall, its top just below the planks that covered the hole.

Stimulated by their pleasing acquaintance with the Mork's, Pehr spent several days walking about the vicinity in quest of other neighbors nearer by. He found them in every direction, but none better ensconced than himself. A mile to the east on adjoining homesteads, two young Norwegian bachelors were building a cabin in which they would live together until they established separate homes. Only half a mile to the south another Norwegian lived in a tent while, single-handedly laying up a log cabin. His name was Gollings. Pehr devoted two days to helping him complete the structure. Pehr did not search to the west, because he knew from Mrs. Lien that there lived a Norwegian family not far from her that lent her continuous and generous help. They would plow a field for her, and, in due course, harvest it for a share of the crop. She also had several relatives in the vicinity. But none had any wheat remaining to be sold. Northward the land appeared to remain empty, except for the intriguing Mormon settlement established some four years before on the north side of Clitherall Lake. Thither he went in hopes of procuring potatoes both for eating and for planting, lest his late-planted ones yield too little or spoiled in storage.

He took his family with him in the wagon to visit the Mormons, but only after lengthy argument with Anna. Some of it went like this:

"I do not choose to associate with people whose men sleep with half a dozen women and call them their wives. It would be sinful to mingle with them."

"No man can support numerous wives in this wilderness! I'll bet no man over there has more than one; and if there be one who has, all I can say is that he's a better man than I am. I believe that their religion, earnestly believed, projects them just as far and in the same direction as ours projects us. I will accept a man for his worth as a man, not because he subscribes to one or other faith. Let's go and see for ourselves whether those people are good or evil."

The Mormons welcomed them with open arms, took them into their homes, and stuffed them with delicious food. Anna was overwhelmed and ashamed; Pehr, his contentions obviously vindicated, beamed with satisfaction. The people appeared to be English, with no comprehension of Swedish. However, a Danish member named Albertson slipped the language barrier half aside, and all conversed through him.

Clitherall, as they called it, was a considerable village, containing numerous log

---

The Clitherall settlement of so-called Mormons were not connected with the Mormons in Utah. The Clitherall folk were Cutlerites, and practiced strict monogamy, according to their gospel.

cabins (several with roofs of shakes hand-rived with a froh), a grocery and dry-goods store, a blacksmith shop, a chair factory, a cobbler's shop, and a wagon factory.

Pehr was amazed and elated at what he was shown. Here were available, at a distance of little more than half a Swedish mile, goods and services of which he would avail himself soon as he had money enough to afford them.

He submitted, through Albertson, his potato and garden seed problems. The men assured him that his late-planted potatoes might yield abundantly and would keep through the winter in a storage pit. In a cellar the tubers should, however, have some ventilation to discourage rot, they said. Pehr remained somewhat skeptical, and, determined to ensure a sufficiency of potatoes, he made arrangement with a farmer named Fletcher to get ten bushels of the tubers when he dug the crop. Hauled to market they would bring two dollars a bushel, but Pehr could come and fetch them for a dollar eighty cents. They shook hands to seal the bargain. Mr. Fletcher would send word when he dug them. It would be quite soon.

When Pehr made known his concern about an adequate supply of garden seeds, several men chimed in at once. Through Albertson, Pehr learned that several of the settlers sort of specialized in the taking and saving of certain garden seeds and could be relied upon each spring for a supply available to others. For instance, one farmer on the edge of town saved and stored the seeds accumulated from Hubbard squash eaten by his family during the winter. Another encouraged a row of onions to head out—for enough seeds to supply the entire community. Everyone volunteered seeds of one kind or another. Pehr was moved to inquire gravely: "how can I remember from whom at what price I can get each sort?"

"I'll fix that," said Albertson. "I'll ask each seed-saver to bring me enough for a good-sized kitchen garden. I'll keep these for you until gardening time next spring. My house is just there to the west on a hill (he pointed). You will not want for seeds, believe me!" (Albertson also kept store in the village, though his farm lay to the west.)

Pehr stood gratified beyond words. Never before, even among his own countrymen in Sweden had he known such generous concern for another man, to say nothing about a total stranger. His enduring faith in the divine destiny of mankind was more strongly reinforced than ever before in his memory.

The sun approached the west before the visitors betook themselves to their wagon and headed for home. Anna and Pehr were jubilant. They were scarcely out of hearing when Anna turned to Pehr and expostulated:

"You were so right, Pehr; and I was so wrong! Those people are, without question, the most genuine Christians I have ever met. I am now ashamed to ever have thought otherwise!"

"Don't ponder your error, Anna," responded Pehr. "We were trained in Lutheran bigotry from childhood. I am neither scholarly nor well-traveled; but I concluded long since that no man can be justly condemned for the manner in which he worships God. All who believe in one supreme being are aiming at the same ultimate destination."

They sat silently contemplative most of the way home; and there stood the faithful Bos awaiting her milking.

Her visit to the Clitherall Mormons had for all time relaxed Anna's fearful concept of the American wilderness! She now felt that she had ready help available to her in any emergency that might befall.

Pehr became more relaxed and cheerful than at any time before since departing Skåne. At times, he even whistled or sang as he worked, recalling Swedish folksongs 'visor' and dances he had learned as a young rustic blade.

He spent two entire weeks of October gleaning from his woods and Mrs. Lien's the wind-thrown trees that remained sound for fuel and the dead or near-dead trees on the root. In order to maneuver oxen and wagon through the forest, he did, indeed, cut down numerous young healthy trees that blocked his passage. Rain showers interrupted the work only twice, briefly. He stacked twenty loads of pole wood by Mrs. Lien's cellar and an equal number by his own cabin, northeast of the structure. He built himself a stout X-type sawhorse and bucked into stove-wood lengths a large pile of fuel. He well knew that the main cut of green wood could not be made before the dead of winter, when the trees stood bare, the sloughs were safely frozen, and the land lay deeply buried under snow for good sleighing.

First night frost had come soon after mid-September, appearing in the morning as a white rime on garden and prairie. The air was notably clear, crisp, and stimulating; the sky looked as if endless in depth, without a trace of cloud.

Pehr had viewed the rime with shock! Why, he never knew, but it called to mind that he had not stacked hay for the widow as he had promised. He was disgusted with himself. Soon as the white glint had gone off the garden, he shouldered the scythe, pocketed his whetstone, and headed for Mrs. Lien's place. He stopped by the cellar to tell her what he was about and to offer his apologies for having delayed so long. She shrugged off his apologies, and thanked him for coming. Then she said: "The best stand of wild hay is on the low flat in my northwest corner. Will you come to the cellar for dinner or shall I bring you a lunch at noon?"

"I'll come in," replied Pehr. "Hot food is always better than cold."

He walked away, pondering the dinner invitation, and even more his acceptance. He wondered whether he should sit with the handsome widow alone, then he thought of Tollef and relaxed. He had no need to fret; when he came for dinner, Anna and the girls were there too. Mrs. Lien had sent Tollef to invite them.

Pehr had laid up two hay stacks such as his own, and was preparing to do another mowing, when Mrs. Lien came and told him that he had laid up all the hay she would need. Pehr looked at her, dumb-founded; so she said: "Tollef and I are coming to eat supper at your place this evening. We have something to tell you."

"Oh," said Pehr, on a note of half surprise and half query. Then, after a moment's hesitation, he added facetiously: "And will you also tell us how you got that sparkle in your eyes?"

She blushed, smiled, and walked into the cellar.

Pehr thought, as he walked home beside his oxen and hay rack: "She's a fine strong woman, and I hope she has caught herself a good man!"

At supper, Anna Lien told her briefly kept secret without prelude.

"I'm getting a new husband, and Tollef a new father. What do you think of that?"

Pehr answered quickly: "It's wonderful news, Anna. No woman handsome as you are should waste her resources living alone. I hope he's as good a man as you deserve."

He's a fine Norwegian homesteader, about my age, whose wife died last year. He has a little daughter. His name is Johann Kladsvik, and he lives several miles west of here. He has a good house, with gables and a shake roof, and we shall live in that."

"What happens with proving up your quarter then?" asked Pehr. "Will that revert to the state?"

"Oh, no," replied Mrs. Lien, "that is not a homestead. It's what they call a war widow's bounty, or freehold. I got title to it after my first husband was killed."

"Then, with your new husband's quarter together with yours, you will be landed gentry, no less. We're genuinely happy for you, dear Anna."

"When and where will the wedding be?" inquired Anna. "We want to come."

"You must come," answered Anna Lien. "You are our closest friends in the whole country. I'll tell you our plans soon as we fix them. We have scarcely talked about them yet."

They toasted the future Mrs. Kladsvik with their second cups of coffee. Mrs. Lien was radiant, as a prospective bride should be.

After the first white frost, the weather became wondrously clear and beautiful. A few light frosts followed, but none dangerous to the garden. Not before mid-October did the family take up their potatoes and root crops; carrots, rutabagas, and onions. Only the turnips had failed; the other crops were of good size and abundance. The late summer weather had been too hot for the turnips!

Immediately after Pehr dug the carrots, the girls gathered them into piles; Anna cut their crowns off just below the shoulder so they would not sprout; and Pehr piled them in the cellar hole behind the ladder. He got two pailfuls. Left in the sun, even briefly, they would have dried, and cracked longitudinally—an invitation to decay. The rutabagas, three pailfuls, similarly beheaded, he piled beside the carrots. (Another day he covered both of these heaps with a tubful of sand dug from the south hill and moistened at the spring.)

The potatoes yielded amazingly well; and they knew them to be firm and tasty from sample hills taken and eaten during past weeks. Never before had Pehr dug "new" potatoes in October. He left them in the sun while they ate dinner; then he and the girls gathered them into piles, gently rubbing the dried dirt off them in the process. He piled twenty pailfuls against the east wall of the cellar, and hoped they would keep. Their potatoes had been planted so late that the bug season was past, and the plants were not attacked.

The yellow onions, also dried in the sun, Pehr buried in hay at the north wall of the stable between the manger and his workshop.

Taking hay from a stack and putting it on the stable floor reminded him that he had made no provision for bedding his cattle when they became confined to their stalls in winter. The upland prairie now lay seared and shimmering in sunlight. The grass cut now might be poor stover for the animals, but it would do well for bedding. The half-dry grass was exceedingly hard to cut, and he swung the oft-stroked scythe two whole days before he had laid down as much as he thought he might need. He left it to dry the third day; then hauled and built of it a stack the length of the stable along the north (basement) wall. The stack was a wind-break without peer.

Only two days after they had dug and stored away their own, Fletcher's teenage son came from Clitherall to notify Pehr that his potatoes were sacked and ready for him. Pehr and the boy immediately lifted the rack from the wagon box and drove to Clitherall, both riding on the seat. They could not converse, but the ride was pleasant nonetheless. They swung by Albertson's store enroute, and he came along as interpreter. Fletcher had four bulging grain sacks full of potatoes for Pehr. He untied one to show that the potatoes were of good size and quality, and uninjured. Pehr approved them enthusiastically.

"I have no sacks," he apologized to Fletcher. "Can you sell me those they're in?"

"I'll be glad to," replied Fletcher. "They're not brand new, but neither are they much worn. Would you think fifteen cents a fair price? They cost twenty-two cents new."

"I would call that a good bargain. At a dollar eighty a bushel for ten bushels, and four sacks at fifteen cents each, I owe you exactly eighteen dollars and sixty cents. Is that right?"

"That's right," answered Fletcher. Pehr counted out the money on Fletcher's palm. He folded the bills and stuck the money into his pocket. They shook hands and loaded the sacks into the wagon box. Pehr thanked both Fletcher and Albertson and prepared to depart. As he mounted to the seat a thought came to him, and he inquired:

"Mr. Fletcher, you have numerous chickens. Would you, perhaps, sell me a half dozen hens and a rooster, next fall after harvest when I have wheat to feed them? I would be obliged." Albertson translated for Fletcher.

"Yes! Mr. Pehrson, I'll sell you that many chickens whenever you want them. They're worth a quarter dollar apiece. These lay quite well, except in the coldest part of winter. I'll save a little bunch for you." Albertson translated for Pehr.

"Thank you, I'll count on it," said Pehr. "Good-by then, 'til we meet again." He called to his oxen and turned them toward home.

"Good-by," called Fletcher and Albertson, and both waved until the wagon was screened from their view.

When Pehr emptied the sacks against the west wall of the cellar he noted that they were of uniformly good quality throughout. He concluded that Mormons were too honest to cheat a buyer by placing choice specimens at the top of the sack. He regretted that certain Lutherans had been known to do so.

Everyone revelled in the beauty and pleasantness of October, which some would, after years of experience, acknowledge the fairest month of the year in Minnesota. Mosquitoes, flies and several other summer pests disappeared, so one could work or idle out-of-doors without suffering annoyance and irritation. Clothes donned for warmth in the morning, one discarded long before noon, as the sunshine warmed the earth to summery warmth through a sky with few obstructions. The mixed hardwood forest stood at its peak of color as the month wore on: the scarlet of black oak, the variegated red and yellow hues of sugar maple, the dull yellow of basswood and the more brilliant yellow of aspen, the gold of birches, and the light dull brown of hornbeam and white oak composed a lovely tapestry of color. At month's end only the aspens, black oaks and hornbeams retained many of their leaves; most other species stood naked, warning of winter. Ruffed grouse and prairie chickens gathered in flocks to mix the summer's broods. Great flocks of waterfowl streamed southward across the sky, some, notably the Canada geese, parading both night and day and cackling so one could hear them a mile away. This was the season in which one went forth to take his share of the year's game crop. Pehr made frequent turns about the prairie and woods, his musket loaded with shot; and rarely did he fail to bring home a brace of prairie chickens, mallards, or grouse. Autumn was the season for feasting on wild fowl, though the grouse and chickens remained readily available throughout the winter, as well. They varied their meat rations with cottontail rabbits and gray squirrels—both populous in and near the woods. The squirrels, fat on acorns, were especially good, soaked in salt water over night, disjointed and fried in a cast-iron skillet.

Chippewa Indians, from their camp in a forest-opening a quarter mile southwest of the cabin came searching for the source one day when they heard Pehr's musket blasts. Without the least malice, two young braves waylaid Pehr and frightened him when they emerged from the brush as if by magic and stood squarely in front of him. They spoke to him rapidly in words he could not understand. Then, by their signs and grunts he understood that they wished to acquire the musket. They would give a great heap of animal pelts for the firearm. Their offer was so extravagant that one reached for the gun as if a bargain was good as made. Pehr swung the musket out of his reach and signalled that he could not part with the piece because it kept his family in meat. Whether the young bucks understood or not, they accepted his mute explanation, and, without any show of hostility, stalked off into the woods. This scene was played time and again later on, until the friendly tribesmen became convinced that Pehr's musket was not available at any price. It contributed a substantial part of the family's food supply. Pehr made no mention of the incidents until a chief and two brawny young braves carrying a great bale of animal pelts came one day to the cabin door and there attempted to bargain for the gun. Anna peaked through the window and was afraid. Pehr, risking the ire of the chief, signed as before that he could not survive without the gun. Finally, at word from the chief, the braves picked up the bale of skins, and all three walked away in the direction of their camp. However friendly they might be, Anna feared the Red Men and her fear fastened on her daughters. Neither buck nor squaw was ever admitted to the cabin, and few came near it. Never did an Indian steal or damage anything on the Homestead.*

In November, days became so short and nights so long that Pehr's industry became much curtailed. He did, however, manage to build two implements of prime importance; a monstrous sledge for hauling during winter and a harrow with which to prepare land for sowing the following spring.

He addressed himself first to the sledge, a major project. He sought and found in his own woods an oak bough that met his specifications: ten feet long, twelve inches in diameter and quite sharply curved at one end. He took down the entire tree to get the bough he wanted. This he split in two with maul and wedges so that each half simulated, however crudely, the runner of a sleigh. These he hauled home, together with all other useful parts of the tree. He carried the two specially selected pieces into his workshop, and there, with broad axe and drawknife worked them into a pair of matched runners, four inches thick and three inches wide, their front ends eight inches off the floor when they were set down on it. Onto these, eighteen inches from each end he bolted risers of oak fifteen inches long, three inches thick and eight inches high. Next he squared two bunks (or bolsters) to lie crosswise of the affair, four-by-four inches in cross-section and long enough to receive the wagon box between stakes set into one and one half inch holes bored through the bunks four inches in from the ends. Next he gouged three-inch holes through the runners six

---

*Indeed, when Pehr, during a siege of blustery winter weather, went to the Chief's lodge and presented him three loaves of Anna's freshly baked bread, the grateful Indian gave Pehr in return an entire haunch of venison. They bartered in such manner frequently, until the Indian removed their camp from the vicinity.

inches back from their up-turned noses. Next he shaped a roller, several inches thick at its midpoint and so tapered toward the ends that it would fit loosely into the holes through the runners and with sufficient shoulders left back from the ends so that it could not slip sideways. He carried these prepared parts out-of-doors and there assembled them, using stout dowel pins to secure the bunks. All now remaining to be done was to chisel a rectangular hole through the roller at midpoint and secure to it a tongue with pins and wedges. When the monstrosity stood thus completed, Pehr examined it critically *(Figure 7.1)*. He said to himself: "If I could attach replaceable treads under the runners, this sledge might wear almost indefinitely." He made a few careful measurements of the curve in the runners. He went into the stable and took up his chopper's axe, peeked into the cabin and told Anna he'd be back before supper, and walked to the Clitherall peninsula. He quickly found a six-inch ironwood apparently with the appropriate bend in it, cut it down, measured the curve and found it suitable, whacked it off about eleven feet long, and carried it home on his shoulders. Darkness came as he walked, and a hot supper awaited him.

Halfway throught his meal he stopped chewing and said explosively: "Fan" (the Devil), a swear word he used only when utterly exasperated.

"What did you say?" demanded Anna, instantly alert.

"Forgive me, dear," said Pehr, calmly. "I just became aware of a blunder I made in the woods this evening. I took home one curved ironwood when I needed two. I shall walk back right away in the morning and get a mate to the one I have." This he did, and with remarkable speed.

He split the rails so that the flat side of one half would fit under a runner with the round side to the ground. He secured one such to each runner with carriage bolts, well counter-sunk into the ironwood tread—six bolts in each runner. Now the odd-looking contraption stood ready. It served him well several winters. He

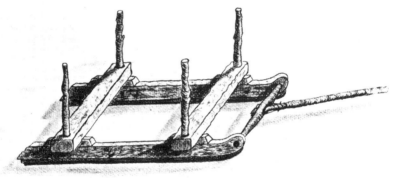

Figure 7.1. Necessity is indeed the mother of invention! It was essential that Pehr have a vehicle for hauling logs and fuel wood in winter. He therefore fashioned a monstrosity such as here depicted. The sledge served well, drawn by a yoke of powerful oxen. When the ironwood treads stood frozen fast it was necessary that they be prized loose before starting, lest the tongue be broken. In deep or heavy snow the sledge had to be turned very gradually, else such maneuver would also break the tongue. However cautious, Pehr was obliged to replace the tongue frequently. The bunk width and stake holes were measured to receive the wagon box when its use was desired. The sledge served its purposes until Pehr changed from oxen to horses, and procured a bob-sleigh.

Artist's conception sketched in charcoal by Julie Wolters.

retreaded it each autumn. Since it was simply a sledge and not a sleigh, it was difficult to turn. However carefully Pehr "Geed" and "Haw'd" his oxen when they were hitched to it they broke several tongues.

Construction of the harrow was a simpler job and more quickly done. The craftsman split out four lengths from a six-foot oak log and worked them with drawknife and plane to three-by-three inch dimensions. From the same log he split out and planed down one piece two-by-four inches, which he sawed to a length of five feet. This heavy piece would be the forward cross-piece and serve as draw-bar, with a clevis to receive the ox chain. He laid these pieces out on the floor, parallel to each other and one foot apart. These would be the business part of the drag (harrow) into which the pins would be set. Now he took up a five-foot oak log, rived from it and planed to size and smoothness three two-by-two inch pieces. These he laid athwart the six-footers, one at their middle and one six inches in from each end. He measured, squared, and marked carefully each point at which an upper member crossed a lower, and at that point, drilled a half-inch hole. He inserted, from the bottom, fifteen half-inch square-headed bolts, nine inches long; laid a washer under each nut on top; and drew them tight with his adjustable "Litchfield" wrench. The harrow now lay completed but for drilling half-inch holes through the lower cross members and inserting the teeth. He drilled the holes, avoiding the upper cross members, and so staggering them that none would track another one in front of it. He leaned the unfinished implement against the stable wall, sawed off a ten inch length of a straight-grained oak bolt, and split from it twenty-five angular pieces that would become harrow teeth. He laid them on a wisp of hay next to the harrow to dry until spring. Then he would shave them to fit the half-inch holes, drive them in, and saw them off to a uniform "working" length of five inches. This tooth-harrow served him many years. Dragged over a plowed field dry enough for tillage, it pulverized the soil and made a good seed bed. The draw bar in front, and, indeed, the entire contrivance, was heavy enough to offset the upward pull of the ox-chain, and work flat to the ground. The oak teeth often broke off on large or land-fast stones; so whenever Pehr used the implement he carried spare teeth in his pocket. With a fist-size stone, he could quickly drive out a broken tooth and insert a new one. Except in low places, built up with erosion silt over the years since glaciation, stones were so numerous that he need rarely search very far for a suitable one.

December came in with miserable weather: overcast skies, cold rain and snow flurries. The ground became sodden, often with an icy crust formed on it overnight. The grasses had frozen and lost their flavor.

Pehr stabled the cattle and fed them hay. He had assumed Anna's milking duties shortly before Bos dried up preparatory to calving. He turned the animals out for a considerable spell each day, so they could go to the slough and drink. He cleaned the stable daily, pitching the manure and spent bedding into a pile down slope from the stable. He used his spade for barn cleaning the first few days, but concluded that handling stable manure with a spade is somewhat akin to eating noodles with a spoon. The first sunny day when he could open the stable door and get sufficient light, he fashioned a four-tined wooden manure fork—the back rib of oak; the tines and handle of ash. It served well for handling hay, bedding, and manure and spared the dirt floor better than did the spade. He promised himself that the stable area occupied by the cattle would have a durable cobblestone floor before a second stallfeeding season arrived. Obviously, he could not lay it while the animals were stabled.

Noting one day at feeding time that Bos was about to calve, Pehr fenced her off from the oxen with a rail barrier and left her untied so she might properly attend to her offspring when it came. He bedded her space generously; which was timely, because she dropped a bull-calf in the night, and when Pehr came to feed and clean next morning the frisky youngster, licked clean and dry, stood sucking and butting his mother with a vigor belying his tender age. Pehr immediately milked out what remained in Bos' swollen udder and held the pail to her for her to drink. She drank little, but perhaps enough to help cleanse her of the after-birth. Then he brought her a pailful of clean water from the spring.

While still at the table, after everyone had eaten dinner, Pehr announced the arrival of their first calf; and the girls fairly whooped with excitement.

"Can we go and pet him, Mamma? Papa?"

"Of course, you may," said Anna.

"Get your coats on," said Pehr, "and your mother and I will carry you down so you don't get your shoes dirty."

Off they went. The little girls saw no baby calf at first because he was hidden behind his mother. Pehr set Elna down on a wad of clean bedding and stepped into Bos' private pen. He stroked the cow on her cheeks and face to reassure her; then he picked the calf up and carried him to the barrier so the girls could reach through and pat him.

"He's so little and pretty," squealed Hanna.

"He's like his mother," submitted Elna, more soberly.

"He's like his mother in color, at least," said Pehr. "Red shorthorn."

"What shall we call him?" asked Anna. "We'll let you girls name him, won't we Papa?"

"Well and good," said Pehr, "but take your time to think up a real special name. Maybe you will agree on one tomorrow." (The girls named the calf "Krull," because the hair on his head was tightly curled "every which way." The name stuck.)

"Is Bos clean and alright?" asked Anna as they started back to the house.

"Almost," answered Pehr. "She drank a little of her first milk, and that should clean her out. Be prepared to bake 'Kalva Dans' pudding. I'll take the milk for it tomorrow morning. I'll let the calf suck for a week or so, to give him a good start. After that he'll have to do with skim milk out of a pail. We shall have butter again, and the girls shall have whole milk to drink."

Then as an afterthought, he added: "Too bad it wasn't a heifer calf. This one can only become a steer and a work animal! With a heifer to help her mother, we could have had a supply of milk year-round."

Early in December, Anna became gravely concerned about their supply of flour. One day as Pehr sat enjoying with his afternoon coffee a well-buttered heel off a hot loaf, she sounded the ominous warning:

"Unless we replenish our supply of flour, we shall be without before Christmas. In the bottom of the barrel is enough for only two or three bakings."

"Relax, woman," said Pehr. "I shall see that we have flour! I'll go this very day to Clitherall and see whether there is some to buy."

He denied that he was worried, but when he departed afoot, Anna surmised that

Page 150

he was skeptical about returning with a bag of flour. He returned well after dark and reported dolefully that neither the storekeeper nor any settler on the route he had walked, had any flour to sell or lend. Next day he walked a wide turn about the neighborhood, with equally discouraging results. He should have to drive his oxen to Alexandria and there procure a barrel of flour, if such could be found even there—by this time a thriving trade center. If his expedition failed, the entire countryside would suffer.

Late November and December thus far had brought heavy rains, snow flurries, and alternate freezing and thawing. The wagon trails lay so deeply mired that scarcely anyone ventured out on them. But Pehr would not be restrained! Flour he must have!

He set out, with oxen and wagon, so early in the morning, Sunday, December twelfth, that the waning moon still shone. The oxen made good progress as long as the night's frost film held; but after that melted they plodded on at a snail's pace through a veritable morass. Wherever possible, Pehr guided his animals about the edges of the low deep-rutted segments of the trail. They passed Swenson's about mid-afternoon, halted only long enough to exchange greetings, and then plodded on. They stopped for neither food nor water before dusk, but then, fortuitously, they came on a settler's establishment at which they got both food and shelter. Pehr estimated that they had come half-way, about twenty American miles. The kind settlers assured him that he was only twenty miles north of Alexandria. In the morning, after a workman's breakfast, Pehr offered his host, a Swede named Lundström, pay for all the accommodations. This was loudly rejected, and Lundström rebuked him even further:

"You will stop with us on your return trip, too, unless you wish us angered by your callousness. We shall be awaiting you; do you hear?"

Pehr acceded, with gratitude, shook hands with Lundström and his comely wife, and was again on his way.

Flour was plentiful in Alexandria. He bought a barrel (196 pounds) but at an exorbitant price, $12.00. He stowed it in the front of the wagon, and laid his lap-robe over it as protection against the elements. He drove to the livery stable and installed his oxen ($.25 apiece, per night or day). He found bed for himself in a rooming house nearby ($.50 per night), and after a good supper, for $.50 he went to his room and counted his money. He had departed home with $32.25 of his own and a two-dollar bill handed him by Anna (the last of her emergency fund) with which to buy a bag of salt. He had deferred the salt purchase until he should know how much his night's accommodations had cost him. After paying for his room in the morning he should have $20.50 remaining, including Anna's contribution. His breakfast would cost only $.25. There would be plenty for salt ($1.00), and some candy ($.25) for the girls besides. He needn't worry, so he slept well.

But in the morning when he looked out the window he was shocked to the very tips of his toes by what he saw. Freezing rain had come during the night and laid a glittering glaze of ice on every surface exposed to the wind. He knew at once that his barefoot oxen could not walk on it without falling; they could certainly not pull a wagon. He hurried downstairs, paid for his room, gulped a twenty-five cent breakfast, and walked, carefully, to the blacksmith shop. The smithy was next door to the livery stable, an arrangement almost universal on the frontier. Pehr came on the blacksmith busily shoeing a horse; and, fortunately for Pehr, the customer was a

Swede. Pehr greeted the men with a half-hearted "good-morning," and got only mumbles in response. He began explaining the urgency of getting his oxen shod; but the Swede interrupted him:

"This here fellow is a Scot, and he can't understand Swedish. If you tell me what you want, I'll try to make him understand. I know a little English."

"Then please tell him that I came here, forty miles, for a barrel of flour; and that I must quite obviously shoe my oxen before I can start home."

The Swede explained, and the Scot replied, now apparently in good humor.

"He says he can shoe your oxen right after he gets through with my horse. He charges two dollars for shoeing a horse and five for shoeing a yoke of oxen. As you probably know, oxen require two half-shoes for each foot, and their hooves are so thin that an ox-shoer must be extra careful not to drive a nail into the animal's foot. Do you have the money?"

Pehr showed him his twenty dollar bill.

(Oxen are difficult to shoe, because of their cloven hooves. Each foot requires a pair of half shoes, each half with caulks at toe and heel. The hooves can splay naturally until the caulks take hold.)

"Good," said the Swede. "If your animals are here in the stable I'll go with you and lead one over while Scotty finishes with my horse. Your steers probably don't like to be separated."

"Thank you very much," said Pehr.

They went next door. Pehr paid his stable bill, untied his oxen, and led Bride, very cautiously, to the smithy. The helpful Swede followed with Buck. The blacksmith straightened from his work a moment to admire Pehr's fine animals. The horse shod and released to its owner, Scotty commenced stroking the oxen and talking to them, by way of becoming acquainted. Soon he was at work on their big feet, beginning with Bride. Apparently the oxen would give him no trouble.

Pehr excused himself with a hand sign, and hurried to the Land Office to formally file his claim. There was the same clerk who had dealt with him before, so this took only a little while. Pehr paid the fee with his twenty-dollar bill, and got his Entry Permit and receipt *(Figures 7.2 and 7.3)* and $6.00 in return. He signed an affidavit of intent to become a citizen *(Figure 7.4)*. He thanked the clerk, folded and pocketed the fourteen dollar receipt, shook hands, and strode out onto the icy walk. He hurried as best he could to the store where he took up a one dollar bag of salt in a sizeable sack, and bought a large bag of mixed candy for a quarter. He had $5.25 left. With the quarter he bought a wedge of cheese to nibble as he drove toward Lundström's. Pehr went to the wagon with the salt and candy, cleared the ice off his lap-robe, laid the sacks atop the barrel, and laid the robe over them. He knocked the glaze off the ox yoke and the wagon seat, and returned to the smithy. His oxen stood ready. He handed Scotty the five-dollar bill, (for which the journeyman Scot nodded and smiled) and led his oxen away. They were scarcely out of town before the oxen stepped out boldly on their new shoes, no longer fearing a tumble.

The day continued so cold that the glaze and mire remained solid. Progress by wagon was far better than possible the day before. Pehr reached Lundström's while candle-light still glowed through the windows. Johann Lundström had, in fact, waited up for Pehr, and kept a candle burning after his family had gone to bed. He greeted Pehr, with a mixture of profanity and vindication:

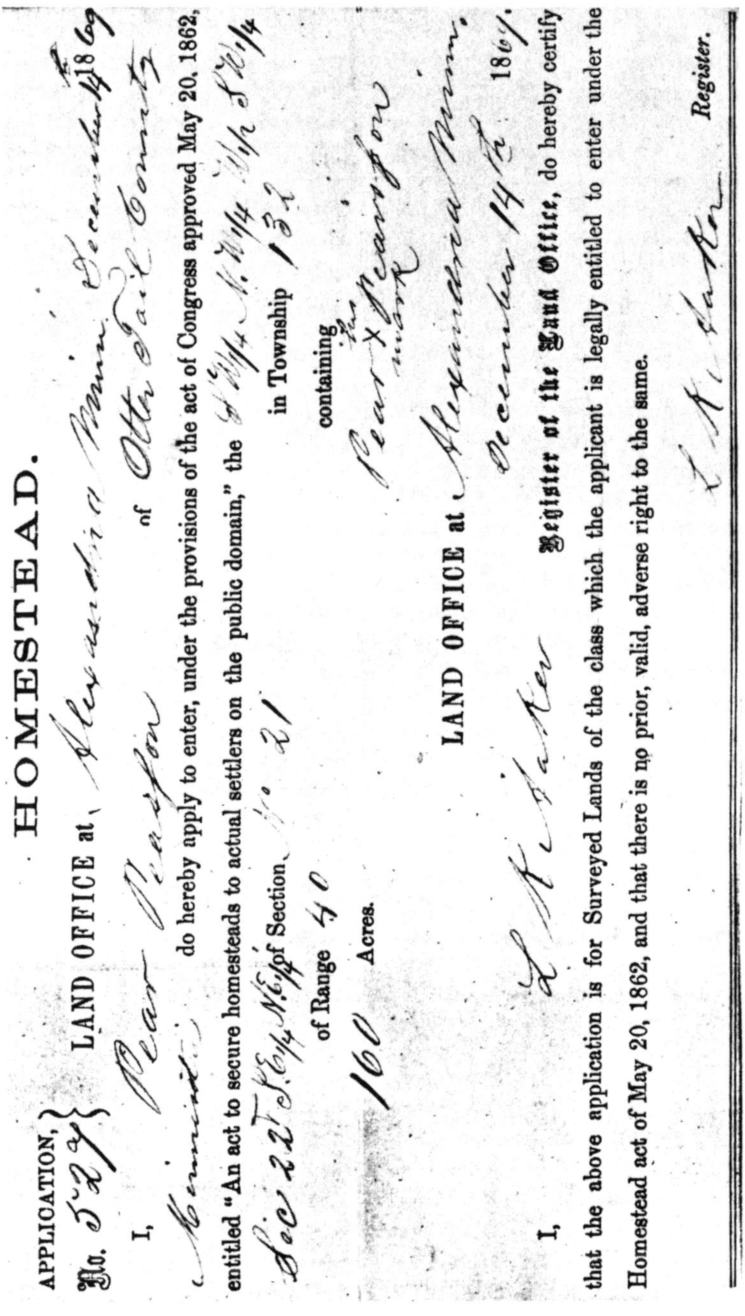

HOMESTEAD.

APPLICATION, No. 5279

LAND OFFICE at Alexandria Minn. December 14 1869

I, Pehr Wrangsten of Otter Tail County Minnesota do hereby apply to enter, under the provisions of the act of Congress approved May 20, 1862, entitled "An act to secure homesteads to actual settlers on the public domain," the $S^{1/2}$ $N^{1/4}$ $N^{1/4}$ $S^{1/4}$ $S^{1/4}$ Sec. 22 & $S^{1/2}$ $S^{1/2}$ $N^{1/4}$ $N^{1/4}$ Section No. 21 in Township 132 of Range 40 containing 160 Acres.

Pehr × Wrangsten
mark

LAND OFFICE at Alexandria Minn. December 14 1869.

I, L. K. Baxter Register of the Land Office, do hereby certify that the above application is for Surveyed Lands of the class which the applicant is legally entitled to enter under the Homestead act of May 20, 1862, and that there is no prior, valid, adverse right to the same.

L. K. Baxter Register.

Figure 7.2. Facsimile of Pehr's homestead entry permit—14 December 1869.

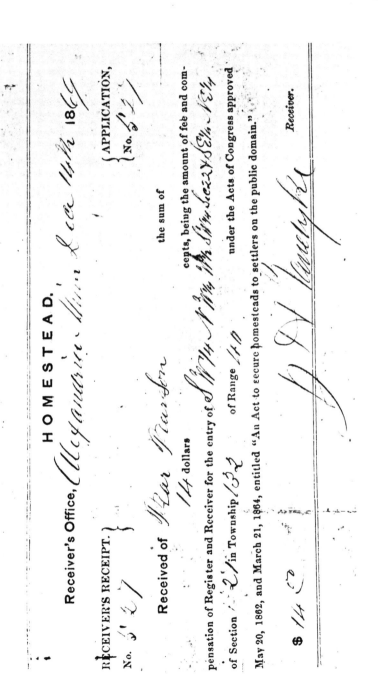

Figure 7.3. Facsimile of Pehr's receipt for fourteen-dollar fee—cost of Entry Permit.

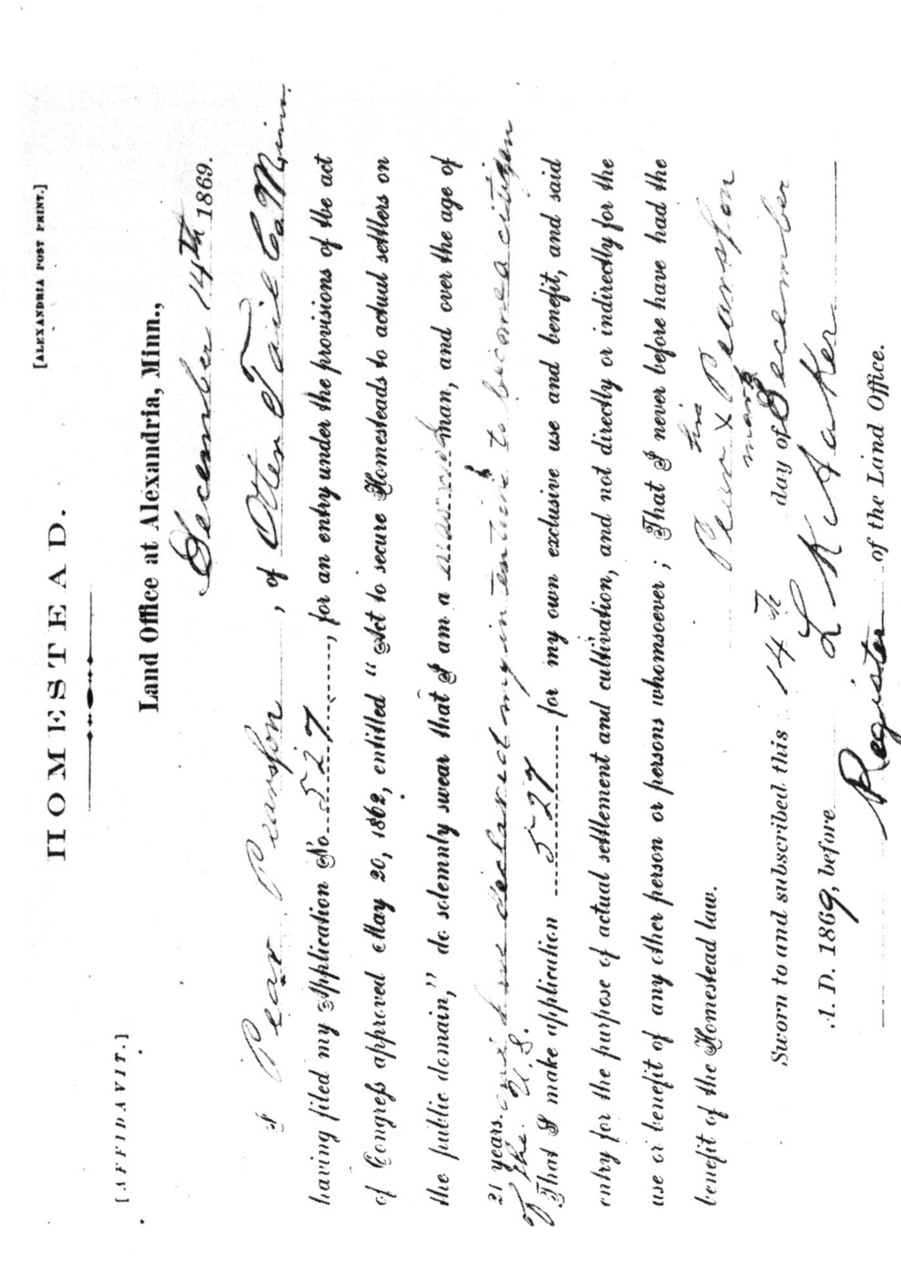

[AFFIDAVIT.]

HOMESTEAD.

[ALEXANDRIA POST PRINT.]

Land Office at Alexandria, Minn.,

December 14th 1869.

I *Pehr Pehrson*, of *Otter Tail Co. Minn.* having filed my Application No. *527*, for an entry under the provisions of the act of Congress approved May 20, 1862, entitled "Act to secure Homesteads to actual settlers on the public domain," do solemnly swear that I am a *widower man*, and over the age of 21 years, *and I have declared my intention to become a citizen of the U.S.* That I make application *527* for my own exclusive use and benefit, and said entry for the purpose of actual settlement and cultivation, and not directly or indirectly for the use or benefit of any other person or persons whomsoever; That I never before have had the benefit of the Homestead law.

Pehr X Pehrson
 mark

Sworn to and subscribed this *14th* day of *December* A. D. 1869, before *L. K. Aaker* *Register* of the Land Office.

Figure 7.4. Facsimile of Pehr's affidavit certifying his status as a family man and his intention to become a citizen of the United States.

"I said, by God, you'd get here, come hell or high water. Go in and warm! I'll water and feed your oxen. What a hell of a spell of weather!"

Pehr was too tired and cold to resent coddling; he went into the house, shed his outer clothing, and began to get warm. Lundström's wife wakened and rose from the bed. She put on a sort of robe and greeted Pehr:

"I didn't think you would be here tonight, because of the ice; but Johann insisted that the purpose of your trip would get you here. I'll warm over some supper for you."

Johann entered and sat with Pehr while he ate.

"I see you had your oxen shod. Did you find a good blacksmith?"

"I didn't have much choice; but those shoes were put on by a Scot that's as good a journeyman as ever I saw in Sweden. The oxen walk as confidently as if the ground were bare."

"Of course, you got the barrel of flour you went for?"

"Yes, Oh yes, I got the flour, and a bag of salt, and some candy for my little daughters. Would you believe that the shoeing of my oxen took my last five dollars. I haven't a penny left to my name?! I'll be entirely without money until I get my wheat harvested late next summer."

"You're far from the first to be in such circumstances. I've known quite a few; and I've never known one to fail!"

They stirred early next morning, at Pehr's apologetic request. As he hurriedly ate his breakfast, he invited his hosts to come and see his Homestead and his family:

"In pleasant weather it would be an easy trip," he encouraged them.

They said they would do it one day.

The freezing weather and frozen ground endured through another day; and Pehr didn't stop his oxen before they were home. Enough light remained so that Anna and the girls came out to meet him when they heard the wagon and the crunch of sharp shoes on ice and frozen ground.

Pehr was so glad to see his little family safe and sound that he came off the wagon almost before it stopped. He hugged all three at once, then he said: "Go in where it's warm, and I'll join you in a few minutes and tell you all about my trip." Then as he unhitched the oxen and lifted off their yoke, he said: "These faithful animals must have water before I do anything else. I'll go with them to the slough and break the ice."

"Oh no! You needn't," said Anna, more loudly than she was wont to do. "We kept Bos in, for fear she would break a leg. We have the tub in the stable, more than half full of water. We carried it from the spring and poured it in.

"What would I do without my girls?" said Pehr. And he led the oxen to the stable. They drank noisily from the tub, almost emptying it. Pehr tied them in their stalls, stroking them and talking to them as he did so. He filled their manger with hay. Enroute the house he took from the wagon the salt and candy and replaced the robe over the barrel.

He gave the girls the big bag of candy and handed Anna the salt. He got a resounding kiss from each. Anna quickly instructed her daughters that they might have only each one piece of candy before supper. Pehr washed his face and hands, combed his hair, felt his stubbly chin, and sat down to the table.

As they ate, he recounted his two-day experience, including the extraordinary kindness of the Lundströms, the high cost of ox shoeing, and the bind he should have fallen into had not his provident wife given him two dollars. He concluded thus: "We must literally live off the land until our first harvest. We haven't a cent with which to buy anything. I believe we can prevail without severe hardship."

"Of course, we'll make it," said Anna, pretending to be no less confident. Then she said further, and tried to sound casual: "Several came today to borrow flour; they had heard that you were going after some. Two young women left for home just before you came. We shall have to lend much of the flour tomorrow!"

"We will lend as much as we dare," exclaimed Pehr. "We will not deny what we have to anyone in need."

In bed, before going to sleep Anna turned to her husband and whispered: "You are such a good man, Pehr. I'm proud you're mine."

Pehr whispered in return: "You are more of a woman than I am a man, my dear. Together, we shall help tame this wild land." Then he was asleep.

Next morning neighbors from near and far converged on the Pehrsons to borrow each a baking of flour. Soon the cabin simulated a doctor's waiting room; Pehr determined to dole out nothing before he had some inkling of the number in need. At Anna's request he shifted the planks over the cellar and took up a generous quantity of vegetables, with which Anna made a large kettle of soup. She would have no one leave her house hungry! (When Pehr refitted the planks over the hole, he remembered to leave cracks for ventilation, as he had been instructed in Clitherall.)

When there were a dozen people waiting, sitting against the walls or standing about the room, he brought out his steelyard and commenced weighing out flour and pouring it into containers brought for the purpose. To each family represented he meted out two pounds for each member—enough for one large loaf apiece.

He kept repeating as he weighed: "How many are you? Then you shall have 'so-and-so many pounds.' Please return them to us when you get some flour."

The tantalizing aroma from Anna's soup soon permeated the small, stuffy room. She announced to the crowd: "When you have your measure of flour, please sit to the table and let me serve you some soup and bread."

Not one disdained the delicious soup, but ate a sizeable bowlful with one or two large slices of bread with fresh butter on it. Each, in turn rose from the table and thanked and shook the hands of both Pehr and Anna, some with tears of gratitude in their eyes, and then disappeared.

When all had been supplied, there remained in the bottom of the barrel only enough for approximately two goodly bakings. Pehr and Anna were both proud and perturbed when they viewed the small residue.

"How shall we know that we get back what we loaned?" asked Anna.

"Dearest woman," said Pehr, "I could not bring myself to take down names as if questioning their integrity. I felt bound to honor the good intent of my fellow man when he is hungry. I would wager that every recipient returns the loan at the first opportunity."

Return of the flour became a cherished chronicle in the Pehrson household. According to Anna's count, everyone returned what he had borrowed, and in extra measure. Some insisted on returning twice what they had borrowed. As if arranged by Providence, someone came with flour every time Anna scraped the bottom of her barrel. Both Anna and Pehr, each in secret reflection, knew that they stood in divine grace! They never came nearer hunger than when Pehr set out, in muck and mire, for Alexandria.

In Mid-December the Pehrsons received house guests—Nils Anderson and Nils Johnson came, and stayed almost steadily until March. Both came looking ill, having worked outdoors for the railway company throughout the inclement weather of November. They were welcomed joyously, being very special friends since their land-selection expedition with Pehr. The fourth member of the quartet, Sven Person, had gone to the pineries for the winter.

The young bachelors brought good-sized bundles of blankets, and with these they made warm and comfortable beds on hay carried into Pehr's stable workshop. Pehr brought his wood-working tools into the house and used the table as a workbench between meals.

"You may sleep in the loft, if you will saw planks and lay enough floor up there to spread your bedding on," Pehr told them. They floored most of the loft during their stay, but they elected to remain in the stable to sleep. It was warmer.

Anderson and Johnson kept the stable clean (partly with selfish motive), and kept the animals fed and watered. The wooden tub became a fixed watering trough in the stable except when Anna required it for washing clothes. (She washed and mended for all three of the men.) The young guests also kept a goodly supply of firewood piled some distance from the stove: bucking, splitting, and carrying it in.

Pehr had more leisure than ever before in his life; but he did not idle it away. First he made Anna a broom of willow switches for use on the dirt floor; whenever Pehr's shavings became dirty, she swept them out. Next he took almost a week to make two spare ox-yokes. The yokes were of basswood, their bows and pins of oak. The bows he boiled, bent them into a U-shape, and inserted them between two spokes of the wagon, there to dry so that they would retain their shape. The complete yokes he hung in the stable on stout wooden pins doweled into an upper log in the north wall—above the manger. Then he fashioned each a pair of wooden shoes for everyone resident in the house. He took careful measurements of everyone's feet and, with a razor-sharp steel spoon on a foot-long shaft, and a cross-tree at its top for turning it, gouged out the inside of the wood blocks to fit. To fashion one shoe sometimes took him from dawn to dusk in short winter days. He also made several wooden scoops or shovels, some long handled, some short, each from a suitable block of basswood. (They lasted indefinitely, without any paint or other wood preservative. The long-handled grain scoops had one grave fault! After sweating hands saturated the ends of the handles, mice inhabiting the granary gnawed the ends off to get the salt.)

When the young boarders discovered that Pehr was penniless, they compelled him to accept from them a quarter a day each, for their keep. Pehr yielded only when resistance seemed futile. He asked that they pay the money to Anna.

After a week of good nourishing food and undisturbed sleep every night, the young bachelors became restless and energetic, in need of exercise and adventure. Sensing their plight, Pehr suggested that they walk to Clitherall and see the remarkable village. (He knew they would find no liquor to buy, but would walk off excess energy.) One day they went; and they returned, not only with earnest praise of the Mormons, but also with several well-selected purchases. They regaled their sweethearts, Elna and Hanna, with each a bag of hard sugar candy, for which they were duly kissed and embraced. For Anna they brought a bright red head shawl having noted that her old one showed wear. Anna thanked most graciously, but did not reward with kisses or embraces. Pehr they brought a new pair of chopper's mittens—his old ones had holes in them, and a four-tined fork for handling hay and manure. For the household they brought a wooden pail with iron hoops, several candles of uncommonly large diameter, a dozen eggs, and a large slab of cured side meat. For themselves they came home with each a pair of lined leather mittens and each a chopper's axe. (They had determined between themselves that they should help Pehr lay up a year's supply of fuel wood and a pile of select logs for craftman's use.) The evening was joyous for all; supper was delicious and long, and all went to bed with warm hearts.

December weather had turned cold—bitterly cold by Swedish standards; the ground had frozen several feet deep; snow had begun to accumulate so that the landscape lay white. A secret dread of Christmas set in: How does one honor and enjoy Christmas in a wilderness?

Anderson conceived innovations and all the elders assisted with their realization. He would see to it that the children had a Christmas! He found and brought home a thick-crowned red haw (thorn apple) for a Christmas tree. He walked to Clitherall and got some papers of various colors; not so bright as he wished, but acceptable. Of this he helped the girls make daisy chains, using flour paste; and with these they festooned the little tree. He bought enough bright-colored calico so Anna could make each girl a new rag doll, which he stuffed with hay. Anna stitched the dolls by candle-light after her daughters lay asleep. They should be surprised!

Anna went to invite Mrs. Lien and Tollef for Christmas Eve, but they were to celebrate with their relatives.

Johnson went to Clitherall and bought a fishing line and a pair of hooks. Anna furnished pieces of pork rind with some fat attached, for bait. He took several pike (walleye) through a hole in the ice, and they served in lieu of lutefisk for supper Christmas Eve. There was no rice pudding and lingonberries for dessert, but no one commented on the deficiency. Egg custard with burnt sugar was eaten instead. After Christmas Eve supper, the assembly sang Swedish hymns and Christmas songs; and deny as they would, their tender thoughts were of the old country almost half a world away. Finally Anderson said so all could hear: "We must sing one last song and then go to bed. We must sing 'Glada Jul Afton' (Joyous Christmas Eve). They sang the old favorite so that the little log cabin fairly vibrated; and not one of the adults concluded it with dry eyes.

On the second day after Christmas a storm deposited more than six inches of new snow.

New Year's Eve they celebrated with a prairie chicken feast. Johnson walked the prairie with Pehr's musket for about half an hour one evening and came home with four—which he plucked in the stable. Anna roasted them in the oven in her largest bread-baking pan. The birds were delicious. (So many were eaten before spring, that they actually became commonplace.)

The old year had ended with deep snow, and the ground cover increased in depth as January progressed. Temperatures often fell well below zero at night, and once dropped to -30° F. Cold was so continuous that little melting occurred during the day. Lake ice became more than two feet thick; sloughs and bogs lay deep-frozen and silent.

"Now, my dear fellows," spoke Pehr one evening after supper, "I believe it's time for laying up a supply of wood for the next year. You have made it clear that you wish to help me and for that I will be most grateful, believe me! But you will not pay board money to my wife while you are doing work for us that would elsewhere yield you a good wage. If I had the money I would gladly pay you, because, as you well know, loading and stacking pole wood is the devil of a job for one man alone."

"Dear Pehr, we are not giving you our labor, but merely lending it," said Johnson.

"Yes," continued Anderson, "when we are ready to build on our claims, we will damn well need your repayment of the loan. We have it all figured out."

"So be it!" said Pehr. "I will help you whenever you call on me. We shall go to the woods in the morning, then. Put on an extra pair of wool socks, so you don't freeze your feet. Frost-bite now would give you trouble all winter. We will work at a leisurely pace, going and coming in daylight."

"The three sturdy men departed for the peninsular woods soon after eight the next morning. They rode astride a hewn plank on the bunks, lengthwise of the sledge. Each held onto his own axe. Anderson sat on the cross-cut saw, laid flat along the plank; but he protected his seat against the coarsely-set teeth with a wisp of hay pulled from one of the stacks. Pehr had the steel wedges in his overcoat pocket. Johnson held in front of him a large kettle, in the middle of which was a half-gallon jug of coffee and cookies for forenoon lunch. The kettle was packed with clothes, to keep the coffee warm. A bunk stake stood two and a half feet tall at each corner of the rig, and onto one of these Pehr had threaded the looped cross-ropes he had used previously on the wagon. They must be used now to restrain a load from pushing the stakes over at an angle and thus breaking out the holes in the bunks.

The snow was so cold and crisp that it complained loudly when trod upon. Steam rose off the oxen, warm from the stable.

When they had felled and trimmed what Pehr deemed a sufficient load for the oxen to pull on the rude sledge, they loaded it up, and Pehr set out for home, riding atop the load. Anna helped him begin a tightly stacked pile, handling the small end of all but the heaviest lengths. These Pehr laid off by himself, one end at a time.

All but the "riding" plank unloaded, and the oxen stalled, Pehr came in for coffee and cookies. Between sips, he said to Anna:

"My friends are good in the woods. They will take down all the wood we need in a few days. They can chop much faster than I can haul. I figure that three trips a day are all I should require of my oxen, since I have no oats to give them."

"Those boys are certainly good and useful guests," observed Anna. "I feared when they came that we could not remain congenial, spending so much time together in so little space. We will miss them terribly when they go away."

Pehr watered all the cattle and filled their manger with hay. He also fed Krull, who was now tied separately, away from his mother. He carried water from the stove and filled the tub, cleaned the stable and renewed the bedding. Then he went inside for early dinner.

While he ate, Anna packed a hot dinner for the choppers in the woods, using the large wooden pail and a small comforter off the girls' bed.

Pehr swallowed his food quickly, hitched the oxen, and with the dinner pail held on the plank in front of him, returned to the woods.

Meanwhile, Anderson and Johnson had set fire to the trimmings and eaten their lunch beside the fire while Pehr was driving home. When he returned they had two or three loads cut and piled. Pehr set their dinner to one side, and all hands helped load the sledge. Pehr took the lunch kettle with him and drove home again, as his choppers sat down to their hot dinner. He returned in about two hours. They loaded the sledge as before, climbed aboard, and headed for home, taking dinner pail and axes with them. (The axes would be filed and whetted before bedtime.) Pehr halted the sledge alongside the stack already a-building; and, while he watered and tied up the oxen, the younger men unloaded the long lengths of wood.

The house felt wondrously warm and cozy after a day in the woods. The men had suffered no ill, though the day had been biting cold. When Anderson took off his leather vest, it had a thick layer of ice on the inside. He hung it on a peg near the stove, inside out, and left it there until morning.

At the supper table, Johnson said casually: "I almost lost my woods partner today."

"What happened?" asked Anna, sensing near tragedy.

"A big timber wolf stalked Short Nils as he stood chopping. I looked up just as the animal was crouching to spring on his back. I let out a yell that shook the woods, and the hungry animal took off through the woods with great leaps and bounds. I spared you some scratches, Nils, if not your life."

"And I am ever so grateful," said Short Nils, gravely.

"Of course," said Johnson with a twinkle in his eyes, "I may also have spared the wolf some frustration. I doubt he could have chewed a tough Swede."

Everyone laughed, and then resumed eating, except the little girls; they sat silent and frightened, gazing at their dear friend, Short Nils, who might have been lost to a wolf. Only when Anna instructed them did they turn their attention to their plates.

The chopping and hauling routine thus established continued for two weeks. All that was needed had then been laid down, and they chopped no more.

But their hauling was delayed a week by a fierce snowstorm that commenced on the fifteenth and blew a gale of cold and snow for three days. A foot of new snow and a foot and a half of prior accumulation became blown into deep, hard drifts as temperatures dropped to a low of -34° F. During the storm no one ventured forth except on the most urgent of missions. Pehr milked Bos morning and night, each excursion a struggle against the elements. Anderson and Johnson, with heroic effort, uncovered enough hay to keep the livestock fed; and they supplied the animals with water by melting snow on the stove and conveying it to the stable, half a pail at a time.

After the storm had spent its fury, and the land lay calm once more, the men worked two days, with such unhandy tools as they had, to clear away snow from the lee sides of house and stable, to dig a path between the buildings, and to uncover hay and bedding litter.

With his new steel fork, Pehr cleared out of the stable a three-day accumulation of manure.

Merely to render the sledge once again available for use required a considerable excavation. This the bachelors accomplished.

At supper the second day after the storm, Anderson proposed that wood hauling be resumed next day. He broached the subject with his customary exuberance:

"The big, hard drifts lie in the open, and we should be able to drive around them. On the marsh the snow may be deep, but it should also be soft, so that the oxen can wade through it. Once we break road, we should be able to haul a fairly good load. If we wait, a February thaw may ruin the sleighing."

Put in Johnson: "We dare not drive the oxen on top of a hard drift, for fear they might break through and become swamped and tangled up in their gear."

"No!" said Pehr, emphatically, "I will not risk my oxen on a snowdrift; certainly not when they're shod. They could do their feet serious injury. And they will need the shoes later on; I don't want to take them off before the ice is gone next spring."

"Why don't you explore the route tomorrow and determine whether you can safely haul a load over it?" asked sensible Anna.

"You have the right approach," said Pehr. "We'll do just that. If we encounter hazards too great, we can turn about and come home. All the fuel in the woods is not worth crippling one of my oxen!"

They made ready for the woods in the morning. Anna insisted that they take along a hot dinner; and for this they would later be grateful. Anderson secured the large wooden dinner pail with ropes from stake to stake in the front bunk so that it could neither tip over nor slide off. They yoked and hitched the oxen, both filthy with dung clinging to the sides of their thighs. Anderson took the fork and Johnson the spade, and the trio mounted astride the plank on the sledge as before. Pehr refused to carry his wooden scoop. It was too soft for use on the hard drifts. He would merely drive and tend the oxen, and spell the other men when one and the other tired of shoveling.

On the first lee slope in the storm, that just east of the farmstead, they encountered their first large drifts. Partly by Pehr's commands and partly by their own instincts, the oxen nicely avoided those places where they might have walked up and plunged through. Everyone became more confident that they would indeed break track and haul the wood.

But the main test lay between them and the marsh—a mile's length over open rolling prairie—where the windward (west-facing) slopes lay almost stripped of snow and the leeward (east-facing) slopes lay piled under great billowing waves of drift. Some of these billows they were obliged to cross, in which event the vigorous young men simply removed the compacted top layer, some ten inches thick, so that the oxen could wallow through. After one such expedient, the task fell into a system: Johnson, with the spade, loosened large blocks by stabbing around them, and Anderson flung the blocks aside with the fork. The two could open a drift in minutes. After a half dozen stops to trench through drifts, the party looked down upon the marsh by which they gained the logging site. As Pehr approached the deep snow that all but buried all marsh vegetation, Anderson hopped off and waded forward to explore the situation. The snow was as he had surmised, quite soft and fluffy; but it reached well above his knees, in places almost to his hips. From one such depth he called back to Pehr and Johnson on the sledge: "She's soft, as I thought, but awfully deep. Do you think the animals will remain calm and push through, or might they struggle and flounder?"

Pehr called back: "I can talk them through and keep them calm, never fear. These animals have yet to fail me."

And he plunged them in:

"Come, Buck, Bride, easy now, steady."

He talked them on, stopping at short intervals to wind them. They literally dragged the sledge through the snow, leaving a trench behind with its middle moulded by the sledge bunks. They reached the woods without mishap. Johnson cleared the snow off a wood pile and the men sat down to eat. After their tense excitement and vigorous labor in the cold, the bachelors had ravenous appetites; the delicious hot food seemed a virtual transfusion. (Pehr sat wishing he had some hay for his valiant oxen.)

All the good food consumed, they loaded about half an ordinary load on the sledge and hauled it home without untoward incident. Anderson and Johnson cleared away snow so that Pehr could pull the sledge along-side the pole-wood previously stacked.

They made two trips per day for five days following, and all their wood lay stacked as they wished.

Now all the men alternated between bucking the wood to stove length and splitting it to convenient size. Nor were they drudges at their work. They took time to hunt and fish frequently, and the young men walked to Clitherall several times on errands for Anna. All three men went one day, while the hard-drifted snow carried them, and walked over Johnson's claim three miles to the northwest. It looked as good to them as it had the first time they viewed it; and Johnson remained delighted with his choice of land. Even so, before the end of February all the wood lay sawed and split, in a huge, pyramidal pile—forty loads of stove wood for a year's supply. It would, in fact, last through a second summer while next year's cutting lay drying in a similar pile.

Early in March, Anderson and Johnson returned to railroad construction, and the Homestead seemed desolated by their going.

Chapter 8

SPRING IN THE NEW LAND

Pehr and his family had witnessed the passing of winter and the slow approach of spring in Sweden several times; but now they would experience its marvelous arrival and passage in intimate contact with natural phenomena that accompanied the season of rebirth in the pristine environment. They would see marvels wrought in the ecotone between tall prairie grassland and mixed hardwood forest on the northerly mid-continental frontier. They were not mere observers, but participants in a wondrous transformation from winter to summer.

Before the end of February the inch-thick rime frost that had built on the window panes during bitter cold of winter, melted and ran down the walls, soaking into the floor. No longer did Pehr keep a fire blazing in the stove all night, but banked it with ashes instead. No longer must Anna thaw the frozen milk and cream before breakfast.

As the sun swung a progressively higher arc to its mid-day zenith, and daylight lengthened appreciably from one week to the next, the virgin land responded to light and warmth as it had each spring for many thousands of years before.

Thaws of February did less than they promised, each in its turn terminated by a cold spell that solidified the snow-melt. Often in February, and even more often in March, water that ran off during the day became solid and stationary at night, thus going step by step toward its downhill destination. Every thaw soiled the landscape by exposing the dirt that had become mixed with the snow by drifting. The dirty aspect was "white-washed" repeatedly by more or less considerable flurries and heavier falls of new snow.

Sleighing remained good to the end of February, and intermittently during much of March.

A full-fledged snow storm raged during the fourteenth to seventeenth of March (1870); and that storm became notable as the first to be called a "blizzard." The name was given it by the *Esterville (Iowa) Vindicator* on 23 April, (Vol. II, No. 6). (Ludlum: with permission, Author-owner of copyright, opus listed among sources.) "Blizzard" became a definitive term in weather reporting many years later.

With each round of snow and thaw the winter's residue on the ground became thinner and more compact, so that by April only solid ice and water remained, the one melting to form the other. Early in April the ground frost went out, so that the melted water began soaking into the earth instead of running off. Just as the ground thawed out so that water could percolate through it, the innumerable temporary sloughs that had formed in low places disappeared as if by magic, leaving where they had stood a quagmire so deep and sticky that neither man nor beast could cross it. At this stage came a two-inch late April snow that lay only a day, initiating a three-part wonder of nature, visited on the midland prairie border, not every year, but now and then: the quick-change from white one day, dark and drab the second, and beginning hints of green on the third. First to show green was the wild spiny gooseberry in woodland edges, quickly followed by heliophytes on the forest floor and equally sensitive forbs at the base of grassland associations on sites best exposed to the sun.

However erratic the progressive warming of March, it commenced the revival and return of wildlife that would be accomplished during April.

In March came the first harbingers of certain spring, the great V-formed flocks of cackling geese, winging northward to their summer nesting grounds. During some nights the noisy parade far overhead seemed almost continuous.

One moon-lit night, Pehr wakened his family, that they might both hear and see the spectacular migration. Quickly bundled up against the chill wet March air, they stood outside the cabin door and watched the sky, one daughter in the arms of each parent. Pehr pointed, and called, "see that!" as one great flock streamed across the moon. The little girls were mute with wonder, and neither of them spoke before they were back indoors. Then Hanna asked the age-old question:

"How do they know their way on a dark night?"

No one could explain, but Pehr submitted that it was one of Nature's secrets not yet revealed to man. Then he added:

"We shall see and hear new and wonderful things here in America. I wish you to become acquainted with them and appreciate them always. Many will be as strange to me as to you; we shall experience them together."

They returned to their beds and fell asleep to the haunting music that moved in the sky. The elders had seen migrating flocks in Skåne, but not of such great numbers.

As spring progressed they heard, by day, the drumming of ruffed grouse, the booming of prairie chickens on their mating grounds, the quacking of ducks and honking of geese selecting nesting places, and the calls of myriad song birds as they built new nests. At night they heard from the marshes a seemingly endless chorus of frogs, punctuated by the ludicrous pump-like call of the bittern. Crows cawed raucously early and late, as if complaining of late snow that fell after their return. (One flurry came even as May was half-spent.)

With the first blush of spring came also the crawling, blood hungry vampires, the woodticks; and not much later the flying blood-suckers, the voracious mosquitos. The ticks compelled each of the family to search clothing and body every night before bed and squash any of the vermin discovered on a stove lid, using the lid lifter as crusher. The mosquitos kept everyone indoors after dusk unless impelled to exit by the most dire necessity. Spring brought not only verdure and bird song but also certain discomforts. One of the most revolting was the invasion of flies, against which there was little defense without screens on door and windows, no poison sprays, not even a common fly swatter. When one sat to eat, flies accompanied him to the table and crawled about on his food. Soon as it thawed, Pehr spread the manure pile on his fields, thus reducing the fly population.

One day during the protraction of winter, Anna Lien and her fast-growing son, Tollef came for dinner at noon and stayed the afternoon. Mrs. Lien had momentous news: "I've decided to remain single, and keep house for my son until he marries. Were I to marry Mr. Kladsvik, there would probably be more children; and I would cheat Tollef out of part of the inheritance for which his father died. This I cannot countenance. We have a good farm; and my son will soon be able to follow the plow behind a yoke of oxen, and do also the other work required to transform the raw land into productive acreage."

"We are pleased that you will remain our neighbors," interrupted Pehr, "but you are a young handsome woman who ought to have a man."

"Tush, tush," retorted Mrs. Lien, "I've now lived two years without a man in my bed, and the yearning has greatly diminished. I am not being particularly noble!"

Despite the slush under foot during March, Pehr hauled home on the sledge several additional choice logs and stood the six-foot lengths in his stable workshop. The ice on lake and sloughs lay firm and safe until late in the month. He also stacked, carefully on fuel-wood blocks, the logs that Anderson and Johnson had garnered for him from the pole-wood pile. He hauled home several loads of oak logs fourteen feet long, which he would later saw off to seven feet and split into fence posts. He cut and peeled more than five hundred aspen rails twelve feet long, but left them stacked in the aspen thicket, for hauling to the wheat field later on.

March prolonged winter so much that it waxed monotonous and vexing. At times the northwest wind whistled about the corners, almost reminiscent of January. At other times the air stilled and became almost balmy, though remaining cold. About nine inches of snow fell on the fifteenth and sixteenth and sleighing remained fairly good until near the end of the month.

The Mork's broke the monotony of protracted winter with an enjoyable visit late in the month. They came afoot, as Willie had said they would, and they arrived just at dinner time. They were welcomed warmly, with handshakes all round. Then Elna and Hanna were greeted, and they curtsied to each visitor in turn. Instantly taken again with the pretty, bashful little girls, Tilda squatted and hugged them both to her. They would once more be intimate confidential friends before day's end. Obviously, Tilda loved children, and the children responded in kind.

Pehr noted, without comment, that Tilda was now even more radiantly beautiful than when he had admired her before; and he thought that he knew whence the bloom.

After the men had settled their dinner, sitting and talking, they inspected the farmstead and toured the entire claim. Willie complimented Pehr on the sturdily built house and stable. He agreed with Pehr's criteria for choosing land, especially the idea of having both woodland and open prairie, combined. As for Willie, he should like to have had more prairie, fewer steep hills, and less grubbing to do. They returned to the house for afternoon coffee with the women and the girls.

No sooner had they sat to the table, than Anna turned to Pehr and said: "Guess what! Tilda's pregnant. My recipe worked. We'll drink to a son!"

Pehr congratulated the happy couple and wished them good fortune with the prospective heir, whether boy or girl.

Willie beamed and blushed at once, and accelerated the stirring of his coffee.

Before dusk, Pehr went to milk Bos, and Willie accompanied him. They discussed a wide range of subjects—all pertaining to farming, animals, crops, and such. Pehr's milking did not interfere with the conversation.

"Pretty little bull-calf you got there," observed Willie. "Are you going to cut him or keep him for breeding?"

"No! No!" replied Pehr, very positively. "I certainly shall not keep him for breeding. I've had him carry tailor-made yokes in his stall since he was a month old. I've made three or four, to fit him as he grew. Could I get you to cut him for me? You said you did your own pigs."

"I cut pigs when I have to, and I do calves, too," said Willie casually. "How old is he?"

"He's four months. That's old enough isn't it?" asked Pehr.

"That's old enough. Can you turn the other stock out to water while we do the job? If he bellers, his mother could get mighty mad!"

"I've been turning them out on clear days. They can drink from the slough edge now. It's had standing water the last week or two. If you're willing, we'll cut him tomorrow. Do you have your knife with you?"

"Of course! I never go without it; and it's sharp as a razor. I need only strop it a few strokes on my boot-top."

"Let's do this secretly, without mentioning it in the house. My daughters would get upset."

Pehr rose from his task and patted Bos on her flank. He had about twelve quarts in the pail.

"Say," said Willie. "You've got a damn good cow there; and her milk looks rich, too."

"She is a good cow. Anna makes more butter than we can fully use. Can we send some home with you?"

"You bet, you can! Our cow is dry right now, so we're without, temporarily! We'll be very thankful."

"Call it your fee for the castration."

"That's a good deal!"

Pehr filled the manger with hay, latched the door shut, took up the pail, and led the way to the house.

At supper the conversation turned to pigs, oats and chickens. Anna began:

"Tilda says we shall need oats or barley to feed our pigs. She says that Willie will lend you oats for seed and enough besides to keep the pigs until harvest. Don't you agree we ought to borrow rather than deny ourselves a pig or two to butcher next fall?"

"Looks as if we'll HAVE to borrow," replied Pehr. Then of Willie he asked: "You got your sows bred, then?"

"Yes, I hauled them to a boar before Christmas. The pigs are due any day now. If you come and help me in about six weeks, we'll make barrows out of the boars."

"I'll come and help you, and gladly; but I can't buy the pigs except on time. My last money went for flour and ox shoes in Alexandria."

"Your credit is good with me, Pehr, for both pigs and oats."

"It'll have to be both or nothing. Don't know what I was thinking about when I spoke for three pigs, with nothing to feed them."

"Oh, I thought about that at the time," said Willie. "You could have fed them a few boiled potatoes once a day, and let them root in the prairie for the rest. Next fall they would have fattened fairly well on acorns. But it will be better to pen them up and feed them, mainly on grain. You ought to sow about five acres of oats. I broadcast one and one-half bushels to the acre; so for five acres you'll need seven and one-half bushels of seed. Ten bushels should be enough to carry the pigs if you'll boil some potatoes with the oats and cut some weeds for them now and again. You could herd them or stake them out on pasture, too. Oats sold for a dollar a bushel two years ago, but I doubt they're worth much more than half that now. I really don't know. Why don't I just lend you your seed and pig feed now and get back the same quantity after you harvest. You should get at least thirty bushels to the acre."

"I would deem that a big favor. Then I'd owe you only three dollars for the pigs. I should have a wheat crop worth almost forty times that much."

"Why don't you drive us home tomorrow, and haul your oats back? It'll soon be time for sowing it."

"Alright," answered Pehr, "if you must go home so soon. We were wishing you'd stay another day."

"No! we must get back tomorrow. A neighbor is feeding the stock, but I'd like to be there when the sows farrow. Sometimes they have trouble."

"I can appreciate your concern. I'll drive you home, but you'll have to let me sleep over."

"That will be fine," Tilda chimed in, "it was a long walk, so I'll be grateful for the ride."

Immediately after breakfast, Pehr took the milk pail and both men went to the stable. Pehr milked Bos as usual, and then turned cow and oxen out. They sauntered off in direction of the slough. Pehr grabbed a goodly length of quarter-inch rope from one of the wall pegs and commenced tying up Krull.

"Do you want him down or standing up?" he asked.

"He's so little, I believe we can best do it holding him on his back. Tie his legs securely, then sort of sit on his head so he can't beller much, and hold his hind legs forward."

Pehr threw the calf on his back as gently as he could and sat down astride him, holding his hind legs. His knife stropped and ready, Willie set to work. A few deft strokes and pulls for each, and the testicles lay on the litter. Willie wiped and folded his knife and returned it to his pocket. Krull's subdued bawls were not heard by his mother. Pehr quickly untied him; he stood up and stamped his hind feet as if flies were biting him. Pehr gave him water at the tub and then tied him in his place. Willie threw the testicles onto the manure pile. The cow and oxen remained in the woods, by the slough. Pehr carried the milk to the house and Willie walked beside him.

"That calf should make a good work ox," offered Willie.

"I hope so," said Pehr, "a spare is good to have in case one of the others gets injured or falls ill."

All had forenoon coffee together, a little early, after which the trio rode off behind the oxen. In the front of the wagon they carried a wooden pail containing a noon-day lunch that Anna had provided. Also in the pail were about two pounds of fresh-churned butter.

Pehr used the wagon for the first time that spring; large bare spots now rendered sleighing very poor. He greased the wagon before departure.

They arrived at the Mork's well before dark, as they had planned. Tilda took the lunch pail into the house; Pehr and Willie stabled the oxen and went to the pig-pen. One sow had farrowed a litter of little speckled pigs and lay suckling them under the straw-built shelter. The other sow, the prospective mother, was rooting the litter about, as if preparing for "lying in."

Willie climbed over the fence and walked over to count the little pigs. The mother (they were both tame as pets) paid him no heed, but remained quiet, proud of her exhibit. He called to Pehr:

"She has seven, and not a runt among them. Looks as if you'll have your pigs!"

The men went into the house and told Tilda the news.

"Seven is quite a litter," she said. "We'll have to cook her a mash of bran or shorts and potatoes so she will have enough milk. When the cow comes in there'll be plenty."

"Yes! You'll have many to cook for now," joked Willie. "That should make you happy."

"I'm happy NOW! I'm almost always happy! Let's say I'll be even happier."

The men exchanged quick glances, and smiled at the handsome, forthright young woman.

Tilda put a shawl over her head and went out to see the little pigs.

"We can do the castrating about mid-May," said Willie to Pehr. "We'll do the job any day convenient for you. Come and stay the night with us. You can pick the pigs you want and we'll bring them to you when they're weaned—before June, maybe. We'll do the traveling that trip."

Tilda returned and removed her shawl. She asked, of no one in particular: "Aren't those little spotted pigs the cutest things?"

No one made reply; silence meant agreement.

"Say," said Pehr suddenly, "you'll have to trust me for the sacks in which to haul the oats. It will take seven for seventeen and one half bushels."

"I'll sell you the sacks or lend them to you, as you wish. Don't fret yourself! Perhaps I could trade the sacks for a long-handled grain scoop, such as I saw in your stable?"

"That you can! And I'll make you one of better-seasoned wood. I'll bring it when I come in May. Did you see anything else you'd like to have?"

"Damn right, I did. I'd give quite a little for a harrow such as I saw in your shop. I dragged two logs over my fields last year, but a drag is no good."

"Would you give three weaned pigs; a gilt and two barrows?"

"I sure as hell would! But, can't I get it before mid-May? I want it for my spring's field work."

"Field work is virtually on us, but you come after two days; I'll either have a harrow made for you or I'll give you mine and make another for myself. The bolts in the harrow cost me about a dollar, and I believe I have enough for another one. There were really no other expenses; just my time. You may be paying too dearly."

"Let me be the judge of that! I'll come for a harrow and be mighty glad to get it. You'll be squared off for everything; and I'll get the big end of the whole deal."

"So be it!" said Pehr, with rare enthusiasm. They shook hands!!

Before Pehr departed next morning, Willie filled the wagon box with hay, and on this they laid the oat sacks. There would be enough to cushion them even after the oxen had been fed at noon. Just as Pehr set foot on the hub to climb up, Tilda handed him the lunch pail, apparently full as before. Pehr learned at noon that it contained more good food than one man could possibly eat at one sitting. What he had to leave, he put back in the pail and took with him home. As he ate, he observed the oxen, debating between the short, new grass sprouts and the dry hay. He would pasture them as soon as he got his grain sown. They could do more work on hay than on tender juicy grasses; but they might reject the hay after a taste of green forage, and thus resolve the issue themselves—which, in fact, they did. Soon as Pehr arrived home he relieved the oxen of their shoes and hung them in the shop by a string. He wondered whether he was man enough to nail them back on when it became necessary.

Pehr made quick work of carving a scoop and building a harrow for Willie, using as patterns those he had made before. April days were now so balmy that the stable door stood open admitting light adequate to work by. In a day and a half of busy splitting, sawing, hewing, planing, bolting, and carving, both items were completed. He drove the oak pegs that would serve as teeth into both his harrow and Willie's, and sawed them off level. (Each implement had thirty.) He shaped two dozen spares for Willie and a few for himself.

Next day Willie came for his implements before noon. He joined the family for dinner, and ate so fast that he was obviously in a hurry. Before he sat to table he thanked Anna for the delicious butter she had sent. At table he reported to Pehr that his second sow had farrowed five good-looking pigs. Then, by way of apology for hurrying, he asserted that the weather holding fair, his new harrow would be put to use tomorrow. He wished to return home and be ready to go to work in the field.

After dinner, Pehr helped him load the new harrow onto the wagon, and stuck the scoop under the seat. As they shook hands in farewell, Willie thanked again for the scoop, the harrow and the extra pins. Then he was off and away.

Neither Willie nor anyone else in the area commenced spring's work next day. A good soaking rain intervened, keeping the eager farmers off the fields three days longer. That the day-long drizzle could be dried off by two sunny, breezy days was reassuring; the sowing time had arrived. Even the sod roof on Pehr's cabin had now grown green.

Pehr first tried out his new harrow on his wheat field. It loosened and smoothed the soil beautifully, and, but for the frequent breakage of pins on stones, was a splendid implement. Pehr reflected proudly that Willie must be pleased with his. By noon-time, he had harrowed the five-acre wheat field, first one way and then the other, so that it lay well pulverized, as a seed bed should be. He leaned the harrow against a tree at the edge of the grove, drove the oxen to water, yoked together, stabled them, and fed them hay.

After dinner he borrowed from Anna a large cooking kettle and a length of stout cord. The cord he stuck through the pot handle and tied into a loop large enough to go over his head. With the cord on his right shoulder and the kettle on his left hip, he could tilt the mouth forward for ready access with his right hand. By deft grabbing of handfuls and by releasing the seed as he swung his arm to right and to left he could broadcast a wide swath as he walked. Sowing grain by hand was a skill he had learned well; he got a remarkably uniform distribution.

His equipment ready, he loaded the seed-wheat in the wagon and drove to the field with his oxen. He unhitched the beasts from the wagon, but left the yoke on their necks. Thus restrained, they grazed the prairie without straying far from the field. Pehr kept an eye on them as he walked back and forth sowing the field. He reserved a two-rod strip across the north end for planting to potatoes. The remainder he had sowed before afternoon coffee time, including several passes made diagonally to expend all the wheat. He called the oxen, hitched them to the wagon and drove to the house. He tied Bride's rope to a tree and left the animals standing thus, while he enjoyed his lunch indoors. Then he unhitched them from the wagon and walked them back to the field. He "after-harrowed" the wheat only the short way of the field (east-west), and had the job done in a little while. He up-ended the harrow where it had stood before, drove the oxen home, unyoked them by the wagon, and laid the yoke in the wagon box. He turned the animals loose and made for the house, calling as he entered:

"Anna, can you help me cut potatoes now, for planting tomorrow? The pieces should dry before being put in the ground. I haven't an 1870 almanac, but I believe the moon is right."

"Of course I'll help you, but let's cut them outdoors in the sun."

She took up her paring knife. Pehr lifted down the tub from its wall-peg outside the door and set it on the ground. (Into this they would pitch the cuttings.) Then he took into the cellar the kettle from which he had sown the wheat, and quickly emerged with it full of Clitherall potatoes, some of them already sprouted. They cut these, and two more kettle-fulls, before they adjudged their cuttings to be enough. Then Pehr said to Anna:

"All we've cut so far came from Clitherall. They were mature when dug. Now I shall take up half a kettle of our own, that were planted late and dug after the first frost. We'll plant the last, the innermost row, of these, just to see how well they do. They have kept as well as the others, and I suspect they will grow and produce as well too."

They kept these cuttings separate from the others and placed them in the kettle after they had emptied it of whole potatoes. Pehr closed his jack-knife and pocketed it.

"Remember I promised you a sufficiency of potatoes; we have an abundance! We have more than enough for ourselves AND the pigs until we take up another crop."

First thing next morning, Pehr and Anna planted the half acre potato patch in the field, and had enough cuttings left over to plant a row across the garden. Pehr plowed and harrowed the garden; then they planted two rows of Clitherall potatoes, of which they would dig and eat, day to day, from early July until the main crop was ready. All this was done before mid-afternoon; so after he had his lunch and coffee, Pehr walked to Clitherall to collect the seeds promised him by Albertson. True to his word, Albertson had virtually every variety of garden seed that would grow and yield in west central Minnesota. How many Clitherall residents had contributed, Pehr never learned.

Pehr sorted out such varieties and such quantities as he would surely use; then asked Albertson:

"How can I ever adequately repay all you good people? I haven't any money!"

"We wouldn't accept money if you had it," replied Albertson. "We wish you to be our friends. Come and trade in our village as you bring your farm into production. That will be our repayment."

"Of that you may be assured," said Pehr. "Perhaps I can DEMONSTRATE my profound gratitude."

He shook Albertson's hand and headed for home.

He took only a few strides, and then abruptly turned about and walked back to Albertson, who remained standing where they had shaken hands.

"I have an important question to ask you, and I almost forgot it: does anyone here in Clitherall have a bull that might service my cow? I should like to breed her during her next heat."

"Yes, sir, there's a bull here, and a fine looking animal he is. It belongs to Whiting. He has a farm some miles east of mine, but you can easily find it. I suggest you just lead your cow over there the next time she's in. I'll tell him you're coming. He won't charge anything."

"That's fine! And thanks for clearing the way for me. Could it be that one of the Clitherall farmers even has a boar pig? I have a gilt I'd like to breed in December or January."

"You're in luck there too, Pehrson. Murdock at Clitherall has a boar. Why don't you go by his place and inquire? I'll go with you; it's not far. I don't know whether he'll want you to come for the boar or leave your sow in his pen for a time. Pigs are slow to mate, as you probably know. The conversation could get complicated, so I'll come along and see that you and Murdock understand each other."

Albertson opened his house door a crack and called in: "I'm going with Pehrson to Murdock's place. I'll be back within the hour."

The men set out and were soon at Murdock's. Albertson introduced Pehr and explained his need. Murdock made reply and Albertson translated for Pehr:

"He says you can come and get the boar anytime after mid-December. He'll have his sows bred before then. You may keep the boar as long as you wish; his feed will be sufficient pay for his services."

Pehr thanked and shook hands with both men. Then he and Albertson struck out in direction of their respective homes.

When he approached his cabin, Pehr saw someone emerge from the woods and come toward him. Before he could well recognize him, at long range, as it were, Nils Anderson commenced waving his arms and calling to him:

"Hallo, Pehr, my good friend and future neighbor. I jumped the claim west of yours."

Now they had met and were shaking hands, one as vigorously as the other.

"You look well, Nils, and I am ever so glad to see you. Can you bide with us awhile?"

"No, I shan't stay more than overnight. I came to bring you something that you may find useful; and you can help me at the same time."

Now they were in the clearing, and Pehr saw, tied to a tree, a beautiful yoke of roan oxen, large as his own.

"So, you will commence breaking sod right away, Nils? We shall be delighted to have you as our nearest neighbor."

"No, Pehr, I need a little more cash before I can settle on the claim. That yoke of oxen, wagon, and plow there cost me a pretty penny, as you well know they might. I didn't win them playing poker. I want you to work the oxen while I return to railroad work and get some money back in my pocket."

They entered the cabin. Nils and Anna shook hands and exchanged affectionate greetings. Nils was full of life and fun, and Anna enjoyed having him with them.

"Nils hasn't come to stay, Anna. He came to lend me a yoke of fine oxen for the summer while he earns a wage on the railroad," explained Pehr.

"I saw the animals, dear. Aren't they a beautiful pair?"

"That they are," answered Pehr. "And I shall make good use of them. Tell me more about your proposition," he requested of Nils.

"Well!, the whole thing is this. Löf lost it to me because he made no improvement within the specified period. If you will plow for me two or three acres and sow them to wheat, I shall have met my obligation, so that no one can, in turn, take it away from me. Are you willing?"

"Of course, I'm willing," replied Pehr, "but what will I use for seed? I just sowed all my wheat in my own ground."

"Oh! I have two sacks of wheat in the wagon. That will sow more area than absolutely necessary for me to show my good intent and some improvement on the land."

"Then it's all settled, said Pehr, "I'll break enough ground for you to use up your wheat sown ordinarily thick. And then I'll break ground for my oats. Where do you wish your first wheat field to be?"

"Why don't you put it on the low flat just over the section line from your fields? That would be handy for everything; and the low prairie should be productive. Break a compact rectangle, if you please; not a long narrow strip."

"You shall have it as you wish, Nils. With two yoke of oxen on a breaking plow, I'll wager I shall turn two acres in a day. I'll do your wheat first, and then my own five acres for oats. Will you come for your oxen next fall before they must be stabled? My stable is rather small for another pair of animals, unless I surrender my workshop?"

"I'll take them off your hands before heavy weather sets in. But perhaps you would be kind enough to put up some hay for them? If you'll help me, we can quickly lay up a stable. I'll show you tomorrow before I leave about where my farmstead will be. The hay should be stacked nearby the stable site. Incidentally, I want you to use my plow as if it were your own. Your's may get dull."

"I have good news for you on that score! At Clitherall, north of the lake only about four American miles from here, is a blacksmith who can sharpen plowshares. I shall wear your plow in your ground only; and I'll grease it after I've done with it."

"Are you going to batch it over there?" asked Anna, with a woman's typical concern.

"My mother will come to stay with me whenever I get a house built. Until then, I beg to stay here as I did before, if you will accept a daily fee for board and room."

"Silly! did you ever hear of room rent on a stable? We'll accept, as before, twenty-five cents a day for board at our table. My cooking will improve as we become able to afford more and better provisions."

"Anna, you've never cooked a poor meal that I know of; and twenty-five cents a day seems to me too little pay for good food. But, so be it! I shall probably find opportunity to compensate you and Pehr in ways other than by cash payment. We may, I hope, be neighbors a long time."

"Before we have supper," said Pehr, "let's carry your seed-wheat inside, in case it should rain."

They brought in the wheat sacks.

Pehr offered this further suggestion: "Suppose we turn my oxen out, and tie your's in the vacated stalls. Before they get settled in a new place, they might stray far away and get lost. Mine never wander far. After they have all worked together a few days, they will probably stay together. Nils, you take yours to water, and I'll turn mine out." This they did before supper.

The girls enjoyed Nils, at table and afterwards, until their bedtime. (Throughout their lives they associated this kindly understanding young man with their first Christmas in America.)

The little girls asleep and the quiet conversation commencing to lag, Nils bade his staunch friends "goodnight" and made his way to his bedding place in the stable.

Next morning, Anna and the girls accompanied Nils and Pehr in their inspection of Nils' chosen building site amid a grove of giant white oaks. All agreed that the place was well chosen. Nils indicated where Pehr might stack the hay, but left the selection of mowing area entirely to Pehr's good judgment.

After forenoon coffee, Nils prepared to depart, but interrupted his bundling and tying to instruct Pehr: "My near ox is Jack, the far one Jim. Those are devilish names for a Swede to pronounce. You'll have to practice sounding the "j," else the animals won't understand. If you sound it soft, as a "g" in certain Swedish words, you'll confuse them. They will obey well when they know you're talking to them."

"I'll practice, replied Pehr, with a grin. "We'll get on alright, never fear."

The girls first, then Anna and Pehr shook Nils' hand in farewell; and he struck out, to resume his railway labors.

April showers postponed Anna's early gardening two days, Pehr's prairie breaking only one. For his oats he stepped off an estimated five-acre rectangle adjoining his wheat field on the west side. Since his upland flat dried more quickly than the lowland Nils had chosen for his wheat, Pehr broke his own field first, with his own plow, with both yoke of oxen hitched in tandem. The four large, well-trained animals drew the plow with such ease that Pehr found himself stopping only now and then, more for his own resting than to wind the oxen. Despite the numerous loose stones that slowed him somewhat, he turned the oat field in only two, long and strenuous, days. Nils' wheat ground took a bit less time because it was of black mellow alluvium, free of stones and rich in humus. This he broke with Anderson's plow, which turned a furrow quite as well as his own. He double-harrowed both fields in half a day, using only Buck and Bride. A good rain delayed his sowing two days; but then, in one day, he sowed both new-broken fields and harrowed them "after," using Jack and Jim. His spring's field work was accomplished and April was little more than half gone.

The remainder of April he devoted to the very considerable enlargement of his fence-post and rail piles, so that he should have enough materials to protect wheat, oats and potatoes within an enclosure. He took one half-day late in the month to lead Bos to Clitherall for service by Whiting's bull. After three quick mountings, minutes apart, he thanked by handshake and led Bos away. Whiting tied the bull to a tree, lest he follow.

May came in rainy, and Pehr spent much of the first week in his workshop at various and sundry projects. He made three ladder-back chairs for the house, the seats and flats of the ladder basswood, the other parts oak. He commenced work on a wooden butchering bench of oak, all parts carefully mortised together—five feet long and two and a half feet wide, with curved cross members so that it swagged down the middle enough to keep a dead animal from rolling off. This he had half done when he volunteered one sunny day to help Anna put in her late garden.

The third sunny, balmy day after the soaking May rain moved Anna to escort her daughters onto the very crest of Discovery Hill, there to admire the beautiful prairie view to the northwest. The girls, little awed by the view, were more taken by short-stemmed and cup-shaped, velvety lavender blooms and tiny yellow buttercups that grew strewn all about on the open hill. Each gathered a fist-full and presented it proudly to her mother. Anna declined, saying, "you carry them home, and we'll set them in water."

(The pretty lavender-purple blooms were "Pasque" or "May" flowers (Anemone ludoviciana), destined to become the State Flower of South Dakota. Gathering of May flowers and buttercups on Discovery (later called May Flower) Hill became a tradition that endured through three generations of children on the Homestead. Mamma's first bouquet in spring was invariably May flowers and buttercups from the hill. Only pussy-willows came earlier.)

As Anna and the girls started homeward, down the hill, Elna suddenly threw her flowers as far as she could and brushed her hands off against her skirt.

Anna, startled, asked: "Why did you do that, dear?"

"They have lice in them," was Elna's quick retort. "They crawled out on my hand. I don't want lice like Hanna got on the train!"

Anna gathered up the scattered flowers, shook them vigorously, and returned them to Elna. Then she did Hanna's the same way.

"Now," she said, "if you see more lice crawl out, blow them off. They will not stay on you, in any case! These are plant lice, and they can't live on people. They continued toward the cabin happily. On the little knoll below the hill they flushed a prairie chicken from her nest, and all squatted down to examine the little brown-flecked, olive colored eggs. Elna counted aloud—"six."

"Mustn't touch," said Anna sharply.

After a few moments of viewing, they arose, proud of their discovery, and went on. Elna thought secretly that she might visit the nest again to see how matters progressed. May in America was a beautiful happy time!

Soon came the fifteenth, and Pehr walked to Mork's to help castrate pigs. He found the Mork's busy planting garden, a garden even bigger than Anna's. He hailed them as he approached and they threw down their tools and seed to greet him. Willie grabbed his right hand with both of his and shook it as he exclaimed: "That harrow you made for me is the best implement I have. I thanked you, mentally, a hundred times, as I used it. I used up all the spare pins, though."

"You shall have an ample supply when you deliver my pigs," said Pehr, and turned to Tilda. She shook his hand more gently than Willie, but smiled her delightful smile. He noted that her "condition" was now becoming obvious.

Next morning the men repaired to the pig pen, prepared for surgery. Willie carried hot water in the tea kettle and a clean towel so that he could rinse and wipe his knife between patients.

Said Willie: "Better I should catch them and bring them to the fence for you. The sows know me. You they might get after when the little ones squeal. A sow can be vicious."

He climbed into the pen and quickly picked up a little boar pig by a hind leg. He handed him to Pehr over the fence. Pehr got him by both hind legs, one in each hand, the pig held so that he hung belly toward the captor. As in one motion, Pehr swung the little fellow between his legs and came to a kneeling position astride him. Thus sat upon, the front end of the animal was quite subdued, and the rear end so firmly held that there was little danger that the patient might kick the knife and injure the surgeon. In about as much time as it takes to tell, Willie removed the little testicles and threw them aside (outside the pen). Pehr rose and lowered the squealing little barrow to the ground, inside the fence.

Proceeding thus, one pig after another, they converted seven boars to barrows before they were through. Fortunately, none had a hernia, so they were spared the delicate task of sewing up with needle and thread, first the sheathe and then the skin, on such a one. For this Willie was glad; castration of a ruptured pig entailed considerable risk. As Willie worked on the last victim, Pehr asked about the peculiar coloration of the little ones:

"What sort of race or breed are these little spotted fellows, anyway?"

"Oh, they're not one breed; they're a double-cross of black Poland China, Chester White, and Duroc Jersey (red). They might be called scrubs; but they combine the lard features of Poland Chinas with the meat and bacon features of the others. I believe you will like them. Now, since you refused to make the selection, I'll pick three good-looking animals for you, one gilt and two barrows, and bring them to you in about ten days. You'll need a little pen and shelter for them if they are to thrive. A little straw shed such as mine is adequate year round."

Willie rinsed and wiped his "scalpel" a final time and washed a little blood from his hands; then they went into the house, where both washed with soap and hot water before sitting down to an early forenoon lunch. Identifying and catching the little animals in a crowd of a dozen had taken an hour, the actual surgery considerably less.

"If I start now and really make tracks, I can be home for a late dinner," said Pehr, rising from the table. "Again I say, 'good luck with the son,' and now I'll be on my way."

They shook hands as usual, and exchanged expressions of gratitude; then Pehr stepped out the door and struck out for home. He halted a short ways off, and called to Willie: "We'll expect you on the twenty-fifth."

Willie called back: "We'll be there!" and waved as vigorously as he called.

Pehr happily rejoined his family, kissing and hugging wife and daughters.

At dinner he asked Anna: "where do you suggest I build a pen and shelter for the pigs? We want them some distance from the house, and down-wind!"

Said Anna in reply: "It seems to me, though the cold blasts may have warped my judgment, that most of our wind comes from the west or northwest. If that be true, the pig-pen should be on the hillside to the southeast. Does that seem right?"

"I believe you're right as rain, and that's where I'll put it! I'll do that piece of work tomorrow; at least I'll begin it.

But first a one-inch snow, and then showers threw Pehr off his pace. May thunderstorms waxed violent, and more than once roused the family from their sleep in the midst of night, to stand before the window and watch the storm expend its violence. Nor did all the violence come at night; more than once Pehr was drenched by a veritable cloudburst as he dashed home from his aspen grove.

To build a pig pen he cut several hundred big-leaf aspen stakes, each about four feet long, and no more than five inches in diameter at the large end. These he sharpened and drove into the ground about four inches apart, closing in an area about a hundred feet square. In the corner nearest the house he placed a feeding trough—a hollowed-out basswood length; and immediately adjacent to it, toward the east, he constructed a framework of rails about four feet off the ground, which he would later cover with hay, leaving only the south side open. The pen contained numerous trees, so the pigs would have shade in which to take refuge during hot summer days. The project took him a week's time of diligent labor.

Days before the Morks delivered the lively little pigs on the twenty-fifth, Pehr had the sty in readiness, lacking only the hay or straw over and about the rail frame, for the shelter. When they arrived, Tilda immediately joined Anna in the house; Pehr and Willie carried to the new pen the gunny sack containing the three pigs; and there they untied the sack and released the animals.

"Say, those are fine little pigs," said Pehr. "They've made good growth even since I last saw them, only ten days ago. I believe you brought me the best of both litters. That you needn't have done Willie!"

"I did a little picking for you well enough, Pehr; but I doubt that I got the best. There's really little difference among them. I might almost as well have taken them at random."

"In any case, I am ever so grateful to you. I have thought ever since first meeting you that I had found the sort of man I would prize as a friend. I'm convinced you are that, Willie."

"I can honestly return the compliment, Pehr. We think alike on many things. Neither you nor I would intentionally cheat any man, nor take advantage of him if we might. Neither of us could live that way."

But for the grunting of the pigs as they explored their new environs, there was momentary silence. Then Pehr inquired:

"Did all the barrows survive their castration?"

"Goodness, yes. They were completely healed days ago. I rarely lose one. By the way, I took these from their mothers only three days ago, so they are barely weaned. For a few days, at least, I would feed them warm oats and potato mash."

"I'll cook a kettle of it after we eat our dinner," asserted Anna. The women and the girls had joined the men; Anna must see the new livestock. She admired the grunting, rooting little pigs. The girls "oh'd" and "ah'd" and pointed.

Ordered Anna: "Come in and wash up for dinner!"

As all walked toward the house, Willie suggested that Pehr might wish to ring the pigs in their noses to discourage them from rooting. Otherwise they would injure the trees that shaded them, and the very trees that, would, in season, supplement their ration with mast. But Pehr, in this case, rejected Willie's well-intended suggestion:

"Pigs are born to root, and I would not deny them their natural inclination. I believe they thrive better when they can root in the earth. I shall, however, stake down their troughs so that they cannot be overturned. I have yet to hollow out a separate large trough for water."

After dinner, Pehr got about a dozen potatoes from the cellar. Anna scrubbed them clean and put them into her black kettle. Pehr poured in two quarts of oats and placed the mixture over an open eye on the stove. Soon the kettle boiled and bubbled, saturating the air with a pungent odor. After half an hour, Anna set it off to cool; and soon as she could comfortably do so, she mashed the oats and potatoes together. Directly, Pehr took up the warm kettle of mash and invited the girls to help him feed the pigs. They accepted enthusiastically, and accompanied him.

When the little pigs smelled the warm mash, they came running and squealing, and were gulping the feed before Pehr could empty all of it into the trough.

"They eat like pigs, don't they?" said little Hanna.

"They ARE pigs, that's why," asserted Elna.

Then she inquired of Pehr: "Papa, won't they eat themselves sick on all that mash?"

"No," replied Pehr, "the hog is one farm animal that never eats itself to death. Swine are really less "hoggish" than cattle and horses."

"What's the difference between a pig and a hog?" asked Hanna.

"That's easy to answer! A hog is just a grown up pig; and they are all swine. Do you understand that?"

"I guess so," replied Hanna, hesitantly.

Pehr was about to suggest that the girls name the little pigs, but thought better of it and remained silent. Butchering time might be sad enough without personalizing the casualties!

Elna did, indeed, establish a certain rapport with the pigs, and called them by name, secretly. While they were little, she often sat down and played with them in an unsoiled place in the pen. They grunted their gratitude when she stroked and scratched their backs. She soon discovered which succulent weeds they most preferred; and these she often fed them—cut with her mother's bread knife. They came to her whenever she called them. She carried water to their trough when she saw it empty—unless she forgot. When they were half-grown, and became hogs, she rode on their backs. By autumn, when they were quite grown, her interest dwindled; but she remained Pehr's most devoted helper with the gathering of acorns for them. In all this swine-herd business, Hanna remained a detached observer rather than an active participant. Never would she venture into the pig-pen.

The Morks returned home next day; their cow had freshened, and Tilda would be busy with butter and cheese making. She had intimated to Anna that the heir ought to arrive sometime early in August. Anna had insisted that she would come and stay a few days, whenever the eventuality—midwife or no midwife. She would cook and keep house for Willie!

"Pehr and the girls can readily do for themselves a few days; so please do not argue. I'll be there!"

Tilda could do aught but acquiesce. In truth, she was tremendously relieved and grateful.

Chapter 9

FIRST SUMMER AND FIRST HARVEST

When June arrived and summer had come on in earnest, Pehr was completing the preparation of fencing materials. Splitting and hewing fence posts in the summer heat was sweaty work, and he was obliged to stop frequently and wipe his face with the large red calico handkerchief so that sweat might not get into his eyes. Often, as he wiped, he thought that he was doing winter work in summer. But the winter had been devoted to other tasks of equal urgency. And the fencing must now be done to protect his growing crops. Animals, both tame and wild, roamed at large; and he dared not risk their potential damage to his fields. He must work hard as he could, despite summer heat and humidity.

Even while he was preparing and sowing his fields he had, by pacing and estimating, determined what he would need to enclose them adequately. Accordingly, he had laid up a thousand stout twelve foot aspen rails and split out three hundred and fifty oak posts—each about seven feet long, three inches thick and eight inches wide at the top. Now, in the heat, he chopped and gouged through each post three oblong holes, each to receive the ends of two rails, one overlapping the other. Thus, each hole must be about two inches wide and at least six inches long (vertically). The holes must be so spaced that when the posts were set two feet into the ground the rails between them would be approximately one foot, two and one-half feet, and four feet, respectively, off the ground. He would build what was commonly known as a "post-and-rail" fence; but its building demanded uncommon application of muscles and simple tools. He would set it two rods out from the plowing on all sides to ensure himself turning space, even with two yoke of oxen in tandem. He had forgotten to allow for turning ends when he calculated posts and rails, so he should have to get a few additional of each.

Also in early June the dreaded potato bugs appeared; and Anna, forewarned by the storekeeper's wife in Litchfield, spotted the black-and-white striped beetles almost at once. The so-called Colorado potato beetles laid large clusters of yellow eggs on the underside of leaves, and these eggs hatched in about a week. Then the ugly, voracious, orange-red larvae set about devouring the foliage, commencing with the heart leaves at the top. Left to feed undisturbed, the larvae would, in a few day's time, strip all the leaves from the plants, and leave standing mere skeletons.

This Anna would prevent, if humanly possible. She equipped the girls and herself with each a small baking pan and a flat stick. They walked every row, daily for several days, beating the larvae off the potato vines into the pans and dumping the crawling vermin into the stove. (Sizzling of the larvae as they fried in the fire gratified the captors.)

Mother and daughters fought three broods of bugs that summer and saved the potatoes. Pehr was proud of their alertness and diligence, and grateful for a good potato crop.

When he had the requisite number of posts ready, he pulled them out on the sledge bunks to spare himself lifting them onto and off the high wagon. The ground was soft, and did no damage to the sledge. He made seven trips, so that the oxen, soft from loafing, need not overly exert themselves. He laid the posts all round the lush green fields, spacing them about eight feet apart. On the last trip he carried with him his spade and a four-foot tamping stick of oak, peeled and smoothed to a diameter of about two inches, tapered to a three-quarters inch thickness at one end and cut off squarely. With this he would pack the earth about each post after it was set into a two-foot hole. He set free the oxen to graze, leaving the sledge standing on the prairie.

Since his spade was six inches wide and only a foot long, he was obliged to dig holes larger than necessary to receive the posts; otherwise he could not remove the earth from the bottom and get the hole deep enough. He was, indeed, obliged to reach an arm down, and remove with his hand the dirt loosened in the bottom. When he had a post-hole begun—deep as he could step the spade in—he completed it from a kneeling position, the more easily and accurately to stab the spade in, and then lever it against the side of the hole to pull out the loosened material. Almost often as not, he struck a stone or two as he dug; these he loosened with the spade, then reached down and got them out with his hands. Digging a single hole took ten to twenty minutes. In some he struck boulders too large to remove, in which case he shifted the hole this way or that, but on the line. With twelve-foot rails and the posts regularly set ten feet apart, he had about a foot and a half leeway for stones.

He set and tamped in the corner posts first, two to a corner, each to receive rails from one direction. The corner posts afforded sighting points by which all sides could be built in straight lines.

At this juncture he called up the oxen and fetched from the poplar grove enough rails for one side of the enclosure. These he laid down outside the posts. He would build one side at a time, alternately setting a post and fitting in rails, thus varying the work enough to rest those muscles most severely taxed. (Digging post-holes with a spade can literally paralyze one's arms.) Now he needed his axe to taper the rail ends enough for fitting into the posts and giving one end enough slipping length to clear the post next in line. Thus a rail was pushed back through one post, then pulled forward and inserted into another. Pehr walked to the house and asked Anna to fix afternoon coffee a bit early to save him the time of another trip. He then went to his stable workshop and got his axe. During coffee he apprised Anna of his progress.

Pehr worked after supper until dark. Days were now near maximum length, and he wasted no daylight. Before darkness compelled him to quit, he had completed half a short side, the east. Next day he completed that side, and began on the south. There, in the southeast corner, he fitted the first series of rails so loosely that they could be shoved clear through the corner post, thus leaving an eight-foot gap for entry and exit.

Though several thunderstorms interrupted the work and drove Pehr to the house for shelter, he completed the enclosure in little more than two weeks of persistent application from dawn to dark. When he had stuck the last rail into place, he stood several minutes and admired the apparent durability of his handiwork. Then he cleaned the spade carefully, laid axe and spade on his left shoulder, picked up the tamper, and walked home. He deposited the tools in his shop, then invited his wife and daughters to come with him and see his first American fencing. No sooner had they reached the fields, than the girls commenced climbing on the sturdy new fence. Anna stood awed, quite aware of the stupendous exertion it represented. Then she said:

"My, what a tremendous lot of work! There's as much material in this as in our house. I hope you won't wear yourself out before you can prove up the homestead."

Then, glancing toward Anderson's green patch of wheat, she asked:

"Will Short Nils come and enclose his field, or help you with it?"

"I don't know. He made no mention of fencing. If he comes, I will help him. Meanwhile, I must mow wild hay, for him and me, before the prairie grasses become too ripe. The grass I mowed for hay last summer had stood too long. The prairie is prime for hay right now. See how it waves there on the hill?"

"Well, then the girls and I will take turns watching over it from a distance during the day-time; though I suppose that marauding animals come more often by night than by day."

"You do that. And if you detect any serious damage, I shall just have to put a rail around it. We shall see!"

On Sunday (mid-June) Pehr invited his family to another exploration of the homestead. They went in the morning, carrying with them a light picnic lunch. Pehr carried his musket, but for what purposes no one knew; he would kill no wild creature while it was rearing a family nor before it was full-grown. They walked over the prairie forties first, flushing several prairie chickens away from their broods. They found several large animal skulls bleached white by the sun, some with horns attached. Pehr identified them for the girls as best he could. Skulls of bison, elk, deer, and moose lay where the animals had fallen, probably killed by hunters—Indian, white, or wolf. Each slough—one on the west forty and two on the north—had a family of mallards. When the exploring party neared home, a meadow lark sang to them from a top rail of the new fence. Now, for the first time, the girls associated the song with the pretty bird. The party walked on, down into the woods. They skirted the first and middle sloughs, on the north side of the first and the southeast side of the second.

They spread their picnic under a small oak on the sharp ridge that separated the middle slough from the largest most southerly one, the larger part of which lay beyond the homestead boundary. (The glacier-built ridge looked as if it had been made for a road.) Thence they climbed after lunch atop the "south" hill to its prairie-covered dome. Below the steep southerly slope lay a deep circular slough of the sort often referred to as a pot-hole or, better, a glacial kettle. At the bottom of the gentler slope to the southeast lay another flat pot-hole. Below the easterly, precipitious slope lay still another, larger kettle hole. Thus, the south (woods) forty contained six perennial sloughs, and every one was home to a family of mallards. The explorers were amazed. Though several times frightened by the whirr of grouse, and scolded by numerous gray squirrels, they were most impressed by the number of ducks that nested on the homestead—altogether nine sloughs and nine families of ducks. Pehr would bag several for the table before the fowls departed for warmer climes in the fall. That evening everyone felt "crawly" with woodticks. Each detected and plucked off two or three before bedtime and dropped them into the stove. Anna found four more on the girls as they undressed for bed. Pehr and Anna examined each other's backs, but found none.

During the stall-feeding season, Pehr had readily observed that his cattle ate with most relish the hay mowed on uplands, and at times rejected entirely stuff taken from a marshy lowland. This year he would stay clear of marsh and slough, and take all his hay from high ground. The upland swaths he had cut last year now bore a heavy stand of new grass; and this he scythed first, four acres in two days. While his first hay lay drying, he spent two days mowing for Anderson on a luxuriant flat in the northwest corner of his square quarter-section. Anderson's grass here stood so thick and tall that a swath yielded almost twice the hay Pehr got from his own prairie. He might cut some of it for himself after he had stacked enough for Anderson.

Pehr soon became acquainted with the dominant, tall, native grasses on sight and also recognized the half-tall ones; but he never learned more than few of their names: Big bluestem (Andropogon gerardi) five to six feet tall; Little bluestem (Andropogon scoparius) about two feet tall; Side-oats grama (Bouteloua curtipendula) tall as Little bluestem; Needle-and-thread grass (Stipa comata) of middle height, and with needles that penetrated one's clothing when he handled hay containing the species.

In fact, he did mow several acres of Short Nils' prairie, and told him about it later. Anderson was delighted because mowing appeared to improve the prairie forage. Of course, he did not neglect the opportunity to jibe Pehr about the relative quality of their claims.

Pehr mowed, raked, hauled, and stacked hay from mid-June into July. Then, with four large stacks by his stable and three by Anderson's stable site, he stopped haying and devoted himself to other endeavors.

First he hauled home on the stone-boat several loads of cobblestones about the size of a man's fist. He leveled the entire stall area of the stable, and laid the stone tightly, side-by-side, from the manger to the south wall, and eastward beyond the door. Then he hauled sand, in the tub, from the south hill, and packed it into the interstices between the stones. This floor held for the life of the stable.

Next he addressed himself to Anna's plea for a floor in the cabin. He chopped, hauled, hewed, planed, and laid in place, thick basswood planks, wall to wall, except for the cellar opening. Over that he laid a fitted trap-door with a gouged-out hand grip by which to open it. For hinges, Anna gave him money from her boarders' fund, and he walked to Clitherall to buy them. While there he also bought some lengths of leather from the cobbler, with which to bind together the handle and swingle of a flail for threshing his grain.

Construction of the flail was quickly done. It required two stout sticks of oak, one about two and a half feet long (the swingle, to strike the grain), and the other three feet long (the handle); the two joined loosely at one end by a thong threaded through a hole bored for the purpose, and tied with a knot to secure it. It threshed quite thoroughly, and wore well, despite the constant abrasion of the thong.

With passage of June the frequency of rain and thunderstorms declined, and hot, brassy days often followed one after another. The time of ripening had come. The oats commenced "turning," first to a pastel green, then yellowish and finally white in the heads. The wheat stood headed out and was turning golden.

When Pehr deemed the oats ripe enough to dry and thresh properly, he commenced mowing them with might and main (second week in July). He knew the day to day risk of letting them stand. A driving rain could shell out many kernels and lodge the straw so it would be difficult to cut and lay straight; a hailstorm could thresh the entire crop where it stood, knocking heads and grain to the ground, beyond retrieval.

Dew delayed him mornings until nine o'clock or later, but after the dew had fairly well dried away, he mowed until dark, stopping only briefly for food. He swung the scythe in long steady strokes, taking a swath of some four feet and moving forward about four inches with each stroke. Each swing performed two functions: it cut down a new width of grain forward while at the same time sweeping to the left side of the swath that grain laid down by the swing before. Behind him the straw lay in a neat, straight windrow, heads forward. It was thus easily gathered for binding.

He bound each swath into sheaves before commencing the next. To tie a sheaf, he grasped with his left hand a handful of straw just below the heads. With his right hand he then gripped half the straw thus held with the left, swung it over the heads of grain and held the knot under the loose grain gathered for a sheaf, then put his knee on the pile so the knot underneath was held tight between grain and ground. Then he gripped with his right hand the half of the straw tie sticking out to the right, and, with a deft twist of his hand, caught with it the half of the tie to the left. Both ends now held tight to the bundle he simply shoved the twist in his right hand under the straw binding the bundle, so that pressure against the bundle held it fast. Thus, he hand-tied the sheaves without any extraneous material.

Had not a rain delayed him, he might have mowed and bound the oats in four days. As it was, the oats stood in shocks with three pairs of sheaves to each, six days after he took the first swath. They would stand so, to dry and "cure," for two weeks at least and longer, if clear weather did not prevail. One shower fell on them, but despite that, Pehr deemed them ready to thresh when the accepted curing time expired.

In preparation for threshing he tramped and compacted a sizeable circular area of stubble in the middle of the oats field, and spread upon it the wagon cover to serve as threshing floor. He took to the field both of his wooden scoops, his steel fork and his wooden rake, besides his new flail and the sacks procured from Willie, Fletcher, and Anderson. With the fork he carried a shock to the threshing floor in two trips. He flailed two bundles (sheaves) at a time, laying them on the floor with heads of one overlapping those of the other. He swung the flail and pounded them flat with the swingle until the heads appeared light and empty. Then he turned the bundles over and applied the swingle to the other side. The grain beaten out onto the canvas, he raked together and piled the straw to one side. He repeated this routine three times for each shock, and he had no less than two hundred shocks. He stopped to count them after flailing out only one. He had before him a very considerable task.

When he had flailed out four shocks, the canvas floor lay so deeply covered with grain that he determined to winnow and sack this batch before beating out another. He lifted and shook the canvas at several points about its periphery, forcing the threshed grain into a pile at the center. Of this he filled his long-handled scoop, stepped to the windward side of the canvas and, holding the scoop above his head, dribbled the grain out of it, down wind, onto the canvas. Thus winnowed, the oats lay in a clean pile, ready for sacking. With some difficulty, he got the grain into two partially filled sacks. He determined to have Anna hold open the sacks for him thenceforth. He went home for his forenoon coffee and delivered the message.

Anna was pleased to help with the harvest. She carried in the bundles as Pehr flailed them, she helped rake and pile the straw, but left flailing and winnowing to her husband. At one sacking juncture she observed:

"Now I know that the prairie wind, however violent and destructive it may be at times, also blows some good! How would we clean the grain without wind?"

"We simply wouldn't," replied Pehr. "We would sack it, chaff and all, and await a windy day. Today, fortunately, the wind is just right for clean winnowing without blowing the oat grains all over."

At dinner time the harvesters went home both happy and puzzled. They had threshed and bagged only a small part of the oat crop, but all their sacks were already full. Where would they store more than a hundred additional bushels?

Pehr resolved the happy issue at the table:

"Soon as I have eaten I'll go and build a bin in a corner of the stable. I'll use six-foot planks and raise the wall high as necessary. We'll haul the oats home in sacks and empty them into the bin. The last seven, packed full, go to repay Willie his kind loan. We must be careful that his grain is most thoroughly cleaned."

He built the little bin, called up Buck and Bride, hauled the oat sacks home and emptied them into the bin. It was then afternoon coffee time.

After lunch the daughters accompanied their parents to the harvest field, and made themselves useful between romps on the fence. They carried in bundles, each one at a time, which was much help because the distance between shocks and threshing floor grew longer as the number of shocks declined. Before the humidity of evening rendered thorough threshing impossible, Pehr hauled to the stable a second load of thirteen sacks (32.5 bushels). The pioneers had done a good day's work!

The weather held, and Pehr flailed less furiously. Yet, in three more days, working only between the drying of dew and the straw-toughening of evening, they threshed all the oats and carefully stacked the straw. The cattle would eat some of the oat straw during winter stall-feeding; and that not eaten would become bedding. None would be wasted!

The oats field had yielded a hundred and sixty bushels; thirty two bushels per acre. The very day after completing the oats harvest, Pehr loaded into the wagon the seven sacks of oats borrowed from Willie, took his family with him, and drove to Morks to return the loan. They departed early and came to the Mork's for late dinner. They would return home in time for evening milking.

Willie's first explosive comment, after all had exchanged endearing greetings was:

"What the hell do I want with more oats? I just threshed out two hundred bushels, and I'm told they are now so abundant on the frontier that one can scarcely give them away. Why don't you take your load back with you, Pehr; and if I become needy, I'll come for it. I don't have any place to store it."

"As you will," replied Pehr, "I built a bin in which I can keep it. If, after I have sold my surplus wheat, you will sell me the oats I got, I'll pay you the market price at the time I got them. As I remember, you suggested fifty cents, so I shall owe you eight dollars and seventy-five cents for seventeen and a half bushels. I should like to settle our account before the snow flies. Indebtedness is a foul way of losing a friend!"

"Alright, Pehr, I would gladly give you the oats without obligation; but I can see that you would not accept them as a gift. Please store them for me until such time as I may need them. I will not jeopardize our friendship with a few damned bushels of oats!"

Tilda was now large with child; and the women talked much in confidence. Tilda estimated that the event would come early in August; and Anna reminded her that she expected notification so she could come and keep house. Tilda would send Willie soon as he had brought the mid-wife. Both women hoped that the birth would not come in the midst of the wheat harvesting.

Pehr and his family (and the seven sacks of oats) returned after dinner, and arrived in time for Anna to milk Bos. The cow stood waiting patiently by the stable door.

On the first Sunday in August, Pehr walked over both his own wheat field and Anderson's to see whether the grain was sufficiently ripe and hard for harvesting. On his upland flat the wheat was more mature than on Anderson's lowland. He would harvest his own first and Anderson's immediately afterwards. He set to work.

The wheat straw was red with rust, whence a dust cloud accompanied him as he mowed. The straw was more stiff and brittle than that of the oats, but it formed straight even windrows. The glumes held the kernels so tightly that one could handle it roughly without shelling it. Pehr debated, as he swung along on his first swath, whether oats or wheat be the most easily harvested. He continued the routine of mowing a swath and binding it before laying down another. The wheat straw was so stiff that its hand-binding was more difficult than had been that of the oats, which he anticipated from past experience.

Because it was less subject to moisture absorption, moulding, and even sprouting, than oats, he set larger shocks of wheat—three pairs of bundles in a row and two bundles on each side—thus ten to a shock instead of six to a shock of oats. The wheat shed rain better and dried more quickly than oats, thus the larger more wind-resistant shocks. Pehr had about half a day's wheat cutting remaining when Willie came for Anna and the girls. They started back immediately after dinner; Willie was too excited to linger.

"We'll be back in a week, or less," promised Anna as she kissed her husband goodby—and, in fact, they returned after only five days. Tilda was not one to lie in bed very long for having borne a child! The new heir had arrived on the seventh, and they named him Ola William. All was well with mother and son.

When Willie returned his housekeepers of several days, he took time to visit awhile with Pehr. He admired Pehr's convenient arrangement of his sturdy buildings, the hay stacks near the stable, and other preparations for the severe winter soon to come. They examined the oats in the bin and the wheat that stood shocked; then went to see Anderson's, still on the root. Willie was duly complimentary of the grain's quality. But on examining one of Anderson's rust-colored straws, he observed prophetically:

"If this damned wheat-rust disease should strike early on, it might so nearly break the straw that nourishment from the root could not get to the head and fill out the kernels. We should have poor shriveled wheat."

Willie turned homeward early enough to arrive and milk his cow before dark.

That night foreshadowed a new era in Pehr's household. When the daughters lay asleep and the parents were settling into bed, Anna turned toward Pehr and informed him in a soft voice:

"Tomorrow night I shall be ready to resume being a wife to you! If Tilda can bear a healthy son in this wilderness and herself also survive, so shall I."

Pehr reached for her, but she pushed him away:

"Tomorrow night, Pehr! Tonight I am not ready."

Anna was almost immediately asleep, but Pehr's anticipation denied him sleep for some time.

August was well advanced before Pehr mowed and shocked Anderson's wheat. It was sown later than his own, but not enough later to account for its late ripening. Its low-lying site appeared to delay its ripening. However, he had it scythed, bound, and shocked before the last week in August. Anderson had a bountiful crop of both straw and grain. And Pehr saw no evidence of damage by animals. Had his fencing been futile exertion? The fertile lowland had produced a taller and heavier stand than had Pehr's upland hill flat. But the rust also appeared to be worse in the lowland than on the upland. (Later on, rust became the scourage of the midwestern and plains wheat farmers, gravely curtailing the crop and raising the risk for many years.) Anna, Pehr, and the girls joined forces in wheat threshing in the same manner as they had done with the oats. There were only about half as many shocks of wheat as there had been of oats, but these were much larger. The wheat was much more difficult to flail out and winnow than the oats had been.

Little Hanna was at one point diverted from her task of carrying wheat bundles by a pretty patch of goldenrods just beyond the rail fence. She crawled through and broke off several stems with brilliant golden plumes, and carried them to her mother. Anna thanked her daughter and hugged her close, but Pehr saw tears welling in the mother's eyes. The flowers caused her to grieve for the Swedish dooryard in which she had nurtured and abandoned a growth of similar kind and beauty.

The wheat was more difficult to flail out, as Pehr knew well from experience, and more of the grain remained in the straw, defying the beating. The little work gang labored diligently for two weeks to thresh Pehr's wheat crop; and everyone was jubilant when the tedious strenuous work was completed.

To receive and store the bulk of his wheat, Pehr built a second bin in the stable corner opposite the first (both in his workshop). But the wheat bin he built smaller, to sacrifice less of his work space. He got ninety bushels, or eighteen bushels to the acre. Five sacks from the last load he hauled home he set in the cabin corner where his seed-wheat had stood before. He would sow three sacks of it next spring—maybe more; perhaps someone seeking seed-wheat would want the other two. With his own seed, he would sow a bushel and a quarter or even a half per acre.

Pehr waxed uncommonly jolly and solicitous, to the delight of mother and daughters alike. Anna pondered whether his light-hearted manner reflected their love-making or the bounty of their harvest. Her ego told her that the harvest was secondary.

At supper one fair late August evening Pehr announced that he would wait no longer for Anderson to come and help thresh his wheat. They would begin the job tomorrow morning soon as the dew dried off. The dew was so heavy next morning and dispersed so slowly that they had forenoon coffee before departing for the field. Then they went, each carrying a piece of necessary equipment. Hanna carried the flail, Elna the rake and scoop, Anna the fork and eight grain sacks, Pehr the wagon canvas, in a large rolled-up bundle.

Pehr prepared a threshing floor, as he had done twice before, this time in the middle of Short Nils' wheat field. All now knew their tasks by rote, and, working thus systematically, they made rapid progress. By noon, two sacks were full and a batch larger than usual lay winnowed on the threshing floor.

The work crew had just sat down to dinner when Nils Anderson popped into the cabin and dropped on the floor a large bundle he unslung from his back. Everyone greeted him loudly and happily. The girls hopped down from their bench at the table and ran to him. He picked them both up in his arms and whiskered them gently. Then he set them down and drew from his pocket a bag of candy. He handed it to Hanna with this admonition:

"This is for both of you to share equally, but not one piece may you eat before you have eaten clean your dinner plates!"

Anna handed him a clean hand towel, saying:

"Here, Nils, go wash your hands while I set a place for you."

Anderson ate and talked with his accustomed gusto and his presence brightened the room for everyone.

"So, how did our crops turn out, Pehr," he asked, through a mouth half full of rabbit stew and potatoes.

"They turned out just fine. Of course, we have yet to thresh yours. We just began on it this forenoon. My wheat and oats both yielded well. I can sell fifty bushels of wheat and have plenty left over for seed, flour and a little chicken feed."

"When are you getting a flock of chickens? I saw none as I came."

"I have a half dozen hens and a rooster spoken for in Clitherall. One day soon I shall go and get them. But first I wish to sell some wheat and get a little cash in my pocket."

Put in Anna: "I have enough board money left to pay for the chickens. The sooner we get them, the sooner may we enjoy fresh eggs."

"Alright," said Pehr, grinning broadly. "If you will finance them, I'll go get them soon! But first we must thresh Nils' wheat. That has priority!"

The men and the girls went to Anderson's wheat field after dinner and resumed the threshing. Soon four sacks stood full; and the need for another storage space was obvious. The crew went home for afternoon coffee. Pehr would resolve the issue:

"I shall rive out rough planking and nail up another bin in the stable—in the southwest corner. The steers rarely go in this time of year, so I can spare the space until stall-feeding time."

"That would be mighty good of you," said Short Nils. "I shall haul and sell my wheat soon as possible, anyhow. It will be out of your way long before you stable the oxen again."

"Alright, then, I'll call up the oxen. You hitch your pair to your wagon and bring what we have threshed and I'll make the bin. Your yoke hangs in the stable on the south wall. Mind you, I haven't worked your oxen in weeks, and they may be pretty frisky."

The oxen gave Nils no trouble, and he had the first load of wheat sacks at the stable door by the time Pehr was four feet up with the bin. He used longer planks in this temporary structure, so that it would hold all of Anderson's wheat without lifting the sacks very high to empty them. After twelve more work days, each greatly foreshortened by dew and evening damp, all of Anderson's wheat was in the bin, ten new sacks lying full on top. Nils had ninety-five bushels of wheat.

During their threshing, the men had exchanged thoughts about the marketing of their surplus wheat. Anderson had come by way of Perham enroute home from the railroad, and he had stopped to inquire into the wheat market. The dealer there had offered him $1.50 per bushel, less any necessary dockage for wild oats or other foreign matter contained.

"There's a good wagon trail to Perham, and dry and firm as the land is now, one should have no difficulty hauling a pretty fair load," concluded Anderson.

Responded Pehr: "I suggest that we load our wagons with eight sacks each and make a trip to Perham. That way we can learn how good the market truly is. It will be a stiff two-day trip—I've heard its almost forty miles from here. We can carry enough food, and we can sleep out. We can mount my canvas on the wagon and sleep under it if it rains. Shall we fill my eight sacks tonight and go in the morning?"

"Suppose we fill your sacks now and have them ready? If the morning is clear, we'll go. If it's rainy or threatening, we wait a day or two for the trail to dry and firm up again. In muddy going, these narrow-tired wagons of ours are bitches to cut in when they are loaded."

"So be it!" said Pehr.

They bagged eight sacks of Pehr's wheat after supper and stood them against the bin.

Next morning the sky was overcast with low heavy clouds, which had released some rain during the night.

The men postponed the wheat hauling. Instead, they drove Pehr's rig, with canvas in place, to Clitherall to buy chickens from Fletcher, with two dollars of Anna's board money. They took with them a gunny sack in which to confine the fowls. This time Pehr went directly to Fletcher's place without availing himself of Albertson's services as interpreter. He had learned a few words of English, and his limited vocabulary included "chickens." Fletcher knew immediately what was wanted; and "shoo'd" his chickens into a pen for easier capture. Pehr held the sack; Anderson and Fletcher caught the birds by their legs and stuck them in it. Fletcher first took a handsome rooster, black-and-white speckled with some shiny golden-red feathers about his neck and in his tail. He was a young bird with short spurs. The six hens were of various colors: one solid black, one reddish buff, the others mixed. All the birds were single-combed. Combs and wattles were blood-red, indicative of good health. Pehr handed Fletcher the two dollars and refused the quarter change that Fletcher attempted to return. The men drove home, with their chickens confined in the sack, laid flat (and lively) on the floor of the wagon box.

Anna took advantage of the men's absence. She and the girls walked over to the Lien's, and Anna delivered her secret message: "I told you that you should be third to know," she whispered to Mrs. Lien. "I've been doing my nocturnal wifely duties for some time now, but I've been too busy to come over."

"Oh, I'm so happy for both of you," said Anna Lien aloud. "Now you may soon have a male heir."

On arriving home, the men released the birds in the stable and sprinkled the litter with wheat. Anna and the girls came to admire the livestock additions, amazed at the vigor with which the birds scratched and pecked for wheat kernels.

"They are thrifty looking," observed Anna, "but won't they soil the grain in the bins?"

"Nils and I will fix that," replied Pehr. "We will cover the bins with hay and weight it down with wood lengths. When we get Nils' wheat hauled out, I'll fasten some roosts across that corner. Until then the birds can roost on the edge of the manger. I'll gouge out two small troughs for them—one for grain and one for water (they will get oats, mostly). We'll search the woods for a fallen hollow log that I can saw in short lengths and set about for laying nests. I do hope those pretty biddies lay many eggs! Let's go in and eat dinner. We'll lock the birds in to get themselves oriented."

Anna's prediction came true. Pehr was obliged to board up the bins containing his grain, almost to the roof, leaving no space wide enough to admit a chicken.

Nils' surplus wheat they hauled to Perham in four days, using two wagons, and making a trip in two days. The ten bushels remaining they stowed in four sacks along-side Pehr's in the cabin corner. Pehr quickly erected roosts for the chickens.

Then they made an equal number of trips hauling Pehr's surplus wheat; leaving him with twelve and a half bushels in the cabin for seed, and about twelve and a half bushels in his bin. They got $1.20 per bushel for all they hauled. Pehr now had a working capital of seventy-eight dollars. His affluence had begun! He had commenced his conquest of the wild prairie border!

At supper one evening Anna raised the issue of flour supply again. The barrel was most empty. The men took heed and set out for the Perham mill the very next day, taking one sack of Nils' wheat and four of Pehr's (12.5 bushels). They arose early and sacked and loaded the wheat before breakfast.

They drove Pehr's oxen on Pehr's wagon. Anna gave them a half flour-sack of food, including coffee, pot, and tin cups.

They reached the woods bordering Rush Lake before dark and camped there over night *(Figure 3.2)*. Pehr kept his musket at hand, primed and ready, in case they were attacked by robbers, for which the place was infamous. They were not disturbed. Next day they got their small grist ground late in the day because many other settlers were there before them with equal or larger loads; they must wait their turn. Pehr paid the miller with cash instead of toll; he had use for all the flour, bran and shorts that his load yielded. He paid the miller ten cents per bushel of wheat and got from each bushel thirty-four pounds of flour, five pounds of shorts and fifteen pounds of bran. (Where went the six pound loss no one knew but the miller). Legal Minnesota toll was one-eighth, or seven and a half pounds per bushel of wheat. Some millers charged one-fifth the value of the wheat to grind it—an old-time rip-off!

Before nightfall of the second day they were once again in the Rush Lake woods, low on hay and oats for the oxen. They bedded where they had slept before, after staking out the oxen nearby. They arrived home on the third day in late afternoon. Now Anna had enough flour to last until spring. The bran and shorts would adequately supplement other rations of chickens and swine until another harvest.

The very year (1870) in which Pehr harvested his first crop of wheat in America, the booming wheat prices consequent upon the Civil War ended. Wheat quotations by the Chicago Board of Trade had gone above two dollars per bushel in 1864

(August and September). During 1870, market reports in Buffalo, New York listed "Number One Spring" wheat, such as grown in Minnesota, at prices ranging from $1.07 to $1.31½. "Number Two Spring" sold for ten cents per bushel less; winter wheats sold for twenty to thirty cents per bushel more than "Number One Spring."

There were in Minnesota in 1870, two hundred sixteen flour mills; but none of them could produce high-quality white flour from Minnesota spring wheat.

But Pehr's American advent was propitiously timed relative to a set of impending developments affecting the price of Minnesota wheat.

The price differential cited above was due to a peculiarity of hard spring wheat:

> Spring wheat has a hard endosperm, rich in gluten, and a very brittle bran which is easily broken and pulverized. Winter wheat, on the contrary, has a tough skin which resists grinding much more effectively than the flouring portions, which crumble very easily. Owing to the ease with which the bran of the spring wheat is pulverized, it was never wholly separated by the old methods of milling. It passed through the bolts, and its presence in the flour always discolored it, and gave to the bread made therefrom a darker appearance. In addition to this fact the presence of the fine particles of bran in the flour caused it to gather moisture much more readily than was the case with flour made from winter wheat. As a consequence, the spring wheat flour would not keep so long nor so well as the winter, especially in a moist or hot climate. These facts about the flour made from spring wheat reduced its price, as compared with that manufactured from good milling winter wheat.
>
> (From Third Biennial Report, Bureau of Labor Statistics, listed among sources consulted.)

During the 1860's and until the mid 1870's the best flour made from winter wheat sold for a much higher price than the best flour made from spring wheat. At one time the excess price differential was as great as $6.75 per barrel. The price of the best spring wheat flour (Chicago quotation) fell to a low of $1.50 per barrel in July and August of 1861. In those same months the best flour from white winter wheat sold for $6.50 per barrel.

But the subordination of spring wheat and the disdain for flour made from it were soon to end; and the change was wrought in Minnesota, with Minnesota wheat and Minnesota mills. It began in Faribault, about 1860, when the founder of the town, Alex. Faribault, engaged a French Canadian named Nicholas La Croix to build and operate for him a flour mill that would make superior flour from hard spring wheat. La Croix had learned the miller's trade in France, where the designs and processes he employed in Faribault had been in use for some time. The Faribault mill had two "run of stones," and employed the principle of "high grinding"—grinding more than once. It was the first such mill in the United States. The first grinding produced middlings, which, when sifted and reground by themselves, became flour of exceptional quality. La Croix supervised the construction and installation of a "purifier" in the little mill, and so produced flour worth two dollars more per barrel than any other flour made in Minnesota.

La Croix's middlings purifier was a simple arrangement of sieves across which air was blown, throwing the bran aside. In more sophisticated form, it was soon an essential part of equipment in all wheat-flour mills.

Soon La Croix's ideas and the "gradual reduction process" or "roller" process, gained from Hungary, became standard practice in Minneapolis and other mills in Minnesota. Rollers replaced stones for grinding; bolting and sifting were improved;

and all commercial mills contained the great labor-saving devices invented by Oliver Evans of Philadelphia—the elevator, the conveyor, the drill, the descender, and the hopper-boy. (The third patent issued under United States patent laws went to Evans, dated December 18, 1790.) With these advantages incorporated, certain Minneapolis mills soon became giants in the flour milling industry.

The Minnesota "patent" or "new process" flour reached markets outside the state in 1873. Its regular reporting by the Chicago Board of Trade began in 1876; but a footnote to the Board's 1875 report stated that the Minnesota patents had, in that year, averaged two dollars higher in price than the best grade of spring wheat flour quoted.

The new process added twenty to forty cents per bushel to the value of hard dark wheat grown in Minnesota. The price of spring wheat far surpassed that of winter wheats. Minnesota gained world renown as the producer of the best flour for baking white bread. Minneapolis became the largest wheat milling center in the world in 1890, and retained that rank several decades subsequently.

Negative factors affecting Pehr's income from wheat came with railroads and grain elevators associated with them. Freight rates were high, and the elevator operators often cheated the farmer on the weight and quality of his load. But despite these unfortunate handicaps, wheat remained for several decades THE stock in trade for Pehr and other settlers like him.

Short Nils and Pehr next bent their energies to the erection of a stable on Anderson's claim. They used Pehr's stable as a model, even to the excavation into a steep south-facing side-hill. The logs, mostly oak, they cut just to the south of Anderson's building site, so the hauling took little time. Working together, one at each end of a log, they handled the timbers easily and quickly. In two weeks time the structure stood completed, including manger, stalls, door, and a thick straw roof. But Pehr deemed the project incomplete without a floor in the stalls; his experience had taught him the need. So they hauled and set in many stone-boat loads of cobblestones, gleaned from the prairie uplands to the southwest. To haul and lay the stones, and haul and pack sand between them took two days. But then both men were content with their handiwork.

Other tasks delayed their plowing until October. One day at mid-September, after a trace of light night frost, they had helped Anna and the girls gather and store such exposed garden stuffs as Hubbard squash and cabbage. They placed in the cellar a dozen large green squashes and a dozen large tight cabbage heads. Now, in October, frosts became more severe; they would soon be compelled to harvest the roots and tubers.

Meanwhile Nils and Pehr plowed with both yoke of oxen hitched to one plow. The men guided the plow by turns, and the oxen went almost steadily, pulling the plow with little effort. Pehr was now feeding his work animals a quart measure of oats morning and night, and furnishing Short Nils a similar quantity for his yoke. (Bos got oats once a day to prolong her period of lactation. Krull got none; he cut enough capers without.) Nils' field they plowed with his plow, Pehr's with his. They had turned Nils' wheat field before a heavy frost prompted them to stop and devote a day to the digging of potatoes and root crops. All were carefully stored in the cellar. The yield was both abundant and of good quality.

After plowing Pehr's fields, they broke about five acres of new ground for each, adjoining the areas previously cropped. Pehr's plow share became so badly dulled by rocks and stones that he left Short Nils breaking alone one half day while he carried the share to the Clitherall blacksmith for sharpening. The smith did an apparently expert job, putting a sharp new edge on the share without drawing it too thin and carefully chilling it to retain its temper. After his skillful repair, the share worked better than when it was new.

Soon the plowing and breaking were done. The neighbors upturned the plows in a shady nook on their respective farmsteads and smeared the shiny working parts with tar and tallow. (This turned into a hard impervious crust, with time, and protected against rust almost indefinitely. The tar was of vegetable origin, tapped from southern longleaf and slash pines.)

The year's work had been done, and the busy autumn season concluded, before November froze the ground and sifted upon its solidified surface one snow flurry after another. Pehr smeared the chinks in the stable walls with fresh cattle manure to defend against the imminent wintery blasts.

Before the rigors of winter held them captive once again, Pehr indulged his family with a two-day trip to Fergus Falls—to see how the little town was progressing and to shop for winter clothing. They took lodging in the new frame hotel and ate their meals there, as well.

Incidental to their search for needed clothing at a modest price, they came on a photography studio, and Pehr insisted that they must don their new clothes and be photographed. The girls posed for one picture; the parents for another *(Figure 9.1)*. Pehr bought three of each, so he might send one set to his mother in Bessinge, one set to Anna's parents, and keep one for themselves. To Anna, he whispered: "Won't the folks at home be pleased to see how well and prosperous we look?" She smiled her agreement.

Late the second day they arrived back at the homestead; and Short Nils was there to greet them—with a good fire in the stove. He had done all the chores during their absence, including the milking of Bos. The girls shared with him the last of their candy.

Figure 9.1. *After harvesting their first crop, in the autumn of 1870, Pehr, Anna, and their daughters drove to Fergus Falls for a shopping spree, and quite incidentally stopped into the photographer's rude studio and had their pictures made—the girls separately from the parents. The photo shows Anna and Pehr. The author has never seen the photograph of the girls, but he assumes that copies of both photos went to grandparents in Sweden.*

Photo courtesy Edna Fletcher, reduced and retouched by Photos, Inc.

Chapter 10

TRAGIC SECOND YEAR

November 1870 came with short gray days and long cold nights. Snow came and went, each flurry seeming to endure a bit longer than the last. Another dark dreary winter was announcing its imminent sway.

On one cold crisp night, after quieting Pehr's passion and lying turned away, Anna asked over her shoulder:

"I suppose you know I'm pregnant? I got that way about mid-September, by my reckoning."

"Yes, I thought you might be; and I'm happy about it. I feel confident that you'll bear a male heir to take over our Homestead when we're old. Aren't you glad, too?"

He turned toward her, put his arm about her, and held her close!

"I'm glad for your sake. As for myself, I have mixed feelings. I'm determined to emulate Tilda, but I remain frightened of carrying and bearing a child in the wilderness. If I were back in Skåne, I would be as glad as you, but here I am full of fear."

"You feel well, don't you, dear? Certainly you've had no morning sickness, or I should have noticed. Be cheerful, and bear a fine son for us!"

"It's for you that I will try. My grieving for home is not your fault, and I wish I could shrug it off. But it stays with me every day and every night. Even now, I sometimes wish I had not come with you. I'm sorry," she sniffled.

"Perhaps Tilda and her young son could cheer you up! Let's drive over to Mork's tomorrow. Bos is so nearly dry that we can let her milking go for a day. I've been stripping her only once a day, anyhow. We'll go and stay over! Short Nils will keep this place warm while we're away. Nothing will freeze up. He can strip Bos for us too, if so inclined. Maybe we can go and see Tilda's midwife, to sort of reassure you. Agreed?"

"That will be fine, I will enjoy a talk with Tilda in any case; and, of course, I should like to see the woman who'll deliver me of a male heir."

They slept well and awakened early. Pehr stripped Bos before breakfast, while Anna readied the girls. They were delighted to go visit Tilda and her little boy again.

They went by wagon, because there were many bare spots whence the snow had blown. The wagon was noisy and rough, as the wheels rolled over frozen ground. Short Nils waved them off.

The Morks sat at dinner when they arrived. Tilda quickly set four additional places, and the Pehrsons enjoyed brown beans cooked with salted side meat.

At the table the elders talked about Anna's pregnancy and the desirability of knowing exactly where the midwife might be got. Pehr and Willie would walk to Mrs. Holm's place and be back for supper—unless the prospective mother insisted upon going along.

"I fear you've had enough shaking for one day," observed Pehr. "That wagon seat sort of threw us about today. I believe that you and the girls had better remain here with Tilda and the baby. Willie and I can be back before suppertime."

"I would like to meet the woman," said Anna, "but I do believe I've had all the shaking I should risk in one day. You go along and reserve me a space of the woman's time—late April or early May. I'll stay here and rest. Off with you!"

The men walked off, Willie carrying his musket. They might get a brace of chickens or grouse enroute. As a matter of fact, Willie shot three chickens on the outward journey and another pair on the return. The first three he presented to Mrs. Holm, who thanked vociferously. He introduced Pehr and stated his business.

Mrs. Holm was a buxom rose-tinted woman about middle age, with a pretty smiling face and a certain aura of daintiness and competence about her. Pehr could assure Anna that her midwife appeared cool and competent. He was to come for the woman whenever Anna felt as if she might go into labor, not after it had begun.

"I'd rather be a week early than five minutes late," asserted the midwife. I charge fifty cents a day and two dollars for the delivery. I'll bring with me everything I shall need, except the tea kettle for boiling water."

"I'll see that you have plenty of hot water. I'll come for you the moment she feels the approach of labor. And thanks for your willingness to help us. My wife has been gravely concerned."

"Then tell her to relax. I delivered a dozen last year and will surpass that number this year. Every one of the youngsters is doing well. The frontier is fertile in more ways than one!" she concluded with a knowing grin.

"Perhaps I shall see you in April then?"

"Yes, you probably will. Goodby, then."

She shook hands with both men, and they commenced their homeward journey.

No sooner were they inside Willie's door than the women were at the task of plucking and drawing the plump prairie chickens.

"We'll have these for dinner tomorrow," said Tilda. "I don't like to eat any meat the same day it's killed. You will stay and have dinner before you start for home! I'll entertain no argument!"

"So be it," answered Pehr. "It will be our pleasure."

He told Anna all about the midwife, and she was greatly comforted.

"I can vouch for her," said Tilda. "She's clean, kind, gentle and efficient. You could have none better! And she will cook and keep your house until you get back on your feet again. Just be sure you don't wait too long before sending Pehr to get her!"

"I'll try to give early notice," asserted Anna. "I feel much more confident, now that I know I shall have competent help."

They stayed for a delicious prairie chicken dinner next noon. The day was cold and brisk, so the girls had remained indoors, building with a box full of wooden blocks that Willie had made for his son—for such time as the infant would be big enough. They begged Papa to make them a box full with which to play at home. He promised that he would.

After eating, praising Tilda's cooking, and exchanging small talk, the visitors prepared for departure. Willie helped Pehr yoke and hitch the oxen. Anna settled the girls in the wagon box, seated on a straw-filled grain sack with a comforter about their legs. The double box sheltered them against the wind. But for the bumpiness absorbed by the seat spring Anna would have sat with her daughters but she wisely elected to ride beside Pehr on the seat, a robe over their knees. When Pehr was ready to start the oxen, Tilda handed up to Anna two bundles tied in clean white cloths.

"Here's something for lunch on the road, and here's a lump of the butter we churned yesterday. Maybe you can stretch it until your cow freshens."

Anna and Pehr thanked in unison. Then, as Pehr talked the oxen into a walk, Anna called to Tilda:

"You've given us more than half of the churning. You are too generous!"

Everyone waved "goodby," including the girls, who stood looking out over the wagon box. Elna lifted Hanna up so she might surely see. When they were out of sight of the Morks, Anna supervised the girls' return to their seat and blanket. Despite the bumps, Hanna soon fell asleep, her head bobbing against Elna's shoulder. Until she too fell asleep, Elna felt protective and superior.

Anna and Pehr rode on in silence, each engrossed with private thoughts. Anna rehearsed, over and over, the pains and risks that accompany childbirth. Pehr envisioned a son, young and strong, laying onto the sledge the big end of a log so heavy that his aging sire could barely manage the little end. He would swing an axe or a scythe with steady, telling strokes. He would roll a salt barrel out of the sledge onto his thighs and walk away with it. He would be a MAN among powerful men!

They waked the girls and handed sandwiches around when they had attained what Anna and Pehr deemed the midpoint of the journey. They ate without stopping. In the cold weather the oxen could readily endure without feed or water until they got home.

Short Nils greeted them as they came to a stop before the cabin. He had a good fire in the stove so the house was warm and cozy. Anna and the girls thanked him for the warmth; they were chilled by the long ride. Nils attended to the oxen, so Pehr might also come in to warm.

Short Nils had driven to Clitherall while his neighbors were away and bought himself a steel fork like Pehr's, a large wooden tub from which to water his oxen in the stable, and two tinned buckets with which to carry water from Pehr's spring.

Next the men hauled in all their wheat straw. With it they doubled the thickness of the stable roofs and banked the north walls right up to the eaves. They fairly buried Pehr's swine shelter, leaving an opening only on the south side. The straw not so utilized they stacked by their stables for use as stall bedding.

When they had hauled all the wheat straw, Short Nils observed curtly:

"That stack of oat straw should be hauled in too, before it becomes buried in snow. The cattle will relish it this winter as a change from hay now and then. I'll gladly help you Pehr."

"Tell you what! If you'll help me, we'll stack half by your stable and half by mine. Are you agreeable?"

"No! I'll accept a third. You have four cattle, and I have only two. Even so, you would be extra generous.

"So be it!"

And they hauled it all home and stacked it conveniently near their stables.

November held cold and snowy. By mid-month the ground was covered well enough for fair sleighing, so the wagons were set aside and the clumsy sledge put in use—newly retreaded with ironwood. The neighbors continued working together, now cutting, hauling, splitting, and hewing oak rails and oak posts, taken from their respective woodlands. They alternated the ox teams from day to day so that all their work stock got exercise. Before month's end they had large piles of finished rails and posts stacked by their patches of plowed ground, each counted sufficient to enclose all the grain sown next spring. Short Nils had his entire enclosure to build; Pehr had only to extend two sides and shift the cross-fence to the northerly edge.

One evening late in November, after the girls were asleep and the adults sat at leisure, talking, Pehr introduced the issue of butchering:

"We should, I believe, butcher one or both of the barrows one day soon. Winter seems to be well enough established so that one might process and store pork without any spoilage."

"You'd better kill both of the pigs now, because I shall be unable to cope with a butchering much later on. We shall, however, need several items of equipment before we can properly preserve the meat and lard. You will have to drive to Clitherall and buy several necessary items. For instance, I shall need a large covered wooden pail for storing lard, two large bread-baking pans for rendering, one or two horn lengths for stuffing sausages, a large wooden bowl and a double-rocker knife for chopping head-cheese, a quantity of black and red pepper, salt petre, and vinegar. I'll think up a complete list." All this from Anna.

Added Pehr:

"We shall need also a tight barrel for scalding and for salting down afterwards and another boiler and two tinned pails for heating and carrying scalding water. We shall need a pair of scrapers and a hook, a large sack or a barrel of salt, and a good willow wisp and corn meal if we wish to take blood for sausage. Can you think of anything else?"

Said Nils:

"Off hand, I can think of nothing else we shall need; but I wonder about taking blood for blood sausage. In her condition, Anna should not see any creature dying, lest it cause her off-spring to be born with "fits." Can you and I, Pehr, stick and catch blood without a third man to hold the pail and stir?"

"Let's try," answered Pehr. "Are you also fond of blood sausage?"

"You bet I am. If we plan our every movement ahead of time, perhaps we needn't spill much."

The list was completed before they dispersed to their beds—Short Nils to his own stable, where no chickens could soil his bedding.

Next morning the men lifted the wagon box onto the sledge and drove to Clitherall with Pehr's oxen to procure the butchering needs. Pehr took along his ox shoes; and while he and Nils bought and carried to the sledge all the items wanted, the blacksmith sharpened the shoes and shod the oxen. They got every item, but had to settle for a large sack of salt instead of a barrel. Nils bought a large bag of hard candy for the girls.

All their purchases stowed in the wagon box, Pehr went to get the oxen. They stood ready, tied beside the smithy.

The smith commented on the gentleness of the large beasts:

"If all the animals I nail shoes on were so well behaved, my job would be easy."

Pehr nodded, though he understood little of what was said. He handed the smith a five-dollar bill and got back three dollars. The good man charged him only twenty-five cents a foot, since he furnished his own shoes. Pehr, ordinarily penurious, pressed on the man an extra quarter.

During the men's absence, Anna and her daughters paid a brief visit to Mrs. Lien, informing her of butchering day and inviting her to come and help. She would, as custom dictated, receive some choice parts of the meat. She accepted enthusiastically, savoring the taste of fresh pork.

The men returned home in time for a late dinner. Anna and the girls had eaten, so this time the youngsters could immediately enjoy Nils' delicious gift. Each in turn hugged his neck tightly.

After dinner, the men stowed all the new equipment and made preparations for butchering next day. Pehr shaped two stout oak stakes by which to hang the carcasses, the ends tapered to thread under the tendons in the hind legs, spreading them firmly apart. (After he had horses and used single trees, a single tree served ideally for hanging a carcass.)

Short Nils sought and found a place near the pig pen where, by arranging several large stones under it, he fixed the tight barrel at such an angle that a dead two-hundred-fifty pound hog might quite readily be shoved into it and pulled out again. Together they selected two adjacent trees with strong crotches about six feet off the ground. In these crotches they laid a stout ironwood rail, spanning the distance between them. About the rail they wrapped and tied a log chain so that the end hooks hung free about four feet apart. Onto these they would slip the loop of light rope tied about the hanging stake of each carcass. They thought themselves ready!

Butchering day dawned gloomy, cold, and desolate, befitting the unpleasant task at hand. Immediately after breakfast the men took to the spring and filled within about three inches of the top, the new boiler and buckets, carried them home and set them on the stove—admonishing Anna to keep the fire hot until the water boiled. The men made another quick trip to the spring and filled the copper boiler.

Pehr nudged Anna, and whispered to her so the girls would not hear:

"We'll kill the animals while the water heats. Give me your wooden pail with some corn meal in it, and the willow wisp with which to stir the blood. Keep the girls indoors!"

He took from Anna the pail she proffered—with corn meal and wisp in it, and took down his musket from his place above the door deliberately, as if he were going hunting. Anna surreptitiously gave to Nils, Pehr's eight-inch sticking knife. The men went to the pig pen. The swine were so restless with hunger that Pehr could not get a sure shot at a doomed one.

"Go get a few handfuls of oats with which we can coax them into position."

Nils went quickly to the stable and returned with a measure of oats. But before he sprinkled the bait, he asked of Pehr:

"Would it be easier to get them over the fence alive and shoot them outside instead of killing them in the pen and lifting the carcasses over?"

"No," replied Pehr. "We shall have to lift them over, dead or alive; and they are easier to handle dead. They weigh only about two hundred fifty pounds apiece. Let's get on with it! Now! We must be systematic and quick, if we are to get most of the blood. The instant I have shot and stunned one I shall lay down the musket and hold his front legs upward and apart so you can stick him. Immediately after you have stuck him, pitch the knife aside and hold him steady as you can while I catch the blood. Are you ready?"

"I'm ready." He waved the knife and threw down a handful of oats. The hogs commenced eating off the ground, their heads down. Pehr stood within four feet of his first victim. He pointed the musket at the middle of the hog's forehead and pulled the trigger. The hog dropped to the ground, completely stunned. Pehr laid down his musket quickly but carefully, grabbed a front leg with each hand, and held him steady. Nils plunged the knife into the thick throat just in front of the fore legs, and, with a practiced twist, severed the main aorta. The blood gushed out in great spurts.

Pehr said loudly:
"You get the pail under and stir like hell with the wisp so the blood doesn't lump. I've got him held, and better not let go."

Nils did as instructed and caught most of the blood. The hog was drained and lifeless in two minutes. The men stood and quieted their breathing, Nils still stirring the blood vigorously. He had blood on his knees and jacket sleeves.

"You did well Nils, better than I had planned. Now we know the routine for the second one. I'll take the blood to the house and get another container. I'll hide the exchange from the girls if I can. Wipe off with straw the best you can; and don't forget the knife."

He took up his musket and leaned it against a tree. He took the blood to the house and returned quickly with a sizeable kettle, wisp, and corn meal. He reloaded the spent barrel of the musket with another ball, powder, and cap, saying:

"Best we kill and bleed the other one at once, so Anna can handle the blood all in one batch. The water is almost boiling. Are you ready for another speed test? We'll use the same routine."

"I'm ready."

Pehr took aim on the second barrow and dropped him as he had the first. This one was more difficult to hold; and try as he might, Nils spilled more blood than before. Once again Pehr marched to the house, stirring as he went. He returned as quickly as he had gone. "Mrs. Lien is in helping Anna," he announced.

"Shall we lift them out before we go in for coffee? You'll have to change your outer clothes so you won't upset the girls."

They lifted the carcasses over the fence, one man at each end; and Short Nils walked hurriedly to his stable. He exchanged his bloodied clothes for clean ones, then rolled up the soiled ones and brought them back with him. He would put them on over the clean ones before he helped scald and scrape the carcasses—splashy, sloppy work.

While Nils was gone, Pehr carried his butchering bench from the stable and set it on a level spot near the hanging rail. Both men washed their hands carefully before enjoying their forenoon coffee.

They did not dawdle. They swallowed the lunch hastily and lifted the boiling containers off the stove. Pehr scooped a fire shovel full of ashes from the ash pit, threw them into the boiler, and replaced the cover. With each a bucket, and the boiler between them, the men returned to the butchering place. A great cloud of steam swathed them as they walked—carefully, lest they slop boiling hot water on themselves. Quickly they poured the water into the inclined barrel and stuck into it, head first, their first victim. Each grasping a hind leg, they sloshed the carcass back and forth several times, and then hauled it clear. They stuck the carcass back in, hind end first this time. Nils stuck the hook into its mouth and pulled it so that its point came out through the lower jaw. One on each side of the hook handle, they sloshed the hind end as they had the fore. Then they hoisted the carcass clear and lifted it onto the bench. Time was now of the essence. They must scald the second hog before the water got too cool. They went quickly to the house for the second boiler full of scalding water. They went through the same end-over-end procedure as with the first hog, but, admittedly, the second carcass was not so well scalded. Steam obscured the entire scalding procedure.

On the bench, they scraped the bristles off each carcass in turn, and rinsed them off with water dipped from the barrel. Pehr slit the back of each hind leg so the main tendon was exposed. He slipped under this his prepared "hanging tree," first one end and then the other, so the carcasses lay with their hind legs spread far apart and secured on the "tree." Now came the test of butchering without block and tackle. They must lift each carcass high enough to engage with the chain hook a loop of the light rope tied at mid-point of the hanging tree. Amid much grunting and puffing, they heaved up and hung both carcasses. They sat on the bench to catch their breath after the strenuous lifting.

Pehr observed between puffs:
"Someone should breed a kind of hog equipped with handles!"
Then he asked:
"Have you dressed out a hog before, Nils? If not, here's the place to learn."
"I never have," replied Nils. "Will you kindly show me?"
"That I will! I'll do the first one and coach you as you do the second. First cut off the head, going deep all around and then twisting it, like this." He severed the head and laid it on a clean spot.

"Next comes the most delicate cut, ripping him open down the belly without touching the sheath underneath that holds the guts in. You must begin here at the top, so, and cut all the way through the fat layer." He cut a deep gash the length of the belly.

"Say! we must have the dishpan to catch the guts, and the bread pan for the second one. I'll go get them from Anna. He picked up a boiler and cover and took them with him. He returned in a few minutes and resumed his post-mortem surgery.

"See! once I am through the "speck" (fat) here at the top, I can hold the insides back and away with my left hand while I rip the belly open with my right, so. Now, hold the pan up against the carcass and I'll roll the guts into it. See? Now, find me a short stick about two inches thick that I can shove into the asshole, so it won't leak anything. That's fine." He plugged the anus. "Now, see, you must cut all around the vent on the outside and along both sides of the big gut, this way." He worked as he explained. "Now you have in the dishpan all the insides except the leaf-lard here. Be careful to hang his asshole over the edge of the pan so it cannot soil anything. That's almost pure lard. I separate that this way with my fingers and take the two halves out together." He did as he had said. "I suggest we take the guts and leaf in to Anna and Mrs. Lien so they can begin the picking off fat and stripping small intestines for sausage casings."

"This looks easy," said Short Nils. "Do you save the liver and lungs?"

"We save neither for our own use. We'll leave the lungs for the wolves; but I'll save the livers and boil them for the chickens, little by little."

They delivered their burdens and went to the spring to refill the boiler and buckets. Anna would need a generous quantity of water to complete her many tasks. Pehr fetched from the stable his handsaw, with which to rip the carcasses in half down the middle of the backbone.

Short Nils eviscerated the second carcass without accident, and they made a second trip to the house with viscera and leaf lard. This time, after putting down their burdens, they washed carefully and sat down to dinner. The house was no less malodorous than any busy abattoir. The girls, vaguely aware that evil had been done, sat to table with downcast faces. Nor could even Short Nils jolly them enough to smile. The pea soup with bread and butter was eaten quickly and in silence.

Now the carcasses should be cut into their proper parts before they froze and stiffened too much. The men must now lift down and make into proper cuts each half carcass; but first they must prepare a brine in the tight barrel into which would go hams, shoulders, and side meat. Nils sloshed the scalding water about in the barrel to partially rinse it and then up-ended it. He rolled it to the house and set it upright by the northeast corner well clear of the eaves. He and Pehr made another trip to the spring, after first rinsing the barrel and then emptying into it the half-full boiler. They took no buckets this time, because Anna had them in use. They filled the barrel a little more than half way and stirred in a generous quantity of salt. Directly Pehr stuck his head in the door and asked of his wife:

"Will you lend me an egg with which to test the brine?"

She handed him an egg from a bowl on her shelf, and he rejoined his butchering partner. From his open hand he eased the egg into the salty water. It sank.

"When the brine floats an egg it is salty enough for packing down pork."

Short Nils added salt and stirred. Pehr tested every minute or two until the egg did, indeed, remain afloat.

They lifted down onto the bench, and cut up each half carcass in turn, carrying to the brine barrel those parts that belonged in it. The meat was now thoroughly chilled; safe to place in the brine. The feet they stacked under the bench. The loins and rib roasts they spread on clean snow to freeze. If the weather turned mild, they would dry-salt them.

Before dark the men carried these parts to Pehr's workbench for safe storage until he could improvise something better. This meat would be eaten fresh or lightly salted, so its storage would not be prolonged. The heads they fetched and set down on the other end of the workbench. These Pehr would split tomorrow to get the brains. Fried brains were one of his favorite breakfast dishes. The jowls, ears, and other meaty parts of the heads would become delicious head cheese when thoroughly boiled, chopped, and placed under pressure to squeeze out excess fat.

The barrel now stood so full of meat that some of the brine ran over the top. Pehr laid atop the meat a large stone, rinsed for the purpose. If wolves or other wild animals ventured to plunder the barrel he would take more stringent measures to protect its contents. He assumed that no local carnivore was strong enough to tip the barrel over. His judgement was vindicated.

At suppertime both men removed their butchering clothes before entering the house, and washed their hands, arms and faces with extra care before sitting to table.

"You killed two of our pigs today, didn't you?" asked Elna accusingly.

Silence was as stone, and it devolved upon Anna to answer:

"We bought them to eat, dear girl. Papa shot them, so they felt no pain. It is not the same as murder. It is a normal necessity among various people. You will see how good the meat is!"

"I shan't want any," grumbled Elna, barely containing her tears.

Nils changed the subject:

"After supper we shall all scrape and clean pig's feet, even my little Hanna. Eh, Hanna?"

"I'll help, if you show me how," answered Hanna.

"That I will! We'll all sit here around the table and scrape all the bristles right off those feet. And, my, they'll be good after your mother cooks and pickles them." To himself he thought: "How can they be so good, after mucking around in slop and manure weeks and months on end?" One should never harbor such reflections!

After supper they all did, in fact, help with the scraping and cleaning of the pig's feet. The girls' help was, in truth, of little consequence, because Anna dared not give them sharp knives for fear they would cut themselves. They scraped with spoons until they grew so sleepy that they could scarcely hold their heads up. Then Anna tucked them into bed, and the adults completed the work.

Mrs. Lien arose from her scraping and said to her son: "Now we go home to rest. We will come back tomorrow to help finish the work."

"Here," said Anna, handing her a generous piece of loin, "this is for your breakfast. There'll be more for you tomorrow."

Pehr opened the door for them and thanked them profusely. Mrs. Lien and Tollef stepped outside and headed for home. Anna stuck her head out the door and called her thanks loudly as mother and son walked away. Everyone turned in early, quite spent by a hard day's work.

First thing next morning Pehr split the heads and removed the brains. He brought them in and washed them free of their seemingly endless mesh of blood vessels that entwined them as hair-like filaments. The brains he ate must be clean; and they must not be adulterated with scrambled eggs or any other "stretching" medium. Clean and straight, fried, with pepper and salt to season them, he thought pig brains utterly delectable.

After breakfast, Nils and Pehr chopped the snouts off the heads and brought them in and cleaned them as they had done the feet the night before. Anna then placed the four halves in the new boiler and Pehr lifted them onto the stove to cook. After about two hours the room was suffused with a pleasing aroma that told Anna the heads were done. At her request, Pehr lifted the boiler off the stove and set it on the floor to cool. When they were cool enough to handle, Pehr, by Anna's instruction, lifted the heads from the boiler and placed them in Anna's new giant wooden bowl. Then Anna took over, separating fat and meat from the bones. Most of this she did with her bare hands; the heads were so thoroughly cooked that the flesh literally fell from the bones. This separation done, Pehr took hold again; this time with the double-bladed chopping knife, made for the very purpose of reducing meat to the texture of headcheese or sausage. Anna added copious quantities of pepper and salt to the contents of the bowl, and Pehr kept chopping and rocking until no sizeable lump remained. Anna now poured the bowl contents into two large baking pans, little more than half filling them. Atop the chopped meat in each pan she laid a clean board, cut in advance by Pehr to fit loosely into the pan, and on the board she laid one of Pehr's splitting wedges, boiled clean for the purpose. The pressure thus applied would squeeze out the excess fat and cause it to rise to the top, whence, when cool and firm it might be easily separated. The headcheese was done! And it would be delicious in sandwiches during the cold winter to come. Mrs. Lien and Tollef had come in time to help.

In like manner, Anna cooked and Mrs. Lien chopped into sausage a considerble volume of odds and ends and trimmings, otherwise quite useless. Anna had ready the casings, lengths of gut cleaned and washed in a dozen waters. Elna and Tollef helped her stuff them, using the tapered horn lengths as funnels, and tying the ends with stout string.

Finally they stuffed a dozen large rings of gut with the blood and meal mixture, speckled with fat lumps garnered by the women off the viscera. They had the mixture thickened to the consistency of cooked breakfast cereal—easily spooned into the casings. The main jobs of butchering and preparing pork had now been done.

To the very considerate gratitude of her men, Anna, with Mrs. Lien's help, had picked the fat off the viscera and rendered it, together with the leaf lard, while they were cutting up and salting down the main parts of the carcasses. She had even, quite understandably, dumped the "innards" into the woods some distance from the house. The women had filled the large pail and several smaller containers with pure sweet lard. One sizeable container would be Mrs. Lien's. The butchering was virtually accomplished; and the entire group enjoyed for supper, thick slabs of fresh light-salted pork, roasted in the oven. Elna had forgotten about the pigs!

Pehr had almost fallen asleep that night, when he suddenly rose on his elbow and whispered to Anna:

"Did you save the bladders for the girls?"

"Yes, indeed I did," replied Anna. "They're soaking. I'll blow them up and tie them tomorrow." (Inflated hog bladders were the only toy balloons known on farms until relatively recent times. They were amazingly strong, and might be kicked about in a home from butchering time until the following spring. Some put dried peas or beans in them so they rattled.)

Pehr's next project was a hog crate or cage, with which to fetch a boar to his gilt, but it was temporarily deferred while he attended to an oversight more urgent—they must have a place to store the frozen fresh pork and sausages.

He turned to, and built a stout tight box of planks about three feet high and two feet square. Nils walked to Clitherall for hinges and hasp while Pehr completed the thing. They placed it beside the brine barrel, loaded it half full of stones pryed off the prairie with the crow bar, covered the stones with straw, and laid the cloth wrapped edibles in the straw. This served well as Anna's ice box until the first February thaw, by which time much of the meat and sausages had been eaten. The remainder would be smoked.

Now to the portable hog cage. Specifications: 3 feet high; 6 feet long; 2 feet wide; hand holds for lifting and carrying; strong, and so built that a five-hundred-pound hog (without nose ring) could not root it apart with his snout; front end solid planking, rear end a solid drop door set behind corner members; solid plank floor, and ribbed top.

Short Nils and Pehr debated briefly and settled on "vertical-bar" design, which would give no snout a lifting purchase.

They set to work. Nils was a willing helper, eager to acquire some of Pehr's skill. First they doweled together two one-foot planks for the floor. This they laid flat, and bored inch-and-a-half holes, centered four inches in from the edges, and at six-inch intervals the length of both sides, so spaced that one hole was in each corner. Into the holes they set three-foot uprights, worked round at both ends to fit snugly into the holes. Next they battened together the boards for the top, spaced four inches apart, then bored holes clear through the boards, spaced exactly to meet and receive the verticals. Before laying the top on they battened and nailed in place the front end, inside the corner members. They built the drop door at the rear exactly as the front end, but had so foreshortened the top and cleated the corners so that the door lifted out easily. Nils, handy with a hammer, drove a nail through each end of the vertical side members squarely across the holes into which they were fitted, thus securing them against pulling out. Finally, they attached to each side, at about mid-height, a light length of rail; flattened the length of the cage; secured with bolts; and projecting round, about a foot beyond the ends. To latch the door, Pehr bored an inch hole through it just below the top cage boards, and stuck a tapered oak pin into it. Now the cage stood ready for its first traveler. It was of clear seasoned white oak, so durable that it out-lasted its senior builder. During Pehr's time, he always set it off ground on stones or wood chunks when not in use, to retard the inevitable rotting of the bottom.

With arrival of December, thoughts turned again to logging. Pehr had promised Short Nils to help build him a cabin; and now was a good time to assemble the requisite materials. Pehr's word was his bond, and never would he shirk from it; but one day at dinner he jibed Nils in this wise:

"I shall have to build a little smoke house before March. Since I will help you cut and lay up a cabin, I assume that you will help me build a smokehouse. It need be only about twice the size of the privy. We had better arrive at an understanding."

Nils struck at the bait:

"Of course, I'll help you. Did you for one minute doubt that I would? Build it big as a house and I'll help you!"

Pehr burst out laughing at Nils' heated retort.

"I knew you would help me, my good neighbor. I was merely amusing myself at your expense. We'll have both structures up before we do our spring planting. Relax and finish your supper!"

They chopped and hauled logs on Nils' place for more than two weeks. Then one day well past mid-month, they loaded the new hog cage into the wagon box on the sledge and drove Pehr's sharp-shod oxen to Clitherall to fetch Murdock's boar.

On arrival, they lifted the cage off the sledge and into Murdock's pig pen. He lured the tame animal into the cage with a handful of oats and dropped the door behind him. Pehr secured the drop door with the oak pin. The boar was heavy, and it was with considerable grunting by both men and hog that they lifted him clear of the fence and into the wagon box. They shook hands with Murdock and departed. At home they repeated the lifting hassle in reverse order, and the gilt had her first romantic companion. She came in heat a few days later, and they coupled several times in the slow deliberate fashion of swine. The boar had served his purpose, but Pehr elected to keep him until year's end, thus compensating Murdock for the services of his animal. Pehr fed the swine well, often cooking for them a mash of bran or shorts and potatoes. The animals kept their straw bedding clean, never deficating except some distance from their straw-built shelter. (Swine are our most cleanly farm animals, much malignment to the contrary notwithstanding.)

They used ten-foot logs for the smokehouse, of various hard species (oak, ash, birch) that grew in the lake woods. They set the structure into the northerly hillside away from the house, siting it in an opening among the trees to avoid large roots. Days were now so short that they made only one trip a day between such stable chores morning and night as feeding and watering the animals, and once a day "mucking" out the manure. They notched and laid up each load as they brought it home. They built it in the manner of the stables and roofed it with hay from the old stack bottom. But for a covered trench to convey the smoke and a fire pit at the lower end of it, they had the affair completed in a week.

Since they had agreed to wait with the laying-up of Nils' cabin until temperatures moderated in the spring, they now had a spell of leisure time until year's end.

Short Nils waxed restless with nothing to do. Pehr suggested they drive to Clitherall and procure some household utensils the young bachelor would need when he occupied his own cabin. This they did and came home with a sackful of items. One day they made for Nils a table and two benches such as he was familiar with in Pehr's house. Then one day Short Nils had a brilliant idea for a project both useful and entertaining.

"Let's break your young steer to lead by a halter and pull against a yoke. The snow is just deep enough and loose enough to curb his antics without injury."

So they commenced. The leading part was easily accomplished. They simply tied a half-inch rope about his neck and secured the other end to the rear bunk of the sledge. When the veteran oxen drew the sledge, the young one was obliged to follow. At first he set his legs in resistance, and was dragged along, his feet splaying out ludicrously. Then he walked along, straining against the rope. At that instant, Nils coaxed Pehr's oxen into a trot, and quite promptly, Krull was also trotting. Pehr slowed to a walk again, and Krull followed, careful not to stretch the rope. They stopped the rig. Nils hopped off and untied the rope around the bunk. Now he need only walk and talk to Krull, and he followed obediently. Perhaps he was halter broken.

Now they would train him to pull a load. Pehr unyoked Buck (Bride was the gentler, steadier of the pair) and Nils led Krull into his place beside Bride. The heavy yoke and bow puzzled Krull, but he was too tired to resist. He shook his head and neck but the yoke remained. Bride stood as if anchored, seeming to enjoy the fun; Pehr called "Come Bride, come Krull;" but only Bride stepped out, virtually dragging his junior partner along. Krull resisted only temporarily, because the bow against his throat threatened to choke him. He walked forward, and the bow fell away from his throat. Now the yoke lay against the neck, as it should, and he discovered that it was a tolerable burden. He fell in with Bride's pace, and offered no further resistance.

"In a week's time I'll bet I can have him responding to Gee and Haw, Get up, and Wo," said Short Nils enthusiastically. "He will make a fine work animal."

"I'll help with it. He needs to learn both of our voices, and to respond to either without hesitation. We'll drive him with Buck and Bride alternately, so he'll behave in either near or off position."

They trained the yearling ox a little each day for almost a week.

Nils suggested they drive him with Bride to Clitherall for Christmas things, but Pehr vetoed the idea. The barefoot young ox was in some danger of injury by the shoes his partners wore. To Clitherall they went—with Buck and Bride. They got candy for the girls and other treats as well; but they failed in their quest for lutefisk. The Mormons were not Scandinavians, and therefore did not stock the odoriferous delicacy.

Nils duplicated his holiday efforts of a year ago. Everyone was jolly and the food was delicious. Nils was busy helping the girls hang each a stocking in the stove corner, early on Christmas Eve, when the door opened and Nils Johnson walked in. Everyone gathered around and greeted him warmly. He said he simply craved a respite from the cold, heavy pinery work, and this was his only sanctuary.

They sat to eat Christmas Eve supper, and the girls said grace in unison. The elders sat and talked long after the girls were in bed. Nils filled the stockings: candy, nuts and other goodies and a doll with a painted glass head went into each.

Nils Johnson yawned and admitted to being tired from his fifty-mile hike.

"Do you have your bedding in that roll?" asked Anna.

"I have some, but can you lend me a blanket."

"Yes, of course!"

She raised the lid of the great chest and took one out.

"Here you are. I regret you'll sleep a bit colder than before. You see we have chickens in the stable now, so we keep no bedding there. Nils has only two animals to take the chill off."

"I sleep in my own stable," explained Anderson proudly, "and you're invited." The bachelors bade Anna and Pehr "Happy Christmas" and walked into the snow-lit twilight of winter night under a dim moon.

As they walked Anderson inquired: "How long will you be staying? Until New Year's?"

"No! I promised to be back on my loading job on the twenty-ninth. I shall have to walk back on the twenty-eighth. I just thought of last winter and felt an urge to see all of you again."

"We're mighty glad you came, even if for a short while only."

"Will you be staying here right on now, or what?"

They walked into Anderson's stable and he indicated a bedding place for Johnson.

"Yes, I'll stay right here and work on my claim. I loaned my oxen here, to Pehr last spring, and he sowed me a patch of wheat. He helped me build this stable and lay up logs for a cabin. We plan to raise that early in the spring. When will you settle?"

"I'm quitting the logging camp in time to dig a cellar house and break some ground for wheat next spring. If I use my earnings sparingly, I can make a go of my claim."

"Of course, you can," mumbled Anderson, half asleep.

Thereafter, only the ruminating oxen violated the infinite silence of winter night on the pioneer fringe.

The three fellow land seekers enjoyed immensely their visit together. Anderson showed Johnson all about his jumped claim, proud of the beautiful, rolling prairie hills he would own. Anna apologized for her cooking; Bos was dry, so they had neither milk nor butter. The men politely shrugged off her apologies.

In the course of their visiting, Pehr inquired about Sven, wondering where he had gone.

"Oh," said Johnson, "Sven works in the same logging camp as I do. He would have come with me, but he was a bit under the weather and dared not attempt the long hike. You know, Pehr, he filed on the land east of yours. He's salting down his wages to come and settle on it next spring. He sends greetings."

"Tell him for me," said Pehr, "if he's not here at sowing time, I'll turn and sow a couple acres for him to demonstrate claim improvement. It would have to be oats!"

"He will certainly be grateful to you; but I expect he'll be here himself. He's a deliberate sort of fellow; but he can also be determined when he sets his mind on something. He'll make you fellows a mighty good neighbor. I sometimes think I should have claimed land nearer by."

Amid all the adult visiting, the girls also had a good holiday. They delighted in showing off their new dolls to the visitors. At one point, speaking from Johnson's lap, Elna said:

"I think I will call Nils and Nils my uncles, since I have no other."

From Anderson's lap, Hanna submitted:

"They will be my uncles too!"

Noting Anna's obvious pregnancy, Johnson wished her and Pehr good fortune with a son.

Sooner than anyone could well realize came Johnson's morning of departure. Anna made fresh pork sandwiches to sustain him on his long walk back to the logging camp. All sent hearty greetings to Sven. "Goodby Uncle Nils," said the girls as they were kissed goodby. The fond wishes and blessings of all went with him. They were glad that Anderson's warm companionship would remain.

After New Year's, the men addressed themselves to the task of chopping and hauling home, each from his own woods, fuel wood sufficient to last a year or more. During the holidays they had constructed for Nils a sledge almost identical to Pehr's, so now they drove two rigs. Whether hauling or chopping, they worked together. On Pehr's land they clear-cut a hill patch in the northeast corner of his woodland forty; on Nils', they cleared a small knoll some distance south of his stable. They walked to the woods when they were felling and trimming, and came home for all their meals. Though they sorely missed Johnson's help of a year ago, the work progressed rapidly. In a week and a half they had a pile of polewood on Anderson's house site deemed abundantly adequate for two years, allowing he would burn it sparingly until next spring. The second year he would have dry wood to burn, during the burning of which he would lay up another year's supply. In such manner he would thenceforth retain a year's supply of dry wood ahead of current needs. A year ago the three men had laid up enough for Pehr so that he was similarly provided. He was now burning wood that had lain sawed, split and piled the year before. About the end of January when Pehr's pile of new wood was adjudged adequate, they made one trip to the lake for a load of sugar maple with which to smoke the meat in the spring. Their own woods were devoid of maple, containing mainly white oak, quaking aspen, and paper birch.

They enjoyed "Kalva dans" (calf dance) pudding for supper dessert their last day of logging. Bos had dropped, two days before, another calf, this one a prettily brindled heifer. This time Short Nils introduced the girls to the little newcomer; and they named her Brindle, befitting her coloration. Anna was pleased that they might soon, by scheduling breeding correctly, be assured of a constant milk supply. Swedish cooking without cream and butter was virtually impossible. While Bos had been dry, swine and cats alike had suffered with their owners.

Pehr now commenced giving each of the cattle a quart measure of oats daily, adding once a week a generous pinch of salt. He gave Short Nils enough oats and salt to feed his oxen a similar ration. So fed, and with a constant manger of hay before them, the work animals would be in good condition for spring's work; and the cow gave milk. Krull came by his oats by default, he neither worked nor gave milk; but his otherwise parsimonious master had not the heart to deny it him.

Throughout February the neighbors bucked into stove wood length and split to convenient size the wood they had hauled in January. They worked separately until Short Nils had his task completed, after which he helped Pehr. They rested one day, to bring Murdock's boar home. While in Clitherall they bought, for Anna, certain condiments and other kitchen items she had requested. Pehr's maple they sawed and split last so that it would lie on top of the stack and ready to hand. Some of it they bucked into six-inch lengths and split it into pieces little more than slivers. This they piled separately, in readiness for meat smoking. There was more on the large pile, in case of need.

After a warm spell in early March had cleared off snow and ice and fairly well dried Nils' building logs, the two beaver-like workers laid up his cabin walls. Roofing it was delayed because the prairie sod remained frozen or water-logged under the surface. The snow was gone, but at depth the ground remained frozen.

They shifted Pehr's wagon box from the sledge to the wagon, put the sledge on wood blocks in a place that would be shady after the trees leafed out, and drove Pehr's oxen and wagon to Clitherall. Nils bought a stove and stove pipe with which to set it up. Pehr bought a quantity of nails and spikes. Soon after the frost went out and the prairie sod lay firm enough to cut and handle they laid Nils' roof and installed his stove. Nils' cabin, similar to Pehr's, stood completed. Anna and the girls came to see and admire.

When Nils came one morning for breakfast, driving his oxen and wagon, he prompted Pehr to inquire:

"And where might you be going?"

"I'm going nowhere, but I've determined to exercise the animals a little every day to harden them for field work. You have seen the signs of spring, yes?"

"Oh, I've seen the signs of spring alright; and if you wish to help me, we shall demonstrate its arrival this very day."

"Are we to violate a military secret, or can you tell me what you have in mind?"

"I intend to hang our meat for smoking. But first we must dig under the back side of the smoke house and run a covered trench about ten feet down the slope to convey the smoke. We'll lay a sort of cobble stone grate at the end. Are you with me?"

"Of course, but first let me drive my oxen home and stable them."

They completed the smoking arrangement before noon. After dinner, Anna wiped each piece of meat dry as the men lifted one after another from the brine barrel. Pehr drove several spikes into the roof supports of the smoke house, from which the various hog parts were suspended by stout cord. By afternoon coffee, all the meat was hung and a good-smelling white smoke was rising through the straw roof of the smoke house. Pehr would, during all his waking hours and a few after he was asleep, keep that smoke filling and slowly escaping from the smoke house. The meat would be delicately flavored and so well sealed that it would keep indefinitely. From the hams, especially, would be delicious meat with which to make sandwiches to sustain one during the strenuous work days of summer. The consumers would prefer the meat sliced raw; they knew not of trichinosis and, in their sublime ignorance, could have no fear of it.

Spring showers ushered in the transitional month of April. On its very first day, Pehr removed the shoes from his oxen and hung them up for use in another season. But for icy mornings in March, he would have taken them off sooner. He knew well that an ox accustomed to shoes fell easy victim to a patch of ice if suddenly barefooted.

April was memorable for the arrival of the homesteader's first litter of pigs. On the tenth the sow gave birth to eight little pigs, more splashed than spotted, and each frisky and rooting from birth. The girls fell in love with them; and soon as Pehr determined that the mother had no objection, the girls were permitted to enter the pen (even the shelter) to play with the "cute" little ones. They called them "little grunts." They were infinitely more genuine and lively than the dolls. Five were males and three females, but the girls made no such distinction. Pehr immediately decided to keep the old sow for a second year, since she farrowed so large a litter. He could sell half a dozen and have two left for the family's pork supply. He wondered what weaned pigs were selling for.

The very day the pigs were farrowed, Anna and Pehr planted a goodly strip of potatoes along the south side of last year's wheat. Pehr plowed and harrowed the garden; and they planted two rows in it, this time at the west side. Anna could not bend, so she dropped the potato cuttings from a standing posture.

In the days that followed, Pehr harrowed and sowed his grain; oats where the wheat had been, and wheat on the remainder, including the new ground (about five acres of oats and ten of wheat). Short Nils borrowed the harrow at times when Pehr was sowing. Both had their crops in and after-harrowed soon after mid-April, despite a few interruptions by welcome spring showers. Anna's early garden was also planted in time, done mostly by Pehr and his daughters; Anna had difficulty kneeling or squatting with her front protruding.

The neighbors worked together at fencing. Short Nils started from scratch but Pehr had only to move the north side far enough out to include the new ground and then build the ends to meet it. They did all the fencing in a six day week—and viewed it with real pride. The girls brought them forenoon and afternoon lunches when they worked in the field. The refreshments and rest were especially appreciated.

Near the end of April Anna waxed extremely uncomfortable; and, though she did not once complain, Pehr became concerned about her. A dozen times a day and whenever he waked at night, he would inquire of her: "Are you feeling alright? Are you sure?"

She was short with the girls, which they had never known before. Finally, her discomfort obviously increasing, Pehr asserted that he would go for the midwife, however long the wait might be. He hitched his oxen early one morning after milking Bos and struck out in direction of Dalton, near which lived the widow Holm. He returned with his passenger the same day, though he arrived late. Nils had milked Bos and fed the stock. Mrs. Lien had come and spent the day with Anna.

Since Sven had not yet made an appearance, Nils and Pehr, their ox yoke in tandem, broke and sowed to oats about five acres of Sven's prairie adjacent to Pehr's middle forty. They would not have him lose his claim because of neglect. It took them until the first of May. Johnson had not been by, but they assumed that he was busy breaking, sowing, and digging a cellar to live in. He would come and see them when his most urgent work had been done.

Mrs. Holm was no less a pillar of strength than Tilda had said. She helped Anna with her work as a hired girl might; but she left to the prospective mother some of the tasks most uncomfortable to her; the discomfort would help bring the fetus down and position it properly. She scoffed at Anna's frequent complaints, and diverted her thoughts with reminiscences of the old country. These took Anna's mind off her discomfort, well enough, but it so intensified her longing for Skåne that she often wept secretly at night. Though she slept beside her, the stout-hearted widow Holm knew naught of her sorrow. Pehr slept in the stable, despite the chickens; each evening laying for himself a fresh bed of straw, and each morning carrying his blankets to the house for safe keeping. He would have slept in Nils' stable, but insisted on remaining within calling distance.

On the afternoon of May second, Anna felt the first twinges of labor, and Mrs. Holm promptly put her to bed. By prearrangement, Nils took the girls and their bedding to his cabin, thus getting them out of the way, and removing them from their mother's inevitable moaning and screaming. Nils explained to them:

"Your mother wishes you safe with me while she is too sick to see about you. She will probably bring you a little brother. Won't you like that?"

"No!" answered Elna, spontaneously. "He has already made her sad and afraid. I would rather not have a brother."

"I should like to have a little brother," ventured Hanna. "But I'll hate him if he hurts my mother!"

"He'll probably come tonight or tomorow; and then we'll all be glad to have him. We shall stay here until he has come."

Nils spread their thick comforters on the floor and their blankets over them. He had even brought their chamber pot.

The girls, now eight and six, were understandably restless and apprehensive, but they felt secure with their Uncle Nils, even so.

Nils delayed supper intentionally, reasoning that late to bed would ensure late sleeping in the morning. When he finally set the table and poured the soup furnished by Mrs. Holm, the girls were yawning. However, with his inducement, they ate quite well, He helped Hanna into her night dress, while Elna, asserting her seniority, changed behind the curtain. Not before he had peeked in and seen them soundly asleep did Nils wash and shelve the cups and soup bowls. Quietly as he could, he put several chunks of wood into the stove, so that the room would surely remain warm. Then he, too, went to bed; but lay awake a long time, visualizing probable events in his neighbors' cabin.

Soon as he awakened in the morning, he fetched wood and built a roaring fire in the stove. He would have the place cozy again before his little guests came awake. (Chilly nights persisted throughout May and well into June.) When he finally heard them stirring behind the curtain, he called to Hanna, asking whether she wished help to dress. Elna called back that she would help her; and soon they emerged, fully dressed.

"Good morning. How are my pretty nieces this fair day?"

The girls responded more cheerfuly than he had anticipated.

"Come, wash your faces before breakfast." He handed them a clean face towel.

"I know you like pancakes, so that's what we shall have. With syrup and butter, too."

His culinary repertoire was limited, but he could mix and fry delicious pancakes. The girls ate several each; and then Nils fried a considerable stack for himself. He was already pondering what he might cook for dinner. He settled on fried bacon and boiled potatoes, both items given him from Pehr's stores. Perhaps the brother would arrive before supper, so the girls might return home and everyone would celebrate the event. He instructed the girls:

"Elna, Hanna, I must ask you to stay in this room quietly while I go over and see how things are going. I shall be back in a little while." The girls, despite long faces, agreed to remain.

When Nils came round the corner of the Pehrson's cabin he saw Pehr standing outside the door. He ran to him, enbraced him, and inquired:

"Pehr, what is wrong? Did Anna die in giving birth?"

Between pitiable sobs, Pehr replied:

"The baby was turned wrong inside her; and before it got born it was strangled to death by the umbilical cord. It was a perfectly formed boy; but now there will be no male heir." His sobbing interrupted the monologue. "Anna has been bleeding terribly inside; the whole bed is bloody. She lost consciousness early this morning—. Mrs. Holm—fears she may die—. Please go and be with the girls. —Don't let them come here. I must go back and sit by my Anna. I'll come for you when there's a change—."

Pehr stepped inside and closed the door behind him. Nils turned on his heel, tears streaming into his beard, and stumbled, half-seeing, toward his cabin. Before the girls could see him he stopped to dry his eyes and beard. He walked in nonchalantly, and greeted them; and in the gloomy room they could not see that he had wept.

"Have we a little brother?" inquired Elna.

"Is Mamma alright?" asked Hanna.

Nils knew he must lie:

"No, you have no brother yet; and your Mamma is very sick. You must stay with me so she can rest in quiet. Your Papa asked me to look after you until he can come."

Meanwhile, Pehr sat at the bedside of his comatose wife, and watched as her precious life literally drained away. While she still had a pulse and breath he bowed his head to the side of her bed and prayed silently. Mrs. Holm, quite helpless in the circumstances, leaned over from her bedside vigil and felt for a pulse-beat in Anna's throat. This time she could detect none. She laid a hand on Pehr's shoulder and said in a husky half-whisper:

"Your wife is dead, Mr. Pehrson. I could not save her. In all my mid-wifery experience I have never failed so badly."

Pehr rose and reached down to stroke Anna's ashen brow. His grief was now beyond tears. He said, half to himself:

"If I had not insisted on coming to the New World, she might have lived to old age. It was my fault that she is dead!"

Mrs. Holm heard his self-incrimination and sought to console him:

"Mr. Pehrson, I know she was unhappy, but who's to say she would have ever been happier in Sweden. You sought a better life for her and your daughters, so you should not assume blame."

Pehr asked: "Will you wash her, please; remove the bloodied bedding and lay her out together with her son? Can you do this without me? I shall go to Anderson's with the tragic news. Please come over there when you have things in order."

The moment Pehr stepped into Nils' cabin, his daughters sensed the grief they must bear with their father. He kneeled down and drew them to him, saying:

"Your mamma and little brother have gone to heaven. You must be brave and strong so they may look down and be proud of you."

The girls sobbed and clung to him, heartbroken. He loaned them his wet hankderchief in turn, and admonished in whispers:

"Cry it out, and you will feel better. We must be strong together."

Gradually their sobbing grew less, and Pehr stood up. But the girls continued to cling to him, as if fearful of losing him too.

"Your Papa and I will not leave you," said Nils, gathering Hanna into his arms as he spoke. Pehr lifted Elna to him at the same time. The girls quieted, but their tears continued to fall. The men held them so for several minutes before setting them down and releasing them.

Anna had died about nine o'clock, and it was almost noon before Mrs. Holm had everything in order. She, too, shed bitter tears at the loss of the young mother. When she arrived at Anderson's, she quickly prepared the bacon and potatoes Nils had scheduled. The girls could not eat and were excused from the table. They went behind their curtain and wept in silence. No one ate with relish, Pehr forced himself to chew and swallow; he had not eaten since the night before, and he had much to do. He spoke in a low voice to Mrs. Holm and Nils, requesting her to remain overnight with the girls in Nils' cabin and Nils to sleep in his stable. To this they agreed without hesitation. He would sleep in the room where the dead lay, so the bodies might surely not be disturbed.

"I shall build a coffin this afternoon, while you, Nils, dig the grave, if you please; and we can bury our dear dead tomorrow morning."

The girls emerged from their place, and begged to go and see their mother. Pehr could not deny them; so everyone went to his place after the dreary dinner. The girls screamed with grief and shock at seeing their mother lying dead. Pehr restrained them from climbing onto the bed where she lay. He was grateful that the dead eyes were closed, and she looked as if asleep.

Pehr turned to Mrs. Holm and asked her to take milk, cream, butter, eggs and whatever else she might wish for supper and breakfast, and return with the girls to Nils' cabin. In a few minutes she did so. Nils and Pehr went out, and when they cleared the south side of the house, Pehr knew exactly where the grave should be. As they walked he instructed Nils:

"Come, and I'll show you where to dig the grave."

In moments they were at the spot; just west of the garden under a splendid young white oak.

"Here it shall be, where the rising sun can strike it. Whenever I build a proper house with more windows to the west, I shall be able to see it even when indoors. I will go and fashion a coffin while you dig. Make the grave six feet long, two feet wide, and five feet deep. Its length must be so; east-west. I'll go build the casket. Remind me later, to go and ask Mrs. Lien and her son to the burial."

Pehr went to the stable workshop and commenced splitting planks off six-foot lengths of basswood. He hewed and planed until he had sufficient material to build a tight box six feet long, sixteen inches wide, and eighteen inches deep, with a snuggly fitted lid on top. The parts ready to assemble, Pehr milked Bos, and the men walked together to supper, carrying the milk. Nils had the grave almost deep enough.

The girls were persuaded to eat a little supper; the adults ate little better than at noon. During the meal Pehr told Mrs. Holm that he would return her to her home tomorrow afternoon. He would take his daughters with him to Mork's and return there to spend the night. His friends must be told of the tragedy.

"Don't let me forget to pay you. I believe I shall owe you for eight days and the delivery, six dollars in all."

"That's how it figures, but I feel unworthy of accepting it."

"You will accept it, and with my gratitude! The tragedy was not your fault."

"Nils, will you kindly milk Bos tomorrow evening and the next morning, and make such use of the milk as you wish?"

"Don't be concerned! I shall milk the cow and skim the cream. Most of it shall be saved for your return. I will also build a fire in your stove each day, so your house will not be stone-cold when you get back. This spring must be unusually cold!"

After supper the men returned to their work. Pehr had exhausted his meager nail supply, so he bored and pegged the coffin together with oaken dowels. It was sturdy and handsome, as a final labor of love ought to be. Nils quickly completed the grave.

Next morning, after a night almost sleepless, Pehr rose early, dressed and washed his face quickly, and came to stand by the strawstuffed mattress on which his beloved lay dead! He stood so, in silent tearless grief, several minutes. Then he stepped to Anna's sewing shelf and took up her scissors. He returned to the bed, and, depressing the pillow beside her head, drew out a lock of her brown hair and snipped it off. He returned the scissors to its place; then dug his large leather wallet from the chest, carefully placed the lock of hair in a secret compartment, and stuck the bulging wallet deep into a corner of the chest.

When he straightened from his secret task, Nils stood by the door, greeting him. Pehr explained:

"I just took a little curl of her hair to keep."

"That's good, Pehr. I came over, thinking we might put them in the casket before breakfast and be ready for the burial. I went and asked Mrs. Lien to come."

"Yes, let's do that. And thanks for going to Lien's."

They walked together to the stable, took up the coffin, one at each end, and brought it into the house. Pehr took from the chest, a beautiful flowered comforter that Anna had quilted in Sweden. He also took a white pillow slip, into which he stuffed one of the down pillows from the bed, and laid it in one end of the coffin. They lifted Anna's body into the box. Pehr at her head and Nils at her feet. (Her rigidity brought tears to both of them.) Her son was held to her shoulder by her left arm, as Mrs. Holm had arranged it. Lying so, the two barely fitted into the casket.

They carried the casket to the grave and set it upon two short lengths of rail laid across the hole near the ends. On the bottom of the grave Nils had laid two thin sticks of firewood, to ensure clearing the ropes by which the casket would be lowered. Nils now went to the stable and spliced together quarter-inch rope until he had two lengths of ten feet each. Pehr went to the house and got the Swedish family Bible, into which he would later enter Anna's vital statistics. Her son he would record without a name.

With some difficulty, Nils threaded under the casket the two rope lengths, about a foot in from the ends. Now all was ready, so they walked together to Nils' house, and brought Mrs. Holm and the girls back for a grave-side ceremony. Mrs. Lien and Tollef were there before them.

At sight of the covered casket, the girls stood bowed, with tears streaming. Nils noted that the casket had tear-streaks on it. Pehr opened the bible to the twenty-third Psalm and commenced reading, Nils beside him. He managed through the fourth verse before his tears blurred his vision so he could not read. He handed the book to Nils, pointing to the approximate place. Nils completed the reading. Then he said to Pehr:

"You take the rope ends on this side, and I'll take them on the other."

When they had the ropes taut under the casket, Nils asked Mrs. Lien to remove the rails on which it had rested. This she did, and the men, slipping the rope through their hands, lowered the casket to the bottom of the grave. The girls screamed hysterically as it went down. Pehr had made sure that Anna lay with her head to the west, so that she would rise on resurrection day facing the sun. (The first time an ordained minister came by the area, Pehr would have him say a proper burial ritual over Anna's grave.) Mrs. Holm took the girls in charge, and returned to Nils' place. Nils and Pehr filled and heaped the grave, taking turns with the spade. (To his dying day, Pehr kept a wooden frame about that grave, filled the depression as it mouldered and sank, and kept on top in summer a clump of red tiger lillies from Swedish seed Anna had brought.)

While Nils returned the spade and ropes to their places in the stable, Pehr sat at the head of the grave and reflected on many of the joys and sorrows he had shared with Anna. Certainly, he thought, the Lord gives and the Lord takes away. Blessed be his name! The wilderness had killed his wife; now he would see that it rewarded her daughters, for whom she had given her life.

The bereaved ones partook of early dinner at Nils' and departed by wagon for Mork's, where Pehr would deposit the girls with Tilda and drive Mrs. Holm to her home.

Tilda and Willie were shocked to tears by Pehr's grievous news. Anna dead! How terrible! Two little girls without a mother!

Tilda insisted that Pehr and Mrs. Holm have coffee and cookies before completing their journey. His spirits lifted by his friends, Pehr almost enjoyed the late afternoon lunch.

He took Mrs. Holm to her place and then returned to Mork's for a late supper. Tilda had fed the girls and put them to bed before he returned. At table, he related how Anna's son had been still-born and how she had bled to death in a few hours' time. Their eyes welled full of tears as he spoke. After drying her eyes and blowing her nose, Tilda asked:

"Would you like to leave your daughters here with me for a few weeks, even indefinitely? We get along well, as you know, and I would be glad to have them stay."

'Thank you! but they'd better come home with me. We shall have to learn how to cope without their mother. We have a good neighbor, Nils Anderson, of whom I know we have spoken. Anna taught him something of cooking, and he really does quite well. Between the two of us, no one will go hungry. The girls are growing fast, and will become increasingly helpful as they gain confidence. I'll remember your kind offer to keep them, should that at anytime seem desirable."

"Remember, they would be welcome!"

Turning to Willie, Pehr inquired:

"Have you any pigs to castrate this year?"

"Yes, I do. I have seven little boars to cut. They're old enough right now."

"Then we shall cut them tomorrow before I go home."

"Very good! do you have any?"

"Yes, I have five little boars, born the tenth of April. They can be castrated in a week or two. My sow had a litter of eight; so I shall have half a dozen to sell. Are they still worth a dollar apiece?"

"Yes they are. Mine have been spoken for at that price. I shall keep two gilts and sell the old sows when the cattle buyer comes round again. Two years are about all a man should keep a sow."

"I shall keep my sow a second year, as you did yours. Perhaps she will farrow a litter of eight a second time. If you hear of someone else wanting little pigs, send him to me!"

"You may be sure I will. Every settler wants a pig or two, because cured pork is the most useful meat on the frontier."

Pehr and the girls drove home next day, after he had helped Willie castrate the pigs. On one, Pehr had practiced the art under Willie's apt instruction, with Willie's carefully honed knife. (Pehr would buy himself such a knife, and do his own castrating thenceforth.)

Short Nils welcomed them home to a warm, clean house, with no visible sign of tragedy. He had even washed all of Pehr's bedding, and refilled the tick with clean straw. He had returned to its customary place, the girls' pallet. Pehr thanked him warmly for setting everything right again. The sorrowing girls stood silent, feeling their mother's absence almost as a physical blow. Without her, life seemed quite impossible.

At supper, Nils' cooking drew compliments from Pehr and his girls, but more from gratitude than for gastronomic quality. Nils did, indeed, persevere, and became a cook with considerable skill. He taught Pehr how to bake highly palatable bread, which, together with potatoes, remained the staff of life for the pioneers. More than ever before, Nils became a participating member of the household, usually taking only breakfast in his own house. Time went on, and everyone adjusted to the changed circumstances. Nils taught Pehr the culinary arts taught him by Anna; and Pehr, in turn, conveyed them to his daughters as they grew ever more confident and capable. Busy association soon meliorated the pain of their loss. Everyone contributed to the common weal. Soon the girls washed dishes after meals competently and independently. Elna learned to churn and salt a batch of butter. Hanna became expert at peeling potatoes, but not without numerous cuts that required very temporary bandages. Hanna became, also, the regular table-setter before meals; Elna served the food, often with Nils' help.

At mid-May all hands turned to and planted the late garden things. The girls learned to soak beans overnight before planting, and to space them about three inches apart in the row—assuming that all would not germinate. Pehr measured and marked rows. Nils made a slight trench by sweeping with the hoe handle; and the girls sowed the seeds. Hanna disposed of the large beet seeds in half a row, so Nils retrieved enough from her excessively thick-sown half to finish out the row. The time was late, even for sowing of the most tender of seeds, but night frosts came frequently; and the spring dragged on a month later than usual. There was no immediate need for weeding the early garden, because temperatures had repeatedly fallen so low that all vegetation was supressed.

Willie and Tilda came visiting May twentieth; he to help castrate pigs and she to see how the widower and his daughters were faring. For the girls it was the happiest day since their mother died. The Morks were pleased to see how Nils, without the least self aggrandizement, helped assuage the family's grief.

Pehr had, in anticipation, equipped himself with a pocket knife of Eskilstuna steel from Clitherall and an oil stone with which to whet it. He played surgeon to his own pigs; and Nils learned to hold them still for him. After the first two had been divested of their testicles, Willie became nothing more than a supervising expert. He was not displeased.

Tilda was delighted to see how punctually and capably the little girls performed various household tasks. They were obviously more help than hindrance to their bereaved father.

During late May and early June, Pehr and Nils chopped, hauled, and stacked logs of various species for the later building of a wood-working shop to stand by itself; the stable was becoming crowded and unpleasant, what with more animals and chickens to populate it.

One day when preparing bread dough, Pehr struck the bottom of the flour barrel with his scoop. It was time for a trip to the Perham flour mill. Nils and Pehr pooled their remaining wheat, some seven or eight bushels, without any question about how much was whose. Nils warned Pehr about hauling to the mill alone. He had heard that thugs frequenting the Rush Lake woods, lying in wait for ox drivers they could rob, were more dangerous than ever before. He would accompany Pehr, "riding shotgun," as it were, with Pehr's musket.

"What shall we do about the girls and the cow?" Pehr wanted to know.

"If we show her how, Elna can get enough milk out of Bos to keep the cow comfortable. We can show her how to replenish the fire with one stick of wood at a time, and keep the damper almost closed. The girls would freeze if they went with us. If they must, they can go to Mrs. Lien for help."

The men departed with their modest grist early on the tenth of June. They gained the woods west of Rush Lake before dark and settled down for the night. Pehr slept with his musket primed and ready, but no one disturbed them. The night was bitter, as Nils had predicted. Enroute the mill, they drove through ice on water puddles. Pehr wondered whether their emergent late garden had been frosted.

At home, the girls remained courageous until dark; then they commenced hearing and seeing such as frightened them. At one point, Hanna whispered:

"I saw something at the window; it was an Indian, I think."

Elna blew out the candle, and whispered to her frightened little sister:

"I'll take most of the stuff out of the chest, and we'll get in and close the cover. There we'll be safe."

They did so, setting the lid on its hasp so they could peek out the crack. They slept in the chest both nights the men were gone.

Enroute home, the men again slept in the Rush Lake woods, without untoward incident. They returned home before dark of the third day, to find the frightened little girls weeping on their mother's grave. So pathetic was the sight that Pehr never again left his girls alone at night before they were grown young women.

Finally consoled and quieted, the girls ate a good supper, their first substantial meal in almost three days, and went to sleep early, safe in their accustomed place.

With arrival of warmer June weather, the potato bugs emerged as they had the year before. But this year, as in every year after, Pehr was ready for combat. He had procured from the Clitherall store a pound of Paris green with which to poison the pests. When he deemed the larvae batch at its peak, he attacked them. He scooped a sizeable earthen bowl full of flour with which to dilute and stretch the toxic material. Into a low round bake pan he measured and mixed the poison and flour—one tablespoon Paris green to six of flour. Then he walked the potato rows while the dew still lay on the vines, sprinkling a pinch or two onto each plant. He mixed several batches before he had all the potatoes treated, using up most of the poison and flour he had ready. The residue of flour he cast out, and carefully washed the bowl with soap and hot water, as he did also the baking pan.

The application was wondrously effective; later broods of larvae attacked only a few plants, and these Pehr rescued, as he had the entire planting earlier. Potato bug poisoning remained an annual chore as long as Pehr lived, and many years after his passing.

Fruition and ripening were slow and late that year (1871), both delayed by a protracted winter and a wet cold spring. But eventually garden and fields yielded fairly well. Pehr sold wheat to the tune of about two hundred dollars, and yet retained an abundance for seed, flour, and feed. He sold fifty bushels of oats to Nils for twenty-five cents a bushel and had a hundred bushels left for his own use. He almost filled the cellar with tubers and roots. He was blessed with abundance!

After harvest, he and Nils plowed their stubble, each with his own yoke of oxen. After that they helped Sven Person log and build a cabin. (He had come in time to harvest his oats that Pehr had sowed for him. He slept under his wagon cover and ate most of his meals at Pehr's until the cabin was erected.)

Finally, that fall of '71, Pehr and Nils drove their oxen tandem again and broke some ten acres of new ground for each. They would be half-rich on wheat. They "had it made," or so they thought.

Chapter 11

MIXED BLESSINGS OF THE SEVENTIES

Though materially blessed by the year 1871, it was also a time of sorrow and trials such as Pehr and his daughters would never again experience. Pehr was doubly saddened because he blamed himself for Anna's demise. (Had he not insisted on their departure from Sweden, his wife would not have grieved herself to death, longing for the home she was never to see again.)

In the face of stark necessity, the girls assumed duties and responsibilities quite beyond their tender age. Under Pehr's tutelage, often awkward and dubious but ever patient, Elna learned to prepare and serve their simple fare as any housewife might; and under Elna's constant guidance, Hanna helped with such routine tasks as table-setting and dishwashing. Elna learned to milk Bos, to skim off the cream when the pail had stood and it had risen, and to churn butter and salt it. Hanna worked the dasher.

Pehr undertook all heavy household tasks. He carried all the water from the spring except when, during busy times, he forgot. Then the girls fetched it with pails half-full. He insisted on a weekly change of clothes, both under and outer and washed all the soiled garments once a week. No one went dirty. He also carried in the stove-wood and took out the ashes—both daily chores in heating seasons. If he forgot and the wood ran out, the girls carried in more; but never did they remove the ashes, because Pehr forbade their trying. He feared they might drop coals on the floor and set the cabin afire. Only he would open the fire door and remove the ash pan! He alone carried the slops, mash, and water to the pigs twice a day and also fed and watered the cattle. When Bos was stabled, he did the milking. Daily he cleaned out the stable manure and spread fresh straw for bedding in the stalls. Hanna fed the chickens and gathered the eggs. When, in the warm season, the laying nests in the stable yielded nothing, she stalked the hens, one by one, to their secret nesting places. On Pehr's advice, she always left one egg as a decoy, lest the hen abandon her nest. When the chickens were confined in the stable, Hanna's chores were simple.

Before cold weather commenced in the autumn of 1871 a third near neighbor was comfortably ensconced on a mile-long string of four forties bordering the south side of the claims held by Pehr and Sven. The latecomer was another Swede, named

Erick Nelson; and all three of his Swedish neighbors helped him lay up his log cabin. He chose to build atop the steep rise that rose from the large slough, part of which lay at the southwest corner of Pehr's woods forty. Erick's claim contained more forest than prairie and never became a desirable property. It had steep slopes and sandy hill crests that produced little. In later years it was owned by absentee landlords and rented on shares by incompetent short-term tenants. Martin Anderson, brother of Nils, owned the farm longer than anyone else, but he disdained living on it. The farm and its tenants grew progressively poorer together until, at last, the buildings stood derelict and fell into ruin.

To the north of Pehr's had come two Norwegian settlers, one with land meeting his north forty, the other adjoining the west forty on both north and west. South of Erick's claim lived another Norwegian, a bachelor named Gollings. These neighbors, though friendly toward the Swedes about them, adhered more intimately to fellow Norwegians to the west and north.

Now, only two years after Pehr's arrival, few forties lay unclaimed in the entire vicinity of his acquaintance. And settlement had so evolved that neighborhood groups could be rather nicely distinguished according to national origins as Danish, Norwegian, or Swedish. Within Pehr's limited perspective the entire countryside was Scandinavian, excepting that part over which the Clitherall Mormons presided. Almost every Scandinavian was a Lutheran, whichever his national origin, and although he might be able to speak fluently only one language, he could quite readily comprehend the other two. Thus, the language barrier between Scandinavians was not really obstructive; and, indeed, it became less with time, as one tongue adulterated another. Where, for instance, Norwegian and Swedish families grew up as neighbors, the young often developed a hybrid speech, partaking of both parent tongues. The erstwhile barrier almost disappeared. But for first generation Americans English remained secondary.

The numerical dominance of Swedish Lutherans to the east, south, and southwest of Pehr and his neighbors was sufficiently extensive in 1871 to attract the attention of Lutheran clergy in the twin cities of Saint Paul and Minneapolis. Early in the summer had come one Reverend Jonas Magny to serve the spiritual needs of the community. He had been welcomed with such religious fervor that he remained a considerable time, staying and presiding over religious services in several homes, one after another. Announcement of one such session up-coming reached Pehr and his neighbors, and all attended, including Pehr's daughters. After the formal proceedings, Pehr inquired of the young preacher whether he might be persuaded to come and perform a proper burial service over Anna's grave. Indeed he would; and a time was set two days hence.

In preparation, Pehr and the girls tidied the cabin as best they could and laid Anna's handsome woven cover on the table.

Erick, Nils, and Sven, Mrs. Lien and Tollef, joined the family for the brief, but touching, ceremony at the grave. Then all repaired to the house, wherein Elna served them coffee and cookies. Before the minister stepped into his buggy, Pehr handed him a lump of butter in a clean cloth and a dollar bill for his kindness. Both items were gratefully accepted; and Reverend Magny shook Pehr's hand before taking up the reins.

Pehr was grateful that his beloved Anna now lay properly committed to her God. The knowledge soothed his sorrow in some degree.

Reverend Magny continued his ministry among the settlers, at various intervals, until autumn. Then word went out that the organization of a congregation would be considered at a meeting in the home of J.G. Lejström (Eagle Lake Township) on the seventeenth of October. Erick, Pehr, and Sven wished to attend. Nils, the young blade in the group, volunteered to stay with Pehr's daughters while their father was absent. The girls were understandably pleased. Meetings they had attended had been utter boredom. Furthermore, they retained their fondness for Nils, now of two years' duration.

The Clitherall Township Swedes attended the historic meeting. Reverend Magny offered a short prayer, and then immediately introduced the recommendation that a congregation be established, citing Conference association and standard framework of organization. The attendants quickly voted to accept his suggestions and determined, there and then, to elect the prescribed officers.

To his utter consternation, Pehr was nominated for Senior Deacon, and elected by acclamation. Pehr arose and, for the time being, simply nodded his acceptance of the three-year term prescribed. But when all other specified offices had been filled, he arose and addressed the assemblage:

"You have honored me greatly, and for that I am genuinely grateful; however, I must reveal to you certain of my idiosyncrasies that may cause you to change your vote. I consider myself a good Christian, dealing fairly with all my fellowmen. Never have I wittingly cheated anyone, nor have I ever lied for my own advantage. I try to live my religion every day, believing that a man must ultimately be judged more by his deeds during the week than by his words on Sunday. Do not expect me to lead you in prayer nor to say aloud in public my own secret prayers. I pray alone and silently, believing that man's contact with his Maker must be private and intimate. I do not apologize for my peculiarity, but neither will I accept election under any pretense."

The assembly sat silent fully a minute after Pehr sat down. Then Reverend Magny spoke:

"Herre Pehrson, I appreciate your point of view and your candor in stating it. Far from disqualifying yourself, I believe you have increased the group's confidence in you."

Then, addressing himself to the group, he inquired:

"Have I expressed the feelings of this assembly?"

His question was answered with a roar of approval. Pehr was Senior Deacon despite his confessed faults. And, without formal proclamation, the passing of his beloved Anna became acknowledged the first death in the congregation, and was so entered in its records.

Winter arrived and progressed. Christmas approached, and Pehr took his daughters to Clitherall and fitted them with new leather shoes. On Christmas Eve, Nils and Sven joined the family for a supper that Elna and Nils had meticulously prepared. However, the evening became a wake for Anna rather than a celebration. After supper, Nils and Sven jointly presented the girls with each a new and very pretty calico frock. A fleeting glow of joy came to their faces and faded quickly. The strained celebration ended early, and the bachelor neighbors departed. Sven accompanied Nils home so they might discuss Pehr's widower status, about which they had become increasingly concerned.

"Pehr must find himself another wife," offered Sven, without prelude.

"Yes, but he hasn't so much as looked at another woman since Anna died. We must see about getting the girls a good step-mother. Can you imagine a girl's experiencing the frightening events of puberty without a mature woman at hand to advise and console her?"

"Never you fear, Nils; I shall persuade Pehr to accompany me the very next time I go courting. My chosen one has a sister who might suit Pehr very well. You'll have to stay with the girls, because it's a long walk there and home, so we shall be quite late."

"I'll gladly care for the girls. Just you make Pehr fall for your scheme."

Sven returned to Pehr's place the very next day and accosted his good friend in the stable. He came, he said, to propose that they work together to lay up their supplies of firewood. Sven had a few trees on his claim, and Pehr was reluctant to cut any of his timber for so mean a purpose as burning. It remained public land, and no one hesitated to log public land, if need be. Hadn't the railroads been given free access to anything on public lands they wished to take and use! Pehr was pleased that they would work together. The silent winter woods became depressingly lonely when one worked in them alone.

The agreement concluded, Sven broached the subject he had, in truth, come to discuss. He commenced cautiously, almost pleading, and then waxed more positive:

"Pehr, you know how I value you as a friend—almost as a brother; and you know I would wish you no ill, but only good! You are too young to remain long a widower. You should find for yourself a second wife, to keep your house and help you rear your daughters. However you might try, you cannot be a mother to them."

"I have thought about it you may be sure," answered Pehr. "I wonder whether a stepmother would be best for the girls."

"In due time, perhaps you could let them decide for themselves."

"You have something up your sleeve! Quit beating around the bush, and come out with it!"

"Alright, here it is, I am courting one Hannah Olsdotter, who lives on the north side of Middle Lake, just west of Eagle Lake. Hannah has a comely old-maid sister about your age, who might, I believe, make you a good wife and your daughters a splended stepmother. Why don't you come with me next Saturday and meet the young woman?

"Why don't I, indeed. If the girls are to have a new mother, I must have her as a new wife. It's that simple. I shall ask Nils to stay with the girls, and I will go with you to visit the Olsons."

Come Saturday evening, Sven and Pehr walked the four American miles to the Andrew Olson cabin, in which lived Andrew, his widowed mother, and three sisters. Two brothers were proving up their own Homestead claims nearby.

Sven introduced Pehr this way:

"This here is Pehr Pehrson, my most esteemed friend and nearest neighbor. I have told you about his qualities before. He lives a lonely life, so I invited him with me for a visit."

Pehr got a warm welcome, despite his shabby awkward appearance. "He looked fierce and smelled worse," confessed Elna, years later. On his feet he had large wooden shoes, onto which he had stapled the legs from his worn-out Swedish boots. On his head he wore a cap that he had sewed from raw muskrat skins, taken in the corner slough with a spear bought in Clitherall. A woman less courageous than Elna would surely have shrunk from him in fear and disgust. Nor was Elna favorably impressed. In the kitchen helping prepare coffee and cookies, she half whispered to her mother: "That man, Pehr, he's not only shabby and awkward. Did you get a whiff of him? He's certainly not for me!"

Her mother half muttered in reply:

"You are getting no younger Elna; and he's a sturdy, kind, and honest man. Certainly you can do away with the smells. Think also about the two little girls, who are in desperate need of a stepmother."

About midnight, when the visitors prepared to say goodnight, the mother invited Pehr to accompany Sven whenever he could, adding that they were proud to have him honor their humble home.

Thus it came to pass that the two neighbors paid numerous visits to the Olsons. And to Elna, Pehr became more tolerable with each trip. At the time of spring's work in the fields he put aside the smelly fur cap, and, of necessity, resumed the weekly baths of summer, to wash away the accumulated field dust. He became quite odorless on weekends, and Elna would sit closer to him. At times she would poke and tickle him and get tight against him; this he enjoyed, but thought it a bit kittenish for a forty-year old woman. He said nothing about it.

One pleasant June evening he took her by the arm, saying:

"Come, away from the others. I have something to say to you that is private."

She came with him without the least hesitation. They seated themselves on a large forgotten log some distance from the house, and he began:

"Elna, you are a handsome woman, and I've grown fond of you. I shall ask you to marry me; but I must first explain my feelings toward you. I loved very dearly my wife, Anna; and such love comes only once to a man, I believe. A second love cannot be quite so great. If you will have me, I will honor you as my wife and share whatever possessions we may acquire. You would have to be kind and helpful to my young daughters, nearly as possible treating them as your own. They must be willing to accept you; otherwise, I will withdraw my proposal."

"Dearest Pehr, of course I should like to marry you, and under the conditions you have stated. I am almost as old as you; and at our age, love is no longer a burning passion, but rather a quiet contentment. I can be a good wife to you; but I, too, must insist that the girls wish me to become their stepmother. When can I meet them and see how they react?"

"I shall ask Sven to bring you and Hannah for a visit next Sunday, a week from tomorrow. If agreeable, you shall then see the girls in their own environment, and see also how we live and what you will have to do with. Now, let's go back to the others."

They stood and he held her close and kissed her—their first kiss.

The memorable visit came to pass, and the girls reacted favorably. After Pehr was again alone with them, he inquired bluntly whether they would like Elna as stepmother, and they reassured him enthusiastically.

"She seemed so good and understanding," said little Elna. "And I believe she liked us, too. But what about two Elnas in one house? Won't that be confusing?"

"We have talked about that," answered Pehr, "and we wonder whether we might call you Ellen until you are grown and married. Then you could change it back. The other Elna is too old to change her name very readily. Would you agree to that?"

"I guess so, if I can get Elna back later on. Ellen is a pretty name too, so I can wait."

"So be it, then. We won't worry if someone slips now and again."

On the next visit to the Olson's the two couples commenced making wedding plans. Pehr and Sven had agreed enroute that the event must be scheduled after harvest and threshing. In any case, the weather in July and August could be too sweltering for the marriage bed; they would wait until early September.

The women had hoped for an earlier union, but yielded to the judgment of their men, especially since the mother of the prospective brides had lectured them about letting the men set the date.

It would be a double wedding, solemnized right there in Andrew's cabin, the first day in September, after noon. Reverend Magny would be asked to perform the ceremony or send a substitute to do so. They could certainly count on him since he would have more than two months notice. Pehr's daughters would be ring bearers; Mrs. Olson would sew them each a new white dress to measurements Pehr would give her. Kjersti, the third Olsdotter, would help the girls get dressed in their finery. Step by step, item by item, the planning progressed, until no one could think of anything to add. The men announced that they would go to Alexandria and buy each a set of matched gold bands, soon as the women could ascertain their sizes according to a jeweler's graduation.

Pehr and Sven walked home early in the evening this trip because Nils had requested it. He had romantic interests of his own, to be promoted on Saturday nights. He took off soon as the others returned.

The men told the girls all about their plans and the parts they would play. The promise of new dresses for the double wedding made them too excited to stand still; but with Sven's help Pehr took the measurements prescribed by Mrs. Olson. He would take them to her and give her money for the dress materials on their next visit.

Nils, Pehr, and Sven mowed and raked their hay, and cut and shocked their grain independently; but for hay stacking and threshing they joined forces. Pehr built the hay stacks; Nils and Sven loaded and hauled. At threshing, the men took turns about flailing and carrying in bundles and stacking the straw. Winnowing and sacking at intervals was quickly done by two of them. In a ten-hour day they flailed out seven or eight bushels; but, regrettably, much grain remained in the straw. If dew was light, or none was on, so they could commence early, they worked twelve hours (until dusk) and beat out eight bushels of wheat in a day. Oats threshing was easier, faster, and cleaner. The 1872 grain yielded well both in quantity and quality; and the year was deemed a good one.

In the first part of July, the three cooperative neighbors met several evenings with others in the community, with the purpose of establishing a public school for the area; and on 16 July the group formally organized and tentatively fixed the bounds for what became Rural School District Number 34, Otter Tail County (County Seat, Fergus Falls, as of 28 February 1872). Comprising the first school Board were: Erick Nelson, Director; John Hovren, Treasurer; and Nils Anderson, Clerk. This Board served until 7 September 1878, at which time the entire Board was replaced with new officers (probably at the urgent request of the first three). (Post Office address for the Board until end of 1881 was Clitherall. The address changed 23 December 1881, when a Post Office was established in Battle Lake.)

When Pehr and Sven went to Alexandria to buy the rings they also got themselves enough clothing to make a respectable appearance at their wedding. The money they had got for three loads of wheat apiece was more than they had ever seen at one time before. They could afford to spend a little to "spruce-up"! In their bins there still remained considerable more grain than they had sold. Pehr felt so flush that he bought a small bottle of fine perfume for each of his daughters and one for his bride.

The big day arrived, and everything went as scheduled until little Hanna dropped the set of rings she was carrying. They were threaded onto a flower stem, and she accidentally permitted them to slip off. She quickly got down on her knees and searched, badly soiling her new dress. With some help, she recovered the rings and replaced them on the flower stem; but the dirt on her new dress caused her to cry during most of the ceremony. Afterwards, her stepmother calmed her feelings with soft-spoken reassurance. She helped her out of the new dress, which she quickly washed and hung out to dry on a line behind the house. In about half an hour she took it down, ironed it, and helped Hanna into it again. Elna had saved the day for her younger stepchild, and both were happy.

After a sumptuous dinner of baked ham, with mashed potatoes, dried fruit sauce and other complements, and with rice pudding and cranberry sauce for desert, the grooms hoisted the bridal chests into their respective wagons, hitched their oxen to the wagons, and set off for home with their happy, smiling brides. Pehr's girls rode, as usual, on a grain sack stuffed with straw, laid crosswise behind the seat. At Pehr's and Elna's place Hannah and Sven stopped for coffee and a chat, before proceeding on to their own premises. They began a long term as friendly, unselfish neighbors.

On Sunday night came the charivari, just as Sven had predicted. He prevailed on Pehr in Alexandria to buy a gallon of wine, as he also did. Pehr did so, though it violated his principles. Now the revelers in the night clamored for it—banging pans and pails, firing off guns and revolvers, and altogether raising a din that might easily be heard a mile away. Pehr and Elna heard them when they serenaded Sven and Hannah—about half a mile distant. They wakened and alerted the girls so they would not be frightened by the loud noises at the door. No less than a score of neighborhood men and women comprised the noisy crew, among them Nils and Erick. Anyone might have guessed that Nils had spread the word. The bridal couple had only to show themselves at the door and hand out the jug. This stopped the noise instantly, and a spokesman wished the couple a long and happy life together. The crowd dispersed into the night, and the newlyweds returned to their bed. An old tradition had been honored!

Main occupation of the settlers during September and October was the plowing of stubble and the breaking of additional new ground. Pehr had about doubled his crop acreage year to year, and he persisted in adding ten to twenty acres per year almost consistently until only some seven acres remained native prairie, from which wild hay was cut until several years after Pehr died (in 1914). It finally fell victim to the fourteen-inch, double-bottom gang-plow with a five or six horse hitch, which became popular in central Minnesota shortly after World War I *(Frontispiece)*. Such a rig, with two lead horses and three or four abreast next the plow, required so much space and time for turning that it wrought drastic change in interior farmland patterns. Fields became larger and rounds longer, and interior fences were shifted accordingly.

In the fall of 1872 Pehr plowed forty acres altogether, of which he would sow thirty to wheat and ten to oats. The twenty acres enclosed by the rail fence would be wheat; the twenty acres of new ground would not be enclosed, the requisite labor adjudged greater than the risk assumed.

The second Sunday in September, Pehr and Sven did their morning milking early, took their wives and Pehr's daughters in Sven's ox rig, and went to spend a pleasant day at the Olson's. They returned in time to do the milking before dark. While milking Bos, Pehr observed that her daughter, the heifer, was in heat again.

Next morning he tied the heifer behind the wagon and drove to Clitherall to have her bred by Whiting's bull. She was now about a year and a half old and almost fully grown. She should carry and drop a strong calf. Henceforth, if he spaced calvings properly, they would have no spell without milk, cream, and fresh butter. He had stolen another march on the wilderness!

The next Sunday Pehr and his daughters took their new wife and stepmother to the Morks for approval. Tilda and Willie were delighted; Ola William made no comment. The discerning Tilda saw the rapport already operative between the girls and Elna, and she was especially pleased. All had a good day together, and the visitors broke away before dusk; but that night Bos was milked long after dark.

Before nightly stabling of the cattle became desirable, early in November, Pehr installed a window in the south wall of the smokehouse and moved thither his tools, workbench, and seasoned wood lengths. With five grown cattle, and calves to come, he had little choice. The stable was full. A workshop was built later.

Before another harvest, he should be compelled to remove the grain bins from the stable, as well. So, during much of November and December he devoted himself to the assembly and preparation of logs with which to build a granary the following summer. He could procure burned lime from one of his new brothers-in-law, Ola Olson, who lived only four miles away, to the southeast. With mortar for laying a stone footing and chinking all cracks, he could build a tight wall without squaring the logs.

Before Christmas of 1872, the girls called their stepmother "Mor" (Mother) more often than Elna, and "lilla Elna" (little Elna) had assumed the pretty name, Ellen.

Several weeks before Christmas, Elna commenced inquiries and planning, determined that her daughters, now beyond the Santa Claus age, should have a proper celebration. She discussed the matter at length with Nils, whom she had readily accepted as somewhat akin to a brother-in-law. He became her willing Christmas champion, with Pehr's infinite, though silent, approval. Nils scoured the woods edges all about in quest of a small, evergreen Christmas tree, but found none. Then one bright day he persuaded Pehr to accompany him on a more distant search. They hitched the oxen to the sledge and set out. They went first to Albertson's place west of Clitherall, and he directed them to the nearest junipers he had seen—a distance northeast of Clitherall. Thither they went, found, and chopped down a handsome little tree, and drove home with it. Pehr bored a large hole in a substantial block of wood and fitted into it the butt of the tree to hold it upright. It stood in the snow without the cabin door until little Christmas Eve (two days before Christmas), at which time it was duly installed and decorated.

Nils walked to Dalton and came home with a large slab of dried "lutefisk" (cod treated with lye and dried). This Elna soaked out and prepared for Christmas Eve.

Pehr and Elna made a special shopping trip to Clitherall and bought a variety of candies and several inexpensive little gifts. Elna bought, at considerable expense, enough wool yarn to make the girls each a pair of new mittens. And during the ride home she suggested to Pehr the acquisition of a few sheep so that she might wash, card, and spin her own yarn. Pehr acquiesced:

"I will get a few sheep next spring after shearing time; but I must remind you that sheep are devilish to fence. And we shall soon have to confine all our herd animals to keep them out of our fields. Anna brought a pair of cards, but you will have to get a spinning wheel."

"I can borrow Mother's wheel. Hannah, Kjersti, and I can arrange to share it. Mother's hands are so rheumatic that she has given up spinning."

Hannah, Sven, and Nils celebrated Christmas Eve with the Pehrsons; and a joyous festive occasion it was. The lutefisk, with drawn butter and creamed mustard on it was most delectable—to the adults. The girls ate little of it, but their constant hero, Nils, gorged himself. The girls appreciated their new mittens more than anything else, which greatly pleased Elna. They were permitted up far beyond their regular bedtime; but when their heads grew heavy with sleep, Elna helped them to bed. The adults sat and talked until eleven; then the visitors took their leave, amid numerous expressions of thanks and good wishes.

To see the New Year in, the same group assembled at Hannah's and Sven's, and enjoyed a feast of ruffed grouse, mashed potatoes and gravy, and buttered biscuits. The girls were asleep on the bed long before the turn of the year; and rather than wake them to stumble home, Nils and Pehr hoisted one each against a shoulder and carried them. Hannah loaned Elna two woolen shawls to wrap about their legs. Nils deposited little Hanna in Pehr's house and betook himself on to his own. Therein he built a roaring fire to welcome 1873, because the room had grown cold during his absence. Nils would not be lonely much longer; he would marry in June.

The year 1873 went down in Minnesota history as the year of the terrible blizzard. Heavy snowfall commenced on Wednesday, the seventh of January. The wind rose before evening, and blew a veritable gale for three days. Snow fell so heavily at times that visibility became almost nil. It was often difficult to determine whether the wind was driving falling snow or drifting that already fallen (a ground blizzard). No doubt both processes operated much of the time. A number of men caught by the violent weather away from shelter, froze to death, presumably during the very first night of the fierce storm. One such unfortunate was Cassius Sherman of the Clitherall community. His body was found on the Everts Prairie the following April.

Little wonder that the early settlers developed a morbid half-superstitious fear of flat stretches on the open prairie. Such places were said to be infested with "troll" (evil spirits), that confused anyone attempting to cross them in the dark or in bad weather. Under their spell, it was said, one walked in circles until the troll released him or he succumbed to the elements. In a snowstorm his tracks drifted over so quickly that he might cross them again and again without detecting them. He dared not sit down and rest, but must stumble on, however exhausted. If he stopped, he would fall asleep and never wake up. His circulation would become slower and slower until he froze to death. Such tragedy had one recommendation: it was a comfortable way to die.

Pehr and his neighbors had hilly land, but at no great distance about them, on three sides, stretched diabolical prairie flats: Dane Prairie to the west, Everts Prairie to the north, and Nidaros Prairie to the east. They were near enough to become steeped in prairie superstition and respect.

The blizzard left snow so deeply drifted that Pehr and Sven experienced unprecedented difficulty in hauling home their annual quotas of firewood. The year was well into February before they completed the task.

Not to be diverted from his plans, Pehr also hauled home twenty long aspen logs eight to ten inches in diameter. By pre-arrangement with one Jesse Burdick, who operated a horse-powered shingle mill in the Mormon settlement, these would be made into shingles next autumn before cold weather set in. For the time being Pehr stacked the heavy logs loosely off the ground, and left them to season through summer. He had promised Elna to replace the leaky aging sod roof with one of shakes or shingles before another winter.

In mid-April Pehr kept his sheep promise to Elna and procured from Ebenezer Corliss, north of the lake, three ewes, each heavy with lamb. He kept his promise, but lived to regret it many times. During the early summer of 1873 he nailed three additional rails between all posts enclosing his entire woods forty, including the stable. Next to the stable he made a gap of removable rails, wide enough to admit the wagon. But the confounded sheep went over, under, or between the fence rails with apparent abandon, and their regretful owner wondered whether he might ever confine them.

The girls adopted the ewes as pets and kept them from straying. When the lambs arrived—two white ones and a pair of black twins, the girls were elated. The lambs were soon so tame and friendly that they followed their little mistresses about. Pehr strictly charged his daughters with the chore of closing the sheep in the stable at night lest the lambs be carried off by fox, coyote, or wolf. When the lambs were almost half grown, the girls forgot and left the door open one night, and next day a black lamb was without his twin.

Early in June came Reverend Magny for a two-day religious affair at Nils' place. On the first day he administered communion, baptized five infants, all boys, and married Nils Anderson to Frederika Belmont, a newcomer girl from Eagle Lake Township. Pehr and Elna stood up with the bridal couple as witnesses. Frederika was a tall quiet young woman, and proved a good damper on Nils' ebullience. She lived out her life with Nils and bore him nine children. The Anderson marriage was entered in the records as the first solemnized under auspices of the Swedish Evangelical Lutheran Church of Eagle Lake.

Before haying time, Pehr built the granary, complete but for its straw roof; this he would lay on at threshing time. The granary had two bins, each large enough to hold a thousand bushels, with a narrow passage between them. In each bin-wall facing the passage was a cutout about six inches square, closed with a little drop-gate snugly fitted into side cleats. When one lifted the gate, the grain poured out at a level just higher than the top of a grain sack stood on the floor. Pehr's vital antagonist, the wilderness, was now confounded even by convenience!

Unfortunately, a financial panic seized the country in 1873; and wheat prices fell to seventy-one cents per bushel at local elevators—the lowest price Pehr had thus far known. Railroad construction came to a standstill, and logging in the great northern pineries was almost quiet.

That summer Pehr also built a lean-to of closely spaced rails against the west side of the stable, with a plank door in the south wall that could be closed securely. He accustomed the sheep to this closed fold several weeks before he covered it with straw.

Haying, harvesting, threshing, and storing went in 1873 much as in the year before; but, at least in Pehr's case, he had much more to do than in any past year. To merely cut and shock his grain took him more than three weeks (including a few days when rain interrupted the work). Threshing took him almost as long, continuing into September. He would not enlarge his fields any more unless he could acquire some implement or implements that would, at least partially, supplant his muscle power. However, on the credit side the year had been good; his new granary stood more than half full of high quality wheat and oats. His new wife, pregnant since April (she thought), grew ever heavier with child as the year waned. Her bulk and discomfort interfered somewhat with the celebration of Christmas and New Year's, although she retained her health and good humor. She commiserated with her sister, Hannah, pregnant since mid-summer.

During October, Pehr completed his plowing, and shingled the cabin roof. He sawed the aspen logs into sixteen-inch lengths and carefully squared each of the bolts with his axe. These he hauled to Clitherall in two wagon loads and laid them off where Burdick indicated, all in one day.

"Come back in four days," said Burdick, "and I'll have your four and a half squares cut and stacked."

Burdick steamed the aspen bolts in a large sheet-iron steam box with a fire under it. Softened by steaming, the aspen wood cut easily and smoothly under the heavy knife, which fell in the manner of a guillotine, shaving off with each fall a shingle thin at one end and a half-inch thick at the other. The bolt must be over-ended each time the horse power mechanism lifted the knife.

A helper stacked the shingles as they were shaved off and tied them into bundles much like those one sees in a lumber yard.

When Pehr came, on the fourth day after delivering the wood, his shingles lay stacked and ready—eighteen bundles. Burdick stopped the horse and greeted his customer: "You brought more wood than you needed, Mr. Pehrson. There's enough of your aspen left over to make a whole square or two. Do you wish me to run it through for you?"

"No," said Pehr, "you keep extra wood." (He outdid himself with the English.)

The three men quickly loaded the wagon—twelve bundles set on edge in the box, and five layed atop these with their bottoms well below the top of the double box. Only three bundles were laid on top, loose; these Pehr must keep an eye on as he drove, lest they shake off the load.

The load ready, Pehr pulled out his leather wallet and asked Burdick: "how much?"

"Ten dollars," replied Burdick; and Pehr handed him a ten-dollar bill. Both men thanked each other and shook hands.

Pehr climbed onto his load, waved to the shingle men, and drove to the store to purchase enough shingle nails to lay his new roof.

Replacement of sods with shingles was less difficult than Pehr had anticipated. Beginning at the eaves, one side of the roof at a time, he simply removed one tier of sod and replaced it with shingles, securely nailed to the rails underneath. Then he attacked another tier of sod. The slough grass and willows came off easily. He pitched sods and all to the ground, to be hauled away later. Proceeding in this

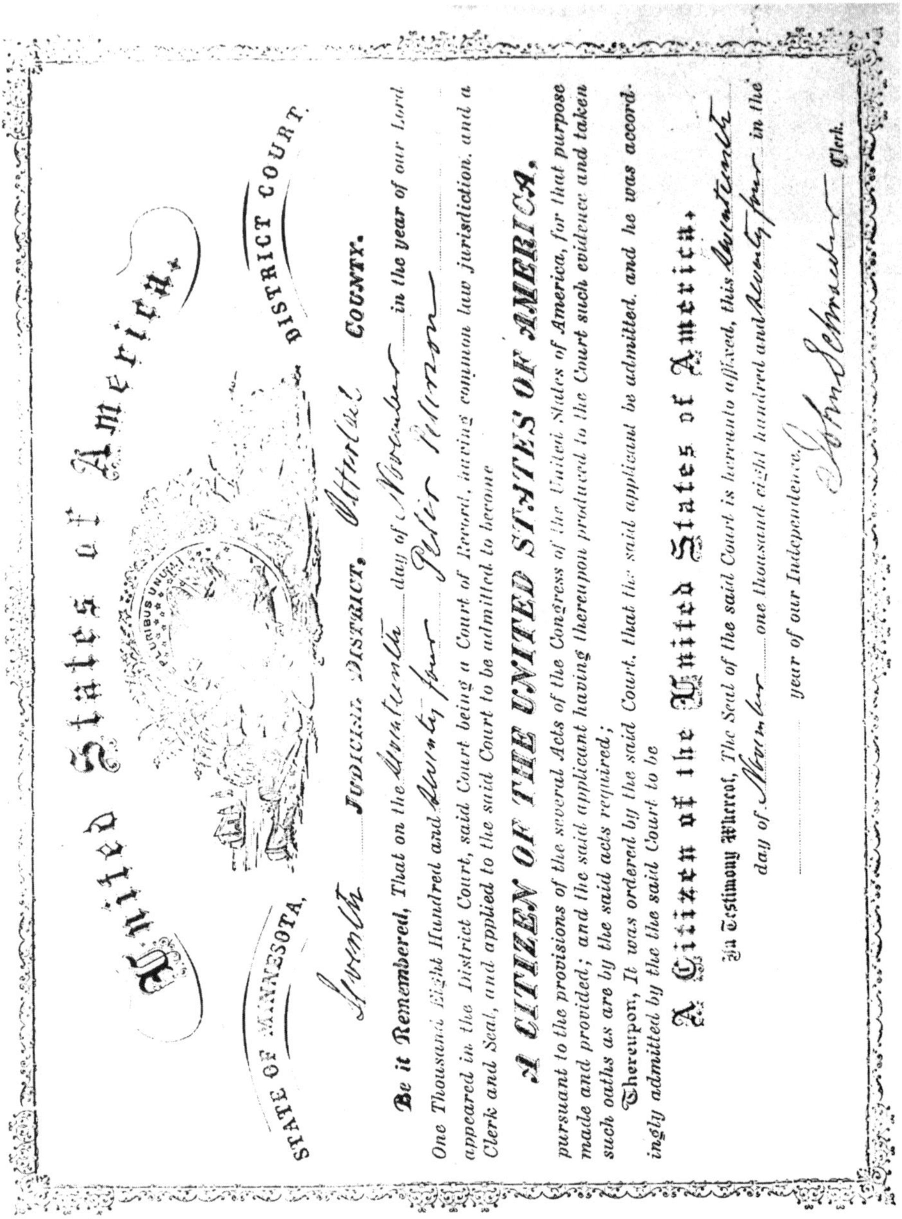

United States of America.

STATE OF MINNESOTA, DISTRICT COURT.

Seventh JUDICIAL DISTRICT, Otter Tail COUNTY.

Be it Remembered, That on the Seventeenth day of November in the year of our Lord One Thousand Eight Hundred and Seventy four Peter Peterson appeared in the District Court, said Court being a Court of Record, having common law jurisdiction, and a Clerk and Seal, and applied to the said Court to be admitted to become

A CITIZEN OF THE UNITED STATES OF AMERICA,

pursuant to the provisions of the several Acts of the Congress of the United States of America, for that purpose made and provided; and the said applicant having thereupon produced to the Court such evidence and taken such oaths as are by the said acts required;

Thereupon, It was ordered by the said Court, that the said applicant be admitted, and he was accordingly admitted by the said Court to be

A Citizen of the United States of America.

In Testimony Whereof, The Seal of the said Court is hereunto affixed, this Seventeenth day of November one thousand eight hundred and Seventy four in the year of our Independence.

John Schroeder Clerk.

Figure 11.1. Facsimile of Pehr's citizenship paper, issued by the Circuit Court, Seventh Judicial District, Fergus Falls, 17 November 1874. This also conferred citizenship on his wife and daughters.

manner, he exposed little of the interior to the weather when he worked, and never left the roof open overnight. He completed the shingling in two and a half days, and used the afternoon of the third day to procure from Clitherall an insulating and waterproofing collar of sheet metal to go around the stove pipe where it stuck through the roof. Elna admired the improvement, and Pehr was justifiably proud.

On 29 January 1874, Elna gave birth to a son, expertly attended by a midwife of Mother Olson's choice. They quickly named the infant Nels, in memory of Pehr's brother, and also to honor their nearest, dearest friend throughout all the trials and tribulations attendant upon their taming a spot of Minnesota wilderness. The boy would be Pehr's only living son, and would, in time, become possessed of the Homestead.

Nels was baptized in the log church built by the congregation on the Martin Nelson place in Eagle Lake, at the first worship presided over by their first resident minister, S.J. Kronberg, in the summer of '74. Hannah and Sven became his godparents.

The year 1874 was for Pehr memorable also as the year in which he became a full-fledged citizen of the United States of America and completed his homesteading obligations. He walked to Fergus Falls and obtained his second naturalization papers on 17 November 1874 *(Figure 11.1)*. He had improved and lived on his claim for five years. He would have walked to Alexandria and proved up his claim but for the sage advice of others in like circumstances. "Wait a year or two," they said, "and save yourself some money. Proving up renders you liable for taxes." The idea seemed to Pehr dishonest and revolting, especially since the taxes amounted to only a few dollars a year, but he agreed to delay and swallow his pride in honesty rather than embarrass his friends. A year or two hence they would go together and prove up three or four claims all at once.

In 1875, both January and February were exceedingly cold, each month with an average minimum temperature lower than -13°F. Lowest temperature in January was less than -30° F. in February less than -32°F. Even March had a low temperature of -15° F. (St. Paul data).

In the spring of 1875 Pehr bought himself two new farm implements from a dealer in Ashby; an animal-drawn seeder and a combination hay mower-grain reaper contraption, also animal-drawn *(Figure 11.2)*.

Purchase of the mower-reaper was most fortuitous because several heavy rains came during the harvest season. Pehr could never have managed to cut his grain crop with the scythe; he would have lost much of the crop. With the scythe he could cut only about two acres per day; with the machine, even when drawn by slow plodding oxen, he could cut six or more acres per day and tie the sheaves before dark. The machine was costly ($175.00), but it paid for itself in only two or three years. (The dealer knocked off fifteen dollars for cash.)

That year he also contracted with Lewis Whiting of Clitherall, a threshing machine owner, to come and thresh his grain. (Never thereafter did he use the flail for anything other than dry peas and beans). The threshing machine was a horse-power affair, activated by long booms pulled round and round by several animals hitched to them. Oxen were said to become dizzy after going around a few times, and they were little used for this purpose. The thresher's fee was seven cents per bushel for wheat and five for oats. The machine worked remarkably well,

Figure 11.2. The McCormick "Advance" combined reaper and mower. This machine was manufactured and sold by McCormick from 1869 to 1879. The "Advance" was a combined reaper and mower, with the automatic rakes built as part of the reel. Platform and reel were removable so the machine could be used as a straight hay mower. The illustration shows it as a reaper.   Photo and above caption courtesy the International Harvester Archives.

Pehr bought an "Advance" in 1873 for $175.00. It took a swath of 5 feet 3 inches. Drawn by oxen, it did not operate well because the slow gait of the animals did not turn the wheels fast enough to activate the sickle at optimum speed. Pehr cut all his wheat with this machine until 1895, for reasons cited in the text. When he pulled it with horses, it functioned well—but it was still necessary to tie the bundles (sheaves) by hand. Statistics from International Harvester Archives.

Reduced in size from original print by Photos, Inc.

leaving little grain in the straw or on the ground. Pehr's threshing took only three days.

In the spring of 1875, Sven's wife, Hannah, also bore a son; and they named him August. He and Pehr's Nels, first cousins, lived as near neighbors and reared each a family on the adjoining homesteads taken by their fathers. August, too, remained an only son, though he had several sisters. Pehr and Elna were August's godparents.

As the year 1875 drew toward its close, Pehr's conscience tortured him beyond endurance; and he determined to prove up his claim before year's end. Let others do as they wished; he would gladly pay taxes on his property. The taxes would amount to only a few dollars per year, he had heard tell.

First Sunday in November Elna bundled up the children, and the family went to visit her brother, Nils, in Eagle Lake. Pehr had a business errand; he asked his brother-in-law to vouch for his eligibility for a deed to his Homestead.

"Of course, I will vouch for you. When do you wish to go? I proved mine up last year."

Pehr did a bit of calendar arithmetic and suggested they go the eighteenth—a weekday.

"Alright," said Nils, "will you drive, or shall we walk? You need another witness!"

"Yes, for my other witness I shall ask Nils Johnson, with whom I walked to choose a claim. He has a team of horses and may be willing to drive. Anyhow, we will come by for you the morning of the eighteenth."

"Very good," said Nils Olson, "I'll be awaiting you."

The family drove home before dark, and Pehr did the milking in good time.

Next afternoon Pehr walked to Nils Johnson's place to ask his friend of more than five years to vouch for his homestead eligibility.

Johnson was delighted to see his friend, Pehr, in his cellar home. They talked over coffee and cakes provided by Mrs. Johnson, who joined them at the table.

Pehr came quickly to the purpose of his visit, and as quickly got the response for which he had hoped, indeed expected.

Johnson would make the trip with his horses and two-seater buggy. The animals were good trotters and should get them to Alexandria in time for late supper. All was arranged! After much friendly conversation, Pehr took his leave, shook hands with both Nils and his wife, and walked home before milking time.

"It's all set," he told Elna and the girls at supper; "we go the eighteenth. Will you manage alone, or do you wish me to ask Short Nils to lend a hand?"

"We'll do fine," replied Elna. "Nils has enough to do."

The three men arrived in Alexandria in time for a late supper, as Nils Johnson had predicted. They quickly stabled the horses in the livery stable and hurried to the hotel in time to eat before the dining room closed. They dined well and paid a dollar apiece for supper, which Pehr thought exorbitant. He paid the entire bill, however.

Then they registered for two rooms, one for Johnson and Pehr ($.75 each, double bed) and a dollar for Olson, alone. They drew straws with broken toothpicks to determine who would sleep alone.

As Johnson and Pehr were undressing for bed (they slept in their underwear), Johnson said: "If Olson had seen my place, I might have proved up tomorrow too, I believe. I could have spared myself a trip."

"Do you have your second citizenship paper?" asked Pehr. "I understand they prefer you to have them, although the first only is required."

"Perhaps I've lost nothing then, because I have only my first paper, the one we both got in Forest City. Hell! I'll just drive to Fergus one day, and stay there until the judge naturalizes a bunch," said Nils.

They slept comfortably and well; Pehr paid for their rooms. They ate a quick breakfast and Pehr paid for it (Pehr, $.25 for mush; the others $.50 apiece for bacon and eggs), checked at the livery stable to see that Johnson's horses were properly fed and watered—and stood in wait before the door when the Land Office Clerk reported for work at eight o'clock.

In the office, Pehr laid on the counter the receipt for fourteen dollars that he had gotten in December 1869, the day of the ice-storm.

The clerk glanced at the paper and asked, curtly; "proving up, eh?"

No one else said a word.

The clerk then pulled out a form such as *Figure 11.3,* asked Pehr a long list of questions, and entered his answers on the form. A time or two, Johnson had to

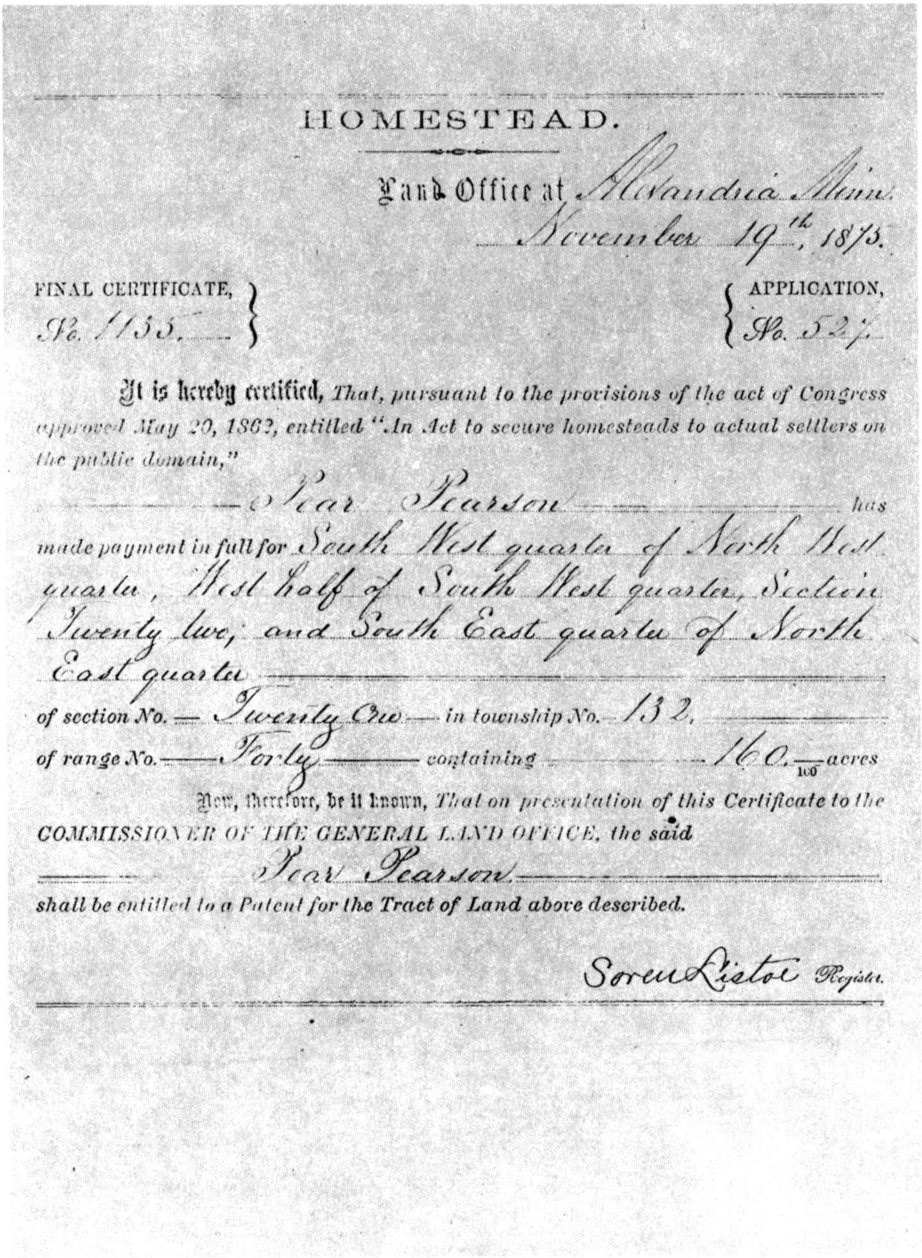

HOMESTEAD.

Land Office at Alexandria, Minn.
November 19th, 1875.

FINAL CERTIFICATE, No. 1135.

APPLICATION, No. 527.

It is hereby certified, That, pursuant to the provisions of the act of Congress approved May 20, 1862, entitled "An Act to secure homesteads to actual settlers on the public domain," _____ Pear Pearson _____ has made payment in full for South West quarter of North West quarter, West half of South West quarter, Section Twenty two; and South East quarter of North East quarter of section No. _____ Twenty One _____ in township No. 132, of range No. _____ Forty _____ containing _____ 160 _____ acres.

Now, therefore, be it known, That on presentation of this Certificate to the COMMISSIONER OF THE GENERAL LAND OFFICE, the said _____ Pear Pearson _____ shall be entitled to a Patent for the Tract of Land above described.

Soren Listoe, Register.

Figure 11.3. Facsimile of Pehr's final homestead certificate, issued at Alexandria, 19 November 1875.

explain to Pehr what he was asked. When all the blanks had been filled in to the clerk's satisfaction, he asked Pehr; "are these gentlemen your witnesses?" Pehr nodded to the clerk and motioned Johnson and Olson to the counter. The clerk turned the paper about and said to the two men, "please read this and tell me whether you will swear that every statement is exactly true." Noting their hesitancy, the clerk read the instrument to them, tracing the lines with his finger as he read.

"That is true," said Johnson.

"Yes," said Olson.

"You swear to it then?" inquired the clerk, holding his right hand up as if taking an oath.

Both men raised their right hands.

"Now, please sign on the lines right there near the bottom, one on each line. He pointed to the exact place, and each witness signed in turn. Then the clerk wrote in their names at the top of the paper *(Figure 11.4)*.

Next the clerk quickly wrote on another sheet, signed it, and shoved it toward Pehr. "Proving up costs four dollars, if you please," he said, his hand on the paper. Pehr took from his wallet four one-dollar bills. The clerk took the money and removed his hand from the paper. "That's your receipt," *(Figure 11.5)* he said. "You are now, for all practical purposes, owner of a quarter section. Congratulations and good luck!" He extended his right hand and shook Pehr's. Johnson and Olson did likewise, in turn.

"Oh!" said the clerk, himself in error, "I need a signed affidavit from you too, Mr. Pehrson." He pulled out another form and filled in blanks hurriedly. "Mainly, this is your sworn statement that you are naturalized and head of a family, and that your name is, in fact, Pehr Pehrson."

"Yes, that is my name," said Pehr, "but you write it. I mark with an 'X'."

"Alright," said the clerk, "put your 'X' right there." He pointed to the exact place and extended the pen toward Pehr. Pehr made his 'X', and the clerk wrote in his name *(Figure 11.6)*.

"Now the business is done, Mr. Pehrson. You will receive your Patent from Washington, signed by President Grant, in four or five months. They have a back-log because so many proved titles are coming in." *(Figures 11.7 and 11.8)*.

Pehr understood only vaguely, but nodded anyhow.

The clerk continued: "I must tell you Mr. Pehrson, that the Patent conveys more than title to the land. Under the Homestead Act of 1862, land so granted to a citizen may not be taken from him to satisfy any indebtedness, whether private or public. Do you understand that?"

"No," replied Pehr, "I do not know what you said."

The clerk motioned to another who had come in. This one came and explained in a mixture of English and Swedish, until Pehr nodded and smiled, apparently pleasantly informed. This clerk also wished the Homesteader well and shook hands with him. "Good-day to you all, gentlemen," he said, "have a good trip back up-country."

The three settlers walked briskly toward the livery stable. Pehr dropped off enroute and bought a loaf of bread and a sizeable wedge of cheddar cheese to sustain them on their return trip. Nils' stable bill already paid, Pehr forced upon him the dollar refund he had intended.

Final Proof required under Homestead Act May 20, 1862.

WE, _Nils W Johnson & Nils Olson_ do solemnly _swear_ that we have known _Pehr Pearson_ for _6_ years last past; that he is _head of a family_ consisting of _wife & children_ and _naturalized_ a citizen of the United States; that he is an inhabitant of the _SW¼ NW¼ W½ SW¼ Sec 22 & S½ NE¼_ of section No. _21_ in Township No. _132_ of Range No. _40_ and that no other person resided upon the said land entitled to the right of Homestead or Pre-emption.

That the said _Pehr Pearson_ entered upon and made settlement on said land on the _14th_ day of _December_, 1869, and has built a house thereon _of logs 16 x 24 feet with shingle roof, 1½ story high, two floors, one door & two windows_

and has lived in the said house and made it his exclusive home from the _14th_ day of _December_, 1869, to the present time, and that he has, since said settlement, plowed, ~~fenced,~~ and cultivated about _40_ acres of said land, and has made the following improvements thereon, to wit: _fenced about 100 rods, built a log stable 22 x 24 feet and a granary built of logs 12 x 16 feet_

Nils W Johnson
Nils Olson

I, _Soren Listoe, Register_, do hereby certify that the above affidavit was taken and subscribed before me this _19th_ day of _November_, 1875

Soren Listoe, Register

WE CERTIFY that _Nils W Johnson & Nils Olson_ whose names are subscribed to the foregoing affidavit, are persons of respectability.

Soren Listoe, Register.
_____, Receiver.

Figure 11.4. Facsimile of Sworn Affidavit by Nils W. Johnson and Nils Olson, certifying that Pehr had completed all homesteading requirements.

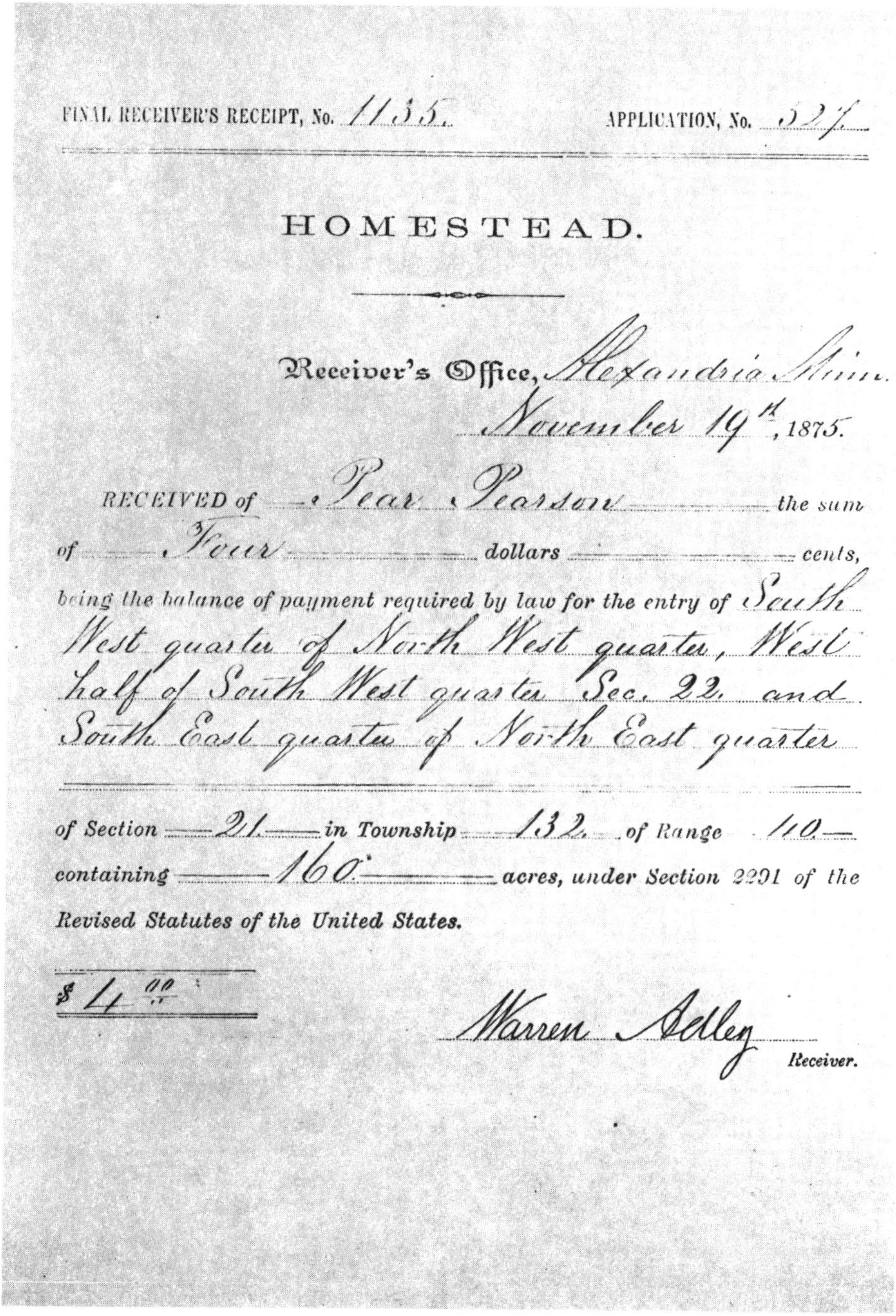

FINAL RECEIVER'S RECEIPT, No. 1135.   APPLICATION, No. 527

HOMESTEAD.

Receiver's Office, Alexandria, Minn.
November 19th, 1875.

RECEIVED of Pear Pearson the sum of Four dollars cents, being the balance of payment required by law for the entry of South West quarter of North West quarter, West half of South West quarter Sec. 22 and South East quarter of North East quarter

of Section 21 in Township 132 of Range 110 containing 160 acres, under Section 2291 of the Revised Statutes of the United States.

$4.00

Warren Adley
Receiver.

Figure 11.5. Facsimile of Pehr's receipt for four dollar fee paid receiver.

Final Affidavit Required of Homestead Claimants.

Act of May 20, 1862.

I, _Pear Pearson_, having made a Homestead entry of the _SW¼ NW¼ W½ SW¼ Sec 22 & SE¼ 18_ section No. _21_ in township No. _132_, of range No. _40_ subject to entry at _Alexandria Minn_ under the first section of the Homestead Act of _May 20, 1862_, do now apply to perfect my claim thereto by virtue of the first proviso to the second section of said act; and for that purpose do solemnly _swear_ that I am _head of a family & naturalized_ citizen of the United States; that I have made actual settlement upon and have cultivated said land, having resided thereon since the _14th_ day of _December_, 1869, to the present time; that no part of said land has been alienated, but that I am the sole bona fide owner as an actual settler; and that I will bear true allegiance to the Government of the United States, _and that my true name is Pear Parson_.

Pear His X Mark Pearson

I, _Soren Listoe Register_, of the Land Office at _Alexandria Minn_, do hereby certify that the above affidavit was taken and subscribed before me this _19th_ day of _November_, 1875.

Soren Listoe, Register

Figure 11.6. Facsimile of Final Affidavit of Homestead Claimant (Pehr Pehrson), 19 November 1875.

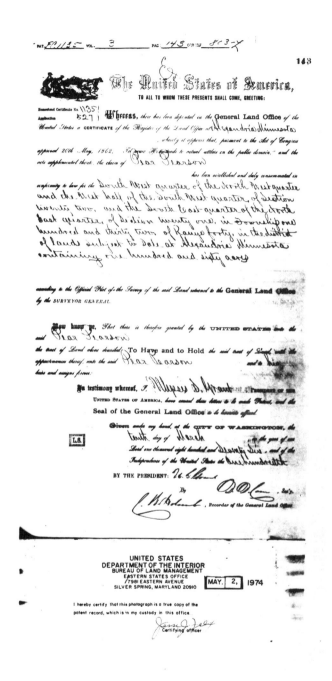

Figure 11.7. Facsimile of Patent as filed in General Land Office, 10 March 1876; now in files of Bureau of Land Management.

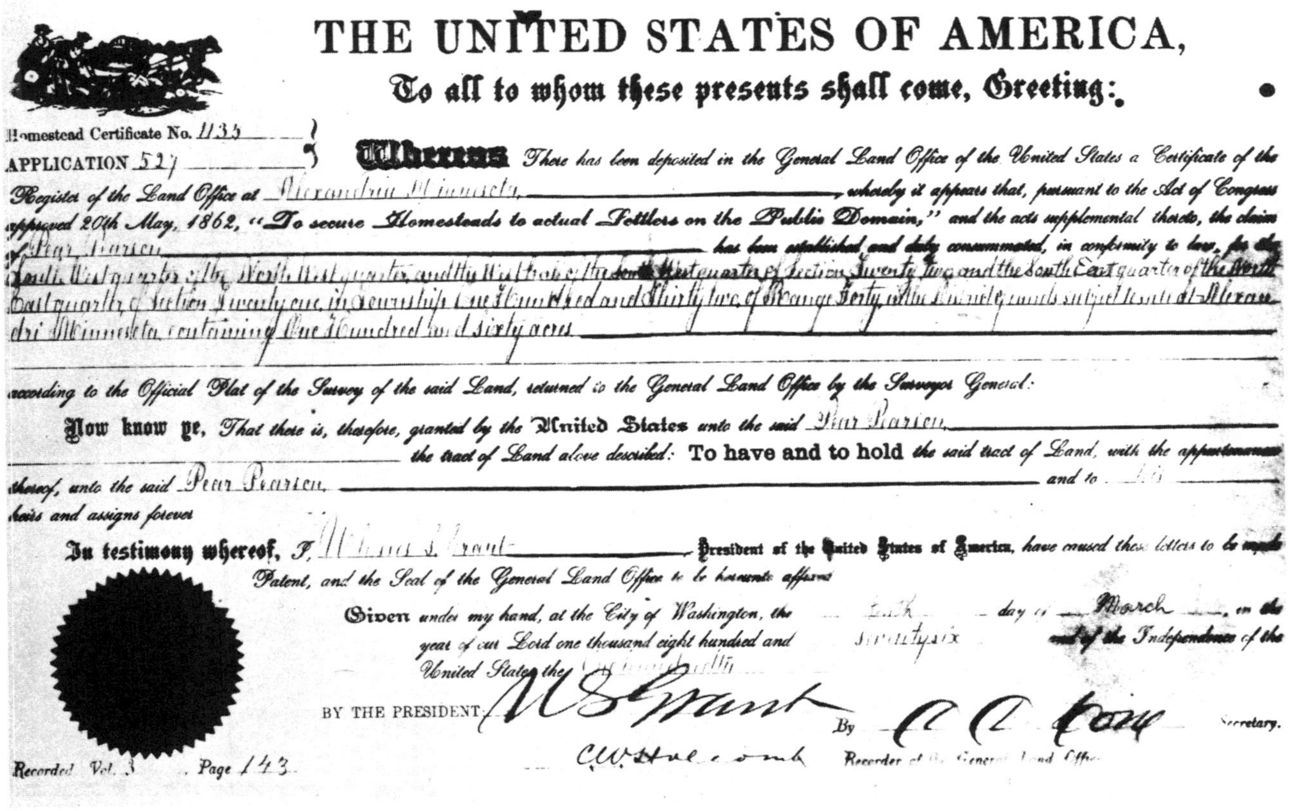

THE UNITED STATES OF AMERICA,

To all to whom these presents shall come, Greeting:

Homestead Certificate No. 1133

APPLICATION 527

Whereas There has been deposited in the General Land Office of the United States a Certificate of the Register of the Land Office at Alexandria Minnesota, whereby it appears that, pursuant to the Act of Congress approved 20th May, 1862, "To secure Homesteads to actual Settlers on the Public Domain," and the acts supplemental thereto, the claim of Peer Pearson has been established and duly consummated, in conformity to law, for the South West quarter of the North West quarter and the West half of the South West quarter of Section Twenty two and the South East quarter of the North East quarter of Section Twenty one in Township One Hundred and Thirty two of Range Forty ... Alexandria Minnesota containing One Hundred and sixty acres

according to the Official Plat of the Survey of the said Land, returned to the General Land Office by the Surveyor General:

Now know ye, That there is, therefore, granted by the United States unto the said Peer Pearson the tract of Land above described: To have and to hold the said tract of Land, with the appurtenances thereof, unto the said Peer Pearson and to his heirs and assigns forever.

In testimony whereof, I, Ulysses S. Grant President of the United States of America, have caused these letters to be made Patent, and the Seal of the General Land Office to be hereunto affixed.

Given under my hand, at the City of Washington, the tenth day of March, in the year of our Lord one thousand eight hundred and seventy six and of the Independence of the United States the one hundredth

BY THE PRESIDENT: U. S. Grant

By C. C. Cox Secretary.

C. W. Holcomb Recorder of the General Land Office.

Recorded Vol. 3, Page 143.

Figure 11.8. Facsimile of Homestead Patent as delivered to Pehr, 17 July 1876.

(All facsimiles reduced in size for this printing by Photos, Inc. Minneapolis.)

When they were on the trail again, homeward bound, it was past nine o'clock. Pehr thanked his friends most sincerely for witnessing in his behalf.

They reached Olson's place soon after dark. At Pehr's place, Elna set out supper for Johnson and her husband while they watered the horses and gave them oats and hay in the buggy box. They blanketed the sweaty animals, lest they chill while standing. Then the men ate supper together, leisurely. It had been a long rewarding day. Pehr showed Elna his Land Office receipt and explained that the Patent would come from Washington later on.

After eating their fill, the men hitched the horses to the rig, and Nils set out for home, with loud exchanges of farewell as he drove off into the dark.

Pehr's Patent reached him by mail, at Clitherall, after mid-March 1876, having been dated and signed by President U.S. Grant in Washington 10 March 1876 *(Figure 11.8)*.

Late in June of the American Centennial year the neighborhood was frightened half to death by news that Sioux, again on the warpath, were about to sweep down upon it, scalping, raping and burning as they came. J.G. Lejström, enroute Fergus Falls, had stopped on the Dane Prairie to feed his oxen, when a horseman rode up to him and announced in a loud voice, "The Indians that killed Custer and his troops the other day have overpowered Fort Abercrombie and are coming this way. Spread the alarm!"

Lejström quickly cut with his pocket knife the ropes by which the oxen were tied to the wagon box, hitched them to the tongue and turned them about, yelling and whipping as a wild man. He drove crazily toward home, cross-country, over fences and ravines, calling out as he went:

"Flee, flee for your lives; the Indians are coming!"

All within hearing heeded his warning instantly. Men in the fields abandoned their work and rushed into their homes and instructed their families. Wives hastily assembled food in cloth sacks, stripped off bed coverings, and deposited all in wagons or carts that would, hopefully, carry them to safety. Pehr poured water on the fire over which Elna had been preparing dinner. Elna took up her young son and such diapers and blankets as he might need. Pehr put some hay and oats into the wagon, to which the oxen had been hitched when Lejström came a-hollering. He lifted his family into the wagon, Elna and Nels to the seat and the girls behind on the hay. He mounted to the seat and cracked his whip over the oxen. Rarely so threatened, the beasts set off at a run, and Pehr urged them on, steering them southward with loud commands.

Soon they came up with others, also hurrying away. Some were driving crude unsprung carts with wooden wheels and axles that squeaked so loudly that Indians might have heard them miles away. A young woman in labor was bedded down in one such cart.

The frightened caravan drivers armed with weapons ranging from high-powered rifles and pistols to knives and meat cleavers, headed for Ashby, where they would take a stand against the savages. The people of Ashby, accepting the risk to themselves, helped the unexpected visitors to bivouac as best they could. The expectant mother was taken into a home, where she gave birth to her first child, a boy. Carts and wagons were arranged as a barricade, behind which men took turns standing guard. Most men remained awake all night, ready to ward off attack at any moment.

But no attack materialized, and the morning broke fair and peaceful. Some there were who turned angry glances on Lejström for having been duped by a stranger on horseback. Before noon the group was enroute again, this time glad to be heading home. When Pehr and his neighbors had arrived back, Nils and Pehr mounted Nils' horses and rode westward several miles to see whether Indians might, indeed, be approaching. They saw no sign of danger; merely farmers busy mowing marsh hay with scythe or machine. They galloped home to report their observations.

When Pehr returned, Elna was gone. Ellen said she had gone to milk the cows that were lowing all around, having missed two milkings.

(Mrs. Johnson and her young daughter, Emily, living in a cellar, heard nothing of the Indian scare before neighbors' cows began complaining. Nils Johnson was away working on the railroad, having departed his cellar after haying.)

Of course, all those frightened away commenced angry inquiry into the origin of the false warning; and gossip soon had it that the cry had been selfishly and maliciously sounded. There was, it was said, a certain Dane Prairie settler who wished to harvest from open (government owned) marsh borders more hay than he had a right to. It was tacitly understood that a man might harvest all the hay about which he could cut a swath without colliding with another; so the unscrupulous fellow had, during the absence of his neighbors, cut in a tremendous acreage of hay, to most of which others had more normal right than he. The man was threatened with legal suit, but nothing came of it. He did not escape punishment, however; he was despised by his neighbors to his dying day.

Greater catastrophe was about to befall. When in July the grain stood headed out, promising a fairly good harvest, great swarms of grasshoppers (Rocky Mountain locusts) came and literally ate up the crop. They ate almost everything green, and some things that were not green, but of organic origin. They took not only leaves, but even bark off trees. They ate the long leather lash off Pehr's bullwhip. If one ventured out during the warmth of the day, they ate his clothing off his back. The diabolical beasts swarmed each sunny day, commencing when the dew had dried off and continuing to eat and swarm until the cool shades of evening stayed them for the night.

There was no grain harvest for Pehr and his neighbors in 1876; and they thanked their good Lord for hay in stack and grains in their bins. They could weather a crop failure. They learned from their Clitherall friends to use as greens or salads a common weed called "lamb's quarter," disdained by the locusts. Fortunately for all, the locusts did little damage to native prairie grasses, so cattle were not deprived of hay or pasture.

In 1875 the little Swedish Lutheran congregation had resolved to build a church. (They had employed a minister in 1874, one S.J. Kronberg.) Before the locusts struck in 1876 church construction was under way on a tract of beautiful oak woods donated for the purpose by Sven Bergstrom. The church would stand on the north side of the town boundary separating Clitherall and Eagle Lake townships *(Figure 10, Chapter 12, Plat Map 1884)*. A master carpenter in the congregation, Martin Evander, was building the structure for a fee of two hundred dollars. The materials were hauled by members, from New York Mills. The church went up, but the locusts came and destroyed the wherewithall to pay for it. Both supplier and carpenter remained unpaid for more than two years.

In 1877 the locusts swarmed again, and despite considerable warfare against them, prevailed much as in the year before. Farmers dragged over their fields great sheet-iron trays with coal-tar or kerosene in them. A mere touch of the oil killed the beasts. But relief was not yet, and our friends again suffered virtually total crop loss.

Now there were those who, less fortunate than Pehr, survived on bread baked of bran and shorts—bread almost indigestible and almost devoid of food value. There were many who counted the grasshopper years more trying than the initial homesteading years.

In 1878 the locust menace appeared to be past, because only a few of the creatures appeared. However, the crop was poor, perhaps because the soil had been excessively enriched by dead insects and two years of partial idleness, and because a blight struck the wheat. The 1878 wheat crop was considerably damaged and reduced by the blight.

(Locusts have invaded the area several times since, notably in 1887 and 1888. In the latter year some 75,000 bushels of locust's eggs and young were estimated to have been destroyed by Minnesota farmers. Several decades ago the author observed in Kansas the combining of wheat so full of locusts that the grain was rejected at the elevator.)

Pehr's last extraordinary act in 1876 was his purchase from Erick Falk and Mary O. Falk, his wife, government lots 1, 2, 3, and 4 (excepting State sublot 7), comprising most of the land on the Lake Clitherall peninsula, Section 14, Range 40, Township 132 *(Figure 13.9)*. He bought this tract, of some hundred and forty-five acres, in partnership with Sven and one P.N. Lundquist. They paid one hundred twelve dollars for the land, from which Pehr and Sven had already taken considerable quantities of building and heating materials. The tract, in oddly shaped lots, some bordering the lake, had been donated to the State of Minnesota in 1874 under the Act of Congress that conveyed land to the states to "provide Colleges for the benefit of Agriculture and the Mechanic Arts."

Now Pehr could log as he wished, without encroaching on another's property, public or private, and without denuding his "home" pasture woods on the south forty. His estate was truly shaping up. The Mortgage Deed was filed for record in the Ottertail County Courthouse, Fergus Falls on 28 October 1876 and recorded in *Book B; Mortgages,* page 317. On 14 December 1877, the Satisfaction of Mortgage was filed, and on 7 December 1877, it was recorded in *Book A; Satisfactions,* page 191.

After several years of desultory and frustrating attempts to operate a school without adequate and continuous housing, the Board took necessary steps in 1877.

On 12 February they bought from Harvey Gollings, for five dollars, a square half-acre in the southwest corner of the northwest quarter of the southwest quarter of Section 27 *(Figure 12.10, Town Plat 1884).*

On this plot of ground, they caused to be erected, during the summer, a splendid school house, twenty-six by thirty-six feet in floor dimensions, and with an entry on the south end, extending ten feet out and twelve feet wide, which was ever known as the "hall." Both main room and hall stood on masonry footings. About the walls of the hall were double hooks on which to hang garments and lunch buckets. The hooks were too high for little children; but older pupils were always ready to help the young. On the front (south) end of the main structure was a short bell tower with a little spire. In this tower was secured in an iron frame a bell more than two feet in diameter, with a beautiful tone that carried, on a calm day, beyond the District boundaries. At the front end of the axle on which the bell swung was a wheel with a rim to receive an inch rope by which the bell could be tolled. The bell rope hung pendant from the ceiling behind the inner door. (The sonorous bell, installed, cost the tidy sum of two hundred dollars.)

In the middle of the main room was installed a large wood-burning stove, its feet almost submerged in sand confined by a four-by-four-foot frame of six-inch planks on edge. The floor was never burned or marred by hot coals. The monstrous stove served well in moderately cold weather, but was no match for temperature extremes twenty or thirty degrees below zero, Fahrenheit.

The main room had a ceiling twelve feet high of patterned sheet metal, boldly coved on all sides. The room was lighted adequately in sunny weather by three tall windows in each of the long (side) walls, and as many kerosene lamps in wall brackets between the windows. Each student was required to have a slate and slate pencil; there was no blackboard.

Martin Evander, who also erected the church and most other frame buildings initially built in the community, contracted to build the school for two hundred dollars. Most District members hauled a load of lumber from the St. Paul and Pacific Railroad in Ashby, or assisted a day or more with masonry or carpentry.

The District assumed a debt of little more than seven hundred dollars, for much of which it was reimbursed with state moneys derived from the sale of school land and disbursed through the county office.

In the area as originally constituted and later adjusted when adjoining districts became operative, District 34 incorporated the entire south central portion of Clitherall Township and a narrow adjacent strip within the northern boundary of Eagle Lake Township.

Elna and Hanna attended several short winter terms, and became fairly proficient in English and arithmetic before each, in turn, withdrew from school in her late teens.

The original School Board was replaced by an election held on 7 September 1878. They received a standing ovation for their conscientious service, but were much pleased to relinquish their responsibilities.

The year 1878 became memorable in the Pehrson household because on 10 July of that year Elna bore a daughter who was named Sadie. She was baptized by the Reverend Kronberg. Nils and Frederika Anderson became her godparents.

No great event befell, nor was any particularly noteworthy project undertaken in 1879. Pehr increased his crop acreage, cattle herd, and sheep flock; but all this came as a matter of course.

The decade of the seventies, with its joys and sorrows, and very considerable accomplishments by our wilderness protagonists, passed into history.

Chapter 12

ERA OF PROGRESSIVE AFFLUENCE
The 1880's

The decade of the 1880's may, by several criteria, be identified as the era of transition from struggling pioneers to established farmers in comfortable circumstances. The settlers had outgrown their fear of hunger and their enslavement to privation. They had attained to levels of prosperity far beyond their wildest peasant dreams. Some sensed in their new-found wealth a certain guilt and degree of sacrilege. Some sought antidotes in church attendance and prayer; but few did penance with generous church contributions. Many thanked the Lord only for the opportunity afforded and credited their success to strong backs and unyielding determination.

Pehr, in his silent dealings with God, acknowledged as a matter of course that everything came from Him—opportunity, muscles, patience, capable hands, determination—everything. He prayed more for worthiness of the gifts than for the gifts themselves.

He would never cheat his fellow man, shirk from an obligation, or measure another by his material possessions. He indulged in no self-examination to gloat over self-righteousness; but he became by others known as an upright, honest, and reliable man; one who never meddled in another's affairs, but who would render judgment candidly when pressed to do so.

In argument, Pehr's piercing blue eyes held his adversary's complete attention; in agreement they appeared mild and smiling.

He came to be respected by all who knew him, despite a severe austerity so deeply ingrained by protracted privation that he could never escape it. His teenage daughters privately called him parsimonious, and their stepmother, Elna, criticized him blatantly for being stingy. The girls remembered how, before Elna came, he doled out their portions of food so sparingly that their hunger was never quite sated. Elna never denied them their fill, contending that they could not be healthy and become grown if not given sufficient nourishment.

When food scarcity was no longer a vital issue, it was the stepmother who appreciated the girls' need of privacy, attractive clothing, and family respect; and it was she who insisted that their father provide the means. She prevailed and he yielded, usually without any considerable resistance. He loved Anna's daughters dearly and would not unnecessarily deprive them. They were blossoming into a pair of beautiful young women, and he took great pride in their appearance. He became less penurious as Elna's demands for the girls became vindicated time and again.

When Pehr spoke of replacing the stable with a large barn and replacing the yoke of oxen with a team of horses, it was Elna who revised his priorities:

"Our fields are large and growing larger. The oxen are too old and slow to do the work anymore. We need a good team of horses if you are to till and harvest so large an area. We need larger and more convenient stable space for cattle and horses: All that I grant! But more than any of these we need a separate comfortable room for Ellen and Hanna, so they may have privacy when they wish it. We cannot, for shame, oblige them to share the intimate problems of womanhood hiding behind a flimsy curtain or in a loft to which they climb a ladder. We are cruelly negligent even now, and our fault must stop! If you would retain the love and respect of your family, now and later on, your next building will be a room added onto our present house, or a new house with a separate room closed off for the big girls! You cannot choose to do otherwise."

Elna had a sharp tongue, and Pehr had learned not to cringe each time she lashed out with it. But this time he must concede that she was right, that he was indeed derelict in duties that should be obvious. He had been so preoccupied with the winning of his contest to subdue the wilderness that needs beyond food, shelter, and clothing had quite escaped his notice. He saw with regret his failure, and determined to make amends quickly as possible.

"This time, woman, I wish you had lectured me sooner. My daughters are becoming young women, and I have continued to think of them as little girls. I will set things right, but it will take time. They, and we, shall have a large new house, the good Lord willing; and I will add to it this room in which we have thus far lived and crowded each other."

True to his word, Pehr began the project at once. He hauled from the lake woods and stacked just east of the cabin the white-oak logs required to build a story-and-a-half structure nineteen by twenty-six feet in horizontal dimensions. Seasoned before laying them up, such logs, winter-cut, would resist rot and stand in a wall almost indefinitely. He brought them home in January and early February, 1880, while at the same time laying up the annual supply of fuel wood. Sven worked with him.

That winter, before bucking and splitting the firewood, Pehr peeled the straight oak logs and hewed them flat on top and bottom sides. Then he stacked them flat on wood lengths laid level, so the logs would not warp, and with slivers of uniform thickness between log layers to ensure air circulation and drying. Lying so for about a year they would be seasoned well enough for laying up.

After cold weather commenced in November 1880, Pehr worked on the logs again, carefully notching the ends so that they would fit together snugly with dove-tailed corners.

After spring's work in 1881 he dug at the north end of the future structure a twelve by seventeen foot cellar and lined it with stones hauled from his field borders. This cellar he vented to both sides (east and west) with square tubes made of planks and projecting through the foundation.

Between haying and harvest in 1881, Sven helped Pehr lay out, dig and pour a masonry foundation on which the logs would be laid. The footings were only shallow, and mostly of stones held together with a spare use of mortar. (Cement could now be bought at lumberyards in towns nearby, but it cost money.)

When crisp autumn weather came in October, Pehr and three husky neighbors, a man for each corner, laid up the walls, doweled on both sides of doors and windows as they went, and sawed out the openings when the walls had reached the desired height. So the bare walls stood, weathering the elements, until the following summer.

In the summer of 1882 Pehr engaged Martin Evander to build onto the logs, gables and roof of sawn lumber hauled from Battle Lake. For the roof he bought mill-made red cedar shingles. When the new structure stood completed, the family moved into it, vacating the original one-room cabin. Now everyone had plenty of space *(Figure 12.1)*. Each of the teenage sisters had to herself a small upstairs bedroom, with a window facing west. Young Nels slept in a small cubicle downstairs, facing east, and little Sadie slept in her parents' room, south of Nels'.

The side walls upstairs were "short walls," about four feet high, from the top of which the ceiling sloped with the rafters to room height and there squared off to the horizontal.

Figure 12.1. Shown above is the "big" house, built of logs in 1882 and covered with drop siding in 1883. The right-hand (north) extension was built of logs salvaged from the original cabin. The porch and shed on the north end were built later. Note rain barrel for catching wash water, the stylish swelling of bricks below chimney tops, the gingerbread trim about the front porch ceiling. Standing in foreground, left to right, are Lillian (5 years old), Lincoln (7), twin sister Ruth (3), Papa Nels (36), twin brother Ruben (3), Mamma Anna (36) and Victoria (11). Anton, age 9, is absent. Sisters Anna and Mabel were not yet born.

Photographer unknown

The living room or "parlor" of the new house served as kitchen while Pehr tore down the original cabin and built it onto the north side of the new structure. The foundation was made ready in advance. With Sven's help, as before, they took down the old walls and laid up the new, tier by tier; and since they had four walls to raze and only three to build they discarded the old bottom logs and a few others showing signs of rot, and yet had enough to complete the new room. Evander came and built the north gable and the ridged roof. His shingling completed, Pehr shifted the stove to the relocated room and fitted the stove pipe into the new chimney *(Figure 12.1)*.

Most remarkable aspects of the new house were the heavy squared oak timbers supporting the living room over the cellar and the seemingly inadequate chimney footings; three-sided boxes of two-by-twelve-inch commercial planks stood atop special floor supports set on large flat stones and leveled with wooden wedges. The chimney proper, of yellow brick masonry, commenced only about three feet below the ceiling, and was unlined. The kitchen chimney support was shelved for convenient open storage; the one flush with the living room wall and protruding into the corner of the "master" bedroom became a cabinet with a door on it. This, the main tall chimney, was vented only in the large upstairs room, so the stove pipe stood straight up through the living room ceiling, in an insulating, double-walled sheet-metal collar to protect against fire. Upstairs, before leading into the chimney vent, the stove pipe had a large double elbow on it, that radiated heat to the upstairs rooms.

The cast iron heating stove that Pehr bought and installed in the living room was literally red hot during bitter cold days.

(Lacking any semblance of wall or ceiling insulation, the upstairs was always cold in winter, almost windy at times, and hot in summer.) The chimney went through the upstairs main room in a leaning posture simulating the tower of Pisa, the bend necessary to gain the roof ridge at midpoint. (Obviously, the part-time mason had wobbled his plumb line.) Both chimneys were built with the modish bulge below their tops *(Figure 12.1)*. In both, the bricks and mortar above the roof became loose and shattered after several decades, and were rebuilt with new bricks and no bulge. However, from the roof down they stand, at this writing (January 1978), exactly as they were built in 1882.

A fancy adjunct to the new house was a cement porch the length of the south wall and five and half feet wide, with four turned supporting posts and a gingerbread facia board *(Figure 12.1)*.

Even as the new house was abuilding, Pehr sold his aged and venerable oxen, and bought horses and harness. The cattle were good only for sausage and brought little money. Bride and Krull went to a local butcher, with an understanding that their horns be returned to Pehr. Of Krull's handsome pair he made one powder horn and one shepherd's horn, the blowing of which could be heard miles away. (The powder horn remains without flaw to this day.) Bride's horns became a wedding gift for Ellen a few years later.

Pehr's first team of American horses were two bays (brown coat with black tail and mane), one a mare named Fanny, and the other a gelding named Blaze. The gelding got his name from a wide splotch of white the length of his face and nose—a blaze. How Fanny got her name one can only conjecture, but it was a popular mare's name in her time. They were well matched in size and build, each weighing an average of sixteen hundred pounds (more in winter when idle, less in summer when worked hard); and they had the trim, though powerful lines of Percherons. They were sound of limb and wind, as the trader had vowed (but one never could believe a horse trader). They had been well broken, to start a heavy load without see-sawing the whipple tree, to ride, but roughly, and to trot nicely on the buggy without breaking into a gallop. They met Pehr's requirements exactly, and he paid for them the same price he had paid for a superb yoke of oxen a decade before. The new leather harness and collars he bought from the Clitherall harness-maker for fifty dollars. He also bought the metal fittings for a whipple tree, neck yoke, and single trees. The wood parts to which these fittings attached he fashioned entirely of white oak. As time at his smokehouse workbench permitted, he made one full set of extras, complete with fittings, and several blanks for each article. He was never long delayed by any breakage of equipment. The harness he oiled thoroughly each spring before field work commenced, and it wore almost indefinitely.

Now, with horse power to drive it at adequate speed, the reaper-mower would function as it should.

But he must also replace the monstrous breaking plow with a lighter, more efficient implement. He bought from the Battle Lake dealer, for ten dollars, a wooden-beam fourteen-inch stubble plow *(Figure 12.2)*. With this he could plow two acres in a ten-hour day, when the soil was moist enough for easy slicing by the share and firm enough to scour freely and turn smoothly from the mold-board.

With the purchase of horses came, of course, also the acquisition of a two-seater platform buggy and a conventional two-bob sleigh *(Figure 12.3)*. Though tremendously costly, the shift to horses, harness, and horsedrawn equipment was

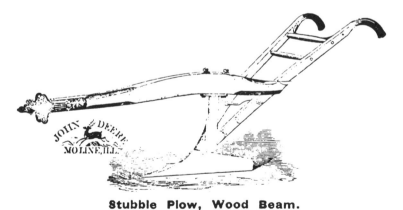

Stubble Plow, Wood Beam.

Landside view, showing patent handle brace and medium landside. Made in sizes from 10 to 16 inches, double or single shin, right or left hand.

Figure 12.2. The wood-beam stubble plow, shown above, was a vast improvement over the monstrous bull-tongue models of earlier years. This plow turned a furrow fourteen inches wide, and two horses could turn stubble with it easily. With a good team on it one could turn two acres in a day. Shown here is the flat landside as opposed to the curved mold-board on the other side. This plow was probably made for the northerly market, since it was designed to turn the furrow to the right-hand side. In the South, left-handed plows became standard.

Photo courtesy Deere and Company.

Figure 12.3. The bob-sleigh such as pictured here, became the winter vehicle for hauling and travel. Stripped to the running gear, as here shown, with stout stakes in bunk holes, it stood ready for hauling high loads of long polewood. Note granary in background and on its lefthand (north) side, the ramp, partially obscured by snow. The ramp served for reaching the unloading door from a wagon load of grain, as mentioned in the text.

Photo by author many years ago.

always deemed by Pehr his major forward step toward making of his homestead a wholly functional farm. With a spirited team of horses he could accomplish in one day the field work that had taken two days or more with the faithful plodding oxen. With horses he could drive to town with a load in the morning and get back before dinnertime.

The year 1883 became as notable for barn building as was 1882 for erection of the new house. The barn project began even before the year, because the ordinarily serene and deliberate Pehr actually waxed impatient, and logged several large white oaks from the woods forty during December of 1882.

In January 1883, he and Sven made their annual assault on the Clitherall Lake peninsula for fuel and materials. Sven had also switched from oxen to horses, so between them the brothers-in-law could, if push came to shove, bring home six sleigh loads in one day. They mixed building logs and fuel wood as was customary, since bole and limbs must come down together. Standard loading practice was to lay onto the sleigh bunks two thicknesses of logs, then slipping the tie ropes over the stakes, and finally building the top of the load with trimmings (pinery men might have called them slash). On one trip Pehr hauled home a stout tree top with a whorl of three branches sticking out almost at similar angles. In his hands the whorl quickly became a tripod onto which he attached a table top *(Figure 12.4)*.

During the winter, Pehr notched the ends of the large logs and hewed them into almost squared timbers. The barn presented a special problem: since it would be more than fifty feet long, it would require two twenty-five foot logs joined together to build the long walls. The short walls required only twenty-six-foot logs, and these he could notch, match, and make ready ahead of time. The overlap at mid-point of the log walls he would fit together as the walls were laid up. Preparation of the oak logs for the barn entailed much more work than had those that went into the house:

the barn logs were larger, and thus heavier. Some squared to as much as fourteen inches on a side.

While winter still held its icy grip firmly, Pehr drove with his horses and naked sleigh to a tamarack swamp in Girard Township, and hauled home across the intervening lakes, a dozen twenty-six-foot logs, almost uniformly ten inches in diameter in the butt end, and eight at the small end after peeling. They were "straight as a candle" and with minimal taper—characteristics for which tamarack was especially prized. These would become the main cross beams holding the long walls in place and supporting the frame structure above them. Ten would be laid in as ceiling joists under the hayloft, and two would become collar beams secured to the plate.

Pehr sited the barn parallel to the front porch (east-west) and about a hundred feet south of it, just beyond the break of the hill sloping quite steeply southward. Between spring planting and haying, helped by both Nils and Sven, Pehr excavated with horses, plow, and slusher a slash across the side-hill six feet deep at the upper side and more than fifty feet long. Some of the earth removed they piled above the cut for later leveling against the north wall; some they simply pushed down the slope, thus extending the exposed platform on which the structure would stand. Against the north (basement) wall they then laid large boulders to hold against the earth, those at the bottom much too large to lift. These they slid off the stone-boat and into place with crowbars. Carefully leaned against the earth, the rocks required no mortar to hold them in place. The upper courses, partially below ground and partially above, were laid with mortar and leveled to receive two log courses to wall height. For the three exposed walls, footings were dug in several inches and built up to a common level above ground with stones and mortar. So the project stood while the workmen did their haying.

After haying, Erick joined the other three neighbors to lay up the heavy logs into walls. When only the top course remained to be laid, Pehr sawed out openings for a door and window at each end and a door and window just east of midpoint in the

Figure 12.4. This tree-crotch table of basswood remains in use (1978). When Anna, wife of Nels, became possessed of it she used it for some of her numerous house-plants, the table against a south or west window for winter sun. Since the three legs did not form a triangle of three equal sides, one side must lean against the window sill.

Photo by E.A. Vievering and Photos, Inc.

south wall. Near the east end of the south wall he cut in another square window that would give on the horse stalls. The next sunny day the crew reassembled, laid up, and leveled the top logs all around.

Before harvest, Pehr hauled from Evert's Lumber Yard in Battle Lake all the needed framing materials; boards and battens for the upper walls, rough-board sheathing and cedar shingles for the roof, and a glazed sash for each window. He almost forgot them, but on his last trip he also brought the sizes and quantities of nails specified by the carpenter. The vertical wall boards were twelve inches wide, the battens two and one-half. The battens were attached over a half-inch space between boards with six-penny, square-point, cut nails, chosen, despite high price, for their superior holding quality. The rough-sawn sheathing boards under the shingles were spaced as much as two or three inches apart "so the shingles might breathe." Some of the pine sheathing boards were two feet or more in width.

The sheathing cost fourteen dollars per thousand board feet; the siding cost twenty-five dollars per thousand; the joist and dimension materials, twenty-five; and the cedar shingles $2.50 per square (100 square feet) and were laid with five-inch exposure to the weather. All the commercial materials purchased for the barn cost Pehr somewhat more than two hundred dollars.

After harvest, Evander kept his appointment to complete the building. With constant help from Pehr, and a hand now and again from the neighbors, Evander had the structure ready in early October. Then he agreed to cover Pehr's log house with drop siding, which he did in a little more than a week. For the barn building he got one hundred dollars; for siding the house, twenty-five.

When the barn stood completed it measured (outside) twenty-six feet in width and fifty-one feet in length. The gable peaks were more than thirty feet high (*Figure 12.5*). On its ridge, a quarter of its length in from each end, it had a pair of sizeable cupolas, louvered on all four sides to ventilate the hay mow. It had, high in each gable, a square window so oriented that its sides were parallel and perpendicular to the roof line—forty-five degrees from vertical. At midpoint of the north wall the barn had a dormer about six feet wide, with a large door, hinged at the bottom and latched on the inside. Through this, wagon loads of stover were pitched in.

Inside, the barn floor plan was arranged this way: The west half was the cow-barn, the animals in two rows facing the north and south walls, respectively. The east one-quarter was the horse barn, these animals, when stalled, facing west to their mangers. Between the horses and cattle was a space for feed and hay, the hay poked down from the mow through a hole, at one side of which was a ladder.

The ladder to the hay mow was doweled of oak. A trap door hinged at one side of the mow hole was used only in winter; at other times it was tied up out of the way. In winter, one propped it up with a prepared pole so that it hung about a quarter open. He then stuck a generous forkful of hay or straw on top of it and closed it up tight, thus cutting off the draft generated when it hung open.

Before the land froze up that fall, Pehr set with cobblestones the stalls of both the cow barn and the horse barn.

The new barn, unpainted for many years, was magnificent in its time, and people came from a considerable distance to see the splendid structure. Since then it has been reshingled and painted several times, and remains standing (though slightly bulged and swaybacked) at this writing (January 1978) (*Figure 12.5*).

(While the barn continued in use, the stones piled up by Pehr at each of the upper corners to hold the earth, remained in place; but now, regrettably, most of those protective stones lie scattered down the southfacing slope at the top of which stands the derelict structure.)

No sooner was the barn built and floored than Pehr determined to have a proper granary in which to store his small-grain crops. The original storehouse with straw roof no longer sufficed. Its capacity was inadequate, and it stood riddled with rat-holes at the bottom, so grain poured out in little heaps.

So, in the summer of 1884, he hired Evander, for fifty dollars, to erect a frame granary, sixteen by twenty feet in floor area and twelve feet high to the roof-line. It stood on oak sills, off the ground, on a large stone at each corner. Inside, the bins were arranged much as those in the original thatched building, with a six-foot alley-way, front to rear, separating the bins on one side from those on the other. In the south wall of the alley was a door with a small window across its top. Each gable had a four-pane square window, oriented as those in the barn. On the south side before the main door Pehr built a three-by-six-foot platform, to which one could back a wagon for loading or unloading. The platform had stairs on the west side. At the north side of the structure was built an earth ramp walled with stones on both sides (always called the "granary bridge") for access to a small door at eaves level. From a load of half-full wheat sacks stopped below this door a man could, with

Figure 12.5. The great barn built in 1883, here viewed from the west, stood many years unpainted, but later boasted a handsome red with white trim. The shed on the south side was added early, and was variously used through the years for sheltering young cattle or brood sows and litters until mild weather came in spring. Enlargement of the big barn door and addition of the projecting peak on the barn were necessitated when the old mechanical hay fork gave way to rope slings, with which one lifted into the mow half a load of hay at one time. Conversion from fork to slings came in the early twenties. Packed full, the barn loft held more than twenty large loads of loose hay (perhaps twenty tons).

Photo by author.

considerable exertion, lift a sack from the wagon and set it in the door. A man in the granary could drag the sack from the door and dump its contents between the joists into the proper bin (only the part of the granary upstairs next to the door was floored, mainly to accommodate a fanning mill, walking plows greased against rust, and other items not immediately or only seasonally useful). In later years, Nels nailed together, side by side, two twelve-inch planks long enough to reach from the wagon box to well inside the door. The hauler then had only to set a sack on this skidway so the granary tender could reach its mouth and drag it in.

The granary had only single drop-siding walls, and had a capacity of approximately four thousand bushels, dry measure. All materials purchased for the building cost less than two hundred dollars, and it serves to this day (January 1978). It stands only about a hundred feet east-southeast of the front porch, and a bit farther east-northeast from the northeast corner of the barn *(Figures 12.3 and 13.8)*.

With house, barn, and granary in place, Pehr's building spree had run its course. Never again need he build so much in so short a span of time. Now he could apply more of his time and energy to the full expansion of arable area, the removal of stones from the fields, and the fencing of the entire quarter section. Many times in ensuing years he helped others build, thus repaying in kind their help to him. He notched the dovetailed corners of many barns, because few settlers had mastered the art as well as he.

Blasting or burial of monstrous land-fast rocks was a more or less permanent riddance, and those no larger than could be dug around, pried out of their holes, rolled or levered onto the stoneboat, and dumped into a slough edge were, indeed, permanently out of the way and never again a hazard to work animals and machinery. But stones no larger than a man could lift up and walk with, even to those of only fist size froze out of the ground each winter and became a nuisance to be countered annually. Stone picking became a seasonal routine in spring or fall when the soil lay bare. Although many—perhaps a preponderance—were thrown into sloughs or rolled into slough edges out of sight, stone piles in fence corners or fence lines, on steep declivities or on unplowed knolls became part of the agrarian landscape, and grew year by year. They became homes for cottontails, ground hogs, skunks, snakes, and other animals tolerant of man's presence and behavior in the land, and they did him little ill.

Less acceptable to the settlers were the pocket gophers and thirteen-striped ground squirrels who became increasingly destructive as native prairie grasses gave ground to cultivated cereals. Pocket gophers became particularly menacing, because often as not their mounds contained sand that dulled the mower sickle, or pebbles that broke it. One could not lift the cutter bar clear of those encountered near the machine where the bar was hinged, nor could he see every mound in time to avoid it wherever it lay. Sickle blades (sections), pitman rods, and costly delays were the toll paid to pocket gophers, besides their burial of crops.

Encouraged and instructed by his father, Nels became, as a young boy, a trapper of pocket gophers every spring. Pehr bought him half a dozen steel traps (No. O Victor) and showed him how to open and clear a burrow, set the trap in it, and cover it over so no light could seep in and warn the busy little beasts. Pehr paid him a penny for every one he caught, and there were days when he made a whole nickel. He checked his traps at least once, and sometimes twice, daily, for reasons partly selfish and partly humanitarian. If a gopher caught only by a foot or leg sat long in the trap he gnawed the caught member off and went his way. A lone fore foot in a trap meant simply that a slow digger was abroad; Nels had lost a penny.

Less destructive, but more fun to catch, were the ground squirrels. These Nels snared with twine or other strong string. He simply tied a slip knot at one end of a six-foot length of string and fitted the noose about the inside of a hole into which his quarry had disappeared. He sat back and whistled, string in hand, until the inquisitive victim stuck his head out. Then he jerked the string quickly and firmly, swung the beast into the air, and slammed him to the ground and killed him; and presto, he had himself another penny.

Eventually the township voted a bounty of ten cents on pocket gophers, but Nels was then grown beyond gopher trapping.

A revolution in farm fencing came on the west-central Minnesota scene during the 1880's; as barbed wire became the standard fence material. In Pehr's protection of his first fields sown in America he used, as previously noted, a "post-and-rail" fence, entirely of wood and laboriously installed *(Figure 12.6)*. Ordinarily, such a fence was of three rails, adequate for turning cattle but not sheep. If sheep were to be confined in an area or excluded from it, it was necessary to use several rails (5 to 6) spaced only eight inches apart. Alternatives were a snake fence or an "angle" ('sne' in Swedish) fence resembling the jack fence popular on western ranges to this day.

The snake and angle fences stood almost indefinitely because they lay entirely above ground, whereas in the post-and-rail fence the posts were set two feet or more into the earth, and rotted off at ground level sooner or later and had to be replaced. Some did, indeed, stand for several decades. (This writer, when young, once removed split oak posts holed for rails that had stood, perhaps more than fifty years, and still remained sound and serviceable.)

First tried as substitute for rails was a heavy gage smooth wire, but unfortunately the animals went right through it. About the same time came wire nails with which one could quickly attach rails to a post *(Figures 12.6 and 13.8)*, and spare himself the drudgery of hewing holes and fitting rails into posts—a major labor saver derived from progress in nail manufacture—a shift from square cut nails with blunt ends, such as used in siding Pehr's barn, to the less costly wire nails, popular ever since certain steel manufacturers installed ingenious machines to make them.

Then came barbed wire, patented by an inventor in DeKalb, Illinois in 1874. When this evolved into a galvanized two-strand material with double barbs spaced five or six inches apart, the handsome rail fence became ornamental rather than functional *(Figure 12.6)*.

In the Old West barbed wire provoked range wars between graziers and intruding farmers, but in Minnesota, when considered together with wire nails and wire staples, it became the means of enclosing and cross-fencing the quarters and forties economically with strong durable fences. Rarely, if ever, had the advance of invention and technology so nearly coincided with necessity in land use and occupance.

From the very beginning of frontier settlement, the fencing of lands, first to exclude livestock from sown fields and shortly to confine the animals within designated woodlands or open pastures, became a progressively greater problem demanding ever more expenditure of money and labor—and materials.

A skilled woodsman could fell a dozen white oak trees, straight for twenty feet

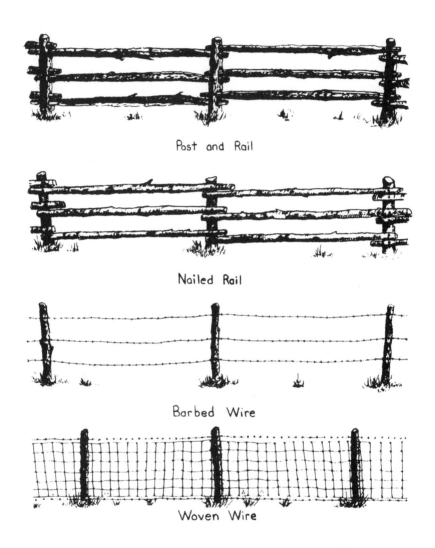

Figure 12.6. Fence types utilized by Pehr, in chronological order top to bottom. The split post-and-rail fence, laboriously built but extremely durable, was the most popular horse and cattle barrier until machine-made wire nails became available at low cost. Round posts and round rails became predominant when cheap wire nails (8, 10, 12 penny) became available. Barbed wire really solved the tremendous fencing problem of the early settlers. It became the least costly fence to build in terms of both labor and materials, and it was both effective and durable. After Minnesota legislators legalized the use of barbed wire in partition fences (1877-1878), it rendered other fencing obsolete. Soon after the invention of barbed wire, came the manufacture of woven wire fencing (netting), the first sure and easy means of confining or excluding sheep or hogs. (Barbed wire had one grave fault; its conductivity of electricity. Numerous cattle and horses were killed by lightning bolts transmitted by the wire.)
From charcoal sketch by Julie Wolters.

and fifteen inches in diameter above the butt flare, trim off the branches for firewood, buck the main stem into two or three lengths of eight feet, and split from each length four or five posts—some one hundred twenty posts—in one day of strenuous labor. From trees already felled and cut off eighteen feet long, such a man could wedge and "maul out" 150 or more sturdy rails in one day.

A three-rail fence with posts set one rod apart required eighty-one posts, two braced corners, and two hundred forty rails per quarter-mile of fence. Hauling and distributing posts and rails, digging post holes and tamping the posts in, lifting into place and nailing on the rails with five-or-six-inch spikes (one at each rail end) took two men two to three weeks, according to hardness or stoniness of the ground.

Total cost of an eighty-rod barrier was some twenty dollars for twenty or more man-days of labor, and 486 spikes, weighing sixteen pounds and worth three cents per pound; not to mention rapid depletion of the choice white oak timber available.

Worst of all, a fence so laboriously built soon fell into disrepair. Rails became loose or rotten and broken, and the fence required constant mending after a few years of service. And the mending was costly and time consuming.

Before 1880 Pehr had fenced his entire section line frontage facing west for three quarters of a mile with sturdy plank-like posts, holed to receive two rail ends in each of three oblong holes as described earlier, obviating the use of nails. He fenced for extraordinary strength and durability, using three stout split rails in posts set only twelve feet apart. He had in similar fashion enclosed his entire woods forty, albeit one side was fenced by his good neighbor on the south and east, Erick Nelson, who willingly assumed his obligation of building one-half the "line" fencing between his homestead and Pehr's.

But there remained four other neighbors with whom he would be obliged to share the fencing of common boundaries *(Figure 12.7)*. He feared that his precious oak stands, already much reduced, would be grievously depleted. He awaited with trepidation the inevitable requests from adjoining neighbors that he build his share of fences to separate their respective pastures. He waited until a neighbor kindly requested his cooperation; then he responded without complaint, however much it grieved him to chop down more of his trees. Close friends and relatives as they were, Pehr and Sven (east of Pehr's middle forty) pooled materials and labored together to erect a division fence from Sven's south corner to the perennial slough that served as boundary for almost one-half the forty line.

Neighbors north and west of Pehr's land, themselves ill-supplied with timber, for several years grazed their cattle at large, herded by a son or daughter. Short Nils, whose land abutted Pehr's west forty on the south, had made only incidental mention of their eventual need for a division fence. Pehr bided his time in the case because he had no immediate desire to drive his cows to pasture on his most remote forty.

Line fencing was never without considerable preliminaries. Since no inside corner of quarter sections was marked by the surveyors, such must be established by the settlers themselves. For this purpose, be they two, three, or four, they met together at an appointed time, and usually, after much sighting on survey posts and bearings and infinitely careful line measurement, agreed on the spot at which a corner should be. And on that spot, all parties in attendance, they dug in, extra deep, a stout and tall peeled white-oak post. For measuring, Pehr contrived, of light aspen rails, a triangle exactly one rod on each side. This simple device sped the task of measuring a forty line, although one was invariably measured at least twice or three times before all parties were content. (In event of disagreement about the placement of a corner, the disputants had legal recourse to the Township Board of settlement on the issue.) Rarely did the measurement and definition of a forty line fail of agreement; but there were, indeed, cases in which tempers flared so hotly that neighbors lived entire lives as enemies, never again speaking to each other.

The homesteaders had read in the *Swedish American Post*, '*Den Svenska Amerikanska Posten*', that a new and revolutionary "barbed wire" for fencing had been patented by one Joseph Farwell Glidden of DeKalb, Illinois in 1874. This might eventually become a solution to fencing problems; but stories of its vicious injury to innocent animals were rife, and as late as 1880 the wire cost ten dollars per hundred pounds (about eighty rods). The settlers had tried heavy gage smooth wire; but it proved quite worthless. The animals simply pushed it out of their way and walked through the fence. The vicious barbed material might be the right stuff, but it was obviously prohibitive in cost. The homesteaders would bide their time, and wisely they did!

So vitally important was barbed wire "armored fencing" to farming, ranching, and railroading in America that its development merits brief recounting here.

The decade of the 1870's was the age of barbed wire and barbed wire machines, mainly in France and America. The invention of main concern to us was that of Joseph Farwell Glidden of DeKalb, Illinois, who was granted Patent Number 157124 on his barbed wire, "The Winner," on 24 November 1874. Shortly, he sold his patent to one Ellwood, also of DeKalb, for a modest cash payment and certain rights. Ellwood's early production attracted the attention of a man named Washburn, associated with a steel company in Worcester, Massachusetts. Washburn and an associate named Moen bought a major share of Ellwood's property, acquired numerous other patents on barbed wire and machinery, and built a sizeable factory in DeKalb. (Eventually, Washburn and Moen Co. (and Ellwood) became part of United States Steel.) Then, as now, the product consisted of two strands of twelve-and-one-half gauge wire, twisted together, and a coil with two three-eights-inch barbs held by the twist at five-inch intervals. In 1876 production was almost three million pounds; in 1950 four hundred eighty-two million pounds (country-wide).

So profitable was the manufacture of barbed wire that numerous illicit (unlicensed) factories infringing upon the Washburn, Moen, Ellwood patents sprang up in the mid-west (139 in Iowa, Missouri, Kansas, Minnesota, and Nebraska, at one time). Only after eighteen years of litigations did Washburn, Moen, Ellwood establish exclusive rights to the manufacture and sale of the product. Other makers electing to remain in business were obliged to pay seventy-five cents royalty per one hundred pounds made; and none must undersell the licensor. Only forty factories became licensed. Feelings against the patent owners ran so high that an Iowa Farmers Protective Association waged a legal war to defend fifteen "free wire" factories that operated in the state in the 70's and 80's (Hayter, with permission of author and publisher; Opus listed). In the end corporate rights prevailed, and the farmers lost the contest. However, supply and demand proliferated at such a pace that the price of barbed wire declined rapidly for more than three decades: from twenty dollars per hundred pounds (about eighty rods) in 1874, to ten dollars per hundred pounds in 1880, $4.20 per eighty-rod spool in 1885, $3.45 per spool in 1890, and to a bottom price of only $1.80 in 1897 (Webb. Opus listed, courtesy the Publisher). During these years, millions of pounds and thousands of miles of fence went up in the young country, mainly in the midwest and plains country.

Not by choice, but because of small-time chicanery, the railroads were the greatest consumers of the product during the 1880's and 1890's. The railroads were held liable for injury to, or killing of domestic animals struck on the tracks. Claims made against the corporations by farmers or ranchers were often decided against the "rich and subsidized" railroads by local magistrates or judges. A raunchy half-starved cow or steer killed on the tracks became a prize specimen in court, with compensation awarded accordingly. The aggregate of such costs became so monstrous that the railroad companies had no other choice than to fence off their rights of way on both sides and install cattle guards at each grade crossing.

Barbed wire had several advantages over board fences for railroad purposes. Board fences were often stolen by settlers for fuel and were also burned by prairie fires. They also caused snow banks on tracks where barbed wire offered no obstruction.

So it was that American railroads built more fencing than did land owners for two decades of our national growing pains!

'Bob wire,' as the Swedish settlers called it, had come into so much use in Minnesota, most notably by the maligned railroads, that the Legislature saw fit to legalize its use in partition fences by an Act of 1878, as follows:

Chapter XVIII
Partition Fences

1. Legal fence defined. All fences four and a half feet high and in good repair, consisting of rails, timber, boards or stone walls, or any combination thereof, and all brooks, rivers, ponds, creeks, ditches and hedges, or other things which shall be equivalent thereto, in the judgment of the fence viewers within whose jurisdiction the same may be, or any such fences as the parties interested may agree upon, shall be deemed legal and sufficient fences.

2. Wire fences legal. In all cases where any law of this state requires to be erected or maintained any fence or fences for any purpose whatever, it shall be sufficient, and a compliance with such law, if there shall be erected and maintained a barbed wire fence, consisting of two barbed wires and one smooth wire, with at least forty barbs to the rod, the wire to be firmly fastened to posts not more than two rods apart, with one stay between the posts, the top wire to be not more than fifty-two inches high or less than forty-eight, and the bottom wire not less than sixteen inches from the ground; or four smooth wires with posts not more than two rods apart, and with good stays not to exceed eight feet apart, the top wire to be not more than fifty-six inches high nor less than forty-eight, and the bottom wire not less than sixteen inches nor more than twenty inches from the ground: provided, that five smooth wires shall be required to constitute a legal partition fence: provided, that any other fence authorized by law shall also be held a legal fence. (1877, c. 107 S 1.)

3. (Sec. 2.) Occupants to maintain partition fences. The respective occupants of lands, enclosed with fences, shall keep up and maintain partition fences between their own and the next adjoining inclosures, in equal shares, so long as both parties continue to improve the same. *(Figure 12.7).*

Settlers were acquainted with and covetous of the wire several years before they could afford to buy it. Almost as soon as the wire became abundant and extensively marketed, machine-made wire nails and fence staples became equally available—at prices as low as two cents per pound (100 six penny nails or 100 one-inch staples).

When the price of barbed wire fell below five dollars per eighty-rod spool (about 1883) the homesteaders commenced buying and erecting fences with it. When the price fell to less than four dollars per spool (about 1886) they bought tremendous quantities. They could now enclose a forty with forty-eight dollars worth of wire (three strands), $6.60 worth of staples, and a handful of nails for securing corner braces. Most ignored the smooth wire legalized in the middle, and used three strands of barbed wire. Neither did many accept the long spacing of posts permissible under law; they set their posts as little as twelve feet apart. They were building for maximum strength and longevity; and, indeed, some of the wire they stretched more than a century ago may be seen in place to this day.

Short Nils, as one might have anticipated, was the first to extol and purchase barbed wire in his neighborhood. One balmy Saturday evening in early May 1885, enroute home from Battle Lake, he swung his team by Pehr's house to show his purchase. He "wo'd" to a stop and called to Pehr loudly, as was his wont: "Come see something we must all get for ourselves!" Pehr sauntered up from his post-peeling job below the barn and looked into Nils' wagon. His eyes fairly popped.

"How much is it now, that you bought a dozen rolls?"

"Would you believe $3.75 a roll for twelve rolls, nails and staples thrown in free? This will be the only horse and cattle fencing from now on."

"I believe you are right. I'll go Monday and get a similar load; then we can build our partition fence on the south side of my west forty. I have 300 posts already split out and peeled. We'll need 220 posts apiece if you are willing to use a twelve-foot spacing. I won't build a permanent line fence according to legal specification, (posts two rods apart and a slat to keep the wires spread, half way between). And I'll never again use a smooth wire as a fence strand! It may be fine for splicing or patching, but not for a good fence."

"I'll match my share of the line fence with yours. I feel exactly as you do about smooth wire and post spacing," agreed Nils. "Do you wish to go at it next Tuesday?"

"Suits me," answered Pehr. "I'll come over right after breakfast, next Tuesday, with my measure and compass. I'll bring my boy with me so he can learn."

"We'll find the corner alright. Never fear. I'll expect you then." Nils shook the reins and clucked his horses off.

Pehr fetched a load of wire the next Monday, as planned. Mr. Everts asked four dollars per spool until Pehr set him straight. "I live across the road from Nils Anderson, and I want the same deal you gave him yesterday." (Pehr's English amazed him more than Everts.)

Said Everts: "On twelve spools you shall have the same deal, yes indeed: $3.75 per spool, with staples and a few ten-penny nails thrown in."

Pehr helped load the spools, which weighed almost ninety pounds each. The lumber dealer pitched into the wagon a sizeable sack of staples and a small one of the common wire nails. Pehr drew his large leather wallet from his inside jacket pocket, counted out four tens and a five and handed them to the dealer. "Thanks for a good bargain," he said.

"Thank you," responded Everts, pleased with another good sale. "Even at that price I can make a satisfactory profit if I can maintain a goodly sales volume."

Pehr and Nels drove home with enough wire to enclose an entire forty. Nels wondered where they could possibly use so much of the fierce looking stuff. He would need much more in time but he would risk that the price would remain stable, or even go down. (Had he lived until 1974, he would have seen the spool of wire bought for $3.75 in 1886 sell for $34.00. (That's inflation, or something!)

After supper Pehr strolled over to talk with Nils—whom he found just arising from his table. They exchanged cheerful greetings, and then Pehr suggested they begin their work next morning at the half-mile point he had marked with a solitary short oak post in his fence line, which stood thirty feet in from the section line—thus leaving the specified width for a road. "I know that the first burr-oak west of my stake is a "bearing" tree noted by the surveyors. I checked it in Alexandria when I proved up my claim. I have a paper on which I wrote down the distance and bearing."

"That sounds good to me," said Nils quickly. "I had wondered where we could start the line from. We'll have to clear away the fringe of willow and aspen to sight across the slough hollow that reaches over on yours. We'd better bring each an axe for the clearing."

"Alright, we'll get at it in the morning. Come by my house on your way. I may need help to carry everything I have to take," and Pehr started toward home. (Nels can come with me too, he thought as he walked.)

"I'll be there about eight," Nils called after him.

Nils was on time next morning, bearing with him a freshly peeled aspen rail about twelve feet long and a sharp axe. Pehr quickly made ready with axe, compass, measuring triangle, a few ten penny nails, and several strips of white cloth.

"What's the cloth for?" asked Nils, a degree insolently.

"That's for marking sighting points at a distance," replied Pehr, no less curtly. "We have more measuring to establish my west corner with you than we thought about before. Christ Nelson's quarter corners on mine AND yours at the same point. We shall have to have him with us before we can fix the corner. To do this right we must run a line straight from my half-mile marker to the northeast corner of your quarter section. And to do that we'll have to sight east from the half-mile marker on Mrs. Lien's and west from the half-mile marker on my hill. Do you see?"

"Of course I see," barked Nils. "Why did you think I brought this rail? to play horse? We may need others before we get through, but we can cut them round the slough. Good morning Nels," he said to the boy.

They walked with quick steps through the dew and laid down their burdens by Pehr's marker stake. Pehr drew from his pocket a worn slip of paper.

"It says here that the first burr-oak west of the corner stands squarely on the east-west quarter-section line. Will you accept that?"

"Let's see how it matches up with the stake I drove in thirty feet west of the section line. I also measured in from the post that once stood in the middle of the road."

They walked together and found Nils' stake. The boy spotted it first.

"Now," said Pehr. "I'll stand squarely west of your stake while you go back to mine and see whether your sight across the two strikes on the tree."

Nils went quickly, hunched down and sighted, one eye closed; then waved his arms and called jubilantly: "It's exactly as you said! But how in hell do we run a sight line through a twelve inch tree?"

"That's what my cloth strips are for. A little wad on each side, nailed on, will be as a continuation of the tree."

"By damn! sometimes you seem too smart to be a Skåning!" And both men laughed, both being from Skåne. Nels, the boy, didn't appreciate the joke. "Now let me contribute a bit of wisdom! If we cut and peel a tall slender aspen and hold it upright on the hill beyond the slough, we may be able to sight it from the oak here, without slaving through the slough thicket. What think you?"

"I'm beginning to think you're wise too," replied Pehr, with a broad grin. "Let's get at it! No! Wait! The branches of the oak will block our view, unless one can climb up and stick a rag out that will show to the west."

"I'll climb if you'll walk," answered Nils. And so they did.

Soon Pehr was on the west hill with a tall aspen sapling held upright. Nils could not see out from the main bole of the oak tree, so clambered down for his axe. After considerable chopping, deft and cautious, he could stick the white rag out so it could be seen from the west. Pehr waved his arms to show that he could see it, then he called loudly to Nils. "Now climb down and see whether you can line me up with my stake, the oak, and the sapling I'm holding. You may have to chop more off the oak."

Nils sighted as told, but even the longest sapling available held beside Pehr's stake failed to clear the tree. Up he climbed again, and whacked off branches until the tree had an open V through its crown. Now they quickly sighted in the line from stake to sapling. Pehr shifted his rail back and forth on Nils' signals until Nils waved both arms in the air, signifying the proper spot. They had spared themselves the laborious task of blindly clearing across the intervening slough. Now they need cut only a gap through the wood and brush on each side.

Pehr quickly walked back and joined Nils, saying as he approached: "Now we can measure to the sapling I just stuck in on the hill, and with stakes east and west of it sight a line to where my land corners on yours."

"How can you swing and turn your measure through the brush and woods in the slough, I should like to know?"

"We shall measure a square off-set over onto my field, entirely clear of the slough, and back to the line on the far side. My triangle makes a square at the top so we can measure a true square by laying it on the ground. Are you ready to try it?"

"Are you quite sure you came from Skåne?" chided Nils, on the same theme as before; and both men laughed again. The humor eluded the boy, Nels, a second time.

"I may be a poor peasant Skåning, but I've learned a few American measurements. The corners of the legs on this triangle measure exactly a rod or sixteen and a half feet, and their sides make a right angle from any point. For measuring rods one need only swing the legs like this, one after the other, over the grass or small bushes, forward to the line. Of course one must keep count as he goes, and for that I shall depend on a certain black-bearded Skåning I happen to know and my young son. Are you ready, my short black-bearded Skåning?" He commenced measuring, and Nils walked along, across the line from Pehr, counting aloud (Nels counted to himself) each swing-over of the measuring device. To the slough brush he had counted sixteen rods and Nils agreed. There Pehr laid down the triangle, squared on the line, and sent Nils out into his field to drive a marking stake perpendicular to the property line they had just measured.

"Here Nils, take this paper and pencil stub and write down your count to the slough, lest you forget it. On the off-set we count only the line that parallels the property line—from the stake you just set to another straight west of it well clear of the slough growth." Soon they had measured the length of off-set and the line to the hill-top sapling. Nils added up his score; they had measured one-half the forty line and a half-rod over. There their fences would meet.

"Now I say this is a good place to stop for dinner," said the younger man, feeling pangs of hunger. "It's a quarter till twelve." Nels was glad!

"Well enough," agreed Pehr, as they set out toward home, "we wouldn't wish to disturb Chris at table. After dinner we'll hunt the post out west while Nels goes and invites Chris to join us. Tell him, Nels, that we'll lay the line corner-wise across his land unless he witnesses our doing," and they turned apart toward their respective houses, snickering. Nels laughed with them this time.

After a quick lunch the neighbors met where they had recently separated, and walked together toward the hill marked by the aspen sapling. As they walked, Nils related that Chris, Mrs. Lien, and he had agreed on the northwest corner of Nils' quarter section. "If you will accept our decision, we can quickly sight in the line between yours and mine. Length of our line will then be the only issue on which to reach agreement with Chris. Sighting in the line from Mrs. Lien's half-mile post I should hate to do again; it is hidden by those hills. We had quite a job."

"If your corner is sited to suit you, it is certainly satisfactory to me. Go get Chris, Nels, while we measure the rest of our forty line. We'll set sighting stakes as we go. We should have the line almost run by the time you get back. Off with you!" Nels hurried away in direction of Christian Olson's house.

When Chris and the boy returned, Pehr had a corner stake tentatively set, and the others agreed that it appeared correctly sighted. But Pehr wished double assurance that they were completely right and that all parties were without any doubt.

Quoth he: "Just for the hell of it, let's all go to your west corner, and from there sight and measure back to this point." They strolled westward, talking together as they went. At the corner, each in turn took a sight over Pehr's stake and the hill-top sapling. Each deemed the line properly drawn.

"Now," said Pehr, "I'll quickly measure back too, so we can feel sure that no one has been cheated." All three counted aloud as Pehr expertly swung and set his measuring triangle. When he arrived at the tentative corner marker he lacked about two feet of reaching the stake with his eighty measured rods.

"We're off, men. What do you say we do to correct this?" Nels marveled, in silence, that it could be so nearly accurate.

Chris spoke up quickly: "I'm not here to split hairs with neighbors. I suggest we move the stake half-way to the foot of the triangle, and call it a perfect and permanent corner. Alright?"

"I'm agreeable," said Nils.

Pehr cast his vote by loosening and withdrawing the stake and driving it back into the earth again where Chris had suggested. The three friendly neighbors had established the meeting point of their three respective properties. (Would that all unschooled neighbors had been able to resolve differences with such regard and respect for each other!)

Chris shook hands with Nils, Pehr, and Nels and struck out for home. Nils, Pehr, and Nels returned to the corner whence they had commenced, gathered up their tools, and headed toward their homes.

"Which half of the quarter-line would you wish to build," asked Pehr as they walked. The east will be a bitch because of the slough; it's so nearly dry in the fall that it will have to be fenced right across. Of course the posts can be driven in instead of digging them, which is some consolation; and once we clear away the vegetation for fencing, it may be less work to maintain than any other part."

"Why don't we build the whole thing together and then draw straws for the half each keeps in repair?" suggested Nils.

"That would be very well, but for one thing," ventured Pehr. "One man's share to maintain should have the wire on his side of the posts so he won't have to disturb his neighbor's field in fence mending. We'd better draw straws now; although I'd like for us to build the first fence together, each using his own materials in his half." He stooped and pulled up a stem of grass, snipped off a short and a long length with his thumb nail, and proffered the ends equally stuck out from the concealment of his hand. "Long straw gets the west half." Nils drew the east *(Figure 12.7)*.

"Now, shall we commence clearing a cut across the slough fringe, or shall we first go home for afternoon coffee. I suggest we go home first and leave our axes here. I'll bring out a ball of twine that we can stretch to help us stay on the line."

By evening the two sturdy workers had chopped a broad clearing into both sides of the slough and trimmed and stacked the trees where they could be loaded on a sleigh for fuel. Nels had piled the slash in neat piles. They selected two six-inch ash trees, chopped off at twelve feet, for corner braces.

"Remember, Pehr, half this wood is yours; it's good for the kitchen stove in summer. Dried aspen burns so fast and hot that it over-heats the house less than hardwood."

"Thanks," said Pehr. "Elna will appreciate it, if I split it fine enough. Do you want me to bring wagon and posts tomorrow, or shall we lay out the entire length before we dig any holes."

"Why don't I bring a load of posts in the morning?" asked Nils. "We can dig them in as far as the slough; then sharpen them and drive them in standing in the wagon. Will you bring your twelve pound maul? Better yet, I'll swing by your place and haul the maul in the wagon, along with my wire."

The men walked wearily toward home, shouldering their axes. They walked in silence until time to turn away, each in his own direction, and Nels with his father.

"If it's not raining, I'll be over before eight," said Nils, by way of farewell. The sun was setting rosy, which might be threatening rain.

Rain fell during the night, but by morning only a mist shrouded the landscape. Nils arrived as agreed, his bottom wagon box full of posts, and a square spade laid on top.

"Pehr, would you mind taking your axe as well as your maul and spade? I forgot to grind mine last night, and I thought it too damned dull to haul along."

"Yes, sure," replied Pehr. "I ground my axe as best I could last night, but the pebbles washed into that slough made big dents in the edge."

Pehr loaded axe, spade, maul, and twine ball, helped his young son up first, and then climbed aboard beside Nils, their feet hanging out over the wagon box. They drove in silence, neither deigning to converse over the wagon noises. When Nils stopped the rig up at the corner, he was first to speak: "You know, Pehr, that we can't drive horses and wagon through our gap in the slough before it gets much drier. How, pray tell, do we drive posts all the way across?"

"I thought about that last night," replied Pehr, "and here's what I suggest: We'll unload all but a few posts for the slough. We'll stretch the twine from the corner all the way across the slough. Then, while I sharpen the posts to be driven in the slough, you can take the twelve-foot spacing rod and with your spade lift the turf or mud where each post will go. This done, we'll wind up the twine, back the wagon with the sharpened posts as far out in the slough as we dare, and drive a post each place where you made a spade hole in the muck. I'll stab the post into the muck and drive it down with the maul, standing in the back end of the wagon. Then you'll pull the team ahead to the next hole mark, and so on until we get to high ground. From there on we'll dig two-foot holes for the posts and tamp them in."

The procedure worked splendidly and was repeated on the west side of the slough. In the midst of the slough were only four posts lacking; these would be put in during dry autumn weather.

By evening they had the posts set and tamped and the braces in place, each with a flat rock, of Nels' choosing, across its bottom end. The brace on the end post was put there to absorb the twist generated by stretching wire in opposite directions on opposite sides of the post—and to mark the half-way point to which each neighbor assumed responsibility for always keeping the fence in repair.

Next morning Pehr drove out with double-box on his wagon, his son proudly driving the horses. His posts were larger than Nils'; fifty-four of them took considerable space. He had also loaded a stout twelve-foot ironwood rail. He had loaded all these materials in the back end of the wagon, the more easily to pitch them out where desired. Nils intercepted him just beyond the grove and Nels stopped the team for him to climb up and stand with him and his father at the front of the box.

Pehr directed Nels to the end of yesterday's post line, then west along the line while Nils pitched the posts out the back end, spaced about as they would stand (twelve feet apart). In a matter of minutes the posts lay in a row, forty rods of them. Here the land lay almost level, with no larger obstruction than an isolated lead plant here and there. Pehr tied the horses to the end post set the day before; Elna would drive them home and unharness them after she had brought the forenoon coffee.

Quickly they stretched the twine to a twenty-rod stake on the line and measured and worked the post holes; then they stretched the twine from the forty-rod stake to the west corner and completed the procedure. Nels wound up the twine and stowed it in the wagon. The men took up their spades and commenced digging holes, one at each end of the line, so they would waste no time talking. Nels investigated pocket gopher mounds in the vicinity. They worked steadily, upending a post in each hole as it was completed, big end of post down. They had made good progress before Elna hailed them for forenoon lunch at nine thirty. How they relished the sandwiches and coffee! After the quick light repast, Pehr took the twine ball from the wagon; they might need that later. He helped Elna into the wagon and she drove home.

When the two sweaty men and the dirty boy walked home for dinner all but a few posts stood in the deep holes dug for them.

"We shall be ready to string wire tomorrow," puffed Nils as they set off for home.

"That we will," agreed Pehr. "We've done a day's work every half day for most of a week. Sunday will certainly be a welcome day of rest." That seemed to say all that was necessary at the time.

Morning came with rain and overcast sky, not a promising day for fencing; but Nils came walking over to Pehr's after breakfast, obviously bent on business.

"I saw when I bought my wire, a mechanical stretcher that I think we ought to have. It was priced at four dollars fifty cents. If you'll go halves with me, I'll take my buggy and trotters to town and get one and be back by noon. What do you say?" asked Nils.

"I'll gladly go halves with you," answered Pehr, "but I saw no such contraption the day I got my wire. Perhaps they were sold out. In any case, you'll get soaking wet if you go."

"That I won't. I have a good rain cape. But, say, do you have a steel crow bar? We need one to shove through the wire spool, so one man can walk on each side to unroll the wire. We must also wear leather gloves. I hear that some people have cut themselves badly."

"I have a good crowbar and a heavy pair of leather gloves, so I'm all set. But I'll not be idle while you go to town. If the rain slacks off a little I'll haul out the wire and crowbar. We shall need a roll and a half of your wire and as much of mine. Rain won't hurt the wire, but we'd better keep the staples dry."

"Alright, my wire is stacked by the new shed. I'll see you about noon," and Nils hurried off, faster than he had come.

The rain virtually stopped at ten o'clock, and Pehr had the wire, crowbar, staples, hammer, axe, and gloves at the east end of the post line a half hour later. He drove his team home, unharnessed them, and turned them out to pasture.

Nils drove up to Pehr's house just before twelve o'clock, his horses fairly foaming with sweat.

"I laid the stretcher by the end post. I'll come with hammer and gloves soon as I've eaten dinner."

"I'll be ready," said Pehr. "Elna, let's eat quickly so I'll not delay the work."

Pehr ate hurriedly, but he had scarcely risen from the table when Nils stood in the door. Off they went to a new experience—stretching and stapling their first barbed wire fence. Elna warned her son to keep away from the work!

"Which wire should we put on first?" asked Nils, as they walked, "top or bottom?"

Pehr quickly replied, "I believe we'd better staple the bottom strand first. That way we can lean over the fence and check post alignment as we go, without getting nicked and tangled by wire higher up. I believe it's the only sensible way."

"That sounds reasonable to me," said Nils. "We might as well space the strands as prescribed by law, too. Did you bring a rule or yardstick?"

"Damn me, No." answered Pehr sharply. "Nels, run back and get it. It stands behind the kitchen door." Nels trotted homeward and soon returned with the yardstick.

They quickly loosed the wire end from one of the spools, drew it tight around the post, secured it with a staple on each side of the post, and twisted the free end tightly about the strand in place, thus averting any twist on the post. Nils stuck the crowbar through the spool; they took up each an end, and with the spool unwinding between them, walked down the line of posts on Nils' side. After rounding the outer post in the slough they skirted the muck as best they could at the edge of the marginal weeds. At times they sank in over their shoes and got almost stuck. This was the dreaded segment of the wire laying; but without serious mishap they gained the outer post on the west side and walked the spool to the south side of it. Now they must hold the spool from turning and haul the wire taut across the slough. Each held the spool with one gloved hand and the crowbar with the other. After considerable heaving and grunting the wire swung free and clear across the slough. The tired partners laid the spool behind a post to prevent its rolling, and sat down to rest and wipe the sweat from their faces.

They sat for ten minutes before they felt inclined to resume their work. Shortly they were at the midpoint post with the brace on it. Now came the trial of the new stretcher, and it lay at the east end. Nels was sent to fetch it, and the men, sitting for another moment, spied Frederika emerging from Nils' grove. She could not arrive before Nels was back, and walking was easier to the spot on which the men were sitting. Nils waved to her and she waved back.

"Your wife brings the coffee today?" Pehr half questioned.

"Yes, I told her to share the chore equally with Elna. Your wife will bring it tomorrow. We'll need it before we get all three of these strands strung!"

"But I think we can be through before supper," ventured Pehr. "The slough is the time-killer. We have to muck around it twice more."

They ate the lunch with speed and enjoyment. There was abundance for men and boy alike. Fredericka complimented them on the straight line of posts they had set. Then, as she gathered up her empty cups and containers and turned to go she said: "Don't get stuck in that slough."

"Now show us how to use this mechanical wonder," said Pehr to Nils, indicating the wire stretcher.

"Well, Everts showed me once, and I'll see if I can remember. The wire is laid in here and this eccentric burled half-wheel catches a barb lump and tightens down on it. Then you move this lever back and forth, far enough so these spring-loaded teeth snap into the notches along the main spine of the mechanism." He demonstrated the procedure. "I was warned to hold a gloved hand over the caught-up barb in case it slips some distance on the wire."

Now they all stood back while Nils manipulated the ratchet lever. Indeed, the gadget did stretch the wire. It was soon stretched so high over the slough that one thought it might break.

"You'll have to back if off some," said Pehr. "If we press the wire down to position this tight I'm afraid it will break. In any event, we could never get the wire over the slough down far enough to reach a post with it."

Nils turned a knob on the stretcher and worked the ratchet lever again. Soon the slough wire hung less than three feet off the muck and water.

"That should do it," said Pehr. "Now we can press the wire down to proper level. Good work! Nils!"

"Now," said Pehr to Nels, as they turned from their manipulations, "you run to the road corner and get a pocketful of staples for Nils. You and I will go and staple that end."

This said, he went to the nearest clump of osier willow in the slough edge, measured, and cut off with his pocket knife, three straight lengths of the prettily red-barked wood, precisely to the legal specification for the height above ground of the bottom wire (sixteen inches). He handed one length to Nils—without superfluous instructions. One he handed to Nels, saying: "This is how far the bottom strand must be off the ground." To both Nils and Nels he said, "don't drive the staples in straight across the wire; that may split the post. Put them in diagonally, and they will hold much better." This was a craftsman's knowledge readily applicable to barbed wire fencing with wooden posts.

Pehr and Nels walked to the road and each stuck a handful of staples into his left front pocket. "Now see how I do it, and then you can practice," said Pehr to his son. At first several of Nels' staples went awry, and Pehr had to withdraw them and drive them a second time. They were easily pulled out by inserting the hammer claws under the wire astride the staple; but Pehr would not so bruise Nils' wire. "Nels my boy, run home and get the pincers. You know where they lie in my workbox. You shall soon learn wire stapling, never fear."

While the boy was gone, Nils and Pehr stapled all the posts and met at the west end. Now they must free the stretcher, cut the wire so it would reach around the post, and leave about a six-inch surplus to twist tightly around that already stretched in place. Pehr clipped the wire off with the pincers, hooked his hammer claws securely behind a barb on the wire, and with hammer handle as lever, drew the wire tightly in place so Nils could staple it. This became automatic procedure, following each line stretching and stapling thereafter. Once done, the task became simple and easy.

"Can we roll out the middle strand to the road before supper time?" queried Nils.

"Oh, I think so," said Pehr. "My watch says only seven. But first we must staple and tie it around the post at specified height above the bottom one. Do you remember what the law says? I don't, but I have it at home. Let's lay the wire around the post about where we think it should be, twist it in place tight enough for stretching, and get the spool rolled out. Nels, you carry the stretcher, hammers, and willow lengths back to the road. Good boy."

The second course of wire they rolled out much more quickly than the first, despite greater mire in the slough edge. At the corner post at the road the wire ended several feet short before stretching. Pehr twisted the end securely to the midpoint of the crowbar, and when both men heaved on it together they soon had it straight across the slough, and several inches to spare at the post.

"I'm glad the spools have on them eighty rods and a little over; otherwise we should be unable to fasten the ends around the posts. Maybe the makers figured on this," thought Pehr aloud.

"That I could well believe," agreed Nils, "and well it is. Now let's wipe our shoes off in the tall grass and go home to supper." Nels had not waded in the muck, but had thrown hundreds of stones into the slough to watch them splash. He was careful to throw none that might strike one of the men.

At table, Pehr said to his son: "If you'll bring a hammer of your own tomorrow, we should, with three staplers, complete the entire forty-line."

"I'm glad I can help, Papa," said Nels proudly, casting a quick glance at his mother. He knew he had been assigned the hoeing of the potatoes.

Elna reassured him: "While you learn to build wire fence I'll hoe for you, but there will be a goodly part of the patch for you to do when the fence has been completed. There will be other days."

Nels gulped his food, excused himself as soon as he dared, and went to get the other hammer—the one with straight claws.

Pehr searched his records drawer and located the copy of the legal barbed wire fence—spacing of strands, etc.

First thing next day Nils stretched the middle wire as he had the bottom one, so they hung over the slough apparently properly spaced. Then he turned to Nels and said, "My boy, if you can now space and staple, your father and I can roll off what we need from my second spool. We might have this whole job done before night." Nels glowed with pride, and filled his left pocket with staples.

"Use my hammer, Nels, it is easier to work with than the one you brought. And remember what I told you: swing a hammer as if its handle were a string; it spares both hand and wrist."

Work progressed apace; and before Elna came with forenoon coffee, the east half of the fence stood completed. Those staples that had gone crooked on Nels he had pulled out and replaced.

"Now you can rest while Nils and I roll out the first strand of my fence. It will take us only a few minutes," said Pehr.

And so it did. They met Elna and her welcome refreshments by the midpoint post at nine-thirty.

"I stapled a whole row," said Nels proudly to his mother.

"That's a good boy; I hoed five rows of potatoes for you, in recompense." The dishes emptied, she gathered them up and began the walk back to the house.

Pehr and Nils were almost jubilant! Unless someone got hurt, the fence would be up for early evening. Unrolling, stretching, stapling; unrolling, stretching, stapling: the routine was now established and work went rapidly. A minor accident did happen, but it interfered but little with the work. Pehr was familiarizing himself with the stretcher, and when the wire was quite taut, it slipped several inches in the eccentric half-spool that wedged it in place. Pehr's injury was a gash in the base of his left thumb. It bled profusely; and he sent Nels for the cloth strips he had brought out for sighting the first day.

Before evening the fence stood completed—their first eighty-rod fence of 'bob-wire.'

"We have done a good week's work, if ever I saw one," proclaimed Pehr.

"Yes, I shall have little difficulty resting on the sabbath," added Nils.

Little Nels said nothing. His right arm ached a little from swinging the heavy hammer, but only he would know it.

They walked the new fence back to the road, Nils on the south (his) side and Pehr and Nels on the north (theirs). They kept an eye out for stray tools, but found none. The half-spent wire spools, Nils' at the midpoint and Pehr's at the far end, they would fetch with team and wagon another time. At the road they gathered up all the equipment they had carried out, Nels loaded heavily as anyone, and walked home at a leisurely pace.

Eventually, Nils would buy Pehr's share in the wire stretcher and Pehr would get one of his own. With barbed wire fences soon a prominent feature of the landscape every farmer needed equipment to deal with it.

They would build several miles of it in the years ahead, not only on property lines but as interior fences enclosing pastures of appropriate area. By the end of the decade almost every farm in the community would be completely enclosed by a stout barbed wire fence.

After building one forty line of partition fence in cooperation with Anderson and another with Erick Nelson, Pehr consulted with each of his other neighbors whose land abutted his to reach agreement on corner locations and for assignment of forty or half-forty lines that each would erect and maintain *(Figure 12.7).*

Two crucial fence problems remained to the settlers after the coming of barbed wire—how to confine swine and sheep without building miniature stockades!

A solution emerged about the end of the decade. In 1883, one John Wallace Page erected on his farm in Lenawee, Michigan, a fence with interlaced wires horizontally and vertically. His neighbors liked the wire so well that he built a factory in Adrian, Michigan.

In the late eighties the woven wire—also called mesh or netting—became available in Pehr's community; and it produced a lesser, though similar revolution as had barbed wire a few years earlier. The netting soon became available in three or four-foot widths (heights) the lower for swine, the higher for sheep *(Figure 12.6).* Indeed, the four-foot netting must have one or two barbed wire courses above it, or the sheep would jump over. Almost as standard practice, the farmers stretched one barbed wire along the ground in hog fencing—the barbs discouraged rooting up the fence. The ringing of swine in the nose finally stopped them from rooting under a fence. The instinctive exercise became too painful.

A good grade of steel wire, thoroughly coated with zinc, might remain serviceable a hundred years, thus outlasting several post replacements. Miles upon miles of line (peripheral) fence rows about west-central Minnesota farms contain lengths of barbed wire, more or less rusted, that were stretched in place when the fence was originally erected. Some that Pehr once stretched and stapled remains in service.

The 1880's were the decade in which Ellen and Hanna completed their schooling and Nels and Sadie commenced theirs. Nels attended, more or less erratically, until he completed the fourth grade. Then Pehr was pleased to have him devote himself to farm work and forget about books.

Twice during the decade it became necessary to deepen the well, previously dug and driven into the spring, so far had the water level fallen in only a decade and a half. The well was fitted with a lift pump manipulated by hand.

The decade was notable as the era during which fruit and vegetable canning came. into practice on the farms. Raspberry jam came into its own, as did other fruit preserves. Prior to this time, dried fruits—apples, pears, prunes, apricots, peaches—were bought and cooked to balance the diet. Off-season vegetables were only those that would keep in the cellar, mostly potatoes and root crops.

During the decade Pehr built of wood his first (one-horse) cultivator, borrowed five hoes off the seeder for use as shovels, and kept the garden clear of weeds with much less hand labor than before.

Elna got her first sewing machine, purchased from a house-to-house salesman. Several neighbors' wives bought at the same time.

Elna bought piece goods spring and fall from an itinerant Jewish peddler and

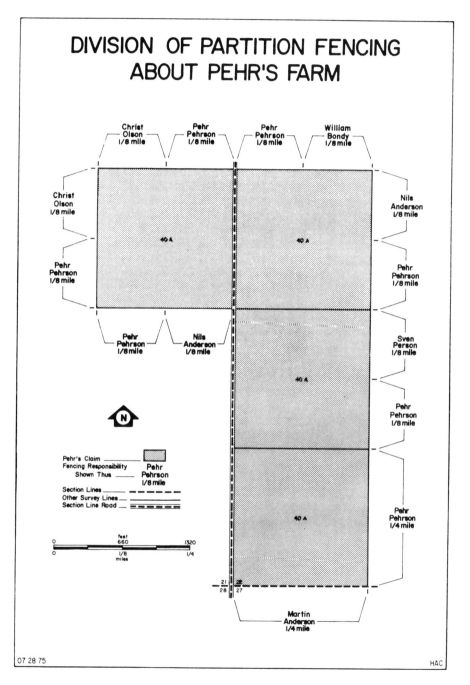

Figure 12.7. Map: Partition fence apportionments with which Pehr became concerned.

sewed most of the family's clothes. She taught her stepdaughters to make both shirts and dresses. (Homespun cloth, from washing, carding, spinning, and weaving wool—a procedure almost endless, would soon be utterly obsolete.)

As the eighties progressed, the Swedish neighbors became increasingly frustrated by the excessive time, labor, and crop loss entailed in their annual harvesting of expanding acreages of grain. Their crops had outgrown their crude equipment. Worst bottle-neck was the hand-tying of sheaves (bundles) raked out loose by their reapers.

Then they learned of a new machine, called a binder, which cast out bundles ready-tied with a slender wire. This must be the answer to their problem!

Sven and Short Nils, in 1877, bought each one of these marvelous machines for the fabulous sum of $250 apiece *(Figure 12.8)*.

Pehr and Erick deferred judgment, partly of necessity. Pehr had only two horses, and the comlex harvester required the power of at least three. He learned also that Minneapolis millers, justifiably fearful of damage to their milling machinery, levied a dockage of ten cents per bushel on wheat in which a wire particle was found. (Sometime later the millers installed magnets over which they passed all the grain,

Figure 12.8. Close-up view of the McCormick Harvester and Wire Binder built in 1876. This machine consisted of McCormick's cutting mechanism and platform and the Marsh type elevator, with the Withington self-binding attachment added. Two steel fingers on the binding attachment packed the cut grain and twisted a wire band around each bundle. Between the years of 1877 and 1885, McCormick put 50,000 of these machines into the grain fields.

Photo and caption courtesy International Harvester Archives. Original print reduced in size by Photos, Inc.

and so removed all iron or steel from the grist before it entered between the precision-set rollers.)

There was considerable talk of injury to livestock by wire gotten into the straw; and threshers so feared damage to their separators that they employed hand cutters to snip the wires off the bundles and cast them aside before releasing the grain into the feeder and cylinder. Some wires inevitably got into the separator, and sometimes wreaked havoc by winding about axles, clogging shaker screens, or fouling concaves.

Indeed, the popularity of the wire binder was short-lived. One wonders why farmers bought them, because the manufacture and sale of twine binders was almost contemporary. It may have been because, at the beginning, twine was more costly than wire, and because wire could not be severed by crickets. In due course, binder twine was oil-treated to repel crickets; and it soon became cheaper than wire.

Although Pehr never owned a wire binder, he gained considerable benefit from such ownership by Nils and Sven. He was regularly aided by one or the other in the harvesting of his small grains other than wheat; and in return he shocked their grain for them and paid them for the wire used in his fields—about two dollars per acre. His wheat he cut with his reaper and tied by hand, assurance against severe dockage at the elevator whence the grain went to a mill.

Most memorable of all family affairs and events during the 1880's were the courtship and marriage of Anna's and Pehr's grown daughters, who had arrived in America as girls aged only three and five years. Elna (Ellen) turned twenty in 1884, and Hanna eighteen. Upon attaining majority, each would receive from Anna's family's estate in Skåne one thousand dollars, an attractive legacy and potential dowry, which they kept strictly secret.

Soon as Elna noted her stepdaughters' blossoming into pretty young women, she concerned herself with their appearance and deportment in public. They would be dressed as ladies and they woud behave as ladies, their peasant heritage be damned! They would marry into the emergent "landed gentry" of the new land; and Elna would see them sought and secured. While they were still in their teens she bought, without Pehr's knowledge, fine dress materials carried by the peddler, and sewed for them stylish skirts and waists for wearing to church, and she saw to it that they missed few opportunities of attending church meetings. How else could they be shown to the public? After harvest in 1884, when Pehr had sold several loads of wheat, Elna insisted that the entire family drive to Alexandria and shop for clothing, especially for the "big" girls. Finally, when Pehr could endure her needling no longer, they went. (Sven and August would come and milk the cows, feed the pigs, etc. evening and morning.) In Alexandria, Elna bought the girls each a long full gown, with bustle, puffed sleeves, and bodice; a corset; a large hat; and a pair of shiny (Sunday) shoes. Amid considerable grumbling Pehr paid the bills, the sooner to return home. Neither of the parents bought anything of consequence for themselves, but they did not neglect to get some "store" clothes for Sadie and Nels.

Elna then insisted that the four children be photographed in their fine new clothes. In this too she prevailed *(Figure 12.9)*. Little Sadie, for want of sufficient candy, threw a tantrum instead of posing.

Observing his well turned-out daughters in church the following Sunday, Pehr was glad that he had been lavish. He sat and wished that Anna might have lived to see them as they were now—handsome capable young women.

Figure 12.9. Left to right: Hanna, Elna, and Nels. Photo probably made in 1884. Photographer unknown.

Original print retouched and reduced by Photos, Inc. Courtesy of Edna Fletcher.

Elna's campaign bore early fruit. The girls drew admiring glances during services and attracted a circle of swains about them soon as church dismissed. Soon young men called on Sunday afternoons, and eventually they came for Sunday dinner, one or two at a time. After each visit by a new admirer, Elna, the matchmaker would render a verdict on his apparent assets and debits. If he failed of her approval, the girl involved would not invite him again. Only once Hanna argued the issue; Ellen agreed with her stepmother in every case.

By the autumn of 1884 each of the girls had a favorite suitor acceptable to her parents; and the foursome shared much fun together. Often in summer the girls, with Elna's ready assistance, packed a huge picnic lunch; and the four happy young people went by buggy to a well-chosen lakeshore site to eat their Sunday dinner and enjoy the out-of-doors. In autumn they went skating if the ponds and lakes had frozen smooth. In winter they went coasting on hills chosen for length and steepness. Sometimes they took considerable joy rides in a cutter loaned by one or other of the young men's fathers.

Then one fateful Sunday late in 1884 each of the young suitors came in his own cutter and set out with his own girl alone. They took off in opposite directions and stopped when they were well out of view. Each in his screened place hugged and kissed the "light of my life" for a considerable time and then asked bluntly: "Will you marry me?" to which each got an affirmative answer without hesitation. Both rigs returned almost simultaneously. The girls were handed down and went into the house. Edwin and Ola unhitched their horses, tied them to the back of the cutter, gave them an armful of hay on the ground, and threw a blanket over each. Then they too entered the house, where the air was already charged with excitement.

The girls had already told their parents: "The boys asked us to marry them, and we want to."

"Then let each of them be man enough to ask me also," said Pehr with mock gravity.

"They will, they will, soon as they come in," squealed the girls.

They came in, caps in hand, and stood awkwardly at the door looking first to one parent and then the other. Both commenced speaking and as suddenly stood mute again.

Pehr broke the tension:

"Are you too cold to talk then; or are you guarding a secret."

"Oh, no, we're not cold!"

"We have no secret."

"We wish to marry your daughters" in unison.

"Have you determined who shall have whom, or are you asking me to decide the issue?"

Everyone, including the bashful young men, laughed at that.

"Of course you may marry our daughters, and with our fondest blessings. Why else would we have tolerated you in our house and fed you our best food all these months past?"

The girls, in turn, hugged Pehr's neck and kissed Elna on the cheek, nor did they forget Nels and Sadie. The house was brimful of happiness.

A double wedding was a foregone conclusion, and the contracting parties agreed on a date while at the supper table—3 January 1885.

Before he fell asleep that night Pehr whispered to Elna: "The young are truly practical. If I had it to do over again, I should also marry in mid-winter to keep warm, not in the sweltering heat of summer. But, perhaps a summer wedding is proof of true love!"

"Silly," said Elna, and turned away.

The double wedding was solemnized as scheduled, the Reverend Kronberg officiating in the parlor. Sadie was flower girl and Nels was ring-bearer. He lost not a ring! Two courting couples, close friends in the young people's affairs at church, stood up with the brides and grooms, one couple witnessing and signing the certificate for each of the bridal couples.

The house was quite full of friends and neighbors. From a distance had come the Morks. All the near neighbors were there, as were the parents of the grooms.

After the ceremony, when the assemblage was partaking of coffee and cake, both bridal couples gravitated to Elna, for her special matchmaker's blessing.

Edwin Lundby, Ellen's new husband, said jokingly to his mother-in-law:

"Thanks, Ma; but for you I might have been rejected."

"I favored you from the start, my dear boy; but let me remind you that you are getting a splendid wife—good-natured, a diligent worker, a good cook and seamstress—if you are not kind to her, I will take her back."

Then she spoke to Ola Peterson, Hanna's husband:

"Ola, your wife is temperamental and frail, demanding much patience and understanding. Her accomplishments are quite equal to her sister's, but she is more sensitive and less serene. But you have known her long enough so I needn't lecture you."

Ola nodded and said merely:

"I know, Ma, and thank you."

Then Elna addressed herself to both Ellen and Edwin, as they stood together:

"Now that you depart from me, my Ellen, you will, I trust, resume your given name of 'Elna.' It is entered so on the marriage certificate. Edwin, you will have to practice the change."

"I've practiced a little already. She told me all about the name problem that emerged when you became her stepmother. I will always call her name kindly and with love, as you both deserve."

At dusk the newlyweds, each couple in its cutter, set off for their new homes.

The girls would live out their lives only about two miles from their parental home, Elna on the west shore of Crane Lake, and Hanna directly south of her father's Homestead, at the northern edge of Eagle Lake Township. *(Figures 3.2 and 13.10)*.

Elna bore and reared five stalwart sons and four pretty daughters, and lived to old age. Hanna bore several children, but only two sons and one daughter lived to maturity, and survived her. She was never strong, and died of consumption (tuberculosis of the lungs) at middle age, 50.

Both Sadie and Nels had cried after the marriage ceremony because they were losing their big sisters. After they were gone the house seemed quite empty. But time meliorated the loss for parents and remaining siblings alike.

The two newly wed couples contributed their share to the mushroom-like growth of Clitherall Township population, land utilization, and agricultural produce. Soon the land that lay devoid of people in 1869 would be largely privately owned and filling with settlers' families *(Figure 12.10)*.

Nels had more chores to do, and Sadie became a pampered brat.

Since early in the eighties decade, Nels and his cousin, August, spent much of their free time together, roaming the woods and prairie hills, observing intimately the wild creatures about them and the fascinating progression of the seasons.

One spring day they almost caught a Canada goose in a fence corner. One sunny day of early spring in the swale between their homes, they came upon a great pile of garter snakes writhing about each other—at least a thousand they thought. (What the boys had seen was, in fact, a mating orgy of the reptiles, and the continuous sound—like that of wind in pine trees—was produced by the rubbing together of their scaly skins as the snakes twisted vigorously about each other. The boys estimate of numbers was probably conservative.)

The boys poked at the pile with sticks, and threw rocks at it to no avail. The snakes would not disperse. Next day the pile had disappeared. The boys marveled at what they had seen, and often told dubious listeners about the snake pile. They never saw another.

Quite often the boys went fishing, walking cross-country to the lake a mile east. They had hooks and line from the Clitherall store, and made their own poles from willow, dogwood, or birch. One of their mothers would pack a lunch for them, and furnish them with pork rind for bait if they were unable to dig up any grub worms or angle worms. For several years their favorite place from which to fish was on a large basswood that leaned, almost horizontally, far out over the water. They caught rock bass, sunfish, blue gills, black bass, perch, even walleye and pike, and the inevitable bullhead, which they threw back. Not once did they return home entirely empty-handed; usually they brought a long string of fish. Their mothers were

Figure 12.10. Plat Map, Clitherall Township, 1884. Both federal and state governments were extravagantly lavish with land grants to railroads in Minnesota. One printed source cites more than twelve million acres granted by the federal government and almost two million granted by the state. Another, equally authentic but more conservative source estimates a "total of more than 10 million acres granted Minnesota railroads," one of the largest aggregate areas granted in any state.

Railroads were given a 400-foot right-of-way by a Congressional Act signed into law by President Lincoln in 1862. This law also granted ten alternate sections per mile of track and permission to use timber, stone, and such materials as required "from adjacent parts of the Public Domain." An Act of Congress of 3 March 1865 liberalized railroad grants to "alternate odd-numbered sections to ten miles, both sides of the track and "lieu" sections to twenty miles if grant land has been sold or impaired in its usefulness to the railway."

The St. P. M. and M. on the map stands for the Saint Paul, Minneapolis, and Manitoba railroad. This line was originally the St. Paul and Pacific (Figure 1.10) abuilding across Meeker County in 1869, heading for Breckenridge. It became the St. Paul, Minneapolis, and Manitoba in June, 1879, and the Great Northern in September, 1889.

The plat map shows that most public domain, school, and railroad grant land had become privately owned before 1884, most of it at ridiculously low prices.

Map from Original in the Library of Congress.

pleased to clean and fry the catch for everyone's enjoyment. Any surplus went to the pigs.

Now and again, with August or alone, Nels walked to Clitherall, carrying eggs and butter to trade for sugar, coffee, and other staples not grown on the farm. A dozen eggs brought ten cents, as did also a pound of butter. His mother allowed Nels five cents for candy each trip. In winter he carried the eggs inside his coat so they would not freeze, and walked straight across the westerly lobe of Lake Clitherall to save time and distance.

But as the decade advanced, the boys' habits changed also. Their leisure time became less and less, their work and responsibilities, greater and greater. At the end of the decade, when they were sixteen, they were long since out of school and working alongside their fathers at such farm tasks as were within their capability. Since the fathers, Pehr and Sven, did much of their heavy seasonal work, such as haying and grain harvesting, in an informal partnership, first on one farm and then on the other, the boys had much time together. They laughed and joked at their work; and not infrequently their stern parents joined in their fun. But work came first; and as the boys grew bigger their share of the labor increased. At sixteen they were almost "filling a man's shoes."

In retrospect, Pehr recalled the decade of the eighties as one of good fortune and satisfying achievement. He had, in fact, built on his homestead a splendid set of buildings. He had seen Anna's daughters married to honest industrious young men; and his only son grown almost to manhood. It had, indeed, been a most gratifying decade.

Though the decade had brought much severe weather, especially in winter, the prairie farmers had suffered little loss other than that of fruit trees, such as apple and pear. But on the plains country to the west, severe winter weather had ruined many a grazier in the "Cattle Kingdom." There, a blizzard raged on New Year's Eve of 1885, a worse one on 7 January 1886, and yet another about ten days later. Extreme cold had come again early in the 1886-1887 winter, accompanied with heavy losses of livestock. During the years of 1886 and 1887, a combination of drought, blizzard, and over-grazing brought such disaster to flocks and herds that the ill-founded "empire" never recovered. A renewed westward surge of homesteading and wheat farming resulted; and this soon caused Pehr and his neighbors to diversify their agricultural land use, lest western competition depress grain prices excessively.

Chapter 13

SONS OF PIONEERS ASSUME PROPRIETORSHIP

The gay nineties brought a degree of gaiety even to the rural rustics of west-central Minnesota. For the sons of the pioneers, it was a time for romance and marriage, and possession of the land. Homesteaders passed on to their heirs, at various prices and by devious agreements, the lands they had brought to fruition. They were realizing a major purpose in their migration to America: independence and freedom from want for their progeny.

In families with several sons, the eldest had a traditional right to inherit the estate by making some reasonable restitution to the other siblings. In event a family had only daughters, the eldest held a certain priority, but not without indemnifying the others. In case of only one child, he or she became sole heir, full possession usually contingent upon "life support" furnished to the parents. A lone daughter might bring to her marriage a dowry of a quarter section or more, free from encumbrance other than the life support proviso. Such a fortunate one was much sought after by eligible young swains. One might, literally, marry a quarter section and get a wife in the bargain. Nels paid court to Emily (Nils Johnson's eldest) ostensibly for romantic reasons, since he was, as an only son, fairly well assured of his own land legacy, but one cannot dismiss entirely some devotion to ulterior motives. (Certainly the sparkle in a young woman's eyes lost none of its brilliance could one see therein a quarter section with appurtenances attached thereto.) (Second generation Americans, with few exceptions, honored no rights of primogeniture.)

Nels turned sixteen in the first month of the 1890's and would arrive at man's estate when the decade was half gone. Pehr was almost sixty as the decade began, well past his prime and ready to shift, more and more, both toil and decisions from himself to his maturing son. Nels assumed added responsibility so unconsciously that he could not have said when it commenced. Pehr was well aware that responsibility was shifting as he wished. By both subtle and overt means he compensated Nels for his work on the farm, lest he quit his home and hire out to someone else. Nels was, even at sixteen, a farm hand so competent and diligent that he might have commanded a goodly wage. Pehr began sharing with him the proceeds from each wheat harvest and each cattle sale, so Nels had money both for jingling and for saving. Infected by Pehr's austerity, he knew the worth of money and never wasted it wittingly.

Before his twenty-first birthday he had often suggested their need of an additional team of horses to speed farm operations, and Pehr had as often shrugged him off. But on his birthday his father stood him to half the price of horses and harness. He bought a sleek pair of blacks, lighter in weight and more slender of limb than Fanny and Blaze. Now Nels owned his first team of horses, ostensibly for farm work, but as father and mother confided between themselves, more obviously for courting expeditions. Soon he bought a top-buggy for the prancers to pull, so his purpose was scarcely in doubt.

The decade was also one of much toil and many accomplishments. In the very first autumn (1890) a new deep well, a windmill, and a large wooden stock-watering tank were installed—the well and mill only a few paces southeast of the house, and the tank inside the barnyard fence. *(Figure 13.8).*

The new water supply system came only after much urging and argument by Nels. He contended that the spring well was no longer adequate to serve the household and the livestock. One could not waste his energy pumping by hand enough water for four horses, thirty head of cattle, fifty sheep, and several swine. The neighbors had windmills, albeit on wooden towers, and the need was obvious. The tank, too, was essential. Carrying water for all the stock up the long hill from the spring was nothing short of ridiculous. The tank could be covered with boards in winter, banked around with horse manure, and kept ice-free with a covering, except in the most severe weather. Then the tank was over-turned to save it from freezing to pieces. Then animals were watered from a tub by turns, a trying task.

Nels' patience gave out during the hot harvest season, and he bought the windmill with his first share of wheat money ($75.00). Pehr paid for the tank and the well materials. (It was by this time tacitly understood that Nels would one day own the farm, so his investments in its improvement would accrue to himself.)

The forty-foot well was sunk part-way by an ingenious method called cribbing, whereby a hole is lined as it is dug, thus preventing caving. Pehr used two-by-ten-inch planking cut into four-foot lengths and nailed securely in the corners. Each course appeared as a bottomless square box. As the first course was undermined and dropped down, another was laid squarely atop it and nailed to it with narrow cleats on the inside, near the corners. As the bottom of the box went lower, its top was kept flush with the ground by adding new courses. The first course laid became the lower end of the crib. Only one man could work in the hole at a time because of restricted work space. He shoveled the spoil into an ordinary bucket, which was hauled up by a small rope for emptying. The glacial material penetrated was mostly fine sand, but with some blue-clay layers. At a depth of twenty feet the cribbing ceased; and the excavator was hoisted up by a rope.

The men completed the well with a drive point (screen), securely screwed onto a pipe. This they lowered into the hole, set it squarely in the middle, and drove it down with a heavy maul, protecting the threaded pipe end against battering by holding across its top a plank length to cushion the blows. When the drive point punctured the aquifer (water-bearing layer) and water rose visibly in the hole, the well was practically completed. A few more blows on the pipe set the screen well into the water layer, forty feet below ground level. They then screwed onto the pipe a so-called 'pump head'—a lift pump with leather-bound piston and simple float valve, manipulated up and down with a handle about three feet long. The pipe driven down to proper height and the pump screwed onto it, Pehr built a plank platform over the hole about six feet square, and raised snug up to the pump base; which he then secured to the planking with lag bolts furnished with the pump. Two planks on the east side of the decking were laid on loose, so one might easily lift them aside and drop down, by a string, any item he wished to cool. In summer the well served not only for water supply, but also as Elna's refrigerator, mainly for butter, cream, and milk.

Next time Nels was in town he procured a hard steel drill to fit his brace. He went down and, by considerable exertion, drilled a quarter-inch hole in the well pipe about two feet above the bottom of the crib. The pump and pipe drained to that level after each use; and since the hole was below normal frost depth, the pump rarely froze fast, even in the most severe winter cold. The well yielded forty-degree (Fahrenheit) water year round. The water was so charged with iron that the kitchen waterpail became lined with a reddish-yellow residue in a week's time. This the housewife wiped with a few swipes of a wet rag loaded with wood-ashes from the stove. The well yielded abundantly and served for many decades without the least modification.

The assembly and raising of the windmill was something of an engineering feat, but was accomplished in three days without damage or injury. Nels hauled the entire affair home in one load, all parts except the wheel and gearing knocked down and crated in wooden boxes. The six-foot wheel he hauled in its open crate, laid atop the wagon box and tied down securely.

The instruction pamphlet, in English, Pehr could not read; but Nels studied it an entire evening. Next day he dug at each corner, measured to the square the tower legs would make, a hole three feet long, two feet wide, and four feet deep. Into each hole he dropped a large flat rock, on which he set the anchor post. He measured, leveled, and corrected until all four anchor posts stood at the same height and spaced exactly as prescribed in the manual.

Next day came the dealer and his expert workman to help assemble and raise the structure, bringing with them several lengths of stout rope, including a three-hundred-foot length of one-inch stuff, a heavy block and tackle, and a pair of twenty-foot shear poles. They began at the top and, flat on the ground, bolted together two entire forty-foot legs (three-inch angle irons), the horizontal girts (lesser angle irons) at intervals of eight feet, and the diagonal cross-wires that would hold the structure square and true. Then they bolted the top sections of the remaining two legs, attached the girts and trusses, and progressed so until the entire tower lay assembled. They then raised the top end off the ground and laid it up on wood blocks so that it was about five feet off the ground. They attached the wheel, vane, and motor unit. They attached the ladder to the side that would face north, and they attached the three-by-three foot platform at the top.

Now the "air engine" lay on the ground, completely assembled but for the loose diagonal truss wires that would be adjusted to proper tension when the tower stood in place.

Now they maneuvered the two legs lying flat to the ground tight against the corner posts on which they would stand, and, through prepared holes in both posts and uprights, tied them together with a small rope threaded through one hole in each member. (Finally, the holes would accommodate two half-inch galvanized bolts in each corner, drawn up tightly.)

Now came the trick—the raising! The dealer indicated where they should be, and his helper drove into the ground three stout stakes, one as dead-man for the block and tackle, the other two for guy-lines to keep the tower from falling sideways or going over. Now they tied the one-inch rope to the tower just below the platform, stretched it over a pair of twenty-foot shear or gin poles, and secured it to the block and tackle gear, which was tied to the dead-man. Now came the test of strength. Two men lifted with poles at the top of the tower to raise it beyond dead-center and two pulled, with all their might, on the block-and-tackle rope. Once the tower started up, the men at the top took hold of the guy-lines and paid out rope as the tower rose, snubbing the lines on the stakes as necessary. In a matter of minutes the mill stood upright. The dealer shifted the legs, in turn, onto the anchor posts and worked them into place so the bolt holes met. The helper inserted the bolts, screwed down the nuts; and the trick had been done *(Figures 13.1 and 13.8)*. There remained the installation of the wooden pump rod and the guides to keep it straight and centered, the attachment of the furl wire and handle (the brake), tightening of the truss wires, and oiling of the mechanism. The furl wire was run down the inside of the leg at the northwest corner—nearest the house. To stop (furl) the wheel, one simply pulled the furl lever down and against the tower leg (past dead-center). Furling turned vane and wheel parallel to each other and parallel to the wind. Thus deprived of "bite," the wheel stopped, and remained so however the wind might shift.

Next day Nels filled the anchor holes with rocks, tamped in hard; then he mixed a rich slurry of sand and Portland cement and poured this over the rocks until all interstices were full and the cement stood almost flush with the ground.

The tower has endured both fair weather and foul for almost a hundred years, and appears about to outlast its third wheel. The early wheels had no oil bath or well and needed frequent oiling. Either because of human negligence or fear of heights, many mills were rarely oiled, and complained so loudly in a breeze that their squealing might be heard miles away, particularly at night. Obviously, a plain iron axle in a plain iron hub wore out quite fast, even had it frequent oilings!

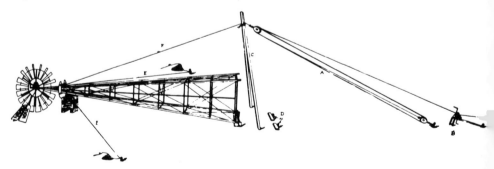

Figure 13.1. *The simple procedure of raising a forty-foot steel tower with mill wheel and power mechanism attached was something of an engineering feat in the olden days. Here we see how it was accomplished—as also described in the text.*

Sketch courtesy the Power Systems Division, Colt Industries.

All the angle irons (legs and girts) in Nels' mill tower were so well coated with zinc (galvanized) that they have yet to become badly rusted (1978).

After almost getting stuck with the mill load in the mud on the section line road, just below the site of Pehr's first fields, Nels took the initiative in another necessary project—gravel in the mud hole. The powers that be had graded the road to something of a crown two years before, but had applied to the dirt no surfacing mettle of any kind. The road became so slippery and muddy after a rain that one dared scarcely venture upon it with horses and rig.

"The devil take me, I shall fix that mud hole," swore Nels.

And Pehr, reluctant to pour oil on the fire, shrugged and agreed to help. He was violently opposed to his son's profanity but this seemed a poor time to labor the issue.

The grader had exposed in the hill west of the house a thick layer of sand, and from this they hauled and put into the mud-hole, load after load, an entire work day. They shoveled the sand into the wagon box and shoveled it out—and they filled and buried the mire so completely that the stretch of road remained firm and negotiable for many years.

In May of 1891 Pehr planted his first corn. Several neighbors had grown it for some years before, and had come to depend on the stover as a supplement or substitute for hay; in good years the ears were better hog feed than barley or rye. Almost every kind of animal on the farm would eat the remarkable cereal and fatten on it. (Pehr had no experience with maize in Sweden; he was there situated too far north. Nor did he hurry to try the unknown in America.)

Pehr eventually reserved enough seed corn from John Høvren one spring to plant ten acres, at an exorbitant price. He planted it on the south side of the west forty, on his most productive land.

In preparation for corn growing both Pehr and Nels made numerous inquiries, and several purchases of equipment. Neighbors who had already grown the native American cereal were pleased to answer their questions. They learned much and made mental note of all the information. Corn might be grown either mainly for stover (fodder corn) or for grain (ear corn), and one must choose his seed accordingly. Fodder corn grew more rapidly than the other, so one might plant it later and cut it earlier, thus avoiding frost risk at both ends of the growing season. Fodder corn grew rank and tall, and yielded heavily almost every year. Ear corn took longer to mature, and must be planted early as possible in the spring, but not so early that the young sprouts became frostbitten. In the second week of May the frost risk was acceptable. The crop must be left standing as long as possible to mature and harden, and even so would produce full ears only about one year in three or four. Most years it yielded only nubbins. In any case, and whatever kind the corn, one must harvest it quickly as possible after the first frost in fall (usually mid-September) "burned" it in the low places so the leaves turned brown, dry, and brittle. One lost much of a frosted crop, and it was miserable to handle. Fodder corn one sowed in rows as he might sow peas or beans. Ear corn one planted in "hills", three or four kernels to the hill, so he could cultivate the field both lengthwise and crosswise, the better to suppress noxious weeds. The hills must be placed accurately. As to row spacing, judgements varied from twenty-four inches to as much as thirty. Pehr settled for twenty-seven.

One fair day he drove to Battle Lake, by then a thriving young town five miles north by road; and bought two two-by-six inch planks ten feet long, one two-by-four inch plank ten feet long, two one-by-six inch boards ten feet long, and a calculated quantity of nails. He bought from the A.C. Hatch Hardware a wooden hand corn-planter that one stabbed smartly into the earth to activate the planting mechanism and as smartly withdrew, straight up. He loaded these purchases into the platform buggy and hauled them home.

Then he set about making a "marker". He sawed off one foot of each two-by-six, wasting material because nine-foot lengths were not sold. He sawed the two-by-four into five two-foot lengths. He laid the two-by-sixes flat on the ground, parallel to each other, and eighteen inches apart on their near sides. Onto them he toe-nailed the two-by-fours on edge, spacing them exactly twenty-seven inches on center. Then he turned the affair over, right side up, and nailed the two-by-sixes securely to the two-by-fours. He nailed onto the two-by-sixes, diagonally, corner-to-corner both ways, the six-inch boards, one sawed in two and shortened to meet the other at midpoint. Finally, he bored a one-inch hole through the upper corner of the middle two-by-four, for attachment of a clevis. There! he had a corn marker, a very ordinary implement on most farms. The seedbed well prepared, it made neat clearly visible grooves when dragged over a field. When preparing for hills, one marked the field first one way and then the other, thus completing a checkerboard pattern. To ensure accuracy, one must run the outer marker in the outer groove made by the last round before, so he marked only four rows with each crossing of the field.

Where the marker grooves intersected was the place to stab the planter for each hill. After a little practice, a man could plant almost as fast as he ordinarily walked—ten acres or more in a day.

For both Pehr and Nels, corn became a staple feed and forage crop, and always remained so. They fed it all to the animals and never sold any. They selected and saved their own seed. They usually stacked the corn just outside the barnyard fence, for convenience in winter. Husking for the pigs was customarily a daily chore from fall until spring, the husked stalks thrown over the fence into a feeding rick for the cattle. In good corn years, a half dozen armfuls would yield a bushel of ears for the hogs; in nubbin years, twice that many might not yield so much.

As utilized during the early years, corn had two distinct disadvantages: the stalks were wasted, except as they augmented the volume of stable manure, and they rendered barn "manuring" (cleaning) almost twice the chore it had been before. Stuck through with a manure fork, the wet stalks in manure were exasperatingly difficult to get off the tines. They simply stuck until dislodged by main force.

Corn in the crop regimen brought a new dimension to seasonality of farm work. It was an inter-tilled crop, requiring frequent cultivation (or plowing) between the rows to suppress weeds and, especially in dry years, to form and maintain a dust mulch that reduced loss of moisture. A good farmer cultivated his corn field three or four times, until the corn stood two feet tall—about the fourth of July, as a rule. In Pehr's time all the cultivating was done with one-horse walking cultivators run between the rows. Pehr bought one with wooden handles, and it outlasted the man by many, many years. His grandsons followed it several years, until two-horse riding, two-row cultivators became available.

The numerous striped gophers (ground squirrels) became a special menance to the corn grower. They found the newly-planted rows or hills as if schooled in geometry and dug up and ate the kernels. Many fields came up with voids at the edges frequented by the beasts—and they were on edges almost everywhere. Pehr bought Nels a .22 rifle with which to decimate the quick little culprits. And Nels obliged his father, delighted to have one assignment that was less toil than sport. He shot gophers by the dozen.

The year 1893 became infamously memorable as the year of the hail. A thunderstorm with heavy marble-sized hail swept over the vicinity and utterly destroyed the standing crops. The storm was of the cold front type, generated as a wedge of cool heavy Canadian air driven under a warm, wet, light air mass drifted in from the Gulf of Mexico. Swept up over the fast advancing northerly air, and cooled to dew-point by expansion, the Gulf air became unstable and rose in a violent up-draft, creating towering storm clouds (cumulo nimbus) as it rose. In the clouds, condensation progressed to precipitation, and frozen rain drops swirled with the turbulence up and down, alternately collecting water and freezing it on. The agatized ice lumps enlarged until their weight exceeded the lift of the upward surge, fell away from their support, and swirled forcibly to earth before they could melt.

The hail beat the standing crops so violently into the ground that the fields, after passage of the storm, appeared almost as if they had been plowed. The storm came between haying and harvest time, so nothing revived sufficiently to produce a crop. The corn, which if struck down a month earlier would have sprouted anew, was too far grown to revive.

The land lay literally ice-covered immediately after the storm. In the lee of buildings and other obstacles, the ice lay several inches deep and took an entire day to melt away; in constant shade, two days.

The crops were a total loss; there was to be no grain harvest in 1893. Pehr eked the forage stored for winter with year-old oat straw and a late clipping of his native prairie area. The grasses, recently mowed, were not much damaged by the storm. Fortunately, father and son had stacked an abundance of hay, both tame (timothy) and wild, before the storm struck; and the granary bins had residues of wheat, oats, and barley to last a year if used with some discretion. The garden regenerated cabbage and kale very nicely. Potatoes and root crops made some recovery but their yield was curtailed in both quantity and quality.

With no harvest to gather in, to what would one apply himself? As several times before, the young man resolved the issue. Said Nels to his father:

"Ma has been wanting a summer kitchen built onto the house. I will haul the lumber and help build a shanty at the north end, if you will pay half the costs."

"That sounds fair enough to me. Shall we ask Evander to be our builder again? If hail hit him too, he may have plenty of time."

"I will take the buggy and drive down (four miles) to see him this afternoon."

Evander had more spare time than he knew what to do with. When should he come?

"Give us three fair days to get the footings in and the framing materials laid down. Then we should be ready to begin the carpentry. How much must you have for the job?"

"I will do all the carpentry for twenty-five dollars. But I'm not a stone or brick mason. Will you need a new chimney, or can we knock a hole in the one already in the wall?"

"We can use the chimney we have. I'll chisel a vent into it if you'll keep an eye on me."

"Can you stable my horses during the day? I need to be here morning and evening for milking and other chores. I'll drive forth and back each day we work, if that's agreeable."

"We can stable your horses; and I will give them hay and water too."

"Alright. I'll be there on Thursday to begin work, unless the weather is foul. If all is not then in readiness, I shall have me a pleasure trip anyhow."

Nels hauled the lumber from Everts' Lumber Yard in Battle Lake, bringing cement for footings on his very first load. Pehr helped him frame up the footings and mix and pour the cement. Nels got the sand from their roadside pit.

Evander came at the appointed time, and they commenced building. Unfortunately for Elna, the hill dropped away where the shanty was to stand, and the footings were too low. She would have two steps to go up and down between kitchen and dining room. Of course, the shanty was for use only in summer!

Evander, with considerable help from both Nels and Pehr, completed the shanty structure in six short work days. It was entirely unfinished on the inside, devoid of ceiling, and with studdings exposed. Elna's brawny men removed the cookstove from the dining room to its new situation and connected the pipes to the new chimney vent, whose ragged edges had been filled and smoothed out with cement about a stub of pipe temporarily stuck in. Pehr erected shelves and nailed up several hooks on which Elna arranged her kitchen equipment. She was pleased, despite the annoying stair steps.

Obsessed by a fear of idleness, Pehr suggested that Nels might busy himself clearing and grubbing out the aspen thicket in the northeast corner of the middle forty. The brunt of the hill facing Sven's slough he needn't bother with; it stood too steep for tilling. They went together to the site, and by much discussion and pointing, agreed which area of trees was to be cleared for plowing and which would remain.

Excepting a few slender Juneberry and pin-cherry trees, the entire stand to be cleared was of quaking aspen ranging in breast-high diameter from four to ten inches. Commonly called "popple" ('aspe' in Swedish) aspen is a soft white wood, easily chopped and sawed; and the trees are neither heavily nor deeply rooted. They are easily grubbed, as grubbing goes; but all grubbing is sweaty back-breaking work. It is work that can utterly fatigue a man unless he learns to pace himself.

All this Pehr knew from experience, and he accompanied Nels when he went to begin the project. Pehr carried axe and spade, Nels the freshly sharpened mattock and the one-man crosscut saw. Pehr selected a young tree at the edge of the thicket amid the raspberry bushes, and showed Nels how to ply the mattock and undermine it. Stumps would be taken out in similar manner.

"If you dig and chop a little trench about a foot out from the base of the tree or stump, all around, you have most of the roots severed. Then if you undercut once around, there should be few lateral roots holding. You may then be able to push the tree over, or lift out the stump, breaking off or pulling up the tap root. Both men pushed and the tree leaned. Pehr gave the tap root one additional whack with the axe, and down went the tree.

"There now, that's how to do it. Now, we cut off the butt end, trim the branches off, stack the boles and slash in separate piles away from each other, roll the stump to the slash pile—and one tree has been disposed of."

They performed all these tasks before stopping to rest.

"Couldn't we leave, for now, the trees in the raspberry brush, and take them later? The berries are abundant and delicious, as you know, and they are approaching their peak of ripeness," spoke Nels, indignantly.

"Leave them if you wish," replied Pehr. "There are not many trees anyhow. If you would shove trimmings and stumps back to the edge of the brunt, we could burn them there after hauling the wood home; and there would be a new raspberry patch. I've noticed that the raspberry and aspen invade a woods opening almost immediately after it is cleared and burned over."

"I'll leave them for now, then."

"So be it! None of this clearing is absolutely necessary. I just thought that when you came into its ownership you would wish no part of the farm lying idle that could be put to profitable use."

Sadie brought them forenoon lunch. Both walked home for dinner, and Pehr remained at home. Nels returned to the aspen stand that would demonstrate his manhood. His days and work became routine. He came home for dinner at noon. Sadie usually, but sometimes Elna or Pehr, brought him forenoon and afternoon lunches. He labored, almost without respite except Sundays, for three months. Then, at the dinner table, one day in early November he said to his father:

"If you'll bring my lunch this afternoon you can see whether I should grub any more. I believe I may have done enough."

"I will be proud to come. I'm sure you have done enough, and done it well. I knew you were making good progress when, repeatedly, even in relatively cool weather, you came home so sweaty and grimy that you must wash yourself all over before supper."

That afternoon Pehr viewed what his son had accomplished, and he was mighty proud of him. Before him lay a dozen or more large stacks of aspen boles, cut to lengths of about twenty feet, and tighty packed piles of trimmings and stumps. Nor had the raspberry patch been spared.

"You have done yourself proud, my son. You shall be a farmer good as any. I'm especially pleased that you have done all this independently without once complaining. I knew from your frequent sharpening of tools that you were not sitting on your hands out here. Let me help you with these three remaining saplings, and we'll walk home together with all the tools. You'll have more bathing time than usual!"

Pehr was justly proud of his son's industry and perseverance. The land he had so precariously claimed and so diligently improved would be in competent hands after he surrendered it to his son—and that time would be soon. He hoped and believed that his male heir might husband and appreciate the land as a divine gift, to be used fully but never abused. It should be so tended that it would serve generation after generation indefinitely, without depreciating. The good prairie soil should be enriched, not impoverished!

At "break-up" time the following spring, roads and sleigh tracks became for a time so icy that one dared not drive horses on them for fear they would slip and break their legs. For the mere continuance of such daily chores as hauling out and spreading the stable manure and bringing home straw for roughage and bedding it became necessary that the heavy horses be shod. Pehr had to have shoes made to size and sharpened for both Fanny and Blaze, also a small hooked horse-shoer's knife with which to clean the frog, a small clinching tool, a large horse-shoer's rasp with which to flatten and level the hoof to receive the shoe, a flat headed hammer little heavier than a tack hammer, a pair of pincers with which to cut off the nails before clinching, and an adequate supply of horseshoe nails, shiny as silver.

Pehr demonstrated the procedure with Fanny's left hind foot and Nels observed. (Of course, Nels already knew how to lift a horse's foot and hold it between one's knees, bottom up, because he had often removed pebbles that became stuck against the frog, causing an animal to limp.) Now Pa showed him how he must carefully clean and trim the inside of the hoof without cutting to the quick, rasp off any slivers on the outside of the hoof, and rasp it flat across so the shoe fitted squarely and firmly, without rocking. He dropped Fanny's foot and straightened his back for a breather. Fanny rested too. Pehr wiped his brow with his handkerchief and stood resting against the stall for several minutes. Before he resumed work, he held up for Nels' inspection what appeared to be nothing more than a four-inch length of iron three quarters inch square.

"This," said he, "is a clinching iron, to be held against the hoof just above the place where the nail should come out. Notice that I hold it against the hoof with my left hand while I nail with my right. It steadies the hoof so I can nail more accurately. Now, grab a handful of nails and hand them to me one at a time as I reach for them. Now, Fanny, we'll finish the job."

He lifted the mare's foot and held it as before, the toe well up toward the fetlock, so she would not lean her weight on him. He slapped the shoe to the bottom of her hoof with his right (hammer) hand, and held it in place with his left. He reached for a nail from Nels, and observed as he stuck the tip into the right second hole from the toe:

"See how those nails are beveled on one side and straight on the other. The beveled side must go toward the inside so the nail will drive toward the outside of the hoof."

He set and started the nail; then commented further:

"Now, note how quickly I bend the nail up after I've driven it home. That's defense against ripping your leg or hand if the horse should jerk his foot free at that instant. It is, in fact, at that very time that a mean or nervous animal is most liable to jerk away."

In a few minutes Pehr had the shoe securely in place, with four nails accurately driven through the hoof on each side and bent sharply upward. He quickly cut the nails off with the pincers, leaving only about three-eighths of an inch sticking out of the hoof. Now he used the little steel gimmick for its special purpose, namely clinching. Held tightly against the projection of a nail while he tapped the nail head, the flat-headed little bar turned the protruding nail tightly back against the hoof, making the shoe's attachment more secure. He released Fanny's foot, straightened his back, and patted the mare's rump in appreciation of her gentle tolerance.

"Now, son, you do her right hind foot and let me hold the nails."

After allowing Fanny a short respite, Nels took up her right hind leg and proceeded step by step under his father's critical supervision. Pehr made few corrections; his son shod the foot more quickly than he had done the other. Nels clinched the nails and released the foot. He looked to his father for final approval.

"You did it as well as I could ever do it, and in less time. I pronounce you a farrier. But do remember this: the shoes should be taken off in six weeks, or less.

Otherwise, they may bind or cramp the foot somehow. If need be, they can be put back on immediately, but one should not use the old nail holes in the hoof."

Nels completed the shoeing. Blaze was as gentle as Fanny, and there was no difficulty. Pehr had driven his last horseshoe nail into a hoof.

A year later, early in the spring of 1895, the first commercial cattle dehorners came round, gory all the way down the front of their jackets and overalls, carrying a giant pair of clippers with handles two feet long and a bloody coil of half inch rope.

"Do you have any young stock you want dehorned?" asked one of the rough looking men.

"I might have. It depends on how much you charge."

"We charge ten cents a horn, but we won't tackle three-year old steers or old bulls."

"Fair enough! Will you give us a hand with herding them into the barn?"

With the two men to help, Pehr and Nels soon had the young stock loose in the cow barn. With a length of half-inch rope the two men quickly had a yearling tied with his head tight against the center post. One man held him so—firmly—and the other lopped off his horns flush with the skull. As each horn came off, blood squirted from the hole in the head as if shot from a water pistol. When released, the young steer bawled, and rushed out the door, shaking his head and gushing blood from both sides.

They took the horns off six young animals in all, releasing without clipping three calves deemed too young. After all was done, the clipper wielder explained that the horn must be big enough to be hollow at the base. If cut off sooner, it would grow back, at least partially. He explained their bloody business further:

"We go around early in spring, before the fly season. If flies get into the holes in the head, the animal may be killed by infection. An animal may bleed several hours, but it seems to do him no injury. The hole will heal over and the skull become smooth in a few weeks."

Pehr took his purse from his pocket and counted out a dollar and twenty cents, which he dropped into the man's palm. The dehorner thanked and dropped the coins into his pocket.

"We'll be around a year from now, if all goes well. The calves will be big enough then," said the holder as he stepped into the buggy.

"If these live, I'll ask you to do the others next year, you bet."

Everyone waved, as the horses stepped out in a trot.

Dehorning became an annual event, and spared many animals (and men) from goring or other injury. One sharp-horned animal could menace a herd, and could not be tolerated. Many farmers sawed the horns off at the base when they were large enough; but it was a strenuous task. Some killed the horns when calves were quite young, just as the emergent horn had pushed up a little bump on the head. A little dab of caustic soda smeared on the bump would, almost without fail, kill the horn, and spare the animal the shock and pain of mechanical horn removal. Muleyness, a desirable cattle trait, appeared on the increase in Pehr's time, but whether by selective breeding, dehorning, or other cause, one cannot certainly say.

Between haying and harvest in the summer of 1895, Pehr and Nels built a machine shed/pigsty combination at the bottom of the gentle slope toward the north, some hundred feet north-northeast of the house. They laid it up with logs hauled home during the annual fuel harvest in January. The structure was about fifty feet long (east-west) and twenty feet wide, and stood only about twelve feet high at the ridge line. The west (lower) end was set below the level of the remainder, but built up to a common ridge height. This was the pigsty, the only part with four full walls; the front of the machine storage part was fully walled on three sides, the south side with only the two upper courses of logs supported by two posts set between the doors. The doors were hinged at the top, and hung free when down to within about two feet of the ground. To open them, one swung them out and up, and propped them up with a rail measured and cut for the purpose. The crude structure stood on boulders dug into the ground to a common level; on these lay the bottom logs. The building was roofed with wide rough-boards and commercial shingles. Cracks between logs were left without chinking, except in the pigsty. The structure was adequate protection for the buggy, the lumber wagon and sleigh in off-season, the seeder (later, drill), the reaper (later, binder), etc. (The pigsty, with south wall knocked out, later became a garage for Nels' first Model T Ford.) Though then gradually falling to ruin, the shed served until gasoline tractors commenced replacing draft horses. Then farm machines became larger, more complex and expensive, and almost entirely of iron and steel. With no wooden parts to rot, they were simply parked in the open air when not in use. In general, only tractors and motorized machines were stored under a roof. The old-style machine shed became obsolete, replaced by a taller building with large sliding doors.

 The year 1895 went down in regional history as the year of the greatest grain crop yields to date; and in the family chronicle as the year of Nels' twenty-first birthday and his first team of horses. The year, as a whole, was considerably dryer than average; but both June and July had unusually heavy rainfall. The summer was abnormally cool, so evaporation was low. Crops matured without any deterrence by hot scorching weather. As previously noted, Nels probably chose the team mainly for courting the handsome farmers' daughters round about; but the team could also pull a fourteen-inch turning plow with comparative ease. And for hauling loads on wagon or sleigh the part-Arabian animals were much faster than Pehr's heavier Percherons. The two teams supplied ample animal power through many years of farm operation.

 After Sven and Pehr, greatly aided by their sturdy young sons, had stacked all their heavily-yielding grain crops, Pehr implored his family to accompany him to Fergus Falls, mainly to have his second family photographed for posterity *(Figure 13.2)*. Nels would drive his prancers on the platform buggy so rain would not defer the trip. But the appointed day broke clear and beautiful. They were off early, to dispatch their business and be home before night. By prearrangement, August would do all the evening chores. (As reward, Pehr bought him a handsome gold watch chain such as worn across one's vest. After all, the young man was his godson! August was proud and greatly pleased.)

 For plowing that fall Pehr bought a fourteen-inch steel-beam stubble plow for Nels' horses to pull *(Figure 13.3)*. With this rig, together with Pehr's old fourteen-inch wooden-beam stubble plow, and his span of horses, father and son, with four willing animals, could easily turn under four acres of stubble (old ground) per day. The annual plowing task spring and fall was reduced to half its previous time. It appeared that everything was accelerating!

 Everyone engaged in farming and every small town business man dealing with farmers in Otter Tail County came to mark the year 1895 as the one of the fabulous

Figure 13.2. Pehr's second family: Pehr, Elna, Sadie and Nels.

Photo made in 1895, in Fergus Falls.

Figure 13.3. Shown here is the model of plow that became used almost exclusively throughout the Middle West, indeed in most of agricultural America, from the 1880's almost to World War I. Most popular were sizes that cut and turned a slice fourteen or sixteen inches wide. For breaking pasture or meadow sod the sixteen-inch with three horses was the standard rig. For stubble plowing, the fourteen-inch with two horses was preferred. The photo shows the steel mold board that turned the furrow (opposite the landside shown in Figure 12.2).

Each plow was variously identified as a "stubble" plow or a "turning" plow. In the off-season, Pehr stored his "walking" plows in the granary loft over the grain bins—share, mold board and landside liberally coated with axle grease.

Photo Courtesy Deere and Company.

grain yields. The yield of small grains were such as never known before, and perhaps never since to this day.

When Pehr and son Nels strolled about their fields one Sunday afternoon a week or so before the oats would commence turning white, they marveled at the fullness and weight of heads and the density of the luxuriant stems that bore them.

"These are the best crops I have ever seen," said Pehr to his son, with a degree of excitement in his voice. "This year's wheat, if it stands to maturity without storm damage, we cannot harvest with the old worn reaper-mower. Nor can we ask Sven or Nils to help with the other grains; they'll have enough work for their machines in their own fields. We shall have to buy a binder."

"You should have bought one years ago; soon as twine binders came out," said Nels, "you have imposed on your good neighbors too long. I'll go halves with you on the cost of a new machine. We are fortunate that so many companies are making them now that competition has driven prices way down."

That very day Nels hitched his trotters to the top buggy, and his father and he drove to Battle Lake. He found a vacant length of the hitching rail half-way up the street on the right (east) side. There he tied his sleek animals by their halters, and the men walked together to the T.A. Ranstad Implement Company, east of the First National Bank. They found what they sought—a Plano twine binder with bundle-carrier—for only one hundred twenty-five dollars *(Figure 13.4)*.

Said Tom Ranstad: "This machine" (pointing to one assembled for show) "I can recommend, Pehr and Nels. It's price will probably go up soon as harvesting begins, because many worn machines will break down in the heavy stuff in field hollows. I also have a stock of twine, and I suggest you buy plenty. It may take a dollar's worth or more to tie two acres this year."

"How about the machine," asked Nels, asserting his impending proprietorship, "if we agree to your price, will you bring one out and assemble it for us one day soon?"

"If you'll help me, I'll haul one out tomorrow and we'll have it put together before evening," replied Ranstad.

"I think we have a deal," put in Pehr. "How much twine will we need to bind eighty acres?"

"You'd better get six sacks. It comes six balls to the sack. This is pure Manila hemp, and oil treated against crickets. It's the best on the market. Each pound has six hundred fifty feet in it and is worth seven and one-half cents. An eight-pound ball should tie three and eight-tenths acres of an average crop; but this year's stand will take twice that much or more. My regular price is sixty cents a ball, which would make six sacks worth $21.60 but since you are buying both the machine and the twine, I'll knock off the $1.60 on the deal. I am sure you'll be pleased with it."

(The so-called Manila hemp was, in fact, not hemp, but the long tough fibers extracted from the leaves of abaca, a plant related to the banana. The gunny-sacks were made in Bengal, India from the jute fiber.)

Aside to Nels, Pehr asked, "do you go halves on the twine too."

"Yes," said Nels, without hesitaiton.

Both took out their wallets, and each in turn counted out on Ranstad's palm $72.50. Ranstad thanked and shook hands with each customer, and assured both that their goods would be delivered next day. He kept his word.

Figure 13.4. A Plano twine binder such as pictured here was Pehr's first specialized harvester. The machine tied bundles with twine, which had become cheaper than wire about 1890, and provoked no dockage at elevator or mill. Although its swath was only six feet wide, one could, with three or four horses abreast, cut ten acres of an average grain stand in a good day—not delayed by dew in the morning, nor often choking the sickle and dragging the bull (traction) wheel among Jerusalem artichokes in low places.

The bundle carrier made possible the dumping of three or four bundles at a time, in rows across the field, thus expediting shocking by sparing the shocker much walking. The machine served several years after Pehr died, but as it became worn it threw more and more loose bundles, despite replacement of the knotter hook. Its size also became outmoded; and Nels eventually replaced it with a seven-foot McCormick-Deering.

Not visible in the photo was a vertical tube of height and diameter to hold two balls of twine, one atop the other. The twine, fed out the top of the can, ran under a spring loaded guide to keep it taut and avert tangling enroute to the tying head, which rose to the knotter when the bundle was sufficiently compressed to trip an adjustable release mechanism. The twine fed out from the inside of the top ball, and it was imperative that the operator replenish the twine supply before the bottom ball was too far spent to be lifted out without unraveling and tangling. While the bottom ball still remained firm the operator must carefully lift it out and tie onto its outside end a fresh ball that he dropped to the bottom of the can, after tying its inside end to the outside end of the ball lifted out. The partially spent ball he then dropped on the new, full one—and he was ready to go again. A careless or dreamy operator might run out of twine and throw out loose bundles by the score before noting his dereliction. The shocker swore at such slovenliness; and carried several lengths of twine threaded through a belt loop on his pants, to meet such an emergency.

The Plano Manufacturing Company was originally situated in Plano, Illinois; later moved to West Pullman (now part of Chicago). Plano joined with four other companies in 1902 to form the International Harvester Company, but I.H.C. for some time marketed certain products under the Plano name.

Photo and last paragraph of caption courtesy International Harvester Archives.

At the hitching rail, Pehr told Nels: "Just wait here, please, while I go get a few articles for Ma at Albertson's."

"Alright," said Nels, and commenced petting his handsome blacks.

The wheat yielded fifty bushels to the acre; the oats, a hundred. Father and son harvested twenty-five hundred bushels of wheat off fifty acres and two thousand bushels of oats off twenty. The remainder of their tilled acreage, some forty acres, yielded comparably well—ten acres of corn, fifteen of red clover and timothy hay, and ten of barley. Nels, with binder, horses, and twine all furnished, spent several working days in the fields of Sven and Nils, respectively. He was determined to make some restitution for the very considerable harvest help given Pehr during many years past. The neighbors were especially pleased to have help with the prodigious 1895 crop.

The fabulous crop so glutted the market that the price of wheat fell to forty-two cents per bushel, oats if one could find a buyer at all, brought only nine to fifteen cents per bushel. Barley for hog or chicken feed sold little better than oats; but barley of malting quality sold better. Corn was fed to the livestock; none was sold.

In January of 1896, father and son again combined the cutting of building logs with the cutting of fuel wood. They hauled from the lake woods enough logs to build the walls of a house sixteen by twenty-four feet. Pehr had insisted that they build a house for him, Elna, and Sadie against such time as Nels would marry and install his wife in the house the family now occupied. Nels had accepted the idea half-heartedly because he had no one in mind for a wife. Pehr hewed, peeled, and notched the logs as he had done for other buildings before. But this would be his last.

As before, he engaged Evander to build the upper part with commercial lumber and cover the logs with drop siding. He and Nels dug and laid the footings with stone. Sven and August helped them lay up the walls after haying and corn cultivation. Evander completed the building in September, with materials hauled from Everts' Lumber Yard in Battle Lake.

The house had two rooms. One large one served as living room and bedroom. A smaller one in the east end served as kitchen and dining room. The only exterior door was to the kitchen. The upstairs was one large room, with short walls north and south, studs and rafters naked, and no ceiling. Pehr made a board cover with which to close the stair well to save heat when the cold upstairs space was not in use. The house had a sizeable dirt cellar under it, reached by a trap door in the kitchen floor. The house stood south of the garden, north of the orginal stable site. In fact, it stands to this day.

A year after the house was built and occupied, Pehr and Nels added a good-sized shed to the east wall, with two windows, an outside door in the south wall, and one door opening on the kitchen. This was Pehr's workshop, in which, amid all his treasured hand tools, he spent much of his latter years, busily shaping and building multifarious items of wood.

When Nels' Anna bore twins in May, 1907, it was in this workshop that Pehr quickly fashioned the necessary extra high chair for the twin boy (the twin sister got the hand-me-down). The chair has three kinds of wood in it—oak, basswood, and aspen: and is so sprung and doweled together that it has not a single nail. (It remains a treasured heirloom of this author.) *(Figure 13.5)*.

In 1897 Nels bought the three prairie forties from Pehr and Elna, but the transaction was not recorded before 27 March 1899, when the three forties became the legal property of Nels and Anna, his bride of six months.

Two land transactions that were finalized early in 1898 transferred to Nels the ownership of the Clitherall Lake peninsula lots acquired by Pehr in 1877. For sublot 1 of government lots 1 and 4 he paid fifty dollars, or five dollars per acre, an exorbitant price between father and son. For sublots 3,8,9,10, and 11 of government lots 1,2,3, and 4, Section 14, Township 132, Range 40 he paid one hundred twenty-five dollars *(Figure 13.6)*. Both transactions were accomplished on 10 February 1898, and Nels was given a warranty deed in each case. His title to sublot 1 was filed on 2 March 1898 and recorded in *Book 51 of Deeds,* page 56, Register of Deeds office, Otter Tail County (Fergus Falls). The Warranty Deed for sublots 3,8,9,10, and 11 was filed and duly recorded in the same book, page 55.

All the foregoing "signed, sealed, and delivered," Nels, nonetheless, deemed his titles suspect, especially as he mistrusted Lundquist. So he later inquired of Mr. E. Frankburg, Register of Deeds, who most kindly replied with a two-page judgment, written long-hand in Swedish. Mr. Frankburg did indeed question the validity of Nels' titles, and recommended that a copy of the original patent issued by the General Land Office be procured from Washington, and that all subsequent ownerships be propery abstracted (which was later done, at Nels' request, the costs shared by August).

Figure 13.5. When Nels' wife, Anna, bore twins on 3 May 1907, Grandpa Pehr saw an immediate duty—the assembly of a second high chair. The chair, shown here was so doweled and sprung together, that it had not a single nail. It became the twin boy's chair, and remains his treasured heirloom. Seat of the chair is basswood, the back aspen, and all other parts white oak.

Photo by E.A. Vievering.

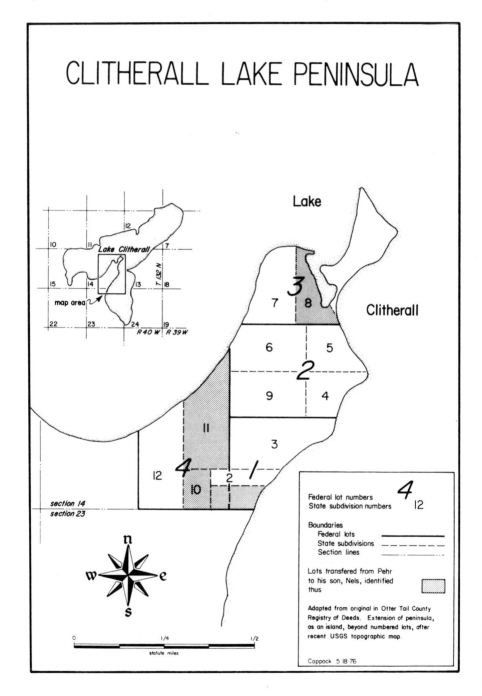

Figure 13.6. Map: Clitherall Lake Peninsula, showing those lots transferred by Pehr to his son, Nels.

Mr. Frankburg also found that taxes for the year 1901 were delinquent for two of the lots, in the amounts of thirty-six cents on sublot one and eighty-six cents on sublot three. Nels paid these back taxes, and promptly sold sublot 3 to August for sixty dollars. Both neighbor-cousins now owned a sufficient standing forest for fuel supply indefinitely.

Not long after this, Nels sold sublot 8 to a conniving chisler for eight dollars. Nels knew only that the lot was a poor area of sand hills and swamp; he did not know that, since it was the outermost numbered lot, the entire stretch of land beyond it (the point of the peninsula) adhered to this lot under the law. (Ignorance was duly penalized.)

The year 1898 became a most important milestone in Nels' life; he got married! Nels had, by dint of his prancers and buggy rig, courted eligible and willing maidens (and a few tarts), as far afield as Lake Christina and beyond; but he had not become sufficiently enamored of one to propose marriage.

Then, in the summer of '98 came his Waterloo, unsought but by suspect fortuity, in the person of one Anna Nelson, who accompanied a family friend of Pehr who came from St. Paul to visit her country "cousins," among them Knut Hanson, Battle Lake banker. By coincidence, her name had also been Anna Nelson before her recent marriage to Nels Lovene. Even had she brought the other Anna with ulterior motive, which one suspects, she would have no further part in this chronicle.

Nels was smitten by Anna even as she stepped off the train at the Battle Lake depot, showing for an instant an uncommonly well-turned ankle. When the Swedish "cousin"—a few times removed—introduced him to his future wife, he blushed, and became so nervous that he almost dropped the luggage he had taken from the visitors. He walked with the ladies to the nearby hitching rail to which his handsome horses were tied. The girls commented on the sleek beauty of the team. Nels stowed the suitcases in the buggy box at the rear of the vehicle, and then handed up the girls—first the cousin, then Anna, to sit in the middle. He untied his horses, climbed into the buggy, and sat down in the driver's place, the right-hand side. The horses pranced as usual.

They spoke of many things enroute the farm: how Anna was gainfully employed as housemaid in a Doctor Cannon's home in St. Paul; how the farmland round-about seemed wondrously fertile and well-kept; how corn was always sown in rows and inter-tilled.

On arrival, the girls were joyously welcomed by Elna, Pehr, and Sadie. They would have the large room upstairs (Nels and Sadie occupied the small bedrooms that had once been Ellen's and Hanna's). Sadie showed the visitors up and Nels brought their suitcases.

After supper, it being June, with long lighted evenings, Sadie and Nels acquainted their visitors with the entire farmstead—buildings, animals, machinery, and all. Both of the girls from Saint Paul were duly impressed. Secretly Anna, eyeing Nels furtively, wondered why some enterprising girl had not picked him off. He was handsome enough, and assured of becoming prosperous. He was, she had been told, two months her senior, a highly eligible bachelor. She would set her cap for him!

The young people did considerable visiting about the countryside. On Sunday all went to church together, and the pert little newcomer from Sweden drew many appraising glances. Nels contrived, with more cooperation then he knew, to walk out with Anna of an evening. The more he was with her the more fond of her he became. In his own mind he knew he would marry her if she would have him, but the right moment to ask her seemed never to come. Eventually the girls had only one day remaining before they must return to Saint Paul. Nels was in a dither. At noon their last day before departure, he needled Anna into bringing his afternoon lunch to him in the field.

"Bring my lunch at three-thirty, and you can see how one cultivates corn. You might also learn a duty of a farmer's wife, should you one day become one."

Nels was cultivating just north of the buildings, but the field stretched over and beyond the first hill, the long corn rows running north-south. At almost three-thirty he glimpsed her coming, but pretending not to see, turned at the end and proceded northward, up the slope. At the hill crest he stopped, ostensibly to rest his horse, turned and saw Anna trudging up the row toward him. His ruse had worked. They would have privacy on the hill.

When she came up to him he took from her the lunch basket and coffee pail, took a few strides to an earth-fast rock projecting well above the surface, and motioned her to a seat. He sat down beside her and commenced eating. She noted the apparent relish with which he devoured the sandwiches, and suspected that he was both nervous and hungry. He offered her none of the food. Convention had it that the wife bringing lunch to her man or men in the field never shared it. She ate before or after the hike.

Anna and Nels sat on the rock long after he had eaten all the lunch. Blaze commenced stomping about in the row, menacing the corn plants. Finally, after much small talk, Nels came to the point.

"You are almost my age, Anna, and getting no younger. Are you not afraid of becoming a spinster?"

"That I am not, thank you. I have had offers now and again," her color rising.

"Would you marry me, then, and come here to live with me?"

"Of course I would. I feared you'd never get up courage to ask."

He rose to his feet, then leaned down and kissed her, squarely on the mouth. Anna rose and stood beside him.

"Will you name the date?" she asked.

"Yes! We shall have to wait until I can, after harvest, help settle my parents and sister into their new house. Never will a wife of mine live under the same roof as her mother-in-law. Let's say the middle of September. Alright?"

"Alright! We'll have a wonderful life together, far from the noise and crowding of the city."

Anna took up her basket and pail and turned toward the house; Nels spoke to Blaze, and walked down the row to the north following the cultivator.

Supper talk was all of the betrothal and impending marriage. Mrs. Lovene seemed smug and satisfied with herself.

Next morning Nels drove the girls to the train, and didn't see his promised wife again before mid-September.

The "proposal" rock became legendary. Not once did Nels so much as consider blasting or burying it. It became, in time, an equally sentimental landmark for his sons. It was a known hazard that remained undisturbed. If one sprung a plow against it, scored the binder platform on it, or broke the mower pitman rod attempting to spare the sickle bar, he uttered not one oath, but went quietly about the repairs. The "proposal stone" protrudes farther out of the ground now than it did in 1898; soil erosion on the hill has exposed more of it as the years have passed.

On 16 September, as planned, Anna and Nels were married, without fanfare. They drove the prancers to Fergus Falls, accompanied by August, who, together with the preacher's wife, would be their witness. They were married in the home of Reverend James Moody, the pastor previously serving the Eagle Lake congregation. Nels, rarely extravagant, slipped him a whole five dollar bill after the ceremony.

Before departing, Nels stopped at a saloon and bought a gallon of port wine, in preparation for the anticipated charivari. The reveling neighbors did, indeed, wake them at midnight their very first night together.

Anna experienced little dificulty settling into her role as a farmer's wife, with her manifold duties. In removal to her retirement house, Elna had quite intentionally left behind numerous items of kitchen equipment she should no longer need; so the young couple was spared the cost of purchasing them new.

Now that he was responsible for a wife and prospective children, Nels determined to formalize his purchase of the three prairie forties. As legal owner he would feel more secure. He mentioned the matter to his father one day, and Pehr was entirely agreeable. Said he:

"Of course you need our transfer officially recorded! If you were to die as things now stand, you would leave your wife destitute. Let's not delay! Let's go tomorrow and have a document written and then recorded. You know my requirements: a thousand dollars to pacify your sisters and life support for me and your mother. That seems to be a practice hereabout, brought over from Sweden."

Although roads were barely negotiable by team and buggy, the entire family went to Fergus Falls to the county courthouse next day. Sadie would go shopping while the others attended to their legal business. At the courthouse, Pehr and Elna, Nels and Anna, were soon seated before an imposing walnut desk, behind which sat Martin Anderson, a brother of Nils. There had been neighborly handshakes all around; Martin now owned land on two sides of Pehr's woods forty. He was also the man designated by the county hierarchy to draw up instruments such as here indicated.

His clients politely seated, he withdrew from a drawer a sizeable legal form that began, in the upper left-hand corner, in bold fancy print: "This Indenture." Martin explained that it was the standard real estate mortgage form. He filled in the blanks left for entry of day, month, and year—27th "day of" March "in the year of our Lord, one thousand eight hundred and eighty" he crossed out "eighty" and wrote in "ninety-nine." There followed, down the sheet, parties of the first part, parties of the second part, and repetitious legal jargon, amid which Martin entered, as instructed, a specification of "one thousand dollars ($1,000.00)" to be paid "60" days after date. In another, long blank farther down the sheet, Martin referred to an "attached sheet" as being a part of the contract. The attachment, typewritten and signed by Nels and Anna, read as follows:

'In consideration of the mortgage hereto attached said first parties agree to and with said second parties to deliver to them anually (mispelled by typist) on said premises 100 bushels of wheat, 300 pounds of pork, 15 bushels of potatoes, necessary stove wood to comfortably care for them ready for use, to feed and care for one cow and one horse on said premises, and to supply all of said articles annually on or before November 1st. of each year so long as said second (smeared and typed over) parties or either of them shall live, except that on the death of either the survivor shall receive only 50 bushels of wheat, and that upon the faithful observance of the terms of this agreement by said first parties during the lives of said second parties or the life of either said mortgage shall be deemed fully paid and thereafter null and void".

The document remained in force seventeen years.

Enroute home, Pehr spoke to Nels so all could hear:

"Whatever the paper says, you needn't fear any time limit on the thousand dollars. You may take as many years as you wish in which to pay it. About the life support provisions, bear this in mind: my horse, Charley, is yours to use; we shall not need him often. If you give me a pig, I will feed it to butchering time. (He built a pen and shelter southwest of the house). After I have enough wheat for flour, I will accept barley or oats for my pig, in lieu of wheat, bushel for bushel. While I'm able, I'll help you cut and haul our entire wood supply, yours and mine. I will buck-saw, split, and stack my own." (He stacked his wood in tight round piles, resembling the circular thatched huts of certain African peoples, similar to wood stacks at railway stations in India for fueling steam locomotives.)

'Tack Far' "Thank you, Pa," said Nels, "you need not wait long for the money. I aim to pay the thousand soon as I have threshed next fall. But I appreciate your kindness nevertheless. You shall want for none of the provisions specified in the paper, and I will make any substitution you may wish. If you find any specified item inadequate, I shall wish to know so that I might furnish an adequate increment. You and Ma shall not want so long as I remain healthy and able to work. My felt responsibility was made neither more nor less by the mortgage document, so we shall not quarrel about the piece of paper."

Little more was spoken on the way home. Nels trotted his horses wherever the road was sufficiently drained so that the wheels would not spatter mud.

Main mid-summer project that year (1899) was the erection of a sizeable chicken house, dug into the same side-hill as the barn about a hundred feet to the east. For fifty cents a day, Nels hired Gustav, one of Nils' younger sons, to help. Pehr cultivated corn and garden while the young men built. They set the structure so deeply into the earth that on its upper (north) side, the eaves cleared the ground by only about one foot. Nels and Gustav built the walls with good-sized stones, hauled in on the stone boat. They laid them with mortar cement and smoothed them on top to receive the sills. Evander came and put up the roof and gables, all with materials from Everts' Lumber Yard. The house was twenty feet long (east-west) and twelve feet wide. Inside, Nels installed sloping trellis-like rail roosts at each end, and a long house-like box compartmentalized into laying nests, at the north wall facing the door. The battened door was at midpoint in the south wall, with a small square window on each side of it.

Nels would have no more chicken "mess" in the barn—dung in the mangers and feed boxes, feathers in the hay, and manure kicked about everywhere. And the chickens would fare better too, with their own water trough and grain, without scratching in manure for it. One wondered how hens could produce good eggs from grain kernels voided whole by cattle.

Before haying time in 1900, Nels had installed in the barn a mechanical hay fork with trolley and track, an ingenious device with which one could fill the hay mow without pitching the hay by hand. Installation entailed the cutting of a large door in the west gable, hinged at the bottom and reaching to the peak of the eaves. It was opened by pushing against it near the top with a pole and dropping it gently by a rope attached to the fork. It was also raised, closed, and secured by tying the fork rope tightly to a roof brace or collar beam. The installation included a two hundred foot length of one-inch rope, a block high in the east gable, and another in the east end of the north wall. Having run the large heavy fork out and down, and stuck it deeply into a hay load, one tripped a catch exposed on top to release a spring-loaded prong on each side, these sprang out and caught in the hay. With luck, one could take in a load of hay with three or four forkfuls. Wild hay clung so poorly that it was pitched in through the small door in the north wall. To power the fork and carriage one used a steady team of horses, hitched by whipple tree to the rope end outside the northeast corner. On relayed called signal from the "fork" man in the load, the driver of this team guided them in direction of the open barnyard gate, carrying the whipple tree until the rope grew taut and raised it three feet or more into the air. One was in lethal danger behind that whipple tree, and Nels always took special care that harness and hitches used for the hay fork were sound and strong. He knew of men and boys gravely injured when a faulty tug, single tree, ring, or clevis broke as a forkful of hay was being lifted to the trolley and the equipment was at maximum stress.

But for one miserable exception it seemed, in 1900, that the farm was completely mechanized. Machinery had now solved the problem of harvesting large fields of small grain; but the laborious hand cutting and loose shocking of corn restricted its acreage and use by Nels, his cousin August, and their neighbors, until one bright day in June of 1900 when the cousins were cultivating a young corn crop on their respective sides of the partition fence between them.

They stopped their animals and stepped over to the fence to pass the time of day while their horses rested.

August, quite out of character, began the conversion: "Now, Nels, we have almost ten acres of corn each, enough to demand at least two to three weeks of sweat and slavery next September, unless we invest in a corn binder. What would you say to the purchase of a McCormick binder on halves. I'm told they cost about one hundred sixty dollars, do good work, and are ordinarily pulled by three horses. I think it's time we spare ourselves the strenuous work of harvesting corn entirely by hand, especially as our fathers are getting too old to help us with such taxing labor."

"You are right as rain!" expostulated Nels, "and I say let's buy such a machine before harvest time. Let's go to town tomorrow and dicker with Ranstad. He'll knock a little off the price if we pay cash." After a little small-talk they continued down their respective rows.

To Battle Lake they went, the very next day, and purchased from Ranstad a McCormick corn binder under good warranty *(Figure 13.7)*. The machine would be stored in Nels' machine shed, so the three men assembled it in front of that building a few days later. The cost was seventy-five dollars each after Ranstad knocked ten dollars off his regular price. So early in the season he willingly sold for less profit.

The machine cut one row at a time, worked well in almost every condition, tied bundles tightly with twine, and deposited them in heavy rows dumped off a bundle carrier. The corn stalks went through the machine standing upright, and when tied, were toppled onto the bundle carrier.

The machine had one grave fault, notable only in tall corn: the tying mechanism

Figure 13.7. This 1900 model McCormick corn binder was deemed the ultimate piece of mechanization a farmer might covet. It tied the bundles with twine. Here shown is the harvest of hilled corn. Photo courtesy International Harvester Archives.

was fixed in place and could be neither raised nor lowered. It tied the bundles about two feet above their butt end, which rendered bundles of tall corn top heavy and prone to "spradle" out above the twine. The fault caused extra work in shocking, and also in stacking, because the off-balance bundles were difficult to pitch with a fork, butt end first!

Despite its fault, the binder, for many, many years, harvested twenty or more acres annually for each of its owners, and similar acreages for Nils Anderson and another neighbor or two. (Many delayed their purchase of one because of its progressively rising price.)

Before Nels and August procured the corn binder, they cut and shocked all their corn by hand, a tedious laborious task. Somewhat facilitating the work, they employed a rail "horse", quickly assembled by Pehr of a dry seven-foot aspen rail with a pair of three-foot legs attached at one end, spread and braced for rigidity. (He made one for August, in event each chopped and shocked alone.) Near the upper end he mounted a box that accommodated a ball of binder twine, and at the very "nose" of the "horse" he attached a sharp section of a mower sickle against which to cut any requisite length of twine drawn from the ball. To build a shock, one gathered against his left thigh with his left arm as many standing stalks as he could comfortably pull together at their midpoint, whacked them off near the ground with the corn knife in his right hand, and leaned the armful, almost vertically, against one side of the rail "horse" at its upper end. Next he braced the horse and corn on the opposite side, etc. etc. When he had a considerable shock (five to six feet in diameter at the base), he withdrew the horse and filled several armfuls of stalks into openings that became exposed—to keep snow out of the shock. Then he stretched a length of twine around the loose shock at shoulder height to gage the necessary length of twine, cut it off to length against the sickle section, again stretched the twine around the shock, tied on it a slip knot, and drew it up as tight as he deemed the twine to hold. By evening one's fingers were sore, if not bleeding, by the wear of the corn and the twine. Little wonder the corn (maize) binder was a welcome addition to farm equippage!

(The rail "horse" or "buck" to aid in shocking corn remained in use by farmers generally until the corn binder became obsolete—replaced by pickers, and later also by field choppers.)

Also in the 1900's, Sadie, married to one Andy Okerlund late in 1899, removed from a rented farm near Christina Lake to a Homestead claim at Kelliher, Minnesota. (Sadie lived a short, sad life. Her husband was a ne'er-do-well. But he sired no less than ten living offspring, each a person of quality.) Poor Sadie lived in poverty and squalor, and died of consumption (tuberculosis of the lungs) at the age of forty-two (2 November 1920). Nels walked to town to hire a car and driver, but none would venture a trip to Kelliher.

Not long after the hay fork was installed, a pair of pigeons, probably Nils', possibly Sven's, found the trolley a good place on which to build a nest; and soon the pair grew into a flock, that soiled the hay and strewed it with feathers. They so filled the trolley (or carrier) that one had to climb a long precariously braced ladder and clear it before each use of the fork. The birds evoked from Nels such a stream of profanity that Pehr determined to remedy the situation. He built several dove cotes and installed them on the east gable of the chicken house under the eaves. However, the remedy was merely a poor palliative. The doves nested in the carrier as before, and filled all the nesting boxes for good measure. The boxes had one advantage: one could take from them the squabs almost fully fledged and eat them, and so delay the multiplication. Nels also helped by nighttime sorties in the hay mow to catch pigeons and wring their necks. All was to no avail; until finally, when Nels' elder sons were half-grown and were permitted a .22 rifle, they shot all the pigeons in one summer. Nels was pleased, until, at next year's haying time, he discovered that English sparrows had stuffed the hay-fork carrier more tightly than the pigeons had ever done. The annual climbing to remove birds' nests persisted; one carried with him an oil can and oiled the trolley wheels after throwing down the nests. The problem of English sparrows in the hay mow would not be solved in Nels' lifetime.

At the turn of the century, the farm was developed and the farmstead built approximately as it would be decades later. Nels had need for only one additional construction. He needed separate shelter for young livestock; his cattle herd had grown until the cow barn (minus a small calf pen to the left of the door) was plumb full of milk cows (fourteen). He had installed in the kitchen shack a De Laval cream separator, through which he cranked all the milk carried in pails from the barn, morning and evening. A considerable part of farm income came from the sale of cream, accumulated in a ten-gallon can. When few cows were dry, he got a can full per week. In summer the can, during filling, stood in a cooling tank, through which went all the well water pumped into the stock tank. A little "pump house" had been built to house the tank, hand tools, etc. *(Figure 13.8).*

So that he might maintain his dairy herd, and also raise to yearling size or better all steers and spare heifers, Nels built a shed onto the barn along the west half of the south wall. He and August built this structure without other help, and covered the nearly flat roof with tar paper, tar, and gravel. Inside they built a manger the entire length of the barn wall and divided the floor space in two with a movable gate. In one end went year-old animals; in the other those younger, even those recently weaned from milk.

Since the shed was only about ten by twenty feet in floor space, it became inadequate after a few years. Then Nels built a straw shed southwest of the barn. He erected a framework (sides and top) of stout rails nailed in place, then stretched across the top and about the walls (but for an opening to the east) woven fence wire (netting). Over this his thresher blew a strawstack at threshing time, from bundle loads of wheat hauled for the purpose.

Season followed season, year followed year, the farm produced and so did Anna—one infant every two years. Pehr was moved to comment privately to Elna: "Anna is certainly a most industrious and capable wife to Nels; but I do declare, she seems bent on filling the house to the bursting point. She's so good a wife and mother that one is obliged to admire rather than criticize."

Nels was so preoccupied with his farm and growing family that he quite forgot that the woods forty was not yet his.

Figure 13.8. The barnyard viewed toward the northeast from the northwest corner of the barn (note stones holding the earth at the barn corner, lower right). The nailed rail fence remained in use for barnyard enclosure because barbed wire often did injury to young colts and to grown horses that rolled themselves near the fence and caught a heel under the wire. The fence shown here stood approximately on the east-west line between the middle and south forties. Note the windmill and the well house in which was a tank containing the ten-gallon cream can, cooled by water pumped through the cooling tank enroute to the wooden stock-watering tank outside. Note front porch looking out on barnyard, young cottonwoods and white oaks left of the wellhouse, and the granary at far right background (painted red, with white trim). Children in foreground: far left, Millard, Sadie's son, staying with his grandparents, then Anton (5), Lincoln (3), and Victoria (7), elder children of Anna and Nels. Anna observes from right end of gate. Date of photo probably autumn of 1906.

Photographer unknown.

Pehr reminded him when they were hauling fuel wood from the lake in January of 1906. Nels sat in front driving the horses; Pehr sat behind him holding his axe, which he was bringing home for sharpening.

"I believe, Nels, that you will wish you had the south forty, however hilly and full of sloughs it may be. I've always thought that you should have bought it with the others when we agreed on terms in '97. It would have been cheap then. Now I must ask a considerable price or the girls will accuse me of favoritism. Ellen and Hanna have confided their belief that the forty is well worth four hundred dollars. I think that is high, but I wish to keep peace in the family."

"I agree, Pa, that the homestead should all be together. The woods have grass for the cattle when my open pastures are too short and dry for grazing. But four hundred paid in one lump would fracture my budget. Can we spread the payment some way?"

"Personally, I care not how you might spread the payment; but let me ask your stepsisters. Perhaps I can work out a plan with them."

The opportunity to devise a plan of payment satisfactory to the girls came sooner than Pehr had anticipated, and he immediately conveyed it to Nels. Nels thought the plan entirely acceptable and much more generous than he had hoped.

Accordingly, on 13 February 1906, Elna, Pehr and Nels drove to Kron's store at Axel, to formalize the purchase. Anna, enjoying a respite from pregnancy, stayed home with her four young children.

The Axel post office was in John Kron's store, at the crossroads west of Eagle Lake Church. There was also a blacksmith shop. Kron dealt in general merchandise, his stock hauled from Battle Lake by a weekly wagon trip. Kron was the best educated man about. Besides being a store keeper and postmaster, he was also a notary public, and prepared many official documents for farmers of the community. He was something of a writer, and his opinion pieces appeared now and then in the Fergus Falls newspaper.

Pehr quickly explained to Kron that they came not to buy but to have a legal paper drawn up; that he was selling to his son the fourth forty of the Homestead. Kron seated himself behind his huge desk in the back of the store, having first politely seated his guests in front of the desk. He took out a long legal form headed, "Know All Men by These Presents," and prepared to ink in the necessary specifics of the contract.

"Tell me again the legal description of the land at issue!"

Pehr recited: "The southwest quarter of the southwest quarter of section 22, township 132, range 40."

"How many acres?" asked Kron.

"Thirty-seven acres, more or less." said Pehr.

Kron resumed writing.

"How much shall Nels pay for this?" asked Kron.

"Four hundred dollars, but only one hundred now, then one hundred fifty dollars each to my daughters Elna and Hanna, when I die."

"I see," said Kron, and resumed writing in beautiul script. Momentarily he glanced up into Pehr's eyes and inquired: "Do you wish this paper to convey part or all of your estate residue to anyone else?"

"Yes," said Pehr, after Hanna and Elna have been paid as I have told you, I wish whatever else I leave behind divided equally between Sadie and Nels." And so it was all arranged *(Figure 13.9)*.

Kron read the document over aloud, entered the place and date (Axel, Otter Tail County, 13th of February, 1906); then turned the document half around and indicated where each was to sign. Elna and Pehr signed with an X, so Kron had to write in the names, labeling the crosses "his X mark" and "her X mark". Then he witnessed and stamped the document. His wife, Julia A. Kron, signed as second witness. Kron would mail the document to the Register of Deeds in Fergus Falls for proper recording, after which it would come to Nels. Nels paid Kron his twenty-five cent fee and the party commenced their return trip. (The Axel Post Office, which had been established 2 April 1897, was discontinued 31 August 1906.)

Enroute, Nels inquired of his parents: "Why have you not learned to write your names in English? You read regularly the "Svenska Amerikanska Posten"; and you can write a little Swedish!"

"We might write some in English, if we dared," answered Pehr. "But since I've been in America, I've seen my name spelled at least seven different ways, none of them correct. I think it wiser, therefore, to simply mark with a cross."

"You may be quite right," said Nels, "I have, hopefully, changed the spelling permanently; this without the least malice, I assure you!"

Nels' name did in fact, remain fixed, though no one could mistake his brogue for any other than Swedish, and southern Swedish at that.

Nels paid the first one hundred dollars on the mortgage soon as he had threshed his wheat in the fall.

It was well that Nels acquired the woods forty because his barn and barnyard were actually upon it *(Figure 13.8)*.

During Pehr's declining years, time wrought many changes in his beloved land, its occupance, and its economy. His own Homestead had flourished quite as he had envisioned that it would. His son kept faith with him and the land he had broken, using it profitably but never wittingly abusing it.

He lived to see binders for harvesting small grain, and others for harvesting corn, with an ingenious knotter-hook that tied a knot in twine drawn tight about a bundle. He saw the use of bundle carriers that could carry three or four bundles and drop them in rows for easier shocking. He saw the practice of stacking grain after a few weeks in the shock become almost universal. Some there were who built giant round stacks containing as many as twenty-four or more bundle loads. The stacks were built in "settings" of four to six, with space one way for a threshing machine to pull between them (Frontispiece). He saw the development of huge threshing separators and massive steam engines on great drive wheels to move the rig between jobs. The great, endless, hundred-foot belt that turned all the separator machinery was so heavy that when it was given one twist and laid over the engine pulley, the engineer pulled it taut by backing the engine "into it." Separator feeders and cylinders were as much as forty to fifty inches or more in width. A threshing crew of a dozen to a score of men could thresh all the small grain on an average-size farm in a single day—dawn to dark.

He saw the village of Battle Lake incorporated 28 April 1891, and a post office established there 23 December 1881. He was served by the first rural mail route operating out of Battle Lake, commencing 1 January 1904. He witnessed the establishment of railway freight and passenger service through Battle Lake (1881)

No. 303. WARRANTY DEED. (Chapter 191, General Laws of 1883.)

Know all Men by These Presents, That the grantor Per Person and Elna Person his wife residing in the Township of Clitherall County of Otter Tail and State of Minn. for and in consideration of the sum of Four Hundred — DOLLARS, to them in hand paid, do hereby Convey and Warrant to Nels Parson of the afore said Town & County

as grantee the following described real estate, viz: The South west quarter of the South west quarter (SW¼ SW¼) of section twenty two (22) in Township One Hundred and Thirty two (132) Range Forty (40) containing Thirty Seven (37) acres more or less according to the Government Survey there of

The Provision of this deed is though that one year after Mr. Per Persons is dead then Mr. Nels Parson is to pay to Mrs. E. C. Lundby and Mrs. Ole Peterson the sum of One Hundred and fifty dollar $150.00 to Each of the afore said Daughters of Mr. Per Person. Then after they Both are dead then what is left of Property Shall be Equaly Divided between Mr. Nels Parson and Mrs. Andy Okerlund.

It is further Stipulated and agreed if Nels Parson Should die before the Old Mr. Per Person then this deed is Null & Void

situate in the County of Otter Tail and State of Minnesota.
Dated at ____ this 13— day of Feb. A. D. 1906
Signed, Sealed and Delivered in presence of
Julia A. Kron   Per + Person   [SEAL.]
                             Elna + Person   [SEAL.]
John Kron   [SEAL.]
                             Nels Parson   [SEAL.]

State of Minnesota,
County of Otter Tail } ss.

On this Thirteenth day of February A. D. 1906, before me personally appeared Per Person and Elna Person and Nels Parson to me known to be the persons described in and who executed the foregoing instrument, and acknowledged that executed the same as their free act and deed.

John Kron
Notary Public
My Commission Expires Nov 1— 1912

Figure 13.9. Facsimile of contract under which Pehr transferred to his son, Nels, the southern (woods) forty of the homestead.

with a branch line built by the Northern Pacific between Wadena and Breckenridge during 1881 and 1882.

He was amazed when, before the turn of the century, his son installed an instrument called the telephone, by which one could speak to distant persons over a battery-powered wire.

Pehr became almost too well acquainted with the horseless carriage. One summer day while walking the road from the house toward the west forty, he was almost over-run by a vehicle that came up behind him. His deafness precluded his awareness of the vehicle before it was upon him. When finally he heard it, he fell headlong out of the track, barely missed, but unhurt. (This author witnessed the frightening incident from a distance.)

He participated in the decline of wheat farming in Minnesota (1890's) as new lands and larger farms to the west usurped much of the wheat market. Replacing dependence on cash grain (wheat) came general or mixed farming, including dairying, beef, swine, poultry and some sheep. Popular cattle strains were of Red and Roan Shorthorns, considered dual-purpose—good for both milk and beef production.

He saw candles for illumination replaced by kerosene lamps and lanterns. In winter, one did his evening milking and other barn chores after dark, lighted by a standard type of lantern. Time and again a lantern accidentally upset caused a barn to burn down.

Whether by sheer good fortune, much devout prayer, or rigid discipline in keeping them away from crowds, Pehr thanked God for sparing his children during the tragic diptheria epidemic that ravaged the community; most severely during the early and middle 1880's.

He had friends who lost their entire families of five or six children in a week's time. He and Elna attended the group burials at graveside in the open air, but they forbade their children to attend.

Pehr observed in 1910 the amazing fire streaks of Halley's Comet, and wondered whenever he gazed at it whether it appeared the same over Skåne as over Minnesota.

Pehr lived to see fabulous rises in land values and taxes. Before he died his Homestead might have sold for considerably more than ten thousand dollars, his land and buildings better than most. It's initial cost to him in money had been only twenty dollars in Land Office fees.

Taxes rose more or less in commensuration with land values. At first Pehr's taxes had been only two or three dollars per forty. As late as 1886, on personal property, homestead, and lakewood lots, his total taxes remained at the modest sum of only thirty-three dollars and ninety-five cents. (In 1930, sixteen years after Pehr's death the four homestead forties and buildings bore a tax of sixty-six dollars and nineteen cents; and by 1974, the same property bore a tax of two hundred eighty dollars and fourteen cents—almost as much per acre as Pehr had once paid per forty.)

Pehr witnessed several economic depressions or "financial panics" during his long American tenure, but ever since the one of 1873 he kept a reserve of food and money with which to endure such events without worry and without severe lack of any family necessity.

He saw crop rotation established, including rotation pasture and hay meadow. He saw red and alsike clover mixed with timothy for heavy hay yields. He saw almost all public land in his vicinity bought by individuals. He saw mustard, Canada thistle,

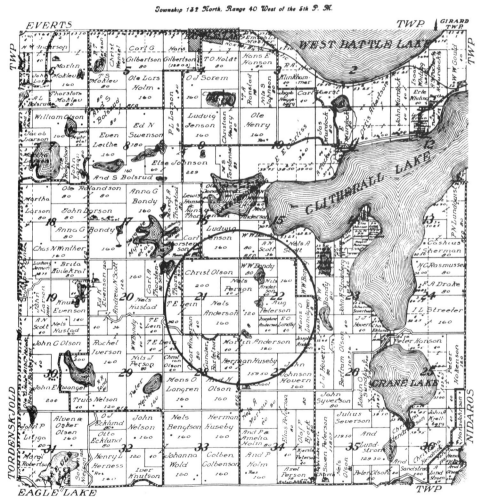

Figure 13.10. Plat Map, Clitherall Township, 1912. (Caption on following page)

and quack grass become dreadful weeds in cropland. Excepting the coyote, he saw large predators almost vanish. He witnessed the search for rust resistant wheat to displace marquis and bluestem strains. He saw the advent of flax for linseed, as a particularly remunerative field crop. He saw Clitherall Township when it supported more than one hundred farm families on farms of one forty to six or seven *(Figure 13.10)*. He lived to hear the rumble of World War I in Europe and feared that his beloved new land would become involved.

He died early on the frosty morning of 5 November 1914. He arose to relieve himself, but could not, and fell on the floor in pain. Elna ran to call her son for help, and he immediately phoned Dr. Haugen in Battle Lake. Then Nels went to his father's assistance, got him back in bed and sought to comfort him. He could relieve his father's pain only by pressing his hand hard against the lower abdomen. "Hold so," whispered Pehr. "That helps." After only a little time, continuously exerting pressure so, Nels felt the hardness under his hand suddenly yield. He withdrew his hand and stood away from the bed, suspecting that his father's bladder had burst. The doctor came in time to verify Nels' suspicion, but too late to save Pehr from poisoning by his own urine. An hour later the old man was dead.

For many years before his passing Pehr had been extremely deaf; but he died, at eighty-three, with most of his natural teeth still retained. He remained active to the very end; he milked his cow, as usual, the evening before he died.

Figure 13.10. Before 1912 essentially all lands in Clitherall Township were privately owned. Few large wooded tracts prevailed, notably the one on the Clitherall Lake Peninsula, but also about sloughs and other lakeshore areas.

The Township supported more than a hundred family farms, and most of the families were large (6, 7 or more children). The Township contained perhaps some seven or eight hundred farm people, and half again as many in the flourishing village of Battle Lake. The Mormon settlement on the north shore of Clitherall Lake (first settlement in the county) had been largely superceded by the new Village of Clitherall at the northeast end of the lake, replete with railroad (Northern Pacific) and post office.

In large part, the farmland was now owned by sons or sons-in-law of the homesteaders, although much remained in transition from immigrants to the American-born heirs. Couples with only one child or two could make a living on less than forty acres of arable land.

But progressive consolidation of lands into larger operating units had already begun as homesteaders purchased scattered tracts of school land in various legal categories, and parcels of railroad land. Ever since these early times, farm land consolidation has progressed, with few and brief interruptions, so that a viable farm of today approaches twice the size of the originally adequate, even extravagant, quarter section. Largest aggregated operation in the township in 1974 was owned by the brothers Hustad, Arvid and Earl—19 forties, or 760 acres.

Dare one speculate that the section will eventually become the ordinary operational unit-area, as was once the quarter section?

Meanwhile, farm families have become smaller because machinery has all but eliminated the usefulness of young farm children. This author's childhood ended the era during which proliferation on the farm had been profitable whether the offspring be of human or other animal species.

Of all the farmsteads denoted by black squares within the circle on the map overside, only four remained actively operational in 1978. Only one was added, several years before, on the land marked "W.W. Bondy," at the eastern arc of the circle. During Pehr's declining years there were, in the circle, a dozen householding operators, each so well known to the old man that any chance meeting evoked considerable conversation.

Map from Original in the Library of Congress.

His good wife, Elna, followed him in death only four months later, 23 February 1916 *(Figure 13.11)*.

If ever Pehr yearned to visit his homeland, he told no one. When he came away he divorced himself from all such as most cherished in the old country, that he might better succeed in the new. He maintained a regular, though far-spaced, correspondence with his dear mother, Sissa, until she died of old age.

Pehr's first wife, Anna, remains well remembered. So that the site of her grave may not be lost, her granddaughter, Edna, placed a simple marker at its head *(Figure 13.12)*.

Pehr achieved his purpose in the new land, but with the sacrifice of his beloved Anna. Often, when working by himself in the fields, he sensed her spiritual presence sharing his pride in the wealth and security won for their children. He was truly a venerable pioneer; and the writer is honored to claim him as his paternal grandfather.

Figure 13.11. Pehr and Elna lie side-by-side in the Eagle Lake Church Cemetery, three miles south by road from the Homestead. Translated, the Swedish inscription reads: "Rest in Peace," and one prays that they do.

Photo by author's wife, Mary Louise.

Figure 13.12. Though for a time within a fenced pasture for calves or sheep, the site of Anna's grave was carefully and surely marked with goodly lengths of steel driven into its corners. More recently, one of Anna's granddaughters, Edna Fletcher, placed on the grave the simple headstone here shown. May Anna sleep a martyr's sleep, her stillborn son at her breast!

Photo by author's wife, Mary Louise.

Appendix

Part I

Printed Sources Consulted

Andersson, Ingvar, *A History of Sweden*. Translated from the Swedish by Carolyn Hannay. Published by: Natur Och Kultur, Stockholm; Weinfeld and Nicolson, London. First published in 1955 under the Auspices of the Anglo-Swedish Literary Foundation. Second Impression 1956.

Andrews, Hon. C.C. (Minn.), *The Conditions and Needs of Spring Wheat in the Northwest*. Government Printing Office, Washington, D.C. 1882.

Ardrey, R.L., *American Agricultural Implements—A Review of Invention and Development in the Agricultural Implement Industry of the United States* (in two parts), published by author, Chicago 1894. (Excerpts from International Harvester Archives.)

Ayer's Almanac, Mass. 1869.

Baker, Roy A., *History of Fergus Falls to January 1, 1893,* Otter Tail County Historical Society, Fergus Falls, Minn. 1935.

Brook, Michael, Compiler. *Reference Guide to Minnesota History: A Subject Bibliography of Books, Pamphlets, and Articles in English*. Minnesota Historical Society, St. Paul 1974.

Brown, Robert Harold, Tideman, Philip L. and Calkins, Charles F. *Atlas of Minnesota Occupancy,* Revised Edition 1966, St. Cloud, Minnesota, Minnesota Atlas Company.

Casey, Patrick J., *The First Hundred Years: A History of Meeker County,* Copyright by Author 1968.

Dana, Samuel Trask, John H. Allison and Russell N. Cunningham, *Minnesota Land Ownership, Use, and Management of Forest and Related Lands,* American Forestry Association, Washington, D.C. 1960.

Encyclopedia Americana, Americana Corporation 1928, N.Y., Chicago, especially Vol. 26.

Folwell, William Watts, *Grasshoppers in Minnesota: A History of Minnesota,* Vol. III, pp. 93-111.

Funk and Wagnalls New Encyclopedia (1973 Edition) Vol. 22, pp. 346-359. Joseph Taffan Morse, Editor-in-Chief. William H. Hendelson, Editorial Director and Successor to Editor-in-Chief.

Gould, Hallie M. Compiler, *Old Clitherall Story Book, A History of the first settlement in Otter Tail County, Minnesota 1865-1919.* Reprinted and published by the Otter Tail County Historical Society, July 1975. (Originally serialized in Battle Lake Review.)

Hayter, Earl W. *The Troubled Farmer,* Northern Illinois University Press, DeKalb, Ill. 1968.

Hendrickson, M.A. "Minnesalbum, 1871-1921, Svenska Ev. Lutherska Eagle Lake Församlingen," Printed and bound by Augustana Book Concern's "Tryckeri och Bokbinderi" Rock Island, Ill.

Israel, Fred L. Editor, Extracts from 1897 Sears Roebuck catalog. Introductions by S.J. Perelman and Richard Rovere. Chelsea House Publishers, New York, 1968.

Janson, Florence Edith, *The Background of Swedish Immigration, 1840-1930.* University of Chicago Press, Chicago, Ill.

Jarchow, Merrill E., *The Earth Brought Forth,* Minnesota Historical Society, 1949, St. Paul.

Jarchow, Merrill E., "King Wheat" *Minnesota History* Vol. XXIX, March 1948, pp. 1-28.

Jennings, Dana Close, *Days of Steam and Glory,* North Plains Press, Aberdeen, S.D., 1968.

Jorgenson, Mrs. Olaf, Compilor and Editor, *One Hundred Years of God's Grace,* Eagle Lake Evangelical Lutheran Church, Battle Lake, Minnesota 1871-1971. Printed by the *Review,* Battle Lake, Minnesota.

Krause, Herbert, *The Thresher,* The Bobbs-Merrill Company, Indianapolis, 1946.

Lindberg, John S., *The Background of Swedish Emigration to the United Stdtes.* An Economic and Sociological Study in the Dynamics of Migration. University of Minnesota Press, Minneapolis, Minnesota 1930. Chapter V.

Lorenzen, Lilly, *Of Swedish Ways,* Illustrated by Dick Sutphen, Gilbert Publishing Company, Minneapolis, Minnesota 1964.

Ludlum, David M. *Early American Winters, II, 1821-1870,* author's copyright. Princeton, New Jersey, 1968. Published by American Meteorological Society. Printed by Lancaster Press, Inc. Pa.

McCallum, Henry D. and Frances T. McCallum, *The Wire that Fenced the West,* University of Oklahoma Press, Norman, 1965.

Michener, James A. *Centennial,* Random House, Inc. New York, 1974, Reprinted, paperback by Fawcett Crest Book.

Murphy, E.C. *The Windmill: Its Efficiency and Economic Use.* (in U.S. G.S. Water Supply and Irrigation Papers, Nos. 20, 29, 41, 42, 1899-1901).

Olson, Sherry H. "Commerce and Conservation: The Railroad Experience." *Forest History,* Vol. 9, No. 4, Jan. 1966 pp. 2-15.

Olson, Sherry H. *The Depletion Myth: A History of Railroad Use of Timber.* Harvard University Press. 1971.

Powers, Legrand G. "Inventions in Flour Making Machinery and the Prices of Wheat, Flour, etc." in Bureau of Labor Statistics, Third Biennial Report, 1891-92, pp. 156-244, extract copy from Minnesota Historical Society.

Riley, Charles V. *The Locust Plague in the United States; Being More Particularly a Treatise on the Rocky Mountain Locust.* (Chicago 1877) The Grasshopper, or Rocky Mountain Locust and Its Ravages in Minnesota.

Robinson, Edward Van Dyke, "Early Economic Conditions and The Development of Agriculture in Minnesota," (Studies in the Social Studies, No. 3) Bulletin of the University of Minnesota, Minneapolis, Minnesota March 1915.

Rogin Leo, *The Introduction of Farm Machinery.* Introduction of Farm Machinery in its Relation to the Productivity of Labor in the Agriculture of the U.S. During the 19th Century. University of California, Berkeley, 1931, Johnson Reprint Corporation, New York, N.Y. 1966.

Ryan, J.C. *Early Loggers in Minnesota,* Minnesota Timber Producers Ass'n. Forester, Author, Historian, Lumberman.

Thomas, Bill, "Oxen Can Do What Nothing Else Can." in *Farm and Home Magazine.* Supplement to the *Sisseton (S.D.) Courier,* Thursday, 7 March 1974.

Tideman, Philip L. *Wheat on the Northern Agricultural Frontier, 1840-1920.* Dissertation for the Ph.D in Geography. University of Nebraska, 1967.

Webb, Walter P. *The Great Plains,* Ginn and Company, Boston 1931.

Several topical extracts reproduced from: Industrial Museum, American Steel and Wire Company, Worcester, Massachusetts.

"Climatic Summary of the United States, Minnesota (Sections 44, 45 & 46)." U.S. Dept. of Agriculture, Weather Bureau, Charles F. Marvin, Chief, Superintendent of Documents, Washington, D.C. 1934.

Commission of Entomologists, 1877, 1879, 1882, Reports on Grasshoppers.

Executive Documents of the State of Minnesota, 1872, Vol. II, pp. 10, 11, 21, 84, 85.

Farm and Industrial Equipment Institute.

Smithsonian Institution.

"The Fence Industry" Wireco Life, Vol. 4, No. 5, May 1940.

"Pioneers of the Past—The Barbed Wire Story," Wireco Life, Vol. 20, No. 4, April 1956, American Steel & Wire Division, United States Steel.

Fergus Falls Advocate, Selected issues 1884 and forward.

Flour Milling, whole issue of *ROOTS,* Minnesota Historical Society, Winter, 1974.

Golden Spike Centennial Issue, a facsimile of the June 1869 Traveler's Official Railway Guide, National Railway Publication Company 1969.

Page 314

"The Heritage of Mechanical Fasteners" The Greatest Story Never Told, "FASTENERS" Spring 1970, Fall 1970, Spring 1971, Fall 1971, Industrial Fasteners Institute.

Historical Statistics of the United States, Colonial Times to 1957, A Statistical Abstract Supplement, Prepared by the Bureau of the Census with the Cooperation of the Social Science Research Council, p. 123 xeroxed, Bureau of the Census, U.S. Department of Commerce.

"History and Development of International Harvester"; undated, but contemporary pamphlet from International Harvester Archives, Chicago.

Development of Immigration and Naturalization Laws and Service History. U.S. Dept. of Justice, Immigration and Naturalization Service, by Charles Gordon, General Counsel, Washington, D.C. (revision of 1 Sept. 1972).

Our Immigration, A Brief Account of Immigration to the United States, U.S. Dept. of Justice, Immigration and Naturalization Service M-85, (Rev. 1972)Y, printed pamphlet.

"Instructions No. 2110L For Erecting, Fairbanks-Morse, Steel Towers for Windmills," Thirteenth Edition, Copyright 1916, Fairbanks, Morse & Co. Chicago, Ill.

Instructions to the Surveyors General of Public Lands of The United States for those Surveying Districts Established in and since the year 1850, containing also *A Manual of Instructions to Regulate the Field Operations of Deputy Surveyors,* Illustrated by Diagrams, Washington, A.O.P. Nicholson, Public Printer, 1855 and 1864 Supplements.

Kartcentrum, Göteborg, Sweden, Mr. Jan-Åke Thurell.

Landsarkivet i Lund, Box 2016, 220 02 Lund 2, Sweden, Ulla-Britt Håkansson, Kansliskrivare.

Landsarkivet i Götaborg, Mr. Gösta Lext fil. dr., landsarkivarie, also Britta Helĕn.

"McCormick Reaper," *Centennial Source Material,* International Harvester Company, Chicago, 1931.

Album of History and Biography of Meeker County, Minnesota, Alden Ogle & Company, Chicago, 1888.

Northwestern Steel and Wire Company, Sterling, Illinois 61081, Mr. D.C. Oberbillig, Merchant Wire Products.

Old Sears Roebuck Catalog, reprint of 1908 issue.

Facsimile of the June 1870 *Travelers' Official Railway Guide,* The first issued by the present publisher, National Railway Publication Company, from whose files the original was reproduced by Edwards Brothers, Inc. Ann Arbor, Michigan, 1971.

Excerpt from: *The Course of Prices of Farm Implements and Machinery for A Series of Years,* by George K. Holmes, Division of Statistics, John Hyde, Statiscian, Misc. Series—Bulletin No. 18, U.S. Department of Agriculture, Government Printing Office, Washington, D.C. 1901.

Lloyd's Register of Shipping, England.

Promotion Pamphlet "Deering Binder Twine, The Very Best," Deering Harvester Co., Chicago, U.S.A. 1898.

"Sveriges Historia Från Äldsta Tid Till Våra Dagar" Vol. VI 1809-1875 by Teofron Säve, Svenska Amerikanska Postens Förlag, Minneapolis, Minnesota 1900.

Digest of "History of Wire nails" American Steel and Wire Histories, American Steel & Wire Company, Worcester, Mass. 17 Nov. 1937.

Part II
Personal Contributors

Allen, M.R. Executive Secretary, Timber Producers Association.

Ash, William F., Proprietor, Photos, Inc., Minneapolis, Mn.

Baker, Dr. T. Lindsay, History Department, Texas Technical University.

Barr, Roger, Reference Associate, Minnesota Historical Society.

Behr, Philip R., Geography Professor Emeritus, Saint Cloud State University.

Britta, Helén, Landsarkivet, Göteborg, Sweden.

Brown, Dr. Luther, Dean, Learning Resources Services, Saint Cloud State University.

Carlson, Einar, Bjälkhult, Sweden.

Carson, E.A., Archivist and Curator, H.M. Customs and Excise Library Services, Custom House, Lower Thames Street, London, England.

Carter, Craig J.M. Editor, *SEA BREEZES,* Liverpool, England.

Clawson, Dr. Marion, Resources for the Future.

Coppock, Dr. Henry A. Chairman, Geography Department, Saint Cloud State University.

Dahlin, Jan, Amanuens, Landsarkivet i Lund, Sweden.

Davenport, Eugene, Assessor, Otter Tail County.

Enersen, Mrs. Gabriella, Public Relations Specialist, J.I. Case, Racine, WI.

Fahl, Ronald J., Forest History Society.

Finster, Jerome, Chief, Industrial and Social Branch, Civil Archives Division, National Archives and Records Service, General Services Administration, Washington, D.C.

Fletcher, Mrs. Edna, Clitherall, Mn.

Fraley, William B., Acting Assistant Director, General Archives Division, General Services Administration, National Archives and Records Service.

Gilbert, Howard A., Assistant Director, Public Relations, Penn Central Transportation Company.

Gray, James H., Fergus Falls Journal Company.

Greene, James F., Deputy Commissioner, U.S. Department of Justice, Immigration and Naturalization Service.

Gronner, John A., Past President, Otter Tail County Historical Society.

Håkansson, Ulla-Britt, Kansliskrivare, Landsarkivet i Lund, Sweden.

Handels-Of Søfartsmuseet, På Kronborg, (Danish Maritime Museum) 300 Halsingør, Denmark.

Hanson, Fred, Advertising Department, Deere & Company.

Hanson, K.W., Auditor, Otter Tail County.

Hargett, Janet L., Assistant Director, General Archives Division, National Archives and Records Service, General Services Administration.

Henn, J.D., Corporate Archivist, International Harvester.

Henningsen, Dr. Henning, Director, På Kronborg (Danish Maritime Museum) 300 Halsingør, Denmark.

Herbert, John E., Secretary, Resources for the Future, Inc.

Hovren, James E., late of Lemhi Lumber Company, Salmon, Idaho.

Hult, Herbert, Executive Secretary, Midwest Old Settlers and Threshers Association.

Johnson, Ronald F., Attorney at Law, Saint Cloud, Mn.

Jørgensen, Harald, Director of Archives, Landsarkivet For Sjaelland M.M. København.

Lennes, Greg, Archivist, International Harvester Archives.

Lext, Gösta, Landsarkivarie, Landsarkivet, Göteborg, Sweden.

Logas, Myrtle E., Clerk, District Court, Seventh Judicial District, County of Otter Tail, Mn.

Lohrentz, W.L., Administrative Vice President, United States Steel Corporation.

Lundberg, Patsy, Librarian, Kishwaukee Junior College, Illinois.

McKenry, Coletta, Librarian, United States Steel Corporation.

Mabry, D.B., Railway Tie Association.

Maunder, Elwood R., Executive Director, Forest History Society, Inc.

National Railway Publication Co., 424 West 33 Street, New York, N.Y. 10001.

Neubert, Mrs. Janet, Secretary, Department of Geography, Saint Cloud State University.

Nystrom, L.A. Manager, Marketing Information Services, Power Systems Division, Colt Industries, 701 Lawton Avenue, Beloit, WI 53511.

Oberbillig, D.C., Merchant Wire Products, Northwestern Steel and Wire Company, Sterling, Illinois 61081.

Parson, Mr. & Mrs. Charles G., teachers, Bemidji, Minnesota.

Parson, Lincoln R., Pehr's grandson and third owner of the Homestead.

Parson, Nels, Pehr's only son and second owner of the Homestead.

Pietz, Pamela, Scholar, Biological Science.

Pietz, Mrs. Mary, R.N., Saint Cloud, Mn.

Price, Ethel L., Chief, Civilian Reference Branch, National Personnel Records Center, General Services Administration, Saint Louis, Missouri.

Ristow, Dr. Walter W. Chief, Reference Department, Geography and Map Division, The Library of Congress.

Schellinger, Francis, retired construction contractor, Avon, Mn.

Severson, David Sr., Land Developer, Battle Lake, Mn.

Skibness, J. Benford, Dairy farmer, Clitherall Township.

Smith, John D., one time procuror of ties for the Central of Georgia.

Smith, J., Liverpool Record Office, Liverpool, England.

Stene, Greer C., Reading Specialist, Bemidji, Minnesota.

Svensäter, Komminister Carl Eric, Östra Sallerup, Sweden.

Thueson, Jim, Minnesota Historical Society.

Thurell, Jan-Åke, Kartcentrum, Göteborg, Sweden.

Tideman, Dr. Philip, Geography Professor, longtime Departmental Chairman, Saint Cloud State University.

Tooker, Irvin W., G.T.A. elevator. Battle Lake, Minnesota.

Turley, Leo, President, Midwest Old Settlers and Threshers Association, Inc., Mount Pleasant, Iowa.

Udy, Lowell J., Director, Eastern States Office, Bureau of Land Management.

Van Brocklin, Lynn, Research Assistant, Minnesota Historical Society, Saint Paul, Mn.

Vaughn, V. Allen, Vice-President, Public Relations, National Railway Historical Society.

Zwach, Hon. John M., longtime Member of Congress, Sixth District, Minnesota.

To order additional copies of
EVER THE LAND
please complete the following.

$16.95 EACH
*(plus $3.95 shipping & handling for first book,
add $2.00 for each additional book ordered.*

Shipping and Handling costs for larger quantites available upon request.

Please send me _____ additional books at $16.95 + shipping & handling

Bill my: ❏ VISA   ❏ MasterCard   Expires _____
Card # _____
Signature _____
Daytime Phone Number _____

For credit card orders call 1-888-568-6329
TO ORDER ON-LINE VISIT: www.jmcompanies.com
OR SEND THIS ORDER FORM TO:
McCleery & Sons Publishing
PO Box 248
Gwinner, ND 58040-0248

I am enclosing $_____   ❏ Check ❏ Money Order
Payable in US funds. No cash accepted.

SHIP TO:
Name _____
Mailing Address _____
City _____
State/Zip _____

Orders by check allow longer delivery time.
Money order and credit card orders will be shipped within 48 hours.
This offer is subject to change without notice.

McCleery & Sons PUBLISHING
a division of J&M Companies

Call 1-888-568-6329
to order by credit card OR order
on-line at www.jmcompanies.com

NEW RELEASES

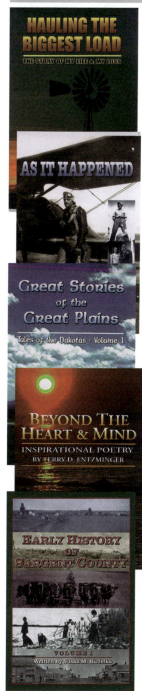

Hauling the Biggest Load - *The Story of My Life & My Loss*
This is an unusual story because of the many changes that have happened since the author's birth in 1926. In May 2002, he lost his son, John, in a car accident. None of those other experiences seemed important anymore... Richard needed something to try and take his mind off that tragedy. "I thought I had hauled some big loads in my life but I never had to have a load as big as this one." Written by: Richard Hamann (144 pages) $14.95 each in 6x9" paperback.

As It Happened
Over 40 photos and several chapters containing Allen Saunders' early years, tales of riding the rails, his Navy career, marriage, Army instruction, flying over "The Hump", and his return back to North Dakota. Written by Allen E. Saunders. (74 pgs)
$12.95 each in a 6x9" paperback.

Great Stories of the Great Plains - *Tales of the Dakotas - Vol. 1*
The radio show "Great Stories of the Great Plains" is heard on great radio stations all across both Dakotas. Norman has taken some of the stories from broadcasts, added some details, and even added some complete new tales to bring together this book of North and South Dakota history. Written by Keith Norman. (134 pgs.) $14.95 each in a 6x9" paperback.

Beyond the Heart & Mind
Inspirational Poetry by Terry D. Entzminger
Beyond the Heart & Mind is the first in a series of inspirational poetry collections of Entzminger. Read and cherish over 100 original poems and true-to-the-heart verses printed in full color in the following sections: Words of Encouragement, On the Wings of Prayer, God Made You Very Special, Feelings From Within, The True Meaning of Love, and Daily Joys. (120 pgs.)
$12.95 each in a 6x9" paperback.

Early History of Sargent County - *Volume 1*
Over seventy photos and thirty-five chapters containing the early history of Sargent County, North Dakota: Glacial Movement in Sargent County, Native Americans in Sargent County, Weather, Memories of the Summer of 1883, Fight for the County Seat, Townships, Surveyed Maps from 1882 and much more. Written by Susan M. Kudelka. (270 pgs.) $16.95 each in a 6x9" paperback.

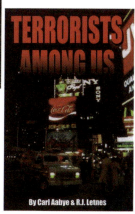

Terrorists Among Us
This piece of fiction was written to "expose a weakness" in present policies and conflicts in the masses of rules which seem to put emphasis on business, money, and power interests at the expense of the people's security, safety and happiness. Shouldn't we and our leaders strive for some security for our people? Written by Carl Aabye & R.J. Letnes. (178 pgs.) $15.95 each in a 6x9" paperback.

THE HASTINGS SERIES

Blue Darkness *(First in a Series of Hastings Books)*
This tale of warm relationships and chilling murders takes place in the lake country of central Minnesota. Normal activities in the small town of New Dresen are disrupted when local resident, ex-CIA agent Maynard Cushing, is murdered. His killer, Robert Ranforth also an ex-CIA agent, had been living anonymously in the community for several years. to the anonymous ex-agent. Stalked and attached at his country home, he employs tools and people to mount a defense and help solve crimes. Written by Ernest Francis Schanilec (author of The Towers). (276 pgs.) $16.95 each in a 6x9" paperback.

The Towers *(Second in a Series of Hastings Books)*
Tom Hastings has moved from the lake country of central Minnesota to Minneapolis. His move was precipitated by the trauma associated with the murder of one of his neighbors. After renting an apartment on the 20th floor of a high-rise apartment building known as The Towers, he's met new friends and retained his relationship with a close friend, Julie, from St. Paul. Hastings is a resident of the high-rise for less than a year when a young lady is found murdered next to a railroad track, a couple of blocks from The Towers. The murderer shares the same elevators, lower-level garage and other areas in the high-rise as does Hastings. The building manager and other residents, along with Hastings are caught up in dramatic events that build to a crisis while the local police are baffled. Who is the killer? Written by Ernest Francis Schanilec. (268 pgs.) $16.95 each in a 6x9" paperback.

Danger In The Keys *(Third in a Series of Hastings Books)*
Tom Hastings is looking forward to a month's vacation in Florida. While driving through Tennessee, he witnesses an automobile leaving the road and plunging down a steep slope. He stops and assists another man in finding the car. The driver, a young woman, survives the accident. Tom is totally unaware that the young woman was being chased because she had chanced coming into possession of a valuable gem, which had been heisted from a Saudi Arabian prince in a New York hotel room. After arriving in Key Marie Island in Florida, Tom checks in and begins enjoying the surf and the beach. He meets many interesting people, however, some of them are on the island because of the Guni gem, and they will stop at nothing in order to gain possession. Desperate people and their greedy ambitions interrupt Tom's goal of a peaceful vacation. Written by Ernest Francis Schanilec (210 pgs.) $16.95 each in a 6x9" paperback.

Purgatory Curve *(Fourth in a Series of Hastings Books)*
A loud horn penetrated the silence on a September morning in New Dresden, Minnesota. Tom Hastings stepped onto Main Street sidewalk after emerging from the corner Hardware Store. He heard a freight train coming and watched in horror as it crushed a pickup truck that was stalled on the railroad tracks. Moments before the crash, he saw someone jump from the cab. An elderly farmer's body was later recovered from the mangled vehicle. Tom was interviewed by the sheriff the next day and was upset that his story about what he saw wasn't believed. The tragic death of the farmer was surrounded with controversy and mysterious people, including a nephew who taunted Tom after the accident. Or, was it an accident?   Written by Ernest Francis Schanilec (210 pgs.) $16.95 each in a 6x9" paperback.

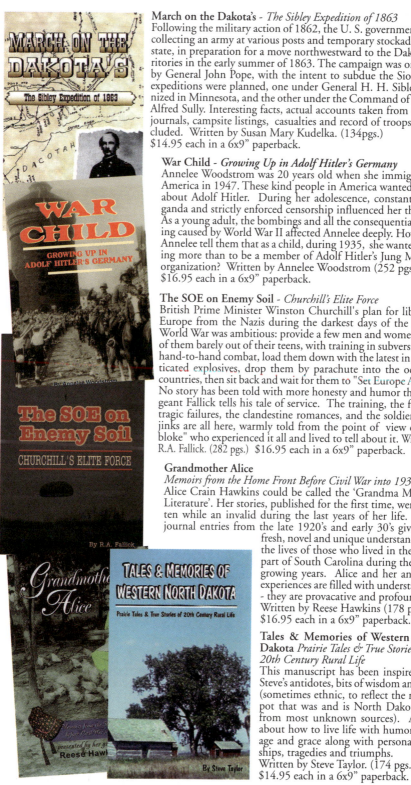

March on the Dakota's - *The Sibley Expedition of 1863*
Following the military action of 1862, the U. S. government began collecting an army at various posts and temporary stockades of the state, in preparation for a move northwestward to the Dakota Territories in the early summer of 1863. The campaign was organized by General John Pope, with the intent to subdue the Sioux. Two expeditions were planned, one under General H. H. Sibley, organized in Minnesota, and the other under the Command of General Alfred Sully. Interesting facts, actual accounts taken from soldiers' journals, campsite listings, casualties and record of troops also included. Written by Susan Mary Kudelka. (134pgs.) $14.95 each in a 6x9" paperback.

War Child - *Growing Up in Adolf Hitler's Germany*
Annelee Woodstrom was 20 years old when she immigrated to America in 1947. These kind people in America wanted to hear about Adolf Hitler. During her adolescence, constant propaganda and strictly enforced censorship influenced her thinking. As a young adult, the bombings and all the consequential suffering caused by World War II affected Annelee deeply. How could Annelee tell them that as a child, during 1935, she wanted nothing more than to be a member of Adolf Hitler's Jung Maidens' organization? Written by Annelee Woodstrom (252 pgs.) $16.95 each in a 6x9" paperback.

The SOE on Enemy Soil - *Churchill's Elite Force*
British Prime Minister Winston Churchill's plan for liberating Europe from the Nazis during the darkest days of the Second World War was ambitious: provide a few men and women, most of them barely out of their teens, with training in subversion and hand-to-hand combat, load them down with the latest in sophisticated explosives, drop them by parachute into the occupied countries, then sit back and wait for them to "Set Europe Ablaze." No story has been told with more honesty and humor than Sergeant Fallick tells his tale of service. The training, the fear, the tragic failures, the clandestine romances, and the soldiers' high jinks are all here, warmly told from the point of view of "one bloke" who experienced it all and lived to tell about it. Written by R.A. Fallick. (282 pgs.) $16.95 each in a 6x9" paperback.

Grandmother Alice
Memoirs from the Home Front Before Civil War into 1930's
Alice Crain Hawkins could be called the 'Grandma Moses of Literature'. Her stories, published for the first time, were written while an invalid during the last years of her life. These journal entries from the late 1920's and early 30's gives us a fresh, novel and unique understanding of the lives of those who lived in the upper part of South Carolina during the state's growing years. Alice and her ancestors experiences are filled with understanding - they are provacative and profound. Written by Reese Hawkins (178 pgs.) $16.95 each in a 6x9" paperback.

Tales & Memories of Western North Dakota *Prairie Tales & True Stories of 20th Century Rural Life*
This manuscript has been inspired with Steve's antidotes, bits of wisdom and jokes (sometimes ethnic, to reflect the melting pot that was and is North Dakota; and from most unknown sources). A story about how to live life with humor, courage and grace along with personal hardships, tragedies and triumphs.
Written by Steve Taylor. (174 pgs.) $14.95 each in a 6x9" paperback.

Phil Lempert's HEALTHY, WEALTHY, & WISE
The Shoppers Guide for Today's Supermarket
This is the must-have tool for getting the most for your money in every aisle. With this valuable advice you will never see (or shop) the supermarket the same way again. You will learn how to: save at least $1,000 a year on your groceries, guarantee satisfaction on every shopping trip, get the most out of coupons or rebates, avoid marketing gimmicks, create the ultimate shopping list, read and understand the new food labels, choose the best supermarkets for you and your family. Written by Phil Lempert. (198 pgs.)
$9.95 each in a 6x9" paperback.

Miracles of COURAGE
The Larry W. Marsh Story
This story is for anyone looking for simple formulas for overcoming insurmountable obstacles. At age 18, Larry lost both legs in a traffic accident and learned to walk again on untested prosthesis. No obstacle was too big for him - putting himself through college - to teaching a group of children that frustrated the whole educational system - to developing a nationally recognized educational program to help these children succeed. Written by Linda Marsh. (134 pgs.)
$12.95 each in a 6x9" paperback.

The Garlic Cure
Learn about natural breakthroughs to outwit: Allergies, Arthritis, Cancer, Candida Albicans, Colds, Flu and Sore Throat, Environmental and Body Toxins, Fatigue, High Cholesterol, High Blood Pressure and Homocysteine and Sinus Headaches. The most comprehensive, factual and brightly written health book on garlic of all times. INCLUDES: 139 GOURMET GARLIC RECIPES! Written by James F. Scheer, Lynn Allison and Charlie Fox. (240 pgs.)
$14.95 each in a 6x9" paperback.

I Took The Easy Way Out
Life Lessons on Hidden Handicaps
Twenty-five years ago, Tom Day was managing a growing business - holding his own on the golf course and tennis court. He was living in the fast lane. For the past 25 years, Tom has spent his days in a wheelchair with a spinal cord injury. Attendants serve his every need. What happened to Tom? We get an honest account of the choices Tom made in his life. It's a courageous story of reckoning, redemption and peace. Written by Thomas J. Day. (200 pgs.)
$19.95 each in a 6x9" paperback.

9/11 and Meditation - *America's Handbook*
All Americans have been deeply affected by the terrorist events of and following 9-11-01 in our country. David Thorson submits that meditation is a potentially powerful intervention to ameliorate the frightening effects of such divisive and devastating acts of terror. This book features a lifetime of harrowing life events amidst intense pychological and social polarization, calamity and chaos; overcome in part by practicing the age-old art of meditation. Written by David Thorson. (110 pgs.)
$9.95 each in a 4-1/8 x 7-1/4" paperback.

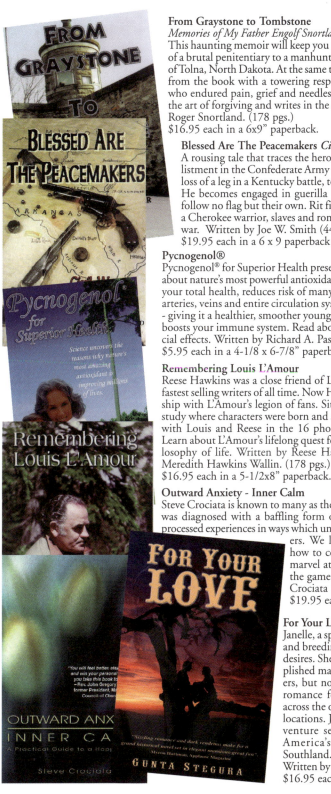

From Graystone to Tombstone
Memories of My Father Engolf Snortland 1908-1976
This haunting memoir will keep you riveted with true accounts of a brutal penitentiary to a manhunt in the unlikely little town of Tolna, North Dakota. At the same time the reader will emerge from the book with a towering respect for the author, a man who endured pain, grief and needless guilt -- but who learned the art of forgiving and writes in the spirit of hope. Written by Roger Snortland. (178 pgs.)
$16.95 each in a 6x9" paperback.

Blessed Are The Peacemakers *Civil War in the Ozarks*
A rousing tale that traces the heroic Rit Gatlin from his enlistment in the Confederate Army in Little Rock to his tragic loss of a leg in a Kentucky battle, to his return in the Ozarks. He becomes engaged in guerilla warfare with raiders who follow no flag but their own. Rit finds himself involved with a Cherokee warrior, slaves and romance in a land ravaged by war. Written by Joe W. Smith (444 pgs.)
$19.95 each in a 6 x 9 paperback

Pycnogenol®
Pycnogenol® for Superior Health presents exciting new evidence about nature's most powerful antioxidant. Pycnogenol® improves your total health, reduces risk of many diseases, safeguards your arteries, veins and entire circulation system. It protects your skin - giving it a healthier, smoother younger glow. Pycnogenol® also boosts your immune system. Read about it's many other beneficial effects. Written by Richard A. Passwater, Ph.D. (122 pgs.)
$5.95 each in a 4-1/8 x 6-7/8" paperback.

Remembering Louis L'Amour
Reese Hawkins was a close friend of Louis L'Amour, one of the fastest selling writers of all time. Now Hawkins shares this friendship with L'Amour's legion of fans. Sit with Reese in L'Amour's study where characters were born and stories came to life. Travel with Louis and Reese in the 16 photo pages in this memoir. Learn about L'Amour's lifelong quest for knowledge and his philosophy of life. Written by Reese Hawkins and his daughter Meredith Hawkins Wallin. (178 pgs.)
$16.95 each in a 5-1/2x8" paperback.

Outward Anxiety - Inner Calm
Steve Crociata is known to many as the Optician to the Stars. He was diagnosed with a baffling form of cancer. The author has processed experiences in ways which uniquely benefit today's readers. We learn valuable lessons on how to cope with distress, how to marvel at God, and how to win at the game of life. Written by Steve Crociata (334 pgs.)
$19.95 each in a 6 x 9 paperback

For Your Love
Janelle, a spoiled socialite, has beauty and breeding to attract any mate she desires. She falls for Jared, an accomplished man who has had many lovers, but no real love. Their hesitant romance follows Jared and Janelle across the ocean to exciting and wild locations. Join in a romance and adventure set in the mid-1800's in America's grand and proud Southland.
Written by Gunta Stegura. (358 pgs.)
$16.95 each in a 6x9" paperback.

Bonanza Belle
In 1908, Carrie Amundson left her home to become employed on a bonanza farm. Carrie married and moved to town. One tragedy after the other befell her and altered her life considerably and she found herself back on the farm where her family lived the toiled during the Great Depression. Carrie was witness to many life-changing events happenings. She changed from a carefree girl to a woman of great depth and stamina.
Written by Elaine Ulness Swenson. (344 pgs.)
$15.95 each in a 6x8-1/4" paperback.

Home Front
Read the continuing story of Carrie Amundson, whose life in North Dakota began in *Bonanza Belle*. This is the story of her family, faced with the challenges, sacrifices and hardships of World War II. Everything changed after the Pearl Harbor attack, and ordinary folk all across America, on the home front, pitched in to help in the war effort. Even years after the war's end, the effects of it are still evident in many of the men and women who were called to serve their country.
Written by Elaine Ulness Swenson. (304 pgs.)
$15.95 each in a 6x8-1/4" paperback.

First The Dream
This story spans ninety years of Anna's life - from Norway to America - to finding love and losing love. She and her family experience two world wars, flu epidemics, the Great Depression, droughts and other quirks of Mother Nature and the Vietnam War. A secret that Anna has kept is fully revealed at the end of her life. Written by Elaine Ulness Swenson. (326 pgs.)
$15.95 each in a 6x8-1/4" paperback

Pay Dirt
An absorbing story reveals how a man with the courage to follow his dream found both gold and unexpected adventure and adversity in Interior Alaska, while learning that human nature can be the most unpredictable of all.
Written by Otis Hahn & Alice Vollmar. (168 pgs.)
$15.95 each in a 6x9" paperback.

Spirits of Canyon Creek *Sequel to "Pay Dirt"*
Hahn has a rich stash of true stories about his gold mining experiences. This is a continued successful collaboration of battles on floodwaters, facing bears and the discovery of gold in the Yukon. Written by Otis Hahn & Alice Vollmar. (138 pgs.)
$15.95 each in a 6x9" paperback.

Seasons With Our Lord
Original seasonal and special event poems written from the heart. Feel the mood with the tranquil color photos facing each poem. A great coffee table book or gift idea. Written by Cheryl Lebahn Hegvik. (68 pgs.)
$24.95 each in a 11x8-1/2 paperback.

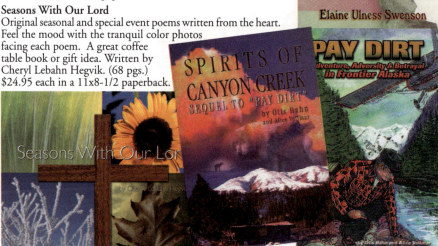

Damsel in a Dress
Escape into a world of reflection and after thought with this second printing of Larson's first poetry book. It is her intention to connect people with feelings and touch the souls of people who have experienced similiar times. Lynne emphasizes the belief that everything happens for a reason. After all, with every event in life come lessons...we grow from hardships. It gives us character and it made her who she is. Written by Lynne D. Richard Larson (author of Eat, Drink & Remarry) (86 pgs.)
$12.95 each in a 5x8" paperback.

Eat, Drink & Remarry
The poetry in this book is taken from different experiences in Lynne's life and from different geographical and different emotional places. Every poem is an inspiration from someone or a direct event from their life...or from hers. Every victory and every mistake - young or old. They slowly shape and mold you into the unique person you are. Celebrate them as rough times that you were strong enough to endure. Written by Lynne D. Richard Larson (86 pgs.) $12.95 each in a 5x8" paperback.

Country-fied
Stories with a sense of humor and love for country and small town people who, like the author, grew up country-fied . . . Country-fied people grow up with a unique awareness of their dependence on the land. They live their lives with dignity, hard work, determination and the ability to laugh at themselves.
Written by Elaine Babcock. (184 pgs.)
$14.95 each in a 6x9" paperback.

Charlie's Gold and Other Frontier Tales
Kamron's first collection of short stories gives you adventure tales about men and women of the west, made up of cowboys, Indians, and settlers. Written by Kent Kamron.
(174 pgs.) $15.95 each in a 6x9" paperback.

A Time For Justice
This second collection of Kamron's short stories takes off where the first volume left off, satisfying the reader's hunger for more tales of the wide prairie. Written by Kent Kamron. (182 pgs.)
$16.95 each in a 6x9" paperback.

It Really Happened Here!
Relive the days of farm-to-farm salesmen and hucksters, of ghost ships and locust plagues when you read Ethelyn Pearson's collection of strange but true tales. It captures the spirit of our ancestors in short, easy to read, colorful accounts that will have you yearning for more. Written by Ethelyn Pearson. (168 pgs.) $24.95 each in an 8-1/2x11" paperback.

The Silk Robe
- Dedicated to Shari Lynn Hunt, a wonderful woman who passed away from cancer. Mom lived her life with unfailing faith, an open loving heart and a giving spirit. She is remembered for her compassion and gentle strength. Written by Shaunna Privratsky.
$6.95 each in a 4-1/4x5-1/2" booklet. *Complimentary notecard and envelope included.*

(Add $3.95 shipping & handling for first book, add $2.00 for each additional book ordered.)

T 182 N R 41 W 5th Mer M.

	North	Between section 27 & 28
		Var 12° 39' E
20.00		Leave timber & enter prairie bears N & S
35.00		Enter a poplar grove
40.00		Set a post for 1/4 section corner from
		Br Oak 10 in diam bears N 29 E 281 links dist
		No other tree convenient
80.00		A White Ash 10 in diam corner to
		sections 21, 22, 27 & 28
		Land 1st rate mostly prairie

	East	On a random line between sec 22 & 27
		Var 12° 37' E
10.00		Enter prairie bear N W & S E
40.00		Set temporary post for 1/4 section cor
80.74		A point 5 lks S of the corner to sec
		22, 23, 26 & 27 from which corner I run

	S 89° 39' W	On true line between sections 22 & 27
		Var 12° 39' 6
40.37		Set post in mound for 1/4 section cor
80.74		To corner to sections 21, 22, 27 & 28
		Land 1st rate level prairie
		Nov 7th 1866

	North	Between section 21 & 22
		Var 12° 39' E
22.01		Leave timber & enter a Large prai
		bears N. E & S. W.
40.00		Set post for 1/4 section corner from
		Br Oak 6 in diam bears N 83 1/2 W 153
		No other tree near
80.00		Set post in mound for corner to
		sections 15, 16, 21 & 22
		Land mostly 3rd rate 21rd on S in
		timber Br Oak & Wh Oak rest of the
		line prairie

T122 N R 40 W 5th Mer Minn

East	Random line between section 15 & 22
	Var 12°39' E
40.00	Set temporary post for ¼ section corner
80.00	A point 30 lks N of corner to sec 14,15,22 & 23
	from which corner N 89°47' W
	On true line between sections 15 & 22
	Var 12°39' E
40.00	Set post in mound for ¼ section corner
80.60	Corner to sections 15, 16, 21 & 22
	Land 2nd rate rolling prairie
North	Between section 15 & 16
	Var 12°39' E
25.00	Leave prairie & enter a round marsh
40.00	Set post in the marsh for ¼ section corner which
	Blk Ash 7 in diam bear N 55 E 4.02 lks dist
	Quaking Asp 6 in diam bear N 79 E 3.16 " "
45.00	Leave marsh & enter Timber
50.00	A marsh with shallow pond in the center
	bear E & W & cross the lake on Ice
80.00	Set post in pond for corner to sec 9,10,15 & 16
	from which
	Bur Oak 8 in diam bear N 20 E 4.41 lks dist
	Wh Birch 6 " " " N 45 W 3.19 " "
	Land 1st rate 1st 25 chs rolling prairie
	rest mostly marsh the marsh where
	the section corner stands extends mostly
	to the W
	Nov 8th 1866
	The line between section 10 & 15 will strike
	Lake Litherall in less than 80 chains
	I therefore run it a true line
East	On a true line between sec 10 & 15
	Var 12°39' E
35.00	Leave marsh